DOWN BY THE RIVER

Archaeological, palaeoenvironmental and
geoarchaeological investigations
of the Suffolk river valleys

Benjamin Gearey, Henry Chapman and Andy J. Howard

Oxbow Books
Oxford & Philadelphia

Published in the United Kingdom in 2016 by
OXBOW BOOKS
10 Hythe Bridge Street, Oxford OX1 2EW

and in the United States by
OXBOW BOOKS
1950 Lawrence Road, Havertown, PA 19083

Hardcover Edition: ISBN 978-1-78570-168-9
Digital Edition: ISBN 978-1-78570-169-6

A CIP record for this book is available from the British Library

Library of Congress Cataloging-in-Publication Data

Names: Gearey, Benjamin R., author. | Chapman, Henry, 1973- author. | Howard,
    Andrew J., author.
Title: Down by the river : archaeological, palaeoenvironmental and
    geoarchaeological investigations of the Suffolk river valleys / Benjamin
    Gearey, Henry Chapman and Andy Howard.
Description: Oxford : Oxbow Books, 2015. | Includes bibliographical
    references and index.
Identifiers: LCCN 2015040529| ISBN 9781785701689 (hardcover) | ISBN
    9781785701696 (digital) | ISBN 9781785701702 (MOBI) | ISBN 9781785701719
    (PDF)
Subjects: LCSH: Suffolk (England)--Antiquities. | East Anglia
    (England)--Antiquities. | Rivers--England--Suffolk. |
    Valleys--England--Suffolk. | Excavations (Archaeology)--England--Suffolk.
    | Paleoecology--England--Suffolk. | Paleoecology--Holocene. |
    Archaeological geology--England--Suffolk. | Geology,
    Stratigraphic--Holocene.
Classification: LCC DA670.S9 D69 2015 | DDC 936.2/64--dc23 LC record available at http://lccn.loc.gov/2015040529

Printed in the United Kingdom by Short Run Press, Exeter

For a complete list of Oxbow titles, please contact:

UNITED KINGDOM
Oxbow Books
Telephone (01865) 241249, Fax (01865) 794449
Email: oxbow@oxbowbooks.com
www.oxbowbooks.com

UNITED STATES OF AMERICA
Oxbow Books
Telephone (800) 791-9354, Fax (610) 853-9146
Email: queries@casemateacademic.com
www.casemateacademic.com/oxbow

Oxbow Books is part of the Casemate Group

This volume has been funded by Historic England (formerly English Heritage)

*Front cover: (clockwise from top left): The excavation of the Ludham medieval boat; The River Waveney near Barsham
viewed from close to water level; Laser scan of the timber from Geldeston showing a high-resolution model of prehistoric
tool marks.*

Contents

4. Archaeological Excavations and Analyses of a Late Prehistoric Timber Alignment: The Beccles Project (2006–2012)

with Michael Bamforth, Kristina Krawiec, Eamonn Baldwin, Chris Gaffney, Emma Hopla, Peter Marshall, Abby Mynett, David Smith, Wendy Smith, Ian Tyers, Cathy Tester and Sarah Percival

5. Archaeological Excavations and Analyses of other Late Prehistoric Timber Alignments in the Waveney Valley: Excavations at Barsham (2007) and Geldeston (2011)

with Kristina Krawiec, Michael Bamforth, Catherine Griffiths, Tom Hill, Kelly Smith, Ian Tyers and Heather Wallis

Contributors

EAMONN BALDWIN
Department of Classics, Ancient History and
Archaeology, University of Birmingham, UK

MICHAEL BAMFORTH
Department of Archaeology, University of York, UK

DR HENRY CHAPMAN
Department of Classics, Ancient History and
Archaeology, University of Birmingham, UK

DR EUGENE CH'NG
School of Computer Science, University of Nottingham
Ningbo, China

DR WILLIAM FLETCHER
Historic England, Brooklands, 24 Brooklands Avenue,
Cambridge, UK

DR CHRIS GAFFNEY
Archaeological Sciences, University of Bradford, UK

DR BENJAMIN GEAREY
Department of Archaeology, University College Cork,
Cork, Ireland

CLAIRE GOOD
Suffolk County Council Archaeological Service, Shire
Hall, Bury St Edmunds, UK

DR CATHERINE GRIFFITHS
University of Wales, Trinity St Davids, UK

DR PAM GRINTER
Birmingham Metropolitan College, Birmingham, UK

DR THOMAS C. B. HILL
Department of Earth Sciences, The Natural History
Museum, Cromwell Road, London, UK

EMMA-J. HOPLA
Geography and Environment, University of
Southampton, UK

DR ANDY J. HOWARD
Department of Archaeology, University of Durham, UK

KRISTINA KRAWIEC
Archaeology South-East, University College London,
Portslade, UK

MICHAEL LOBB
Geography and Environment, University of Southampton,
UK

DR PETER MARSHALL
Historic England, 1 Waterhouse Square, 138–142
Holborn, London, UK

ANDY MOSS
Geography, Earth and Environmental Sciences,
University of Birmingham, UK

ABBY MYNETT
Wessex Archaeology, 7–9 North St. David St.,
Edinburgh, UK

SARAH PERCIVAL
Suffolk County Council Archaeological Service, Shire
Hall, Bury St Edmunds, UK

DR IAN TYERS
Dendrochronological Consultancy Ltd., Lowfield House,
Smeath Lane, Retford, UK

DR IAN PANTER
York Archaeological Trust, 47 Aldwark, York, UK

DR EILEEN REILLY
School of Archaeology, University College Dublin,
Ireland

DR DAVID SMITH
Department of Classics, Ancient History and
Archaeology, University of Birmingham, UK

KELLY SMITH
The Natural History Museum, Cromwell Road, London, UK

DR WENDY SMITH
Department of Classics, Ancient History and Archaeology, University of Birmingham, UK

CATHY TESTER
Suffolk County Council Archaeological Service, Shire Hall, Bury St Edmunds, UK

DR EMMA TETLOW
Wardell Armstrong LLP, 2 Devon Way, Longbridge, Birmingham, UK

HEATHER WALLIS
206 Woodcock Rd, Norwich, UK

DR INGRID WARD
School of Social Sciences, The University of Western Australia, Perth, Australia

Acknowledgements

The authors would like to thank the following: Beccles Town Council for their help and support in granting access to Beccles Marshes; Beccles Amateur Yacht Club for allowing the use of their clubhouse as a 'dig hut' during the excavations in 2007 and 2009; The people of Beccles and Geldeston whom attended the open days at the sites; English Heritage, for financial support and advice, especially Magnus Alexander, Dr Jane Siddell and Dr Jen Heathcote. Halcrow/Besl, part funded the work at Beccles in 2006 and at Barsham in 2007 and Christian Whiting acted as liaison; Suffolk County Council Archaeological Service for their role in the excavations at Beccles and Barsham and also in the various commercial projects described in Chapter 3; The Broads Authority for their support and interest in the excavations at Beccles and for funding the information panel now in place at Beccles Marshes; Helen Moulden who drafted additional figures; The Institute of Archaeology and Antiquity students whom took part in the excavations at Beccles and Geldeston for all their hard work. Finally, we thank the anonymous referee for providing useful and constructive advice on an initial draft of this book.

The research presented in this book includes data from the Ordnance Survery © Crown Copyright and database rights 2015. Ordnance Survey (Digimap Licence) and the British Geological Survey (Geological Map Data © NERC 2015). BG gratefully acknowledges the financial support of the Research Publication Fund, College of Arts, Celtic Studies and Social Sciences, University College Cork.

Summary

Whilst East Anglia has long been known as a key area for the preservation of important Palaeolithic archaeological and palaeoenvironmental deposits, relatively little study of the Holocene record has previously been carried out. This volume presents the results of palaeoenvironmental, archaeological and geoarchaeological investigations focused on the Post-Glacial record preserved in the Suffolk river valleys. The work discussed includes two phases of Historic England/Aggregate Levy Sustainability Funded palaeoenvironmental assessment (pollen, radiocarbon dating, beetle and diatoms) under the auspices of the Suffolk River Valleys Project (SRVP); various environmental archaeological commercial projects across Suffolk largely carried out by Birmingham Archaeo-Environmental, University of Birmingham, under *PPG* 16 and subsequent legislative frameworks; and the archaeological excavation and associated palaeoenvironmental analysis of three late prehistoric timber alignments on the floodplain of the lower Waveney Valley at Beccles, Barsham and Geldeston (Norfolk).

Five sites were selected on the Rivers Waveney, Little Ouse, Lark and Blackbourne (Beccles, Hoxne, Hengrave, Ixworth and Brandon) by the SRVP, with cores from floodplain contexts recovered for palaeoenvironmental assessment following desk based assessment, including interrogation of archaeological information derived from the Sites and Monuments Record and topographic data from Light Detection and Ranging analyses (Chapter 2). The palaeoenvironmental assessments showed that Holocene sequences were preserved at all of the locations except Brandon, but that the chronological range and state of preservation of palaeoenvironmental proxies was variable across the sites. An initial programme of radiocarbon dating also produced a series of anomalous determinations. This led to SRVP Phase II, which included a second round of sampling and radiocarbon dating of multiple samples to investigate this issue. The results indicate that a range of factors associated with the formation processes of floodplain peats may be responsible for the significant age differences between samples from the same depths observed in the SRVP sequences.

Chapter 3 presents a summary of the results of palaeoenvironmental and geoarchaeological investigations carried out in Suffolk between 2005 and 2012, as part of archaeological mitigation associated with commercial developments in the river valleys of the Gipping, Stour and Lark and along the east coast. The scale and scope of these studies varied but typically included some form of stratigraphic recording accompanied by assessment of palaeoenvironmental potential if appropriate, alongside recommendations for further work if needed. However, only one of the sites investigated (Stowmarket Relief Road, River Gipping) was taken to full analysis (beetles, plant macrofossils, molluscs and radiocarbon dating). Here an 8m floodplain sequence, provided evidence of Holocene environmental change and human impact *c.* 9000–*c.* 1100 years BP. Whilst the level of analytical detail provided by the SRVP and the commercial projects restricts comprehensive conclusions regarding landscape evolution, the results demonstrate the largely untapped research potential of the river valleys in Suffolk and also provide hypotheses concerning the timing, pattern and process of fluvial development, human activity and landscape change during the Holocene.

Bank realignment work at Beccles in the lower Waveney Valley resulted in the discovery of three late prehistoric wetland archaeological sites at Beccles, Barsham and Geldeston (Suffolk), which were excavated as part of commercial (Beccles, Barsham), University of Birmingham training excavation (Beccles, Geldeston) and Historic England funded research projects (Beccles) (Chapters 4 and 5). These sites all consisted of triple alignments of timber stakes that were constructed across the floodplain of the River Waveney during the later Iron Age but with evidence for continuing activity in the Romano-British period. The most detailed and comprehensive study was carried out at Beccles and included geophysical survey, palaeoenvironmental analyses, assessment of the condition of the archaeological wood and palaeoenvironmental proxies, geochemical analyses and a 2-year period of hydrological monitoring of the *c.* 500m long monument (Chapter 6). These data indicate that the greater proportion of the site and associated organic deposits are above the water table for much of the year and hence the potential for the preservation of the archaeological and palaeoenvironmental record *in situ* over the long term is threatened.

The final chapter (Chapter 7) presents a summary of the current state of knowledge of Holocene environmental change and the archaeological record in Suffolk, focusing on the evidence from the various river valleys. The possible form and function of the Waveney timber alignment structures is discussed and compared to other similar sites from around the United Kingdom. It is suggested that these structures may have acted to delineate routeways to, from and across the river and also as territorial markers associated with river travel, both local and perhaps into the southern North Sea. The Barsham and Geldeston sites may have formed a single monument that stretched across the River Waveney. The final chapter concludes with a discussion of specific techniques employed during the work at Beccles, including the trialing of a novel geophysical approach at the site, laser scanning to record wet-preserved archaeological wood in three dimensions, the use of digital approaches to provide 'virtual reconstructions' of the timber alignments and to hence improve public engagement with wetland archaeological sites, which are otherwise 'hidden' from public view. The volume concludes with a brief summary of research questions that future palaeoenvironmental and archaeological study of the Suffolk river valleys could seek to address.

Zusammenfassung

Während es bereits seit langem bekannt ist, dass East Anglia hinsichtlich der Erhaltung archäologischer und paläo-ökologischer Befunde ein Schlüsselbereich ist, wurden bislang nur recht wenige Studien zum holozänen Denkmalbestand durchgeführt. In diesem Band werden die Ergebnisse paläo-ökologischer, archäologischer und geoarchäologischer Untersuchungen des nach-eiszeitlichen Denkmalbestands, der sich in den Flusstälern Suffolks erhalten hat, vorgelegt. Die hier behandelten Arbeiten umfassen zwei Phasen einer von Historic England/Aggregate Levy Sustainability Fund geförderten Untersuchung im Rahmen des Suffolk River Valleys Project (SRVP); verschiedene, von der Firma Birmingham Archaeo-Environmental der University of Birmingham in Suffolk durchgeführte, kommerzielle umweltarchäologische Projekte, die durch den staatlichen Notgrabungsfond *PPG-16* und nachfolgende gesetzliche Regelungen finanziert wurden; sowie die archäologische Ausgrabung und die damit verbundene paläo-ökologische Auswertung von drei Pfostenreihen der vorrömischen Eisenzeit im Niederungsbereich des unteren Waveney Tals bei Beccles, Barsham und Geldeston (Norfolk).

Im Rahmen des SRVP wurden entlang der Flüsse Waveney, Little Ouse, Lark und Blackbourne fünf Fundstellen (Beccles, Hoxne, Hengrave, Ixworth und Brandon) für die Entnahme von Bohrproben für paläo-ökologische Untersuchungen ausgesucht, die zuvor in Archivstudien unter Zuhilfenahme archäologischer Informationen des amtlichen Fundstellenregisters und topografischer Daten von LIDAR-Analysen ausgewählt worden waren (Kapitel 2). Die paläo-ökologischen Untersuchungen zeigten, dass sich holozäne Schichtfolgen an allen Fundstellen außer in Brandon erhalten hatten, dass aber chronologische Bandbreite und Erhaltungszustand der Indikatoren für die Paläo-Umwelt zwischen den Fundplätzen variierten. Außerdem lieferte ein zu Beginn durchgeführtes Programm von Radiokarbondatierungen eine Reihe von ungewöhnlichen Ergebnissen. Dies veranlasste die Durchführung von SVRP Phase II, in der u. a. mithilfe einer zweiten Runde von Beprobungen und Radiokarbondatierungen zahlreicher Proben dieses Problem untersucht werden sollte. Die Ergebnisse deuten darauf hin, dass eine Reihe von mit den Entstehungsprozessen von Torfen im Niederungsbereich zusammenhängenden Faktoren für die signifikanten Altersunterschiede verantwortlich sind, die zwischen Proben aus den gleichen Tiefen in den SRVP-Schichtfolgen beobachtet wurden.

Kapitel 3 fasst die Ergebnisse paläo-ökologischer und geoarchäologischer Untersuchungen zusammen, die in Suffolk zwischen 2005 und 2012 als Teil archäologischer Schutzmaßnahmen im Rahmen kommerzieller Erschließungen in den Tälern der Flüsse Gipping, Stour und Lark sowie entlang der Ostküste durchgeführt wurden. Ausmaß und Umfang dieser Untersuchungen variierten, sie umfassten aber für gewöhnlich eine adäquate Form von stratigraphischer Dokumentation und, sofern angebracht, eine Bewertung des paläo-ökologischen Potenzials sowie, wenn nötig, Empfehlungen für zukünftige Arbeiten. Nur eine dieser Fundstellen (Stowmarket Relief Road, River Gipping) wurde allerdings vollständig ausgewertet (Käfer, pflanzliche Makroreste, Mollusken und Radiokarbondatierungen). Hier lieferte ein 8m langes Auenprofil Belege für Umweltveränderungen sowie menschliche Einflüsse für den Zeitraum zwischen ca. 9000 bis ca. 1100 Jahren vor heute. Wenn auch das im Rahmen des SVRP und der kommerziellen Projekte gewonnene Ausmaß an analytischen Details nicht erlaubt, umfangreiche Aussagen zur Landschaftsentwicklung zu machen, so demonstrieren die Ergebnisse dennoch das größtenteils unangetastete Forschungspotenzial der Flusstäler in Suffolk, und sie bieten darüber hinaus Hypothesen zu zeitlichem Ablauf, Struktur und Prozessen fluvialer Entwicklung, menschlichen Aktivitäten und landschaftlichem Wandel im Holozän.

Im Zuge von Uferverlegungsarbeiten bei Beccles im unteren Waveney-Tal wurden drei archäologische Feuchtboden-Fundplätze der vorrömischen Eisenzeit bei Beccles, Barsham und Geldeston (Suffolk) entdeckt, die als Teil von kommerziellen Ausgrabungen (Beccles, Barsham), von der Universität Birmingham durchgeführten Lehrgrabungen (Beccles, Geldeston), bzw. von Historic England geförderten Forschungsprojekten ausgegraben wurden (Beccles) (Kapitel 4 und 5). An all diesen Plätzen fanden sich dreifache Holzpfostenreihen, die zur Überquerung des Niederungsbereiches des Flusses Waveney während der späteren vorrömischen Eisenzeit errichtet wurden, die aber alle auch Hinweise auf eine fortlaufende Nutzung während der romano-britischen Periode lieferten. Die detaillierteste und umfangreichste Untersuchung fand bei Beccles statt und umfasste geophysikalische Surveys, paläo-ökologische Analysen, Beurteilungen des Zustands von archäologischen Hölzern und Indikatoren der Paläo-Umwelt, geochemische Analysen und eine über zwei Jahre laufende hydrologische Beobachtung des 500 m langen Bodendenkmals (Kapitel 6). Diese Daten deuten an, dass der größere Teil der Fundstelle und der damit zusammenhängenden organischen Schichten für die meiste Zeit des Jahres über dem Grundwasserspeigel liegt und daher das Potenzial für die *in situ*-Erhaltung des archäologischen und paläoökologischen Bodenarchivs auf lange Sicht gefährdet ist.

Das Schlusskapitel (Kapitel 7) fasst den derzeitigen Kenntnisstand über die holozänen Umweltveränderungen und den archäologischen Bodendenkmalbestand in Suffolk zusammen, wobei der Schwerpunkt auf den verschiedenen Flusstälern liegt. Die mögliche Form und Funktion der Waveney-Holzpfostenreihungen wird diskutiert und mit ähnlichen Fundplätzen aus ganz Großbritannien verglichen. Es wird vorgeschlagen, dass diese Strukturen der Markierung von Wegeverläufen zum, vom und über den Fluss gedient haben und darüber hinaus auch als territoriale Markierungen für den Flussverkehr, sowohl den lokalen als vielleicht auch jenen in die südliche Nordsee, fungierten. Die Fundplätze in Barsham und Geldeston gehörten möglicherweise zu einem einzelnen Bauwerk, das sich quer über den Fluss Waveney erstreckte. Das Schlusskapitel endet mit einer Diskussion der spezifischen, in Beccles angewandten Techniken, zu denen u. a. die Erprobung eines neuartigen geophysikalischen Ansatzes am Fundplatz, Laserscanner zur dreidimensionalen Dokumentation von feucht erhaltenem archäologischem Holz sowie die Nutzung digitaler Methoden für virtuelle Rekonstruktionen der Holzpfostenreihungen gehörten, und die so der Öffentlichkeit eine bessere Beschäftigung mit ansonsten dem Blick der Allgemeinheit verborgenen archäologischen Feuchtbodenplätzen ermöglichen. Der Band schließt mit einer kurzen Zusammenfassung von Forschungsfragestellung, die im Rahmen zukünftiger Forschungen in den Flusstälern Suffolks untersucht werden könnten.

Übersetzung: Jörn Schuster

Résumé

Alors qu'on connait depuis longtemps l'Est-Anglie comme zone clé pour la préservation d'importants dépôts archéologiques et paléo-environnementaux du Paléolithique, on n'a jusqu'à présent que relativement peu étudié les vestiges de l'Holocène. Ce volume présente les résultats d'études paléo-environnementales, archéologiques et géo-archéologiques concentrées sur les vestiges post-glaciaires préservés dans les vallées fluviales du Suffolk. Les travaux discutés comprennent deux phases d'évaluation paléo-environnementale (pollen, datation au C14, coléoptères et diatomées) financées par Angleterre Historique et Levée sur la Durabilité des agrégats sous les auspices du programme des Vallées Fluviales du Suffolk (en anglais SRVP), divers projets commerciaux environnementaux et archéologiques menés dans tout le Suffolk en grande partie par Birmingham Archéo-Environnemental de l'université de Birmingham sous le plan *PPG* 16 et les cadres législatifs qui lui ont succédé; et les fouilles archéologiques et analyses paléo-environnementales associées de trois alignements de bois de construction de la préhistoire finale dans la plaine alluviale de la basse vallée de Waveney à Beccles, Barsham et Geldeston (Norfolk).

Cinq sites furent sélectionnés sur les rivières Waveney, Little Ouse, Lark et Blackbourne (Beccles, Hoxne, Hengrave, Ixworth et Brandon) par le SRVP, avec des carottes de contextes de plaine inondable extraites pour une évaluation paléo-environnementale suite à une évaluation reposant sur un travail de bureau, y compris une interrogation des renseignements archéologiques provenant des Archives des Sites et Monuments et des données topographiques provenant d'analyses de détection et de diffusion de la lumière (chapitre 2). Les évaluations paléo-environnementales montrèrent que les séquences de l'Holocène avaient été préservées sur tous les sites sauf à Brandon, mais que l'échelle chronologique et l'état de conservation des proxies paléo-environnementaux variait d'un site à l'autre. Un premier programme de datation au C14 a également donné une série de déterminations contenant des anomalies. Ceci a conduit à SRVP phase II, qui comprenait une deuxième tournée de prélèvements et de datations au C14 de multiples échantillons afin d'examiner ce problème. Les résultats indiquent qu'une gamme de facteurs associés aux procédés de formation de la tourbe de la plaine alluviale pourraient être responsables de ces importantes différences d'âge entre des échantillons de même profondeur observées dans les séquences SRVP

Le chapitre 3 présente un résumé des résultats des recherches paléo-environnementales et géo-archéologiques menées dans le Suffolk entre 2005 et 2012, dans le cadre de la mitigation archéologique associée à la construction d'une zone commerciale dans les vallées fluviales de Gipping, Stour et Lark et le long de la côte ouest. La taille et la portée de ces études variaient mais en général comprenaient une forme quelconque d'enregistrement stratigraphique accompagné d'une évaluation du potentiel paléo-environnemental si opportune, ainsi que, si nécessaire, des recommandations pour des travaux supplémentaires. Cependant, un seul des sites étudiés (la déviation de Stowmarket, rivière Gipping) a été soumis à une analyse complète (coléoptères, macrofossiles de plantes, mollusques et datations au C14). Ici une séquence de 8m de plaine alluviale a fourni des témoignages de changements environnementaux et d'impact humain de l'Holocène ca 9000-ca 1100 ans avant le présent . Tandis que le niveau de détail analytique fourni par SRVP et les projets commerciaux restreint les conclusions générales en ce qui concerne l'évolution du paysage, les résultats démontrent le potentiel de recherches, en grande partie non exploité, des vallées fluviales du Suffolk, et nous fournit aussi des hypothèses en ce qui concerne la chronologie, la configuration et le procédé de développement fluvial, l'activité humaine et les changements dans le paysage au cours de l'Holocène.

Des travaux de réalignement de la rive à Beccles, dans la basse vallée de la Waveney ont conduit à la découverte de trois sites archéologiques marécageux de la fin de la préhistoire à Beccles, Barsham et Geldeston (Suffolk),qui furent fouillés dans le cadre de fouilles commerciales Beccles, Barsham) de formation sous l'égide de l'université de Birmingham (Beccles, Geldeston) et de programmes de recherches financés par Angleterre Historique (Beccles) (Chapitres 4 et 5) Ces sites consistaient tous en de triples alignements de poteaux de bois qui avaient été construits à travers la plaine alluviale de la rivière Waveney au cours de la deuxième partie de l'âge du fer mais avec des témoignages de continuation de l'activité à la période romano-britannique. L'étude la plus détaillée et la plus exhaustive fut menée à Beccles et comprenait une prospection géophysique, des analyses paléo-environnementales, une évaluation de la condition du bois archéologique et des proxies paléo-environnementaux, des analyses géochimiques et une surveillance hydrolique pendant une période de deux ans du monument d'environ 500 m de long (Chapitre 6). Ces données indiquent que la plus grande partie du site et des dépôts organiques associés se trouve au-dessus de la surface de la nappe phréatique pendant une grande partie de l'année et de ce fait la possibilité de préserver ces vestiges archéologiques et paléo-environnementaux *in situ* dans le long terme se trouve menacée.

Le dernier chapitre (Chapitre 7) présente un résumé de l'état actuel de nos connaissances des changements environnementaux de l'Holocène et des archives archéologiques dans le Suffolk, se concentrant sur les témoignages des diverses vallées fluviales. Nous discutons de l'éventuelle forme et fonction des structures d'alignements de bois de Waveney et les comparons à d'autres sites similaires de tout le Royaume Uni. Nous suggérons que ces structures avaient peut-être servi pour délimiter des voies de passage vers, de et à travers la rivière et aussi comme marqueurs territoriaux associés à des déplacements sur la rivière à la fois locaux et peut-être jusqu'au sud de la Mer du Nord. Les sites de Barsham et de Geldeston auraient pu former un seul monument qui se serait étendu des deux côtés de la rivière Waveney. Le dernier chapitre se conclut par une discussion des techniques particulières employées pendant les travaux à Beccles, y compris l'essai d'une approche géophysique novatrice sur ce site, l'utilisation d'un scanner laser pour enregistrer en trois dimensions des bois archéologiques préservés en milieu humide et des approches numériques pour créer des 'reconstitutions virtuelles' des alignements de bois et donc améliorer la relation du public avec les sites archéologiques marécageux qui autrement se trouvent 'cachés' à la vue du public. Le volume se termine sur un bref résumé des questions de recherches que de futures études paléo-environnementales et archéologiques pourraient être amenées à aborder.

Annie Pritchard

1. Introduction: Archaeological and Palaeoenvironmental Research in East Anglia

1.1 Introduction

The potential of the lowland river valley floors of England to preserve deposits of archaeological and palaeoenvironmental value (the archaeo-environmental record, *sensu* Chapman and Gearey, 2013) has long been known (Limbrey and Evans, 1978; Fulford and Nichols, 1992; Needham and Macklin, 1992), although research and associated knowledge is spread somewhat unevenly geographically. Commencing in the 1970s a series of English Heritage funded surveys beginning in the Somerset Levels, but subsequently encompassing the Fenlands, North-West Wetlands and finally the Humberhead Levels, provided significant audits of these wetlands, which have largely been reclaimed by drainage for agriculture since the mid-18th century (e.g. Pryor *et al.*, 1985; Coles and Coles, 1986; Hall *et al.*, 1987; Van de Noort and Ellis, 1987; Lane, 1993; Cowell and Innes, 1994; Hall *et al.*, 1995; Van de Noort and Ellis, 1998). These studies have formed the basis for further investigations and syntheses (e.g. Van de Noort, 2004; Bamforth and Pryor, 2010; Brunning, 2013).

In addition to English Heritage sponsored projects, the minerals industry has funded numerous investigations of valley floor environments beyond tidal influence in advance of sand and gravel extraction, both informally through the funding of rescue excavations during the 1960s and 1970s and more formally since the early 1990s as part of planning processes, as well as indirectly between 2002 and 2011 through the Aggregates Levy Sustainability Fund (Brown, 2009). The corpus of literature resulting from developer-funded research is significant and includes major thematic studies, for example of the Thames Valley (Lambrick *et al.*, 2009; Morigi *et al.*, 2011), the Lugg Valley (Jackson and Miller, 2011), Trent Valley (Knight and Howard, 2004), and the Milfield basin (Passmore and Waddington, 2012).

This monograph describes the results of over eight years of research focused on palaeoenvironmental and archaeological archives preserved within the river valleys of the county of Suffolk, eastern England (Figure 1.1). Previous studies of palaeoenvironments, archaeological sites and associated cultural assemblages within East Anglia predominantly focused on its Pleistocene history and Palaeolithic heritage (e.g. Tallantire, 1953, 1954; Singer *et al.*, 1993; Lewis *et al.*, 2000a, b; Rose, 2009; Boismier *et al.*, 2012) and the region includes four stratigraphic type-site localities for the British Pleistocene (i.e. the Cromerian, Anglian, Hoxnian, and Ipswichian; Wymer, 1999). Recently, fluvial deposits exposed on the North Sea coastline at Pakefield in Suffolk (Parfitt *et al.*, 2005) and Happisburgh in Norfolk (Parfitt *et al.*, 2010) have yielded lithic evidence for the earliest human occupation of Britain, which is believed to be at least 780,000 years ago, reinforcing the importance of the 'ice-age' heritage of East Anglia.

Although clearly of great international significance, these Pleistocene and Palaeolithic records have perhaps somewhat deflected focus away from the later and potentially more extensive Holocene archives within the region. To the north of the River Waveney, the county boundary of Suffolk, research on the Holocene record has a long history within Norfolk and Cambridgeshire, with much of the early impetus provided by the coordinating forces of the Fenland Research Committee (Smith, 1997) and the Sub-Department of Quaternary Research (SQR) at the University of Cambridge, the latter under the initial leadership of Professor Sir Harry Godwin (West, 1988) and subsequently Professor Richard West (Turner and Gibbard, 1996). In Norfolk, relatively long Holocene palaeoenvironmental records have been recovered from a number of meres, notably at Diss (Peglar *et al.*, 1989, Peglar, 1993) and Hockham (Bennett, 1983).

In Cambridgeshire, the work of the Fenland Research Committee and SQR provided substantial foundations for the Fenland Archaeological Project (e.g. Pryor *et al.*, 1985; French *et al.*, 1993; Waller, 1994) and a number of major later prehistoric archaeological excavations, notably at Fengate (Pryor, 1980), Flag Fen (Bamforth and Pryor, 2010), Etton and Maxey (Pryor, 1999); these seminal studies have shaped our knowledge of wetland environments and methodological approaches to their study. More recently, the site of Must Farm near Whittlesey is providing significant new evidence for Neolithic and Bronze Age settlement and palaeoenvironments on the western edge of the Fenland Basin (Knight, 2009; Gibson *et al.*, 2010).

It is hoped that the work presented in this monograph will go some way towards re-dressing the imbalance of geoarchaeological and palaeoenvironmental research undertaken in Suffolk in comparison to adjacent counties in East Anglia. This monograph summarises the work of a number of projects and programs of study: the *Suffolk River Valley Project*, (SRVP) undertaken by Birmingham Archaeo-environmental (BA-E) and funded by the Aggregates Levy Sustainability Fund (ALSF; administered for this project by English Heritage), excavations and associated analyses at Beccles in the Waveney Valley funded by English Heritage's Historic Environment Enabling Programme (HEEP), excavations at Barsham and Geldeston, also in the Waveney Valley, funded by the Broadland Flood Alleviation Project (BFAP) and a number of projects of varying scope and extent delivered largely under *Planning Policy Guidance* 16, often as part of wider programmes of archaeological mitigation associated with various commercial developments. The work outlined therefore represents the result of partnerships and collaborations with a wide range of stakeholders and funders, including English Heritage, the Environment Agency, the Broads Authority, Broadlands Environmental Services Ltd, Suffolk County Council Archaeology Service, Beccles Town Council, local community groups and a number of other companies and organisations.

The results and conclusions of this work are diverse; they range from site-specific data regarding patterns and processes of Holocene environmental change and human activity in eastern England to methodological developments and protocols for radiocarbon dating of alluvial deposits and geophysical prospection for wet-preserved organic archaeology. Furthermore, the work offers perspectives on the management, protection and preservation *in situ* of the often fragile and threatened archaeo-environmental records preserved in these river valleys. Suffolk is an aggregate–rich, relatively low-lying region with a growing population and therefore its landscape is under pressure from a variety of directions including quarrying, intensive arable agriculture, infrastructure development and climate change. In addition to addressing the themes described above through archaeological survey, recording and excavation, it is intended that this work should contribute to the wider goal of protecting the fragile and threatened records preserved within river valleys of England and other areas of north-west Europe.

1.2 Physical setting and the Suffolk rivers

Cretaceous Chalk dominates the solid geology of East Anglia with less extensive deposits of Greensand, Gault Clay and (Jurassic age) Kimmeridge Clay in the north-west of the county (Chatwin, 1948). Following the Cretaceous, the Tertiary age Thanet Beds provide evidence for further marine conditions, before regional uplift resulted in fluvial deposition (the Reading Beds); however, both these units are restricted in their spatial extent to the extreme south-west of Suffolk, around the Brett, Gipping and Deben valleys. Towards the end of the Tertiary Period and spanning the Pliocene-Pleistocene boundary, shallow marine conditions returned, marked by the deposition of the shelly sands of the Coralline, Norwich and Red Crags that crop out along the coastline of East Anglia.

Further inland (and especially in the central and northern regions), the solid geology is overlain by superficial sediments comprising a mixture of glacial tills, fluvio-glacial and fluvial sands and gravels and coversands ranging in age from the early to late Pleistocene. About two-thirds of the county (the 'claylands') is covered by chalky boulder clay, with two large areas of sandy soils flanking this area. The area of sands on the east coast, south of a line from Woodbridge to Orford is referred to as 'The Sandlings' and that to the west as 'The Breckland' (Dymond and Martin, 1999). In low-lying areas such as the river valleys, coastal fringes and at the eastern edge of the Fenland basin, the Pleistocene deposits are covered by a veneer of peats, estuarine and riverine alluvium of Holocene age (Figure 1.1). The variability of surficial deposits has significant implications for land fertility and fragility, which in turn has implications for settlement, land use and the archaeological record.

The complex natural evolution of East Anglia area over the Pleistocene Epoch and underlying solid geology have played a major role in shaping the physiography of the contemporary landscape (Rose, 2009; Boreham *et al.*, 2010). The Anglian glaciation (MIS12), which occurred around 450,000 years ago was particularly important in this respect since ice eroded and created the Fen Basin and destroyed the major eastward draining river systems that previously flowed across the region, forerunners of the River Thames and Trent as well as an artery flowing from the south Midlands known as the Bytham River (Rose, 2009; Bridgland *et al.*, 2014). Following this glaciation, the drainage network observed today largely became established, although with minor modifications over the last 400,000 years (Boreham, 2010), some possibly as a result of newly recognised post-Anglian glacial incursions that affected eastern England (White *et al.*, 2010; Gibbard *et al.*, 2009a, b, 2012).

The Chalk outcrop, although now much subdued by glacial erosion, still forms an important north-south escarpment and drainage divide, separating those rivers that flow westwards into the Fen Basin (the Lark, Little Ouse, Wissey and Nar) and those flowing east directly to the North Sea (the Gipping, Waveney, Wensum, Yare and Bure). Whilst most of these rivers established new courses, the Waveney Valley from a few kilometres upstream of Diss follows the alignment of the Bytham River (Rose, 2009; Boreham *et al.*, 2010). The Holocene drainage network of Suffolk consists of low-energy river systems with cohesive channel banks, which transport fine-grained sediments (Howard and Macklin, 1999, 534). The rivers are characterised by low valley gradients (<2m km^{-1}), well-developed floodplains and low-angle valley-side slopes.

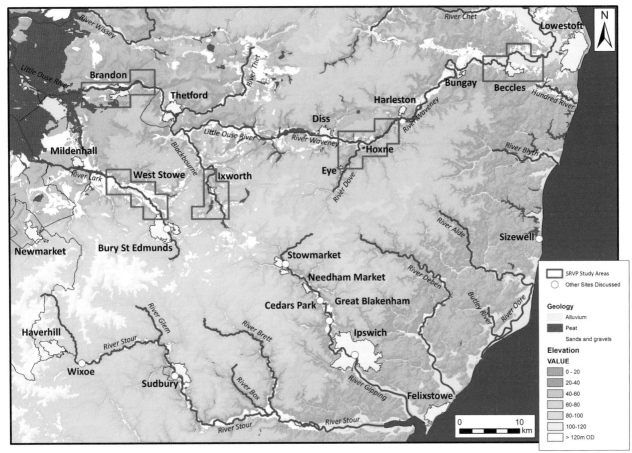

Figure 1.1: Map of Suffolk and part of south Norfolk showing alluvial, peat and sand and gravel deposits in the river valleys.

Whilst rivers of the Lateglacial period (13–10,000 BP; Lower and Walker, 1997) were typified by variable discharge and the creation of multi-channel braided river systems across Britain and north-west Europe (Collins *et al.*, 2006; Gao *et al.*, 2007; Howard *et al.*, 2011) climatic amelioration during the early Holocene reduced discharge, promoted vegetation growth, and subsequently reduced the erosive potential of the river systems (Brown *et al.*, 1994). The reduction in fluvial energy commonly resulted in the abandonment of secondary channels, which became infilled with organic deposits over time. The archaeological and palaeoenvironmental work described in this monograph includes the valleys of the Rivers Waveney, Blackbourne, Gipping, Lark, Little Ouse and Stour. With the exception of the Rivers Gipping and Stour, selected study areas along these channels were examined as part of the ALSF-funded *Suffolk River Valleys Project*.

The River Waveney

The River Waveney rises near the village of Redgrave and for a considerable part of its 90km course, it forms the county boundary between Norfolk and Suffolk. In its upper reaches as far as Hoxne, the river is single thread with a

slightly sinuous planform and it flows generally eastwards in a confined valley floor, which includes the largest remaining area of river valley fen in England (Redgrave and Lopham Fen National Nature Reserve). From Hoxne, the site of famous Lower Palaeolithic discoveries (Singer *et al.*, 1993), the valley floor begins to widen and the river turns to flow north-eastward towards Bungay, the upper navigation limit of historic river trade. The increased width of the valley floor has allowed the river greater mobility within its floodplain and within this reach it is increasingly sinuous, though it is still a single thread channel.

The wider valley floor has also been the focus of aggregate extraction (see Chapter 2). Downstream of Bungay, the river flows in an easterly direction, past Geldeston and Beccles as far as Camps Heath; as in the previous reach, the valley floor is wide, which has allowed the single channel to become highly sinuous. South of Camps Heath, the Oulton Dyke links the river with Oulton Broad and ultimately the North Sea at Lowestoft, but the river continues northwards to its confluence with the River Yare to the west of Great Yarmouth in the Belton Marshes. A second artificial channel, the 'Haddiscoe Cut' starts approximately 6km upstream of the confluence at St Olaves, and links the Waveney to the Yare at Reedham.

Both these cuts, together with the construction of weirs and locks at various points along the channel were made with the intention of allowing greater use of the waterways for transport and trade, a process that started with an Act of Parliament obtained in the 1670s but which continued into the 19th century. Other structures were emplaced to generate power for the numerous mills along the river. Today, the Waveney forms an important part of the network of waterways associated with the Broads National Park.

The River Gipping

The River Gipping rises near Mendlesham Green and flows in a generally south-westerly direction to Stowmarket before turning towards the south-east and flowing to Ipswich, a total distance of around 36km. Below the tidal limit at Stoke Bridge within the town, it becomes the River Orwell, which drains via its estuary into the southern North Sea. Upstream of Stowmarket, the single channel river is relatively confined within its valley floor and has a relatively straight planform. Downstream of Stowmarket, the floodplain is wider and the river becomes more sinuous and there is significant evidence for aggregate extraction across the wider valley floor, a pattern that is repeated as far as the outskirts of Ipswich. Around Needham Market and several other points downstream, the river bifurcates into two channels and together with numerous locks, this indicates the river's importance for trade and power in medieval and post-medieval times.

The River Stour

The River Stour rises to the north of Haverhill and takes a generally south-eastwards, though sinuous 76km long route to the North Sea coast at Harwich. For most of its course, it forms the county boundary between Suffolk and Essex. Throughout its course the single channel river is regularly bifurcated and there are numerous locks reflecting its improvement for transport, trade and power generation. Downstream of Haverhill, gravel extraction becomes a notable feature of the floodplain. Below Dedham in its lower reaches, the river flows through an Area of Outstanding Natural Beauty (AONB; Dedham Vale), an area synonymous with the Romantic landscape paintings of John Constable (1776–1837).

The River Lark

The River Lark rises on the Chalk high ground between Bury St Edmunds and Sudbury and flows in a generally north-westerly direction to its confluence with the River Great Ouse near Ely; it is the first of the Suffolk rivers described here to drain via the Fen Basin and Wash. The Lark is single thread throughout its course and shows a range of sinuosity, which is dependent on the width of the valley floor. Downstream of Bury St Edmunds, as it widens, the river shows greater signs of movement across its floodplain, which has also been the focus of aggregate extraction, notably around West Stow. However, downstream of Mildenhall, as the river enters the Fen Basin, it becomes notably straightened and canalised, and together with locks and sluices, reflects the influence of drainage projects associated with agricultural and transport improvements within the wider region.

The Little Ouse and Blackbourne

The Little Ouse rises close to the River Waveney but in contrast flows in a sinuous east-west course across the sandy heathland of the Breckland through Thetford and Brandon to join the River Great Ouse north-east of Littleport. As with the Waveney, for much of its length is defines the border between Norfolk and Suffolk and in total it flows approximately 65km. As with the Lark, its natural sinuous planform is overprinted west of Brandon as it enters the Fen Basin and it is replaced by canalised channels, dykes and drains. Historically, the river has been important for transport and trade and it was navigable as far as Thetford in the mid 17th century AD. The valley floor has also been the focus of aggregate extraction, notably upstream of Thetford and downstream of Brandon. South of Thetford, the Little Ouse is joined by a south bank tributary, the Blackbourne, which flows for approximately 32km from its source near Bradfield St George. Overall, the river has a south-north orientation, though this is sinuous, and although a relatively small valley floor, it does expand and bifurcate in places to include larger areas of wetland, for example, that at Ixworth (see Chapter 2).

1.3 The Suffolk Rivers: archaeo-environmental potential and threats

The accretion of sequences of fine-grained alluvium and associated valley floor peat deposits occurred across many floodplains during the Holocene. High-quality *in situ* multi-period archaeological remains can be preserved within these sedimentary archives, whilst associated organic deposits can provide a record of landscape evolution. However, variations in geomorphological processes and sedimentation styles can have significant implications for the techniques that can be effectively employed for archaeological geoprospection in these alluviated environments (Challis, 2006; Challis and Howard, 2006; Linford, 2006; Jordan, 2009; Challis and Howard, 2014). The large-scale land drainage and channelisation of many valley floors is likely to have had a significant impact on the fluvial stratigraphic archive of certain areas, but the overall extent of any such impact on the preservation potential of archaeological and palaeoenvironmental archives in the Suffolk river valleys was unknown at the beginning of this project.

Across the UK, the expansion of infrastructure, settlement, mineral extraction and the intensification of agriculture continues to put considerable pressure on both cultural and environmental archaeological remains in valley floors (Darvill and Fulton, 1998; Howard and Macklin, 1999) and the situation in Suffolk is little different. The principle mineral exploited in the county is sand and gravel with the majority of resources concentrated in the river valleys especially the Gipping; in 2007, 20 active quarries and three inactive sites were operational within the county (Suffolk County Council, 2008). In 2003 sand and gravel demand was estimated to be 1.73 million tonnes per annum (mtpa), although in 2006 this was revised down to 1.67 mtpa, providing nationally required county reserves until at least 2015 (Suffolk County Council, 2008).

Although a largely rural county, strategic development plans highlight the Felixstowe (Haven Gateway sub-region) and Lowestoft areas as the focus of planned expansion, which will include new residential and commercial developments (Suffolk County Council, 2008); quarrying to meet these growth plans will focus on the Gipping Valley/ A14 corridor, the Sudbury area and north-east Suffolk, although local borrow pits will also be developed as needs arise (Suffolk County Council, 2008). Therefore, whilst with the exception of the Gipping Valley, development pressures have not been significant or widespread to date, there is the potential for much greater pressure with planned growth and that earmarked for the Felixstowe area will impinge directly on the lower Waveney Valley. However, a more direct immediate threat to the valley floors and one which was highlighted by archaeological discoveries at Beccles and Barsham is the 20 year programme of flood alleviation works being undertaken along the tidal parts of River's Yare, Bure, Waveney and their tributaries under the auspices of the Broadland Flood Alleviation Project (http://www.bfap.org) (Figure 1.2).

Prior to the work of the *Suffolk River Valleys Project* knowledge of the Holocene history of the fluvial network of Suffolk was comparatively sparse, although excavations and palaeoenvironmental studies at Scole in the Waveney Valley (Ashwin and Tester, forthcoming), at Brandon on the Little Great Ouse (Carr *et al.*, 1988; Wiltshire, 1990), and at Sproughton on the River Gipping (Rose *et al.*, 1980) had shown significant potential for the preservation of archaeological sites and deposits of palaeoenvironmental value. Whilst the study by Rose *et al.* (1980) provided a benchmark publication for studies of lowland river evolution during the Lateglacial and early Holocene, rather little was known more generally concerning the timing and character of landscape development and the nature and extent of deposits associated with floodplain environments during the early to mid-Holocene.

1.4 Outline of this monograph

This monograph begins with a discussion of the background to the various phases of archaeological and palaeoenvironmental work undertaken in the Suffolk river valleys (Chapter 1). Chapter 2 summarises the results of the *Suffolk River Valleys Project* whilst Chapter

3 provides a discussion of the various commercial palaeoenvironmental projects carried out by Birmingham Archaeo-environmental (BA-E) in Suffolk between 2005 and 2012. This is followed (Chapters 4 and 5) by the results of excavations of later prehistoric sites in the lower Waveney Valley at Beccles, Barsham (Suffolk) and Geldeston (Norfolk). Chapter 6 discusses research into the preservation of the archaeo-environmental resource at Beccles reflecting on the implications of this for the *in situ* preservation of the site. The final chapter (Chapter 7) provides a summary and discussion of the entire corpus of work, considering the broader implications of this in terms of current understanding of the archaeological record, human activity and environmental change in east England. This final chapter also reflects on issues related to the investigation, understanding and protection of wetland archaeological sites and deposits within a broader national and international context.

1.5 The Suffolk River Valleys Project (2007)

The initial investigations of the Suffolk river valleys described in this volume began through the work of the *Suffolk River Valleys Project* (Fletcher *et al.*, 2006) funded via the Aggregates Levy Sustainability Fund (ALSF). Other research funded through the ALSF in Suffolk had previously begun to address the identification and quantification of the archaeological record in the minerals resource areas (Plouviez *et al.*, 2007), but no provision had been made within this project for the investigation of the palaeoenvironmental and geoarchaeological record, which too had the potential to be affected by aggregate extraction and other development pressures (see Figure 1.1). With the core objective of the English Heritage funded part of the ALSF scheme being to 'reduce the impact on the historic environment of aggregate extraction', a number of the ALSF priorities were identified as being directly related to the threats posed on the Suffolk lowlands:

- To contribute to 'developing the capacity to manage aggregate extraction landscapes in the future' through resource assessment.
- To contribute to 'delivering to public and professional audiences the full benefits of knowledge gained through past work in advance of aggregates extraction' through outreach as well as popular and academic publications.
- To contribute to 'promoting understanding of the conservation issues arising from the impacts of aggregates extraction on the historic environment' through the identification of areas of geoarchaeological significance worthy of preservation and conservation.

In addition, the project and related work aligned closely with the headline objective of promoting environmentally friendly extraction and transport:

- To contribute to 'research to enhance the understanding of the scale and character of the historic environment

Figure 1.2: New soke dyke excavated as part of the Broadland Flood Alleviation Scheme

in current or likely future aggregate producing areas in order to provide the baseline information necessary for effective future management' through the assessment and characterisation of sediments at threat through future aggregate extraction.

- To provide 'support for the development of management and conservation strategies for the historic environment in current or likely future areas of aggregate production' which would aid in the development of future geoarchaeological prospection strategies undertaken in response to aggregate extraction' through extensive literature reviews of both published and grey literature relating to the county.

The *Suffolk River Valleys Project* subsequently developed through the identification of this major gap in knowledge with the project designed to:

- Provide baseline data addressing the geomorphological character of selected Suffolk valley floors and the potential of the landforms and sediments recorded within them for palaeoenvironmental reconstruction of the surrounding archaeological landscape.
- Provide an assessment of the potential for the preservation of archaeological remains within Suffolk valleys through an understanding of their geomorphological history.
- Review and collate both the grey and published palaeoenvironmental and archaeological literature into a single review.

The project was linked to *The Aggregate Landscape of Suffolk: The Archaeological Resource* (PNUM 3987; Plouviez *et al.*, 2007), and both had common goals and themes:

- To provide additional data to enhance the themes identified in the regional research frameworks and enable the continued formulation of the regional research agenda.
- To use the findings of this study alongside the data provided by the *Aggregate Landscape of Suffolk* project to enhance the county HER, providing other heritage managers with information to assist them in the decision-making process associated with development activities.
- To provide a framework for the development of a closer working relationship between: Suffolk County Council, English Heritage, the University of Birmingham, and other stakeholder organisations such as the Environment Agency. Policies over the coming decades, such as the development of Catchment Management Plans (CFMPs), which shape strategies for flood, water quality and abstraction management, particularly in the light of the European Water Framework Directive (European Commission, 2000), and managed retreat, will have significant implications for the archaeology of the river valleys and coastal margins of Suffolk. However, archaeology also has the potential to play a valuable role in contextualising past change and therefore planning for the future impacts of processes such as those brought about by climate change (e.g. see Van de Noort, 2013).

Suffolk River Valleys Project Structure

Dr William Fletcher for Suffolk County Council Archaeological Service (SCCAS) coordinated this project and Birmingham Archaeo-Environmental (BA-E) undertook the research under the direction of Dr Benjamin Gearey, Dr Andy J. Howard, Dr Tom Hill and Dr Emma Tetlow. In addition to core project staff, a steering group was established to oversee the project and consisted of senior members of Suffolk County Council Archaeological Service (Keith Wade, County Archaeologist, and Jude Plouviez, Archaeological Officer), stakeholder partners from English Heritage (Tom Cromwell and Dr Jane Sidell) and the Environment Agency (Phil Catherall, deceased).

A major desk-based literature review of previous archaeological and palaeoenvironmental research was undertaken as part of the *Suffolk River Valleys Project* and this forms the basis of the concluding discussion (Chapter 7). Both published and unpublished (grey) literature was reviewed to enable an assessment of the current state of knowledge of the environmental history of the river valleys and to indicate areas of high and low archaeological potential. The results of the literature review enabled the identification of sites with potential for further study through the *Suffolk River Valleys Project*. The original draft assessment report of the *Suffolk River Valleys Project* was submitted to English Heritage in March 2007; a second phase was approved and commissioned in July 2007. An overview of both phases of study is outlined in Chapter 2.

1.6 Commercial palaeoenvironmental and geoarchaeological study in the Suffolk river valleys (2005–2012)

As well as the targeted work carried out by the *Suffolk River Valleys Project*, BA-E undertook a number of other palaeoenvironmental and geoarchaeological investigations in Suffolk between 2005 and 2012. These works were generally part of archaeological mitigation associated with commercial development projects carried out under *PPG* 16 and hence varied in scope and extent. In the main they consisted of stratigraphic recording of boreholes and trial trench surveys of sites and deposits associated with the valleys of the Rivers Gipping, Stour and Lark, as well as investigations of areas on the east coast around Ipswich and Sizewell. Some of these studies were associated with wider programs of archaeological work, such as trial trenching and excavation, whilst others were 'stand-alone' projects. Most of the studies, which identified deposits of palaeoenvironmental potential subsequently, included some level of assessment (typically pollen, plant macrofossil, beetle and occasionally diatom analysis), often but not always supported by radiocarbon dating of suitable organic material (see below). Occasionally, recommendations were made at assessment stage for more detailed analyses of those sequences, which were regarded as of high potential, but very few of these proposals were ever subsequently carried through. The results of these various commercial projects are presented in Chapter 3.

1.7 Archaeological excavations and analyses in the lower Waveney Valley (Beccles, Barsham and Geldeston)

In 2006 excavation of a 'soke dyke' as part of a wider scheme of flood alleviation works on behalf of the Environment Agency in the lower Waveney Valley unearthed wooden archaeological remains in the form of large timber stakes within the floodplain peats. The site was located on Beccles Marshes, adjacent to the River Waveney, just under 1km due north of the edge of the town of Beccles (NGR TM29156413). Subsequent archaeological excavations were undertaken under *PPG* 16 by a joint team of archaeologists from BA-E and SCCAS between 19 July and 5 August 2006.

The area of disturbance by the flood alleviation works defined the initial phases of excavation (approximately 20 × 5m). An auger survey of the floodplain and associated palaeoenvironmental analyses were undertaken as part of the *Suffolk River Valleys Project*. This work provided a context

for the archaeological excavations and also demonstrated the depth and extent of the floodplain peats, indicating the potential for preservation of archaeological remains beyond the area of initial disturbance. The following year (2007) a second season of work was carried out as part of a University of Birmingham undergraduate training excavation, which also included members of SCCAS. Both seasons of work incorporated an integrated sampling strategy for palaeoenvironmental assessment and dendrochronology.

Following the results of these two seasons of excavations, English Heritage funded a subsequent project based at the University of Birmingham: *The Beccles Triple Post Alignment, Beccles Marshes, Suffolk: understanding, contextualising and managing a later Iron Age wetland site.* During the 2007 excavations at Beccles, the ongoing flood alleviation work on the River Waveney also unearthed a second site at Barsham, approximately 4km upstream. A subsequent season of excavation and analyses of this site under *PPG* 16 was undertaken by BA-E and SCCAS in 2007. A third site was identified during continuing flood alleviation work on the north (Norfolk) side of the River Waveney just across from Barsham, just to the south of the village of Geldeston. Following initial investigations of this site by Heather Wallis, further excavations were undertaken as a University of Birmingham undergraduate training excavation in 2011. Chapters 4, 5 and 6 summarise the results of these excavations and associated palaeoenvironmental and geoarchaeological research in the Waveney Valley at Beccles, Barsham and Geldeston, whilst Chapter 7 provides a synthesis and discussion of the combined archaeological and palaeoenvironmental studies carried out. The following section outlines the project aims and structure of the research at Beccles.

Project structure: the Beccles Triple Post Alignment, Beccles Marshes, Suffolk: understanding, contextualising and managing a later Iron Age wetland site

Wetland sites and deposits of palaeoenvironmental potential such as those preserved in river valleys present a range of problems for archaeological managers and related policy frameworks. As well as aiming to produce a specific management plan for the Beccles site, all elements of the work described in this monograph ultimately contribute to discourses regarding the management and protection of the archaeo-environmental resource. In 2012, English Heritage published a *Strategy for Water and Wetland Heritage* (Heathcote, 2012), but when this project was undertaken, there was no overarching agenda or framework specific to wetland archaeology and hence reference was made to related documentation:

- English Heritage's *Strategy for Wetlands* (Olivier and Van de Noort, 2002: www.english-heritage.org.uk/upload/pdf/wetlands_strategy.pdf).
- East Anglian Regional Research Frameworks

(Glazebrook, 1997; Brown and Glazebrook, 2000); in the case of Beccles, particularly the Iron Age sections by Bryant (1997, 2000).

The Beccles project was influenced by the '*Strategy for Wetlands*' and from lessons learnt from other key wetland archaeological projects, notably that at Sutton Common, south Yorkshire (Van de Noort *et al.*, 2007). The '*Strategy for Wetlands*' is for the most part an overarching document without specific reference points for individual cases on a site-by-site basis. The main principles of the strategy (Olivier and Van de Noort, 2002: 2) are to: promote better management though practical conservation mechanisms; undertake better research and outreach; and develop wetlands policy through the work of local authorities, national agencies and intergovernmental bodies. The final chapter (Chapter 7) outlines reflections on the prospects for the preservation *in situ* of the later prehistoric sites in the lower Waveney Valley and also the implications of the research for broader concerns regarding wetland sites and landscapes in the face of a range of threats and management concerns (Heathcote, 2012).

The Beccles project was funded through the Historic Environment Enabling Programme (HEEP) and organised according to the *Management of Research Projects in the Historic Environment* guidelines. The project had the following aims:

- Investigate the efficacy of novel non-intrusive geophysical techniques in the identification of wetland sites of this and related forms.
- Establish the full extent, form and chronological phasing of the site.
- Generate baseline data on the state of preservation of the archaeo-environmental resource.
- Obtain data regarding the groundwater regime and assess the implications of this for the current preservation of the remains and the continued *in situ* preservation of the site.
- Determine the relationship between the quality of preservation of different archaeological and palaeoenvironmental source materials, the hydrological regime and soil chemistry.
- Develop a sustainable management strategy for the site and contribute to agendas relating to 'best practice' in the preservation and management of similar sites elsewhere.

The strength of this project with regard to these issues was that the initial phases of work had indicated that the archaeological structure was linear and potentially passed through several different land-use regimes across the marshes. Factors that were regarded, as potentially having a detrimental effect on the burial environment and preservation of the archaeological remains included:

- The on-going flood alleviation works in the Waveney Valley.
- The range of current land-uses along the known and

projected alignment of the site, which included rough grazing, improved pasture, small-scale cultivation and recreation (yacht club).
- The distance of remains with respect to the River Waveney and the implications of this for water table drawdown.

The project was arranged around three main phases of work (Survey, Recording and Analysis), each of which was followed by an updated project design. The associated methods to address these aims included a combination of remote sensing and survey, sediment coring, modelling within the framework of a Geographical Information System (GIS), archaeological excavation, palaeobiological and wood analyses, geochemical analyses, scientific dating and preservation assessment. The first phase of the project (Survey) consisted of a programme of capture and analysis of remote sensing data, followed by geophysical survey and an associated programme of borehole drilling, which aimed to generate data for a three-dimensional digital elevation model (DEM) of the lithostratigraphy and underlying pre-peat landscape. These methods were intended to inform the subsequent programme of archaeological excavation (Recording). A subsequent phase of Analysis followed with final project completion and reporting and publication represented by this monograph.

1.8 Methodologies

The various phases of work described in this monograph employed a variety of standard archaeological and palaeoenvironmental techniques and methodologies. This section outlines these methodologies with additional information regarding specific sites or phases of the different projects provided in the relevant sections.

Borehole excavation, stratigraphic recording and sampling

Boreholes were excavated as part of all the phases of work described in this monograph and unless otherwise stated, borehole excavation was carried out using an Eijkelkamp gouge auger with a range of different head attachments depending on local ground conditions. Certain projects, particularly those that were developer-funded, utilised mechanical coring rigs such as windowless samplers and these are described in the relevant sections. Where possible, borehole locations were recorded using differential Global Positioning Systems (dGPS), but less accurate handheld GPS devices were also employed. Stratigraphic recording was carried out in the field with samples recovered as appropriate for further assessments and analyses. In the case of on-site sampling for the archaeological excavations in the Waveney Valley (Chapter 5), this was achieved from open sections using monolith tins and where appropriate, by the collection of bulk samples during excavation.

Pollen assessments and analyses

Pollen assessments and full analyses were carried out on peat and other organic deposits sampled both from boreholes and archaeological excavations at Beccles, Barsham and Geldeston (Chapters, 3, 4 and 5). Pollen preparation followed standard techniques including potassium hydroxide (KOH) digestion, hydrofluoric acid (HF) treatment and acetylation (Moore *et al.,* 1991). For assessment level counts, at least 125 total land pollen grains (TLP) excluding aquatics and spores were counted for each sample, although this was not always achieved for samples with low concentrations or poor preservation. A total of 300 TLP were counted for those samples that were subsequently analysed in full (Chapter 4). The results from the pollen analyses are generally presented in the form of pollen diagrams produced using the computer programmes TILIA and TILIA*GRAPH (Grimm, 1991), although not in the case of several of the commercial assessments (Chapter 3) for which relatively few samples were counted.

All percentage figures quoted are of TLP unless otherwise specified. Pollen concentrations were calculated with the addition of *Lycopodium* tablets (Stockmarr, 1971) but these data are only referred to in the case of the palynological studies at Beccles. Pollen nomenclature largely follows Bennett *et al.* (1994). *Cerealia*-type includes all grass pollen grains over 40μm in diameter, a group which as well as cultivated cereals can include wild taxa such as *Glyceria fluitans, Aira caryophyllea, Ammophila arenaria, Leymus arenarius* and *Elytrigia. Glyceria fluitans* is the most probable in the fresh water environments of the Suffolk river valleys and this plant may thus be represented in the *Cerealia*-type curve. *Corylus avellena*-type includes hazel as well as sweet gale/bog myrtle, but the latter is unlikely for the majority of the sampling locations discussed.

Plant macrofossil and beetles

Assessments of bulk sediment samples for wet-preserved plant macrofossil and beetle remains were carried out as part of the *Suffolk River Valleys Project,* as well as for certain commercial projects and the excavations at Beccles and Barsham. These were processed using standard methods (Kenward *et al.,* 1980). Insect remains were sorted and identified under a low-power binocular microscope at a magnification between ×15–×45. For full analyses, where possible, the insect remains were identified to species level by direct comparison to specimens in the Gorham and Girling Insect Collections housed at the University of Birmingham and The Hope Collection at Oxford University Museum of Natural History. In the case of the plant macrofossil analyses at Beccles, flots were collected over a single 0.25mm sieve, rather than a stack of sieves of decreasing apertures. Plant macrofossil identifications were made at magnifications up to ×50 using reference material and standard botanical keys (e.g. Cappers *et al.,* 2006).

Archaeological excavation and sampling

Archaeological excavations at Beccles, Barsham and Geldeston (Chapter 5) followed standard methods for wetland sites unless otherwise indicated. All trenches excavated were located using dGPS and superficial deposits were removed using a tracked excavator fitted with a ditching bucket. Archaeological deposits were then excavated by hand and planned using a dGPS established grid. Worked wooden material was numbered, recorded and sub-sampled as appropriate. In trenches where additional sections were not excavated (Trenches 3, 4, 5 and 6 at Beccles, 2009) natural (un-worked) roundwood, roots and worked material such as wood chips were planned. In Trench 4 at Beccles (see Chapter 5), a 1m test-square was excavated from which all material was collected, following a methodology implemented at Flag Fen during the later phases of excavation (Taylor, 2001). All archaeological data from the excavations and associated studies was stored within the project GIS. Sampling for palaeoenvironmental analyses (pollen, beetles and plant macrofossils) was carried out and outlined in further detail in the relevant chapters.

Archaeological wood recording

The system for recording and analysis of archaeological wooden remains from Beccles, Barsham and Geldeston (Chapter 4) followed Taylor (2001). Archaeological wood was recorded using *pro-forma* sheets and samples retained where appropriate for further analyses. The significant quantities of waterlogged wood encountered during the Beccles excavations necessitated the design and implementation of a trench specific sub-sampling strategy to recover material for detailed recording and analysis. The collection of this material was determined by subjective sampling, complimented by total collection within defined sections. Although this strategy is likely to have produced a bias towards larger, worked items, a sizable sample of smaller, wood-working debris and other bulk material was also collected. Converted material was described according to the method of splitting, radial, tangential, half or quarter split and the worked ends of timber classified on the basis of the number of sides worked to produce pencil, wedge or chisel shaped ends. Other features such as jam curves (where a tool had come to a stop in the wood leaving a clear mark) were also recorded.

The Beccles excavations in particular produced a large number of wood chips. Wood chips were planned and numbered as groups with larger pieces of timber debris recorded individually. Roots were individually numbered but were not always sampled. Preliminary wood species identification, sub-sampling and recording was carried out on-site with a subsequent discard policy. A number of the upright stakes from Beccles (see Chapter 5) were retained for formal preservation assessment (see below). Samples of *Quercus* (oak) and *Fraxinus excelsior* (ash) were identified as such on the basis of observable macroscopic features with additional verification as necessary through thin-section analysis using a standard binocular microscope (×400 magnification).

Radiocarbon dating

A range of archaeological and palaeoenvironmental material was radiocarbon dated as part of work described in Chapters 2–5. Four laboratories were used: the Scottish Universities Environmental Research Centre (denoted by the prefix code SUERC); Beta Analytic Inc., Miami, Florida (denoted by the prefix code Beta); the Oxford Radiocarbon Accelerator Unit, University of Oxford (denoted by the prefix code Ox-A) and the Centre for Isotope Research Groningen, the Netherlands (denoted by the prefix code GrN). All four laboratories have quality assurance procedures and participate in regular international inter-comparisons (Scott, 2003), which indicate no laboratory offsets and demonstrate the validity of the precision of the dates quoted. Radiocarbon samples were obtained on plant macrofossil, humin and humic fractions and in the case of the work described in Chapter 2, all three fractions where these were available. Rowena Gale and David E. Robinson carried out identification of the plant macrofossil samples reported in Chapter 2.

Samples submitted to the Scottish Universities Environmental Research Centre (SUERC) were pre-treated following methods outlined in Hoper *et al.* (1998). CO_2 from the pre-treated samples was obtained by combustion in pre-cleaned sealed quartz tubes (Vandeputte *et al.,* 1996) and the purified CO_2 was converted to graphite (Slota *et al.,* 1987) and the samples were then measured by Accelerator Mass Spectrometry (AMS), as outlined in Xu *et al.* (2004). Samples submitted to Beta Analytic were pre-treated using the acid/base/acid protocol (Mook and Waterbolk, 1985) and dated by AMS. The Oxford samples were pre-treated using a standard acid/base/acid method followed by an additional bleaching step (Brock *et al.,* 2010), then combusted, graphitised and dated by AMS as described by Bronk Ramsey *et al.* (2004). The Netherlands (GrN) samples were prepared using the acid/alkali/acid method (Mook and Waterbolk, 1985) and measured using gas proportional counting (Mook and Steurman, 1983).

The results are expressed as conventional radiocarbon ages (Stuiver and Polach, 1977) quoted in accordance with the international standard known as the Trondheim Convention (Stuiver and Kra, 1986). All calibrations used in this volume have been calculated using the calibration curve of Reimer *et al.* (2009) and the computer program OxCal version 4.1 (Bronk Ramsey, 1995, 1998, 2001, 2009). The date ranges cited in the text are those for 95% confidence quoted in the form recommended by Mook (1986), with the end points rounded outwards to 10 years.

Bayesian chronological modelling

In the case of radiocarbon dates from archaeological contexts (see Chapters 4 and 7), the dates for specific 'events' can be estimated using the scientific dating information from the radiocarbon measurements, but also by using prior information about the relationships between specific samples. Methodology is available that allows the combination of these different types of information explicitly, to produce realistic estimates of the dates of interest. It should be emphasised that the posterior density estimates produced by this modelling are not absolute, but are interpretative estimates, which can change as further data become available. The technique used is a form of Markov Chain Monte Carlo sampling, applied using OxCal version 4.1 (http://c14.arch.ox.ac.uk/); details of the algorithms employed are available from the on-line manual and in Bronk Ramsey (1995, 1998, 2001, 2009). Bayesian modelling (see e.g. Gearey *et al.*, 2009) of the radiocarbon chronology of the palaeoenvironmental sequence from the Stowmarket Relief Road (Chapter 3) did not produce a robust model and hence the chronology proposed for this sequence, based on simple linear interpolation, must be regarded as highly tentative. It is likely that the AMS determinations for this sequence have been affected by the incorporation of older or younger organic material (see Chapter 2 for discussion of the problems associated with radiocarbon dating of floodplain sediments).

Dendrochronology

Selected samples of wood from the excavations at Beccles, Barsham and Geldeston (Chapter 4) were submitted for dendrochronological dating. Each sample was collected as a complete cross-section and assessed for the wood type, the number of rings it contained, and whether the sequence of ring widths could be reliably resolved. For dendrochronological analysis it was preferable to have samples of *Quercus* (oak) with 50 or more annual rings, and for the sequence to be free of aberrant anatomical features such as those caused by physical damage to the tree whilst it was still living.

Standard dendrochronological analysis methods (see English Heritage, 2004) were applied: the sequence of ring widths in each sample was revealed by preparing a surface equivalent to the original horizontal plane of the parent tree with a variety of bladed tools. The width of each successive annual growth ring was revealed by this preparation method. The complete sequences of the annual growth rings in the suitable samples were then measured to an accuracy of 0.01mm using a micro-computer based travelling stage. In some instances two or three radii were measured, particularly on samples, which appeared somewhat distorted. Due to the remarkably uniform character of the assemblages, a decision was made to attempt to analyse material with less than 50 rings, though only from samples that were complete to bark-edge. This strategy described above could not be continued for the southern trenches of the 2009 excavations (Chapter 4) as the preservation of this material was poor.

The sequences of ring widths were plotted onto semi-log graph paper to enable visual comparisons to be made between sequences. In addition cross-correlation algorithms (e.g. Baillie and Pilcher, 1973) were employed to search for positions where the ring sequences were highly correlated. Highly correlated positions were checked using the graphs and, if any of these were satisfactory, new composite sequences were constructed from the synchronised sequences. Any *t*-values reported below were derived from the original CROS algorithm (Baillie and Pilcher, 1973). A *t*-value of 3.5 or higher is usually indicative of a good match, although this is with the proviso that high *t*-values at the same relative or absolute position needs to have been obtained from a range of independent sequences, and that these positions are supported by satisfactory visual matching.

Condition analysis: archaeological wood, geochemistry and sediment sampling

Whilst it is clear that the conditions that control long term preservation of remains in wetland environments are highly complex, Brunning (2013: 23) has recently stated with some justification that: "As a rule, if an archaeological site continues to remain permanently below the water table, and there is no significant contamination of the water supply, then that site is safe from rapid degradation." In addition to the qualitative and semi-quantitative assessment of the condition of organic archaeological remains at Beccles, Barsham and Geldeston (Chapters 5 and 6), formal quantitative analyses of samples from Beccles were also carried out with additional study of samples of archaeological wood from Barsham. The condition assessment studies aimed to produce a picture of the physical and chemical characteristics of the archaeological wood (Panter and Spriggs, 1996). This was to formulate an understanding of the history of the structure, both pre- and post-deposition; and establish a profile of the chemical and physico-chemical make-up of the wood, thereby establishing a 'baseline' condition of the current state of preservation of the structure.

The density of a sample of wood can be determined by the amount of 'wood substance' (cellulose, lignin, short chain sugars etc.) present per unit volume (Dinwoodie, 1989). It follows therefore that a reduction in the amount of 'wood substance' resulting from decay will be reflected in a reduction in the density of the sample. By comparing the sample density with that of un-decayed wood of the same species (termed the 'normal' density) it is possible to quantify the amount of decay of any given sample. Decay and breakdown of the cellular structure gives rise to an increase in the porosity of the wood as more and more voids are created, leading to an increase in the amount of water retained; in effect, increasing water content equates to increasing wood decay.

A Sibert drill was used to assess the condition of two samples of archaeological worked wood from the Barsham site (Chapter 6). The Sibert drill (probe) is a handheld device, which produces a graphic representation of the rate of penetration of a high-speed probe into the sample of wood (Panter and Spriggs, 1996). For the assessment of the horizontal archaeological timbers from Beccles (Chapter 4), an 8mm diameter incremental auger was used to extract core samples (0.05m) at selected locations from the two oak stakes. Each core was assessed visually before further sub-sampling. To ensure full saturation (in order to determine maximum water content) each sub-sample was degassed in water and under vacuum (Hoffman, 1981).

The maximum water content was determined by oven drying each sub-sample from each timber until a constant dry weight was obtained. The maximum water content (µmax) was calculated and expressed as a percentage of the oven dry weigh (such values can exceed 100%, depending upon the level of wood decay). The density of each sub-sample was also calculated from the maximum water content, which can be compared with the 'normal' density of fresh wood of the same species and the amount of material lost. For English *Quercus* (oak) the normal density is taken as 0.56g per cubic centimetre (cc) and for *Alnus glutinosa* (alder) the density is 0.42g/cc.

At Beccles, sediment samples were collected and analysed for the principal redox sensitive parameters (sulphate, sulphide, nitrate, nitride and ammonia) as well as for pH and organic matter content to provide baseline data on the nature of the burial environment, indicating whether conditions were reducing (and therefore suitable for *in situ* preservation of organic material) or oxidising (aggressive towards to organic preservation). This work was intended to complement the subsequent groundwater-monitoring programme, also discussed in Chapter 6.

Water table monitoring

A range of projects over the last two decades have developed approaches to understanding the preservation of wetland archaeological sites and deposits, including monitoring of the groundwater table, determinations of redox potential, soil moisture content and acid buffering capacity (e.g. Freeze and Cherry, 1979; Faulkner *et al.*, 1989; Caple, 1996; Welch and Thomas, 1996; Corfield, 1993, 1996, 1998; Caple and Dungworth, 1998; Brunning *et al.*, 2000; Raiswell, 2001; Hogan *et al.*, 2002; Cheetham, 2004). Following the establishment of the extent and character of the archaeological remains through excavation at Beccles, a network of piezometers was installed to permit fluctuations in the groundwater table at the site to be recorded over a two-year cycle. These data were modelled within GIS to investigate relationships with the patterns of preservation observed in the archaeo-environmental sequence (e.g. Chapman and Cheetham, 2002; Van de Noort *et al.*, 2002) and these results are discussed in Chapter 6.

2. The Suffolk River Valleys Project (SRVP) Phases I and II (2006–2008)

With contributions from
Tom Hill, Peter Marshall, William Fletcher and Emma Tetlow

2.1 Introduction

As outlined in the previous chapter, The *Suffolk River Valleys Project* (SRVP) was funded by the ALSF (Brown, 2009) and designed as an assessment of the archaeo-environmental potential of selected river valleys in Suffolk (Hill *et al.*, 2007). Following a desktop review, five areas were selected for further investigation on the Rivers Blackbourne (Mickelmere), Little Ouse (Brandon) and Lark (Hengrave) in the west of the county and the River Waveney (Hoxne and Beccles) in the east (Figure 2.1). Two phases of fieldwork followed at these sites: Phase I (2006) resulted in the recovery of core sequences and subsequent palaeoenvironmental assessment, with associated programmes of radiocarbon dating intended to establish robust chronologies for these sequences. However, this radiocarbon programme produced a number of marked age inversions. It was unclear whether these data demonstrated that the deposits in question had been disturbed or re-worked and/or if the anomalous radiocarbon dates could be attributed to other factors, such as contamination during sampling or processing. Phase II of the project (2008) therefore aimed at using a revised methodology for radiocarbon dating of the sediment sequences to investigate the possible reasons for the anomalous radiocarbon dates with new sampling undertaken immediately adjacent to Phase I core sites (Hill *et al.*, 2008a, see also Howard *et al.*, 2009). This chapter therefore presents a synthesis of the Phase I palaeoenvironmental assessments alongside the results of Phase II radiocarbon dating programme, which provided a provisional chronology for the deposits and the associated palaeoenvironmental assessments.

2.2 Study site selection and methodologies

The Suffolk County Council Sites and Monuments Record (SMR) was provided as MapInfo MIF files and incorporated into the project GIS during Phase I. The SMR provided information relating to the spatial distribution and diversity of archaeological sites and finds throughout Suffolk. A number of GIS 'layers' that proved useful to the identification of potential sites suitable for the preservation of palaeoenvironmental deposits were also available in the form of soil and geology data, which indicated the character of the drift deposits within specific valley lowlands (referred to in the following section). In addition, the location of parish boundaries, which were officially recognised in the Anglo-Saxon period (but commonly in use long before) provided potential evidence for spatial and chronological patterns of river channel change.

Aerial photographs, supplied by Suffolk County Council, included vertical photographs from the 1940s as well as those taken in 1999. Subtle changes in vegetation type and colour identified on aerial photographs, for example, could imply variations in the underlying soil type and moisture content, a common indicator for the presence of palaeochannels (Baker, 2003). Comparisons were also made between aerial photographs taken in the 1940s and in 1999 to identify palaeochannels and other significant landscape features that were not visible on the later prints because they had had been destroyed by gravel extraction or other forms of development.

Once the five site research locations within Suffolk had been identified, project partners The Environment Agency provided Light Detection and Ranging (LiDAR) data. LiDAR has become an essential part of the archaeologist's geoprospection toolkit (Challis, 2006; Crutchley and Crow, 2009) providing high-resolution altitudinal data that can be used to construct Digital Terrain Models (DTMs) and Digital Surface Models (DSMs). The topographic information can then be analysed to identify subtle variations in the topography of the study areas, which may relate to palaeochannels or areas of river terrace. The resulting data were supplied as 2m spatial resolution elevation product and provided as ArcGIS ASCII grid files, which were converted to ArcGIS raster grid format. Site selection (see below) was thus informed by a combination of archaeological, topographical and remote-sensing derived data sources

Fieldwork took the form of the excavation of transects of cores across the selected locations and the recovery of samples for palaeoenvironmental assessment. Palaeoenvironmental assessments were carried out on sub-samples from three of the five sites investigated (Beccles, Hengrave and Ixworth). This included pollen and beetle assessment on three of the four sequences (Beccles Core 1, Hengrave and Ixworth). Full Coleopteran analyses would generally require *c.* 10 litre samples to obtain sufficient faunal assemblages for reliable palaeoenvironmental interpretations (Kenward *et al.*, 1980). For this reason, combined with the qualitative nature of Phase I of this project, core samples were 'bulked' to provide limited quantities of sediment for assessment purposes. Diatom assessments were carried out on Beccles Core 1 with more detailed analysis of Core 2. All assessments were carried out following the methods outlined in Chapter 1.

Phase II of the project was initiated to assess the issues raised regarding the chronostratigraphic integrity of each of the sequences identified in Phase I; specific protocols for the sample recovery, sub-sampling and radiocarbon dating were developed in collaboration with Dr Peter Marshall (English Heritage). To enable close comparisons between the radiocarbon dating results of Phases I and II, the new sample cores were taken from close proximity to those locations used in the original phase of fieldwork. Due to the suggestion that potential dating anomalies may have resulted from disturbance to the upper layers of peat, it was proposed that trial trenching of the locations be undertaken to allow detailed inspection of the stratigraphy of these uppermost deposits. Monolith tins were then used to subsample the open trench faces. Core extraction using a Russian Corer was then undertaken to sample the remaining stratigraphic sequences to depth.

An initial round of radiocarbon dating was undertaken on samples from the top, middle and bottom of each sequence (i.e. similar stratigraphic units and comparable depths to those sampled during Phase I). At each radiocarbon sample depth, individual plant macrofossil samples were submitted if possible, in addition to bulk samples. Prior to radiocarbon sample submission, samples were assessed for their pH and total organic content (determined by loss on ignition). All radiocarbon dating protocols followed the procedures outlined in Chapter 1.

2.3 SRVP fieldwork, palaeoenvironmental assessments and radiocarbon dating

The Waveney Valley and Beccles Marshes

The Beccles Marshes study area (TM 642355 291900) was located on the southern bank of the River Waveney (see Chapter 1) on an area of pasture to the north of the town of Beccles (Figure 2.2). The drift geology comprises glaciofluvial sands and gravels and chalky till, providing a mix of acidic soils and slowly permeable loamy and clayey soils. The early to mid-Holocene clastic deposits that overlie the terrace gravels in the Waveney Valley and associated rivers (Yare and Bure) have previously been referred to as The Breydon Formation (Jennings, 1951; Coles, 1977; Coles and Funnell, 1981, Alderton, 1983; Moorlock, 2000). Jennings and Lambert (1955) divided the Formation into five Members: the Lower Peat, Lower Clay, Middle Peat, Upper Clay and Upper Peat. These deposits represent the influence of changes in relative sea level on the environments prevailing in the valley and associated tributaries.

The precise timing and character of these changes across the Holocene remains the subject of some debate (e.g. Peterson, 2007), as there is local variation in the stratigraphic sequence across the area, a relatively limited number of associated radiocarbon determinations and other complicating factors, including evidence for erosion of the peat units during deposition of the clays. Alderton (1983) proposed an alternative scheme to that of Jennings and Lambert (1955) based on comprehensive radiocarbon dating of five palaeoenvironmental (pollen and diatom) sequences from the Waveney valley; however, this doctoral study remains unpublished.

Broadly, the Breydon Formation consists of a Lower (woody) Peat deposit (–19.5m OD at Great Yarmouth to *c.* –9.5m OD inland) indicating fen and reedswamp, followed by saltmarsh development in and close to the incised channel of the Waveney and Bure. A determination of 7580±90 BP (HAR-2535, 6600–6245 cal. BC) is available from the top of the peat from near Great Yarmouth (Coles and Funnell, 1981). The Lower Clay (base *c.* –20m to –6m OD further inland, top *c.* –5.5 to –8m OD) contains foraminifera indicative of low intertidal marsh through to high intertidal flat and finally reed swamp, apparently reflecting a period of positive sea level tendency prior to a transition to the Middle Peat, which is found in the valleys of the Waveney, Yare and Bure and thins out markedly towards the coast. Alderton (1983) dated the transition to the Middle Peat to *c.* 2850 cal. BC and suggested that this unit represents a relatively rapid fall in the rate of relative sea level rise. A further episode of rising relative sea level resulted in the deposition of the Upper Clay (*c.* –3.75 to 4.5m OD) which fills the full width of the valley at the seaward end of the Brue, but thins markedly inland becoming restricted to the proximity of the current channel of the Waveney above Gillingham (Alderton, 1983). Coles

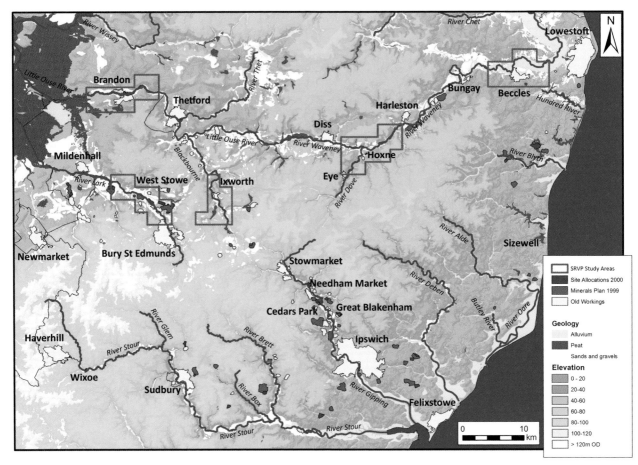

Figure 2.1: Map showing SRVP study areas in relation to areas of aggregate extraction

and Funnell (1981) report that at its maximum extension, the Upper Clay reached some 23km inland to within 7km of Norwich.

This shift from peat to estuarine conditions is dated to 1985±40BP (Q-2184; 90 cal. BC–cal. AD 140) at Stanley Carr just to the north-east of Beccles (Alderton, 1983). Wells and Wheeler (1999) also presented evidence from Norfolk Broadland for a marine transgression during the Romano-British period. Although there are various data indicating a period of rising relative sea level in East Anglia during this period (see also Clarke *et al.*, 1981), Peterson (2007) has cast doubt on the precise extent of the estuarine environment in this period. The final member of the Breydon Formation, the Upper Peat unit, is described as discontinuous and restricted to the downstream valley margins in the Waveney Valley (Alderton, 1983), whilst in the Yare it is only present in the poorly drained upper valley (Coles, 1977).

The study area

The Beccles Marshes study area was selected on the basis of the discovery and subsequent excavation of the archaeological site on Beccles Marshes in 2006 (see Chapter 4). Stratigraphic survey during Phase I demonstrated the

presence of peat deposits ranging in depth from *c*. 2.50m to *c*. 6.50m, with estuarine clays and silts overlying the floodplain peat unit at the northern end of the study area. Two cores were extracted for palaeoenvironmental assessment during Phase I; the first core was taken adjacent to the archaeological excavations at Beccles (Beccles Core 1, 2007); the second core from *c*. 100m to the north of Trench 1 (see Chapter 4) (Beccles Core 2, 2007). Two cores were subsequently taken from the site during Phase II (Beccles 2008 Core 1; Beccles 2008 Core 2) for the second round of radiocarbon dating.

A 10km stretch of the River Waveney floodplain centred on Beccles was also assessed for other potential sites, but no palaeochannels could be identified using LiDAR with the exception of a possible feature north of Shipmeadow, *c*. 4km west of Beccles (TM 637714 290888). In addition, no parish boundaries deviated from the present river course and few field boundaries suggested patterns that might be interpreted as providing evidence for palaeochannels (see Chapter 6).

Beccles Core 1 (2007) palaeoenvironmental assessments

A transect of cores from adjacent to the archaeological

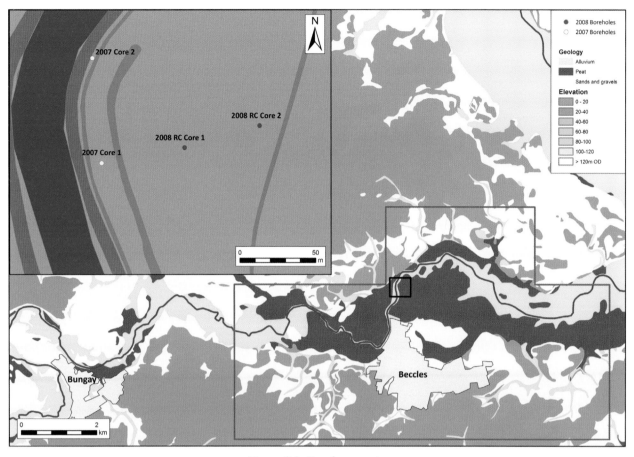

Figure 2.2: Beccles mapview

excavations at Beccles (Trench 1, 2006) (see Chapter 4) and Beccles Core 1 were recovered for assessment. The Beccles Core 1 sequence was 5.50m thick, consisting of well-humified, silty peats, with occasional wood fragments and a grey organic silt layer (0.10m thick), in turn underlain by basal sands and gravels (Table 2.1).

Pollen

The pollen assessments are presented as a percentage pollen diagram (Figure 2.3). Pollen concentrations and preservation were highly variable with a general deterioration in preservation and associated reduction in concentration towards the middle/top of the sequence. For this reason, pollen counts are very low above *c*. 2.90m in particular, and any interpretation must thus be considered tentative.

The basal zone (BCC-1) is dominated by *Pinus sylvestris* (Scots' pine), which seems to have been growing locally during the earliest stages of floodplain sedimentation. This

Table 2.1: Beccles Core 1(2007) stratigraphy and associated data

Depth/m	m OD (top unit)	Description	Pollen Zones code/depth	Other samples
0–0.90	−0.41	Dark grey brown herbaceous well humified slightly silty peat	–	–
0.90–1.0	−1.31	Light grey organic silt	–	0.88 and 0.96m: Diatoms
1.0–1.90	−1.41	Dark grey–brown herbaceous well humified slightly silty peat	BCC-1: 1–2.50	–
1.90–4.50	−2.13	Dark red–brown well humified herbaceous peat with wood fragments	BCC-2:	2–2.60m: (Bulk)
4.50–5.50	−4.91	Dark brown well humified peat	2.50–4.50	4.80–5.40m: (Bulk)
			BCC-3: 4.50–5.0	
>5.50	−5.91	Gravels	–	–

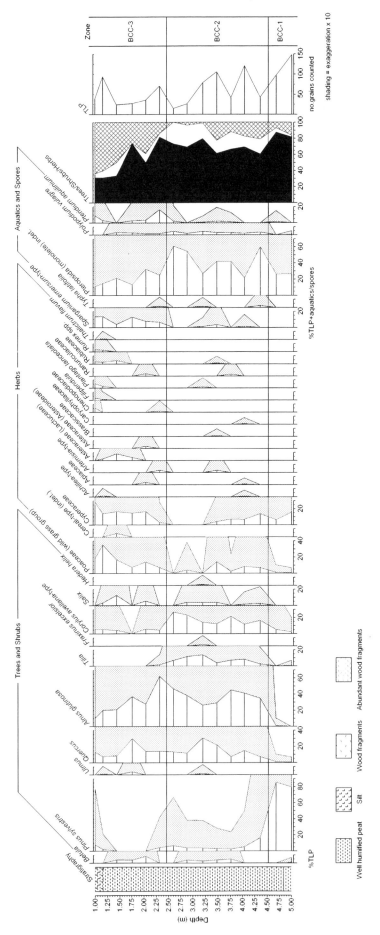

Figure 2.3: Beccles Core 1 Pollen diagram

presumably reflects the availability of sandy soils suitable for this tree on the pre-peat land surface. The subsequent zone, BCC-2 opens with a marked decline in *Pinus* and concomitant rise in *Alnus glutinosa* (alder) and other trees including *Quercus* (oak)*, Corylus* (hazel)*, Salix* (willow) and *Tilia* (lime). Poaceae (wild grasses) also increases whilst Cyperaceae (sedge) declines steadily across the zone and Pteropsida monolete (indet.) (ferns) remain well represented. This zone therefore reflects both local and extra-local vegetation change, with alder and willow replacing pine locally, probably as paludification affected the sandy substrate of the pre-peat landscape of the valley floor. Lime, hazel and oak were probably expanding onto drier soils around the valley. The Poaceae curve is likely to reflect local wetland grasses such as *Phragmites* (common reed), with few other herbs recorded at this time.

The final zone BCC-3 sees an abrupt fall in *Tilia* and steady reductions in other trees and shrubs including *Alnus*, *Corylus* and *Pinus. Salix* and *Betula* are the only woody taxa to increase at this time. Herbs including Poaceae and Cyperaceae increase with other indicators of open ground such as Lactuceae (dandelion-type plants), *Galium*-type (bed straws) and towards the top of the zone, *Plantago lanceolata* (ribwort plantain) and *Rumex* (docks). *Sparganium emersum*-type (bur-reeds etc.) also displays a steady increase. The data would therefore appear to reflect a general opening up of the woodland canopy on the floodplain and beyond. The increase in bur reeds, sedges and willow may suggest that locally, conditions had become wetter, favouring the expansion of willow over alder. The disappearance of lime and decline in the other arboreal components alongside rising grasses and other herbs suggest significant changes on the dryland, with lime dominated woodland being replaced by open grassland.

Beetles

Two bulk samples were assessed for beetle remains from towards the centre of the core (2.00–2.60m) and the base of the core (4.80–5.40m); both samples were from dark brown to red-brown herbaceous, well-humified peat. A restricted assemblage of well-preserved and identifiable Coleopteran remains was recovered from 2.00–2.60m. Species included *Pterostichus* spp., *Trogophloeus* spp.*, Philonthus* spp. and *Aphodius* spp., but their abundance never exceeded 1–2 individuals. The limited nature of this assemblage prevented any meaningful palaeoenvironmental interpretation. The sample from 4.80–5.40m contained no Coleopteran remains.

Diatoms

Diatom analysis in Core 1 focused on the organic-rich silt horizon at 0.85 1.00m with two samples from 0.88m and 0.96m (Table 2.1). At 0.88m, diatom abundance was relatively low and the frustules were commonly disarticulated. The species *Diploneis interrupta* almost wholly dominated the diatom assemblage encountered during the initial assessment. Fragments of species including *Diploneis bombus*, *Rhophalo diagibba*, *Nitzschia navicularis*, *Paralia sulcata* and *Nitzschia punctata* were also present. The dominance of *Diploneis interrupta* may be a consequence of preferential diatom preservation, as diatoms composed of weaker biogenic silica may have been destroyed. However, the overall abundance of *Diploneis interrupta* is an indicator of the influence of intertidal conditions on the development of the sedimentary unit. The aerophilous nature of *Diploneis interrupta*, supported by the presence of *Diploneis bombus*, suggests deposition occurred on the coastal zone proximal to an upper tidal flat or saltmarsh.

Diatom abundance was slightly higher at 0.96m than at 0.88m, with a higher overall diversity in species. However, as with 0.88m, *Diploneis interrupta* dominated. Species including *Diploneis ovalis*, *Nitzschia navicularis*, *Cyclotella striata* and *Nitzschia punctata* were also encountered, whilst the common fragmented nature of the frustules restricted the identification of disarticulated *Navicula* spp., *Pinnularia* spp. and *Cymbella* spp. The majority of identifiable species thrive in brackish water environments, whilst the abundance of *Diploneis interrupta* confirms deposition is likely to have occurred within an intertidal estuarine setting.

Beccles Core 2 Palaeoenvironmental Assessments

Beccles Core 2 was located *c.* 80m north of Beccles Core 1. The stratigraphy at this location was markedly different to that of Core 1, consisting of *c.* 3m of grey-brown to blue-grey clays and silts overlying *c.* 2m of red-brown herbaceous peat (Table 2.2). Samples were retrieved during Phase I for palaeoenvironmental assessment and radiocarbon dating, but due to the highly cohesive nature of the minerogenic sediments, it was not possible to sample using a Russian corer and an Eijkelcamp gouge corer was thus used. This sampling methodology probably accounts in part for some of the anomalous radiocarbon dates subsequently obtained during Phase I.

Beetles

Two bulk samples were assessed for Coleopteran remains; one from towards the base of the core within dark brown herbaceous, well-humified silty peat (3.20–3.80m) and a second sample from towards the centre of the core (2.00–2.30m) within grey-brown organic-rich silts and blue-grey clayey silts. The sample from 3.20–3.80m provided a small but well-preserved and interpretable assemblage. Species included *Elaphrus cupreus*, *Pterostichus* spp., the aquatic *Cercyon* spp. and *Hydrothassa glabra*. The insect remains from this sample suggest well vegetated, standing water surrounded by grassland. The Carabid *Elaphrus cupreus*

Down by the river

Table 2.2: Beccles Core 2 (2007) stratigraphy and associated data

Depth/m	m OD (top unit)	Description	Diatom samples	Other samples
0–0.16	–0.08	Unsampled	–	–
0.16–0.89	–0.24	Blue grey organic clayey silt	–	–
0.89–0.96	–0.97	Grey brown organic silt with rootlets	–	–
0.96–1.35	–1.04	Blue grey clayey silt	1.34m	–
1.35–1.56	–1.43	Grey brown organic silt	1.55m	–
1.56–1.74	–1.64	Blue grey clayey silt	1.73m	–
1.74–2.23	–1.82	Grey brown organic silt	2.22m	2–2.30m: (Bulk)
2.23–2.51	–2.31	Blue grey clay rich silt	2.50m	–
2.51–2.55	–2.59	Grey brown organic silt	2.54m	–
2.55–2.58	–2.63	Blue grey clayey silt	2.57m	–
2.58–2.76	–2.66	Grey brown organic silt	2.75m	–
2.76–2.84	–2.84	Blue grey clayey silt	2.83m	–
2.84–3.74	–2.92	Dark brown herbaceous well humified silty peat	–	3.20–3.80m: (Bulk)
3.74–3.88	–3.82	Wood – core not bottomed	–	–
	–3.96 (base)			

is found at the muddy margins of standing waters in reedy swamps and bogs (Lindroth, 1974). The aquatic members of the Hydrophilid family, *Cercyon* spp., are also found amongst wet, decaying organic material at the margins of standing and slow moving waters (Hansen, 1987). At 2.00–2.30m, a well-preserved and identifiable but restricted assemblage of Coleopteran remains was recovered. Species included *Helophorus* spp., *Stenus* spp. and *Aleocharinae* (gen. and spp. indet.), although counts rarely exceeded one or two individuals. The limited nature of this assemblage precluded any detailed interpretation.

Diatoms

The interbedded layers of organic-rich silts and blue-grey silts and clays in Core 2 were suggested to reflect the influence of relative sea-level change in the lower Waveney Valley. Nine samples were taken for diatom analysis from the lower stratigraphic boundary between the organic-rich silts and the clayey silts (Table 2.2). Two samples contained very low species abundance and diversity (2.50m and 2.57m). A count of only 110 frustules was achieved for the sample at 1.55m. The diatom frustules from these samples may have experienced post-depositional biogenic silica dissolution as a consequence of fluctuations in the local water-table. Enhanced redox conditions within lowland deposits have been shown to precipitate iron oxides that influence diatom preservation (Mayer *et al.*, 1991). The other six samples yielded counts of 200+ total diatom valves (TDV; Figure 2.4).

2.83M Dominant species: Nitzschia navicularis, Cocconeis placentula, Paralia sulcata and Epithemia turgida.

Marine brackish epipelon species contributed *c*. 31% TDV, with *Nitzschia navicularis* dominating. Marine-brackish aerophilous species such as *Diploneis ovalis* and *Diploneis interrupta* were also present in relative abundance (12.6%

TDV). There is also however strong influence from brackish-fresh and fresh-brackish epiphytic species (26% TDV combined), whilst fresh epiphytic species (*Epithemia turgida* dominating) contributed 11.5% TDV.

Sample 2.83m was located at the base of blue-grey clayey silt that immediately overlies fen peat. Although the overall dominance of marine brackish epipelon and aerophilous species initially suggest sedimentation in an upper mudflat intertidal environment, the influence of brackish-fresh and fresh-brackish and fresh epiphytic species underlines the maintained influence of freshwater conditions. Consequently, classification according to Vos and de Wolf (1993) suggests deposition may have occurred within pools on the supratidal salt marsh

2.75M Dominant species: Epithemia turgida, Cocconeis placentula and Epithemia zebra.

Brackish-fresh (13.5% TDV), fresh-brackish (17.6% TDV) and fresh (24% TDV) epiphytic species dominate, with *Cocconeis placentula*, *Gomphonema constrictum* and *Epithemia turgida* contributing respectively. Marine-brackish epipelon species also contribute.

There is a distinct increase in the influence of diatom species that thrive in environments with lower salinity levels when compared to the underlying assemblage. This, in turn, is supported by the enhanced organic content within the sedimentary unit, indicative of deposition at a higher altitude on the salt marsh. However, based on Vos and de Wolf (1993), deposition was still occurring in pools within the salt marsh, as this depositional environment is the highest altitudinal zone relative to tidal level available within the classification scheme.

2.57m: Very low diatom abundances were recorded. Based on sedimentology, it is hypothesised that the shift from underlying organic-rich silt to blue-grey clays and silts is indicative of a positive sea-level tendency. The abundance of organic matter within estuarine deposits commonly

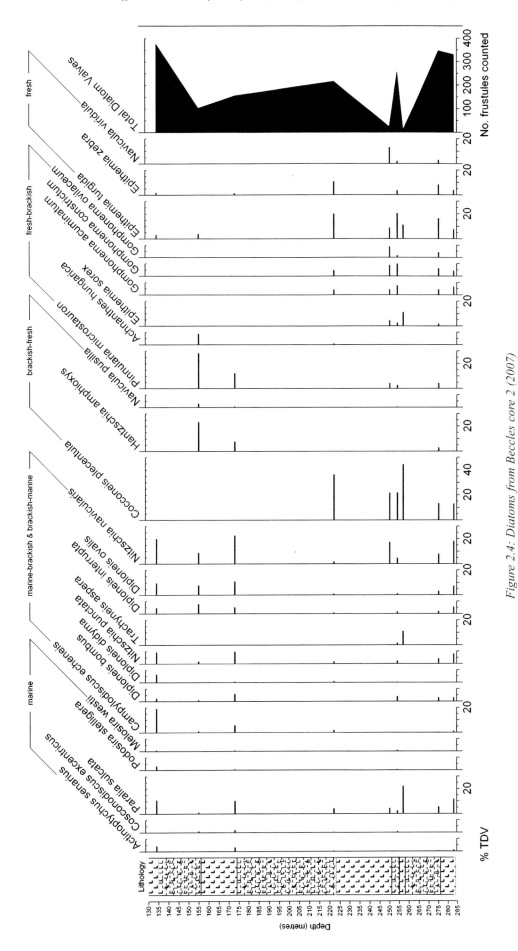

Figure 2.4: Diatoms from Beccles core 2 (2007)

decreases with distance down the tidal frame (Hill, 2006). If deposition occurred at a lower altitude on the tidal frame, marine encroachment may have caused the shift in the depositional environment

2.54M: DOMINANT SPECIES: COCCONEIS PLACENTULA, EPITHEMIA TURGIDA AND GOMPHONEMA CONSTRICTUM.

As at 2.75m, brackish-fresh, fresh-brackish and fresh epiphytic species dominate, with *Cocconeis placentula*, *Gomphonema constrictum* and *Epithemia turgida* dominating the respective contributions. The influence of marine planktonic and tychoplanktonic species remains low, indicating a restricted input from tidal influence. Deposition of the organic-rich silt continued to occur perhaps within pools on a salt marsh, similar to samples at 2.83m and 2.75m. If deposition of the underlying sample at 2.57m had occurred further down the tidal frame, it is likely that a negative sea-level tendency resulted in enhanced freshwater terrestrial sedimentation within the coastal lowlands.

2.50m: Very low diatom abundance was recorded within this sample. Consequently, as with the sample at 2.57m, no reliable palaeoenvironmental interpretations were possible. It is however suggested that a shift from the deposition of the underlying organic-rich silt to blue-grey clays and silts is once again indicative of a positive sea-level tendency.

2.22M: DOMINANT SPECIES: COCCONEIS PLACENTULA, EPITHEMIA TURGID AND EPITHEMIA SOREX.

Brackish-fresh epiphytic species (*Cocconeis placentula)* and fresh epiphytic species (*Epithemia turgida* and *Epithemia sorex)* dominate the assemblage. Less than 15% TDV are diatom species requiring marine, marine-brackish or brackish water conditions to survive. The low abundance of saline-tolerant species, combined with the lack of planktonic and aerophilous species within the assemblage, is indicative of the restricted influence of tidal conditions on the sedimentary environment. If deposition of the underlying blue-grey clays and silts occurred in conditions of enhanced marine influence, this horizon reflects a negative sea-level tendency and a return to supratidal conditions.

1.73M: DOMINANT SPECIES: NITZSCHIA NAVICULARIS, DIPLONEIS OVALIS, PARALIA SULCATA AND NITZSCHIA PUNCTATA.

Marine-brackish epipelon species dominate this assemblage (42% TDV), with contributions from *Nitzschia navicularis*, *Diploneis didyma* and *Diploneis bombus*. Marine plankton species (e.g. *Paralia sulcata)* are much more influential (15.4% TDV) when compared to the underlying assemblage. Marine-brackish and brackish-marine aerophilous species, including *Diploneis ovalis* and *Hantzschia amphioxys* respectively, are also influential within the diatom archive.

The abundance of marine-brackish epipelon species,

combined with the influence of saline-tolerant aerophilous species indicates sedimentation occurred lower down the tidal frame when compared to the underlying assemblage. This is also supported by the comparable reduction in organic content within the unit. Although the diatom species present suggest deposition may have occurred on intertidal mud flats, according to Vos and de Wolf (1993) the maintained presence of brackish-fresh aerophilous species indicates deposition slightly higher up the tidal frame, on salt marshes around Mean High Water (MHW). This however indicates a positive sea-level tendency when compared to the underlying diatom assemblage, resulting in the enhanced influence of estuarine conditions within the depositional environment.

1.55M: DOMINANT SPECIES: PINNULARIA MICROSTAURON, HANTZSCHIA AMPHIOXYS AND NITZSCHIA NAVICULARIS.

Brackish-fresh aerophilous species dominate the assemblage, contributing *c.* 57% TDV. *Pinnularia microstauron* and *Hantzschia amphioxys* dominate this group. Whilst marine-brackish epipelon species such as *Nitzschia navicularis* and marine-brackish aerophilous species including *Diploneis interrupta* and *Diploneis ovalis* are also present, their abundance is relatively low. Very low populations of marine planktonic and tychoplanktonic species are also evident within the assemblage.

Although a count of 200 diatom valves could not be achieved for this assemblage, tentative conclusions can be made regarding the palaeoenvironmental conditions present at the time of deposition. Based on the influence of marine-brackish epipelon and aerophilous species, combined with the overall dominance of brackish-fresh aerophilous species, deposition is suggested to have occurred in the supratidal zone, on salt marshes *above* MHW. This would therefore indicate a negative sea-level tendency has occurred in relation to the underlying depositional environment.

1.34M: DOMINANT SPECIES: NITZSCHIA NAVICULARIS, CAMPYLODISCUS ECHENEIS, PARALIA SULCATA AND NITZSCHIA PUNCTATA.

Marine-brackish epipelon species such as *Nitzschia navicularis* and *Campylodiscus echeneis* dominate the diatom assemblage, contributing *c.* 54% TDV. Marine planktonic species (e.g. *Paralia sulcata)* contribute 17% TDV, whilst marine-brackish aerophilous species including *Diploneis interrupta* and *Diploneis ovalis* contribute 14% TDV.

The overall dominance of marine-brackish epipelon species, supported by the enhanced influence of marine planktonic and aerophilous species, suggest that deposition continued on the supratidal area, but lower down the tidal frame on a salt marsh around MHW. A positive sea-level tendency is therefore indicated due to the enhanced influence of marine environmental conditions on the diatom assemblage.

Table 2.3: Beccles RC Core 1 (2008) stratigraphy and radiocarbon samples

Depth/m	m OD (top unit)	Description	Radiocarbon samples/m/material/ lab code
0–0.40	0.03	Made ground	–
0.40–0.45	–0.37	Dark red brown very well humified peat	–
0.45–0.62	–0.42	Dark red brown herbaceous well humified peat with wood fragments	–
0.62–3.30	–0.59	Dark red brown herbaceous well humified peat with wood fragments & *Phragmites*	0.84-Humin (GrN-3116) 0.84-Humic (GrN-31151) 0.84-*Alnus* twig (SUREC-15973) 0.84-*Alnus* twig (SUREC-15974)
3.30–3.60	–3.27	Dark brown black very well humified peat with sparse *Phragmites*	3.30-Humin (GrN-31117) 3.30-Humic (GrN-31152) 3.30-*Alnus* twig (SUERC-15975) 3.30-*Alnus* twig (SUREC-15976)
3.60–4.60	–3.57	Dark brown very well humified peat with occasional wood fragments	4.60-Humin (GrN-31118) 4.60-Humic (GrN-31153 4.60-*Alnus* twig
	–4.57 (base)		(SUERC-15981)

Table 2.4: Beccles RC Core 2 (2008) stratigraphy and radiocarbon samples

Depth/m	m OD (top unit)	Description	Radiocarbon samples/m/material/ lab code
0–1.0	0.02	Made ground	–
1.0–1.38	–0.98	Dark brown well humified peat with occasional wood and mollusc fragments	1.37-Humin (GrN-31119) 1.37-Humic (GrN-31154) 1.37-*Alnus* twig (SUERC-15982) 1.37-Alnus twig (SUERC-15983)
1.38–2.75	–1.36	Dark brown well humified herbaceous peat with *Phragmites* and wood fragments	–
2.75–3.10	–2.73	Dark brown well humified detrital peat	–
3.10–3.60	–3.08	Dark brown well humified peat	3.59-Humin (GrN-31120) 3.59-Humic (GrN-31155) 3.59-*Alnus* twig (SUERC-15984)
3.60–4.0	–3.58	Dark brown well humified peat with monocotyledonous remains	-
4.0–4.30	–3.98	Dark brown-black very well humified peat with *Phargmites* remains	4.30-Humin (GrN-31121) 4.30-Humic (GrN-31156)
	–4.28		4.30-*Alnus* twig (GU-6796)

Phase II Chronology: Beccles RC Core 1 and Core 2 (2008)

Following the problems with the radiocarbon dates derived from all the Phase I SRVP cores outlined in the introduction, re-sampling at Beccles was carried out with two cores taken further away from the original sampling site to minimize any disturbance to the sediments by human activity in antiquity. Core 1 was taken from 50m and Core 2 from

Table 2.5: Beccles RC Core 1 (2008) radiocarbon dates and associated data

Lab code	Sample ID/ depth m	Material	Organic Content	pH	δ13C (‰)	Radiocarbon age (BP)	Weighted mean	Calibrated date BC (95% confidence)
GrN-31116	0.84	Peat (Humin)	79%	3.9	−28.9	2130±40	2142±32 BP (T'=0.2; v=1; T'(5%)= 3.8)	360–50
GrN-31151	0.84	Peat (Humic acid)			−28.9	2160±50		
SUERC-15973	0.84 A	Plant macrofossil: *Alnus* twig,	–	–	−29.5	2065±35	–	190–10
SUERC-15974	0.84 B	Plant macrofossil: *Alnus* twig	–	–	−28.1	2015±40	–	160–70
GrN-31117	3.30	Peat (Humin)	78%	6.2	−28.0	4590±30	4590 ±26 BP (T'=0.0; v=1; T'(5%)= 3.8)	3500–3340
GrN-31152	3.30	Peat (Humic acid)			−28.7	4590±50		
SUERC-15975	3.30 A	Plant macrofossil: *Alnus* wood	–	–	−30.8	3885±35	–	2480–2210
SUERC-15976	3.30 B	Plant macrofossil: *Alnus* wood	–	–	−30.7	3970±35	–	2580–2350
GrN-31118	4.60	Peat (Humin)	72%	4.8	−28.4	8460±50	8427 ±43 BP (T'=1.6; v=1; T'(5%)= 3.8)	7580–7370
GrN-31153	4.60	Peat (Humic acid)			−28.0	8340±80		
SUERC-15981	4.60	Plant macrofossil: cf. *Alnus* twig	–	–	−28.4	5660±35	–	4560–4400

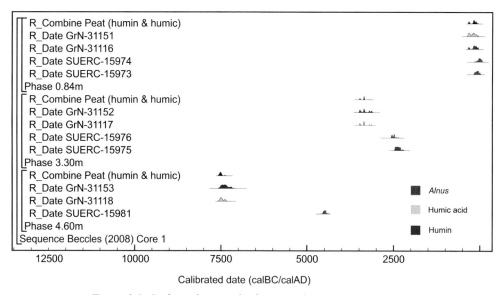

Figure 2.5: Radiocarbon results from Beccles RC Core 1 (2008)

100m to the north-east of Beccles Core 1 (2007). Eleven radiocarbon dates were obtained from Beccles (2008) RC Core 1 (referred to as RC Core 1) (Table 2.3). Duplicate dating of humin and humic fractions were carried out on samples from 0.84m, 3.30m and 4.60m with dating of macrofossils also undertaken at both 0.84m and 3.30 m. A fragment of *Alnus* twig was submitted from the sample (2.39m), but the low carbon yield of this fragment prevented successful dating. Ten radiocarbon samples were

submitted from a second core, Beccles (2008) RC Core 2 (referred to as RC Core 2) (Table 2.4). These included duplicate humin and humic measurements and duplicates of *Alnus* macrofossils (twigs) at 1.37m and triplicate measurements from 3.59m and 4.30m (humin, humic and *Alnus* roundwood/twig) although the latter sample failed.

The results of Phase II radiocarbon dating of RC Core 1 (Table 2.5; Figure 2.5) show no age inversions and all four dated samples from 0.84m are statistically consistent.

Table 2.6: Beccles RC Core 2 (2008) radiocarbon dates and associated data

Lab Code	Sample ID/ depth (m)	Material dated	Organic content	pH	δ¹³C (‰)	Radiocarbon age (BP)	Weighted mean
GrN-31119	2–1.37	Peat (Humin)			−28.7	2230±30	–
GrN-31154	2–1.37	Peat (Humic acid)			−28.6	1830±40	–
SUERC-15982	2–1.37A	Plant macrofossil: *Alnus* twig, 1 growth ring	76%	5.6	−28.7	2275±35	–
SUERC-15983	2–1.37B	Plant macrofossil: *Alnus* twig, 1 growth ring			−28.4	2215±35	–
GrN-31120	2–3.59	Peat (Humin)			−28.6	5060±30	5060 ±24 BP (T′=0.0; v=1;
GrN-31155	2–3.59	Peat (Humic acid)	70%	6	−28.0	5060±40	T′(5%)= 3.8)
SUERC-15984	2–3.59	Plant macrofossil: *Alnus* roundwood, c. 8 growth rings			−29.0	4765±35	–
GrN-31121	2–4.30	Peat (Humin)			−27.6	7740±40	7735 ±35 BP (T′=0.1; v=1;
GrN-31156	2–4.30	Peat (Humic acid)			−27.7	7720±70	T′(5%)= 3.8)
GU-6796	2–4.30	Plant macrofossil: *Alnus* twig, c. 1 growth ring	31%	4.3	–	Sample failed	–

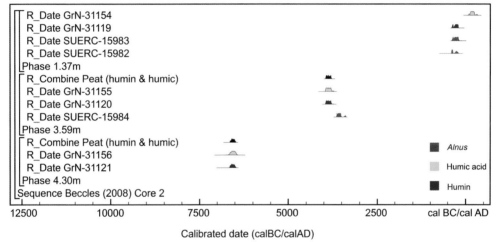

Figure 2.6: Radiocarbon results from Beccles RC Core 2 (2008)

Although the four dated samples from 3.30m are not statistically consistent with one another, the humic acid and humin fractions are consistent, as are the two plant macrofossil fragments. However, in two cases (3.30m and 4.60m) the *Alnus* fragment(s) were younger than the bulk sediment measurements from the same depth. The stratigraphic consistency of both sets of data when analysed independently thus raises the possibility that either could be regarded as accurate reflections of associated depositional processes (see below).

The humin and humic acid fractions from RC Core 2 are statistically consistent at 3.59m and 4.30m (Table 2.6; Figure 2.6), whilst statistical consistency is evident between the two macrofossil and humin dating results from 1.37m. The overall consistency between humin and humic acid fractions implies that these data provide the more reliable age estimates for each dated sample depth. The chronology of this core is perhaps less robust than that for RC Core 1, due to the lack of duplicate measurements from all horizons (resulting from the failed plant macrofossil dating at 4.30m depth). Although the *Alnus* fragment from 3.59m is younger than the bulk sediment sample from the same horizon, the offset is smaller, perhaps indicating less movement of macrofossil material down the profile. Alternatively the humin fraction may incorporate older woody material around which finer fractions of peat have accumulated. This hypothesis might be supported by the presence of occasional wood fragments at this level.

Brandon

Brandon is located on the western margin of the Breckland in

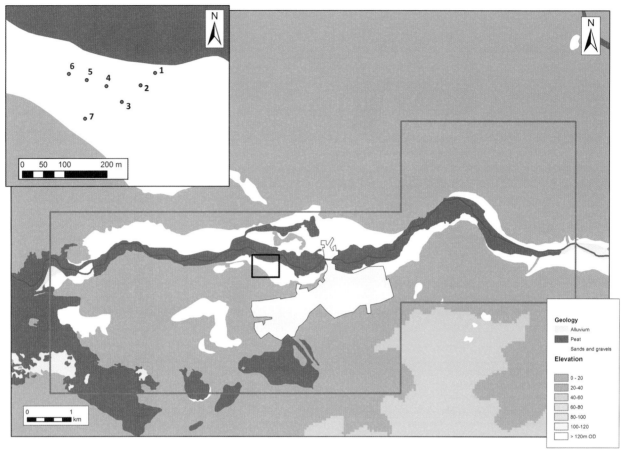

Figure 2.7: Brandon mapview

north-west Suffolk, where the River Little Ouse flows west into the Fenlands (Figure 2.1; Figure 2.7). Less than 10km west of Brandon, marine alluvium is recorded, reflecting the inland limit of Holocene sea-level transgressions; to this end, processes of Holocene environmental change at this location must be seen within the context of those in the wider Fenland (Waller, 1994). The river is steeply incised into the Breckland and consequently its floodplain is very narrow until its emergence into Hockwold Fen. To the west of the Breckland, the low-lying and flat topography has encouraged the development of thick sequences of fen peat proximal to the Little Ouse, whilst the floodplain and fens are composed of a mix of minerogenic sediments and peat.

Seven cores were excavated to investigate variations in topography identified in aerial photographs, 1.4km west of Brandon, in the grounds of Brandon Hall (TL 576949 286751). The majority of cores revealed *c*. 2.0m of yellow-brown sands with varying abundances of disarticulated shell fragments and occasional humic mottling. Below *c*. 2.0m, saturation of the sediment prevented further core extraction. Organic deposits were only encountered in two of the cores (5 and 6) and comprised thin, well-humified sandy peat interbedded within the yellow-brown sand. The relatively shallow stratigraphic sequence encountered, combined with the overall absence of organic-rich sediments within

the deposits, suggested the Brandon site did not contain sediments of significant palaeoenvironmental value and hence no further survey was carried out.

Hoxne

Hoxne is located in north Suffolk on the southern valley side of the River Waveney and is best known archaeologically for the Lower to Middle Palaeolithic deposits and artefacts, which have long been a focus of study (e.g. Wymer, 1985; Wymer and Singer, 1993; Singer *et al.*, 1993; Lewis *et al.*, 2000). To the west of Hoxne, excavations of more recent deposits have also been undertaken on the Waveney floodplain during highway improvements at Scole. These studies included environmental analyses of palaeochannel deposits demonstrating sediment accumulation from the early Bronze Age (Ashwin and Tester, forthcoming: see Chapter 6). The River Dove and a number of smaller tributaries drain the higher ground to the south, converging with the River Waveney to the west of Hoxne. The topography of the landscape has clearly been influenced by the rivers in the immediate vicinity of Hoxne, with the floodplain of the River Waveney to the north, the River Dove valley to the west and smaller tributary valleys to the south. The village of Hoxne is located on slightly

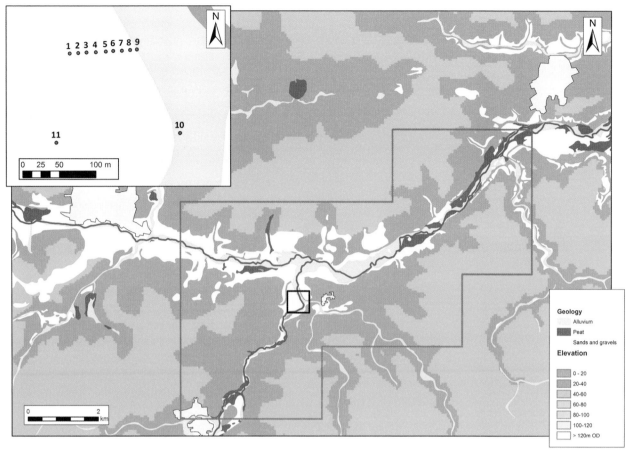

Figure 2.8: Hoxne mapview

permeable calcareous soils, whilst the floodplain of the River Waveney is composed of fen peat and river alluvium overlying basal gravels.

Phase I fieldwork was undertaken on the floodplain of the River Dove (Figure 2.1; Figure 2.8) around 1km south of its confluence with the Waveney (TM 617381 277145). A transect of 11 cores were excavated, across a possible palaeochannel feature identified from LiDAR data during desk-based assessment. The deposits were found to be relatively shallow, consisting of coarse brown sands around half a metre thick, resting upon sandy gravel. However, one location (Core 10) revealed a *c*. 3.70m thick sequence of black, well-humified silty peat overlain by dark brown silty sand. This core was located *c*. 100m east from the potential palaeochannel identified from LiDAR imagery and discussions with the landowner indicated that the area in question contained a pond that had been deliberately infilled. Given the potential for disturbance to the deposits, no further work was carried out at this location, although this area in general has demonstrated potential for the preservation of archaeological and palaeoenvironmental sequences in the river valleys.

Hengrave

Hunt *et al.* (1991) carried out previous investigations, which had identified Late Devensian and Holocene deposits in the Lark Valley between West Stow and Lackford, indicating that this area had clear potential. The selected study area focused on a *c*. 10km reach of the River Lark at Hengrave, north-west of Bury St Edmunds (Figure 2.1). Around the study area, the valley floor is narrow, although generally increases in width downstream from *c*. 0.20km to *c*. 1km. The surrounding catchment geology comprises predominantly glaciofluvial sands and gravels overlain by well-drained sandy calcareous soils. The valley floor comprises alluvium within the upper catchment, whilst beyond West Stow (north of Hengrave) deposits of fen peat are recorded.

Aerial photographs revealed variations in vegetation and surficial sediments implying the presence of a substantial palaeochannel feature 1km south-east of Hengrave (TL 583424 268323), whilst field boundary positions implied other potential palaeochannel features further north, 1km north-east of Hengrave, at Flempton. Immediately east of Hengrave, the parish boundaries separating Hengrave, Culford and Fornham St Genevieve dissect the western River Lark floodplain (TL 829505 691752). Cropmarks interpreted as a Neolithic cursus monument are located 0.40km to the south of this location.

The study area was under pasture (Figure 2.9) and a transect line of six cores were excavated east-west over 200m, close to the position of the parish boundary (described above) (Figure 2.10). The general sequence

consisted of organic sediments between *c.* 2.20m and 3.70m thick overlying sands and gravels. There was considerable variation in stratigraphy between cores, but the sedimentary archive was typified by silty peat, with thin interbedded minerogenic horizons with occasional shell fragments. The minerogenic horizons varied from silts to fine sands and rarely exceeded a thickness of a few centimetres; they were also characterised by relatively sharp upper and lower contacts, implying erosional episodes. It seems likely that the accumulation of peat occurred as a result of the aggradation of a former channel of the River Lark, whilst the thin minerogenic units reflect ephemeral flooding of the channel in response to periods of increased river discharge or perhaps enhanced run-off from disturbance to the dryland soils. A core was recovered for palaeoenvironmental assessment (Table 2.7).

Pollen

Pollen concentrations were assessed as moderate to good for most samples from this sequence (Figure 2.11) although counts for the samples at 2.40m and 2.64m were low due to poor preservation. The pollen sequence clearly represents a mid to late Holocene landscape. Poaceae and Cyperaceae dominate HEN-1 with a range of other herbs including

Figure 2.9: Photograph of the Hengrave study area showing current landuse

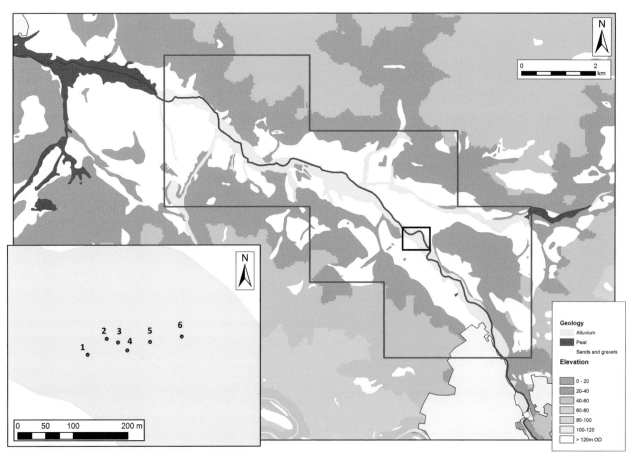

Figure 2.10: West Stow and Hengrave mapview

Table 2.7: Hengrave Core (2007) stratigraphy and associated data

Depth/m	m OD	Description	Pollen zones code/depth	Other samples
0–0.24	20.61	Dark brown very well humified slightly silty peat	–	-
0.24–0.60	20.37	Grey brown very well humified peat		–
0.60–1.0	20.01	Dark red-brown humified peat with wood fragments	HEN-1: 0.25–0.95	0.60–1.0 m: (bulk)
1.0–1.51	19.61	Dark brown well humified peat with monocotyledonous remains		
				1.40–1.80 m: (bulk)
1.51–1.64	19.09	Dark grey brown very well humified slightly sandy peat	HEN-2: 0.95–2.55	–
1.64–2.0	18.97	Dark grey brown monocotyledonous peat with occasional sand horizons		–
2.0–3.0	18.61	Dark grey brown monocotyledonous peat with wood fragments		2.60–3.0 m: (bulk)
			HEN-1: 2.55–3.0	
3.0–3.75	17.61 16.86	Grey brown silty humic sand	–	–

Lactuceae, Brassicaceae (cabbage family), *Cerealia*-type (cereals) and *Plantago lanceolata* recorded, whilst arboreal taxa are very low. The data therefore reflect an open, damp grassland landscape, with evidence for the cultivation of cereals. Few trees can have been present in the near vicinity of the sampling site, other than some alder possibly on the damper soils of the floodplain.

Changes at the opening of the subsequent zone (HEN-2) are fairly subtle, consisting of increases in *Plantago* and other herbs including *Chenopodium* (fat hen), *Filipendula* (meadow sweet), *Rumex*, *Urtica* (nettles), *Polygonum* cf. *aviculare* type (knot weed etc.) and *Cerealia*-type. The impression is of the development of an open agricultural landscape with an expansion in arable cultivation and associated weed floras (e.g. mugwort and fat hen), as well as plants suggesting a range of other semi-natural vegetation communities such as tall herbs (meadowsweet and the carrot family), disturbed grassy places (knotweed) and pasture/meadow (ribwort plantain, dandelions, meadow-rue, docks and nettles). Vegetation on damper soils near to the sampling site and probably also on the edge of the floodplain included Cyperaceae, *Equisetum* (horsetails), *Typha latifolia* (reedmace), which expands towards the top of the zone, whilst aquatic vegetation and standing water is evidenced by *Potamogeton* (pondweeds). As with the previous zone, no substantial woodland cover is indicated, with perhaps some alder and scattered oak-hazel scrub possible.

The final zone, HEN-3, is mainly defined on the basis of the virtual disappearance of tree and shrub taxa from the record, with only *Corylus* recorded as a continuous curve at very low percentages. Changes in the ground flora consist of an initial spike in Poaceae, followed by reductions in *Rumex*, *Polygonum* cf. *aviculare*-type and *Filipendula*. Other herbs including *Plantago* and Lactuceae remain well represented, whilst there are slight increases in *Artemisia*-type (mugwort) and *Urtica*. The spectra therefore indicate the demise of any remaining woodland communities in the pollen source area at this time, with hazel the only woody component that might have persisted after the opening of the zone. This as well as the changes in the representation of herbaceous taxa is probably a reflection of a shift in the nature of the local agricultural regime at this time.

The suite of herb pollen in all three zones includes relatively high percentages of cereal-type pollen, as well as weeds of cereal plots and those suggesting grazed swards and disturbed habitats. The final zone (HEN-3) would appear to reflect an intensification/change in the nature of local farming activity, leading to the demise of certain herb communities including knotweed, docks and tall herbs, and the expansion of taxa typical of heavily disturbed habitats such as nettles and mugwort. It might be speculated that the maintenance of a steady hazel curve in the context of an open, farmed landscape at this time suggests some form of woodland management.

Beetles

Three bulk samples were assessed for beetle remains (Table 2.7). One bulk sample was from towards the base of the core within dark brown to grey-brown herbaceous humified silty peat (2.60–3.00m), a second sample from the dark grey-brown sandy peat (1.40–1.80m) and a third from the dark brown to red-brown herbaceous humified peat (0.60–1.00m).

The beetle assemblage from 2.60–3.00m is primarily composed of aquatic and hygrophilous beetle taxa. This suggests a pool or stream filled with slow moving water fringed by tall reed swamp was present at the time of deposition. For example, *Hydrobius fuscipes* and *Chaetarthrias eminulum* are both found in standing stagnant waters. *Hydrobius fuscipes* is found at the margins of standing water amongst dense vegetation (Hansen, 1987), whilst *Chaetarthrias eminulum* prefers the muddy

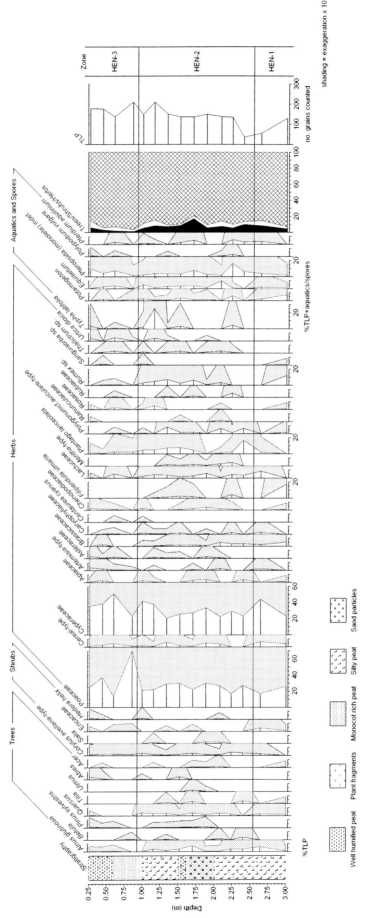

Figure 2.11: Pollen diagram from Hengrave

Table 2.8: Hengrave RC Core (2008) stratigraphy and radiocarbon samples

Depth/m	m OD	Description	Radiocarbon samples/m/ material/code
0–0.20	20.51	Made ground	–
0.20–0.38	20.31	Dark grey-brown well humified silty peat with occasional pebbles	–
0.38–0.47	20.13	Dark brown herbaceous well humified peat	0.47-Humin (GrN-31113) 0.47-Humic (GrN-31148) 0.47- Moncot stem (SUERC-16385)
0.47–0.80	20.04	Dark grey-brown herbaceous well humified silty peat with occasional sand	–
0.80–1.02	19.71	Dark brown herbaceous peat with detrital remains	–
1.02–1.05	19.49	Dark brown herbaceous peat with detrital laminations and *Phragmites*	–
1.05–1.51	19.46	Dark brown herbaceous peat with abundant detrital material	–
1.51–1.62	18.99	Dark brown very well humified silty peat with occasional *Phragmites*	1.61-Humin (GrN-31114) 1.61-Humic (GrN-31149) 1.61- Macrofossil Monocot stem (GU-6786)
1.62–1.95	18.89	Dark brown herbaceous well humified peat, with occasional grass and *Phragmites* remains	–
1.95–2.77	18.56	Dark brown herbaceous humified peat with abundant *Phragmites*, occasional wood fragments	–
2.77–2.95	17.74	Dark brown very well humified peat with light grey sand laminations and occasional *Phragmites*	2.76-Humin (GrN-31115) 2.76-Humic (GrN-31150) 2.76-Monocot culm (SUERC-15972)
2.95–3.20	17.56	Light grey-brown sand with humic horizons	–
3.20–3.60	17.31	Dark brown sandy peat with *Phragmites*	–
3.60–3.70	16.91 16.81	Light grey-brown sand with occasional humic lenses	–

periphery of standing water, particularly in bogs and fens (Friday, 1988). A further indicator of fen vegetation is the Chrysomelid, *Plateumaris braccata*, a monophagous taxa exclusively associated with the common reed (*Phragmites australis*; Menzies and Cox 1996). Vegetation in the wider environment is also suggested by the presence of the Curculionid, *Apion* spp., a family of weevils associated with a variety of plants found in both meadows and disturbed ground, such as vetches and mallows (Koch, 1992).

In sample 1.40–1.80m, whilst the beetle assemblage is similar to that encountered in the previous sample, the local environment appears to have become drier. Aquatic taxa are absent and are replaced by the Hydraenidae, a family of hygrophilous taxa associated with muddy, ephemeral pools (Hansen, 1987). The Chrysomelid *Plateumaris braccata*, which feeds exclusively upon the common reed, increases in abundance (Menzies and Cox, 1996), suggesting the spread of tall herb fen across the site. A single specimen of the Scarabaeidae (dung beetle) family was also recovered from this sample; *Geotrupes* spp. (the 'Dor' beetle) is found in the dung of large herbivores (Jessop, 1996).

During the deposition of sample 0.60–1.00m, wetter conditions on the sampling site are indicated. Distinct aquatic species such as the hydrophilid *Hydrobius fuscipes*

and the Dytiscid *Noterus* spp., were recovered, which are both found in standing, stagnant water (Nilsson and Holmen, 1995). In addition, the lower abundance of Hydraenidae suggests a contraction in muddy pool environments. Beetles indicative of tall reed environments, have been replaced by species associated with lower growing and aquatic vegetation. The Chrysomelid *Plateumaris sericea*, is found on sedges (*Carex* spp.), water-lily (*Nuphar* spp.) and yellow flag (*Iris pseudocorus*; Menzies and Cox, 1996). Increased numbers of the Curculionid, *Apion* spp., suggest drier grassland habitats.

Phase II Chronology – Hengrave

A duplicate core was extracted from 2m to the east of the 2007 Core. Nine radiocarbon dates were obtained, consisting of triplicates (humin, humic and macrofossils) from 0.47m, 1.61m and 2.76m (Table 2.8). The results demonstrate that there are no age inversions in the sequence (Table 2.9; Figure 2.12) and the humic acid and humin fractions at 1.61m and 2.76m are statistically consistent. The plant macrofossil and humin fractions dates at 0.4m are also statistically consistent. The lack of duplicate measurements from all horizons (due to the failure of plant macrofossil dating at 1.61m depth) makes interpretation

Table 2.9: Hengrave RC Core (2008) radiocarbon dates and associated data

Lab code	Sample ID/ depth (m)	Material dated	Organic content	pH	$\delta^{13}C$ (‰)	Radiocarbon age (BP)	Weighted mean	Calibrated date (95% confidence)
GrN-31113	0.47	Peat (Humin)			−29.1	715±30	–	cal. AD 1260–1380
GrN-31148	0.47	Peat (Humic acid)			−29.7	540±40	–	cal. AD 1300–1450
SUERC-16385	0.47	Plant macro-fossil: stem fragment	44%	6.0	−25.1	660±35	–	cal. AD 1270–1400
GrN-31114	1.61	Peat (Humin)			−28.9	1430±35	1442±23 BP (T′=0.2; v=1; T′(5%)= 3.8)	cal. AD 570–655
GrN-31149	1.61	Peat (Humic acid)	60%	6.4	−28.5	1450±30		
GU-6786	1.61	Plant macro-fossil: herba-ceous stem				Sample failed	–	–
GrN-31115	2.76	Peat (Humin)			−29.8	2310±40	2319±34 BP (T′=0.2; v=1; T′(5%)= 3.8)	410–360 cal. BC
GrN-31150	2.76	Peat (Humic acid)	47%	5.7	−30.5	2340±60		
SUERC-15972	2.76	Plant macro-fossil: monocot culm			−27.5	2095±35	–	210–1 cal. BC

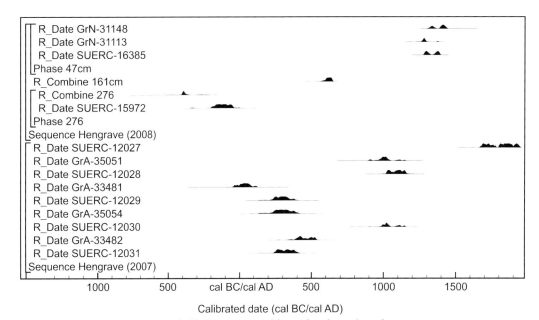

Figure 2.12: Hengrave calibrated radiocarbon dates

slightly less robust, as the date on the *Alnus* macrofossil from 2.76m is younger than the bulk sediment sample from the same horizon, although the offset between the bulk and macrofossil dates is smaller than observed for Beccles (see below).

The statistical consistency between the determinations from the humin and humic acid fractions at 1.61m and 2.76m imply that there was overall water table stability within the floodplain during the accumulation of the deposits, which possibly prevented the vertical movement of certain sediment fractions. In contrast, explanations for the age difference between the humic acid and humin/ *Alnus* fragment at 0.47m depth may include the upwards movement of humic acid or the intrusion of younger

material perhaps down rootlet channels during periods of lower water table and the opening up of desiccation cracks (see discussion below).

The date from 2.76m, which is over 1m (17.739 m OD) above the base (16.81m OD) of the Hengrave RC Core, produced a combined age estimate of 410–360 cal. BC (R_combine GrN-3115 and 31150) demonstrating that accumulation of the well-humified peat had begun by the Iron Age. The combined radiocarbon dates from 1.61m of cal. AD 570–655, (R_combine GrN-31114 and 31149) show that the upper section of the sequence can be assigned to the early Anglo-Saxon period. The three Phase II radiocarbon dates from 0.47m are not statistically consistent (T'=12.198; v=2; T'(5%)= 6.0), although

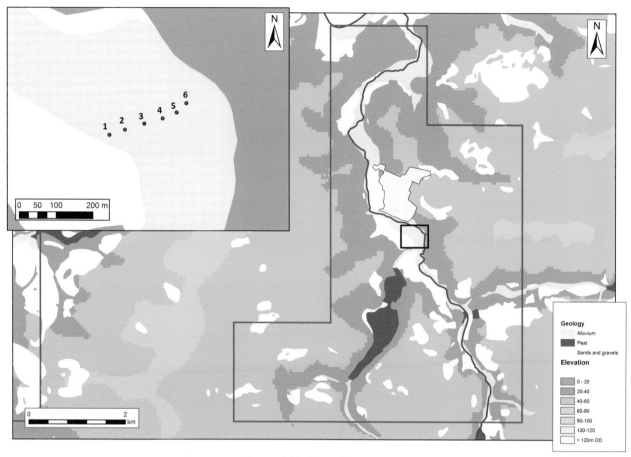

Figure 2.13: Ixworth mapview

the plant macrofossil and humin fraction are (T'=1.4; v=1; T'(5%)= 3.8), indicating that the upper deposits at Hengrave date to the later medieval period.

Ixworth (Mickle Mere)

The village of Ixworth is located on the eastern floodplain of the River Blackbourne, approximately 10km north-east of Bury St Edmunds. The valley floor is relatively narrow varying in width from *c.* 0.25km to 0.50km. The surrounding catchment is primarily composed of Chalk bedrock, chalky till, and glaciofluvial sand and gravel. Deep fen peat soils are present along the floodplain of Pakenham Fen to the west, whilst sandy and peaty soils are found on the valley floor of the Blackbourne proximal to Ixworth. Immediately south of Ixworth, the floodplain is *c.* 0.30km wide at Mickle Mere (TL 593767 269749). There is a Roman Fort on the western valley side and a Roman Villa to the east, whilst Palaeolithic and Neolithic archaeological remains have been found at Pakenham Fen, *c.* 0.50km to the south. Historically, Mickle Mere was once one of a corridor of grazing marshes running along this reach of the river Blackbourne, but the construction of the Ixworth bypass across the north-west corner of the site has resulted in frequent flooding of the area. Previous palaeoenvironmental assessment of deposits carried out

Figure 2.14: Augering at Ixworth (Mickle Mere)

in advance of the construction of the bypass, identified an organic-rich deposit overlain by a minerogenic unit; the sequence was radiocarbon-dated to 1290±100 BP (HAR-5936, cal. AD 580–970; Murphy and Wiltshire, 1989) and interpreted as material deposited through soil erosion associated with agricultural activity on the valley sides.

Standing water on the surface of Mickle Mere prevented the collection of reliable LiDAR data. During Phase I fieldwork, a borehole transect *c.* 300m long was drilled on the western side of the river approximately east-west across the site (Figure 2.1; Figure 2.13; Figure 2.14). The thickness of the deposits varied from *c.* 2.50 to 3.50m

Table 2.10: Ixworth (Mickle Mere) Core 2007 stratigraphy and associated data

Depth/m	m OD	Description	Pollen zones code/depth	Other samples
0–0.57	27.13	Light grey gravelly silt	–	–
0.57–0.87	26.56	Dark brown well humified peat with occasional monocotyledonous remains		0.50–0.90m: Bulk
0.87–1.38	26.53	Dark grey brown silty well humified peat	IX-3:	–
1.38–1.41	25.75	Light grey brown humic sand	0.60–1.45	–
1.41–1.50	25.72	Dark grey brown silty well humified peat		–
1.50–2.50	25.63	Dark brown well humified peat with monocotyledonous and wood fragments		1.90–2.30m: Bulk
2.50–2.64	24.63	Grey brown slightly gravelly organic silt		–
2.64–3.45	24.49	Dark brown well humified peat with occasional monocotyledonous remains		2.70–3.10m: Bulk
			IX-2: 1.45–3.15 IX-1: 3.15–3.40	
3.45–3.50	23.68	Grey silty sand	–	–
	23.62 (base)			

and there was considerable variation between cores, but layers of peat intercalated with lenses of sand typified the stratigraphic archive. Silty-sand horizons including a 0.50m thick organic-rich silt layer capped the sequence. A core 3.45m deep, consisting of well-humified silty peat with occasional wood fragments and overlain by *c.* 0.60m of grey gravelly silt, was recovered for palaeoenvironmental assessment (Table 2.10).

Pollen

Pollen concentration and preservation were assessed as good to moderate and the record suggests that a near complete Holocene record is preserved at Mickle Mere (Figure 2.15). The basal zone (IX-1) records a peak in *Betula* with lower values for *Pinus*, *Salix* and *Quercus*. Cyperaceae is well represented with other herbs including Poaceae, *Thalictrum* (meadowrue) and *Plantago lanceolata*. The impression is of an open birch-willow scrub dominated environment, with the suite of herbs implying disturbed/skeletal soils. These pollen spectra clearly demonstrate that sediment accumulation began during the early Holocene (see below).

Pollen zone IX-2 is marked by a reduction in *Betula* and *Salix* and increases in the other arboreal taxa including *Alnus*, *Ulmus*, *Tilia* and *Corylus*. *Pinus* also increases to a marked peak at 2.28m prior to falling to low values. Indicators of open habitats are reduced and in the case of certain of the herbs in the previous zone, disappear from the record. Other than Poaceae and Cyperaceae, herbs tend to be recorded in low and sporadic quantities in IX2, whilst Pteropsida (monolete) indet. increase towards the top of the zone. The pollen spectra reflect the *Alnus* rise and growth of alder carr on and around the wetter soils of the sampling site and the spread of mixed woodland in the wider landscape. Lime and hazel appear to have been the major components of the tree/shrub cover on dryland soils, with oak and elm less significant.

Birch was clearly out-competed following the spread of the other trees in IX-2, but pine appears to have remained present on some areas of the floodplain, and even expanded, perhaps as a result of a dry phase, which favoured this tree over alder. This was clearly a relatively brief event, as pine is subsequently reduced whilst alder re-expands. The nature of the understorey on the drier soils beyond the floodplain is unclear, but it seems probable that the canopy was dense with few clearings or open areas away from where high soil moisture favoured wetland vegetation. It is possible that some of the Poaceae reflects open dryland communities rather than wetland grasses on the floodplain, but it is likely that the pollen spectra are biased towards on-site vegetation in any case with ferns and sedges probably forming the alder carr understorey.

The final zone IX-3 is marked by an abrupt decline in *Tilia* with *Alnus* and *Ulmus* also reduced at this time. Other trees including *Corylus* and *Quercus* initially display small increases but subsequently decline across the zone. Pronounced rises in Poaceae and Cyperaceae are accompanied by the record of other herbs including Lactuceae, Apiaceae (carrot family), Asteraceae undiff. (thistles etc.), Caryophyllaceae (the pink family) and *Chenopodium*, with *Cerealia*-type and *Plantago lanceolata* towards the top of the zone. This can be interpreted as indicating a significant opening up of the lime-dominated woodland followed by disturbance to the alder carr on and around the sampling site.

The initial enhanced values for hazel and oak are probably a result of the increased representation of extra-local vegetation following the reduction in alder rather than an actual areal expansion of these taxa. The subsequent decline in all the arboreal components and the rise in *Cerealia*-type and indicators of disturbed habitats and grassy places towards the top of the diagram reflect the demise of much of the woodland on both dry and wetland soils as a result of the expansion of arable cultivation.

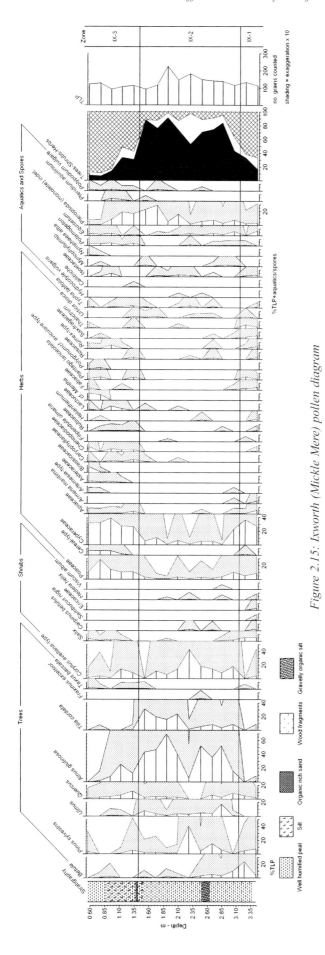

Figure 2.15: Ixworth (Mickle Mere) pollen diagram

There is no clear evidence for human disturbance to the vegetation until the final zone IX-3, when an abrupt and large-scale clearance of lime woodland seems to have been followed by the clearance of other components of the arboreal vegetation. Initially, the pollen spectra suggest predominantly pastoral activity (dandelions, docks) in the vicinity of the sampling site but with the relatively high values for cereal pollen subsequently indicating arable agriculture, presumably relatively close to the sampling site. By the close of the diagram, an open, agricultural landscape with few trees other than perhaps oak and hazel is inferred. The impression is of both arable and pastoral farming activity during IX-3. The relatively high values for *Cerealia*-type pollen suggest that cultivation was taking place reasonably close to the sampling site. Again, the absence of secure dating control makes further comment difficult but it seems likely on stratigraphic grounds that this dates to the later Holocene.

Beetles

Three bulk samples were assessed for beetles. One was taken from towards the base of the core within dark brown herbaceous well-humified woody peat (2.70–3.10m). A second was taken from within the dark brown, well-humified peat with occasional wood fragments (1.90–2.30m) and a third from within the dark brown herbaceous well-humified peat towards the top of the stratigraphic archive (0.50–0.90m). Only a single beetle sclerite was recovered from the basal sample (2.70–3.10m). At 1.90–2.30m, well-preserved and identifiable beetles were recorded, but species abundance and diversity was restricted to the Staphylinidae, *Lathrobium* spp. A restricted assemblage of well-preserved and identifiable Coleopteran remains was also recovered from 0.50–0.90m depth and abundance and diversity was greater than from the underlying assemblages, with species such as the Staphylinidae, *Stenuus* spp. and the Curculionidae, *Apion* spp. However, the limited nature of these assemblages precluded any firm interpretations.

Chronology Phase II Ixworth, Mickle Mere

A core was extracted from adjacent to the location of the Phase I sample core. A lack of identifiable plant macrofossil material in this second core meant that radiocarbon dates were obtained from humin and humic fractions only for the Phase II dating programme (Table 2.11; Figure 2.16). The results indicate that no age inversions are present and all humic acid and humin fractions are statistically consistent implying that the radiocarbon results provide a reliable chronology for this sequence (Table 2.12). The date of 6460–6360 cal. BC from 2.39m (R_combine GrN-31112 and 31147) indicate that peat inception at Mickle Mere (24.83m OD) began in the earlier Holocene, whilst the dates from the central section of the core (1.24m) produce a combined estimate of 910–800 cal. BC (R_combine GrN-31111 and 31146). The uppermost (0.71m) combined

Table 2.11: Ixworth (Mickle Mere) RC core (2008) stratigraphy and radiocarbon samples

Depth/m	m OD	Description	Radiocarbon Samples/m/material/code
0–0.70	27.23	Light grey-brown clayey silt	–
0.70–0.89	26.53	Dark brown well humified peat with occasional monocotyledonous remains	0.71-Humin (GrN-31110) 0.71-Humic (GrN-31145)
0.89–0.95	26.34	Dark grey brown silty well humified peat	–
0.95–1.25	26.28	Dark brown well humified peat with occasional sand and silt lenses	1.24-Humin (GrN-31111) 1.24-Humic (GrN-31146) 1.24-*Alnus* wood (GU-6798) FAILED
1.25–1.57	26.07	Medium grey brown, well humified silty peat	–
1.57–2.40	25.66	Dark brown well humified peat with monocotyledonous and wood fragments	2.39-Humin (GrN-31112) 2.39-Humic (GrN-31147)
	24.83		

Table 2.12: Ixworth (Mickle Mere) RC core (2008) radiocarbon dates and associated data

Lab Code	Sample ID/ Depth m	Material Dated	Organic content	pH	$\delta^{13}C$ (‰)	Radiocarbon Age (BP)	Weighted mean	Calibrated date (95% confidence)
GrN-31110	0.71	Peat (Humin)	55%	5.6	–29.6	1740±35	1779±27 BP (T'=2.9; v=1; T'(5%)= 3.8)	cal. AD 130–340
GrN-31145	0.71	Peat (Humic acid)			–29.2	1830±40		
GrN-31111	1.24	Peat (Humin)	14%	7.0	–29.3	2670±40	2700±29 BP (T'=1.1; v=1; T'(5%)= 3.8)	910–800 cal. BC
GrN-31146	1.24	Peat (Humic acid)			–29.3	2730±40		
GrN-31112	2.39	Peat (Humin)	53%	5.9	–28.9	7530±50	7520±36 BP (T'=0.1; v=1; T'(5%)= 3.8)	6460–6260 cal. BC
GrN-31147	2.39	Peat (Humic acid)			–28.3	7510±50		
GU-6798	1.24	Plant macrofossil: *Alnus* wood			–	Sampled failed	–	–

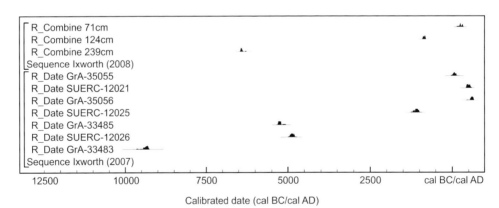

Figure 2.16: Ixworth calibrated radiocarbon dates

dates produce an estimate of cal. AD 130–340 (R_combine GrN-31110 and 31145) indicating that the top of the organic sediments at Ixworth dates to the Romano-British period. The Mickle Mere sequence is therefore an extensive Holocene record. The greater depth and associated pollen spectra (Figure 2.15) may actually suggest that the base of this core is somewhat earlier than that attested to by the radiocarbon dates for the base of the RC Core.

2.4 Discussion

Beccles

The palaeoenvironmental assessments at Beccles produced contrasting results (see also Chapters 4 and 5 for further palaeoenvironmental study of the site). The pollen counts were very low due to poor concentration, especially in the middle to top section of the sequence. Beetle assemblages

Depth (m)	Altitude (m OD)	Sediment	Supratidal		
			Around MHW	Above MHW	Pools in SM
1.34	-1.42	clayey-silt			
1.55	-1.63	organic silt			
1.73	-1.81	clayey-silt			
2.22	-2.30	organic silt			
2.5	-2.58	clayey-silt	?		
2.54	-2.62	organic silt			
2.57	-2.65	clayey-silt	?		
2.75	-2.83	organic silt			
2.83	-2.91	clayey-silt			

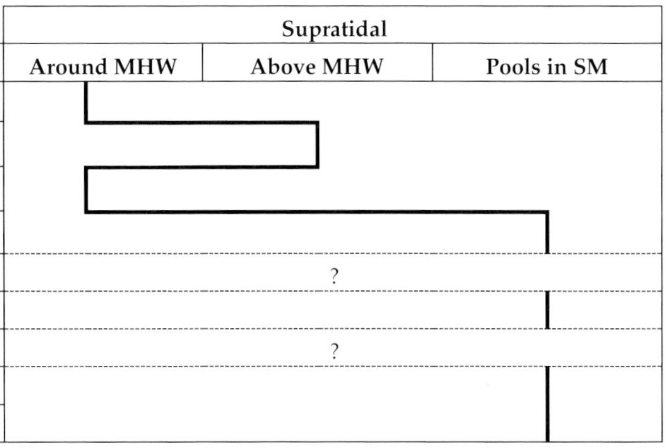

Figure 2.17: Qualitative reconstruction of ground surface altitude relative to the palaeo-tidal frame from the diatom assemblages in Beccles Core 2. Higher palaeo-ground surfaces are indicated towards the right of the diagram and lower palaeo-ground surfaces towards the left

were relatively small, due in part to the restricted sample size, but demonstrated the preservation of beetles in some sections of the peat. The Phase II radiocarbon dating programme demonstrates that whilst a provisional chronology for peat accumulation can be established, there are a number of issues concerning the lack of consistency between different sediment fractions (see below).

Dating of the humic acid and humin fractions from the basal deposits (Tables 2.5 and 2.6) produced age estimates of between 7580–7370 cal. BC in RC Core 1 (4.60m, –4.57m OD) and 6640–6480 cal. BC in RC Core 2 (4.30m, –4.28m OD). Humin and humic acid dating of the samples from the middle of the cores produced estimates of 3500–3340 cal. BC in RC Core 1 (3.30 m, –3.27 m OD) and 3960–3785 cal. BC in RC Core 2 (3.59m, –3.57m OD). Finally, the upper age estimates vary between 360–10 cal. BC in RC Core 1 (0.84m, –0.81m OD) and 400 cal. BC and cal. AD 320 in RC Core 2 (1.37m, –1.35m OD). Given the differences in the depths and absolute heights of the sequences, these data indicate a very broadly coherent chronology for floodplain peat accumulation at Beccles Marshes although this is hampered by the lack of consistency between dates on humin/humic fractions and plant macrofossils and these data should hence be interpreted with some caution.

The basal radiocarbon date of 7580–7370 cal. BC for RC Core 1 (4.60m, –4.57m OD, R_Combine GrN-31118 and 31153) indicates peat inception during the early Holocene. The basal date for RC Core 2 (4.30m, –4.28 m OD) of 6640–6480 cal. BC (R-Combine GrN-31156 and 31121) indicates that peat inception began slightly later at this marginally higher area, around 100m to the south-west of RC Core 1. It is very likely that sedimentation was occurring partly in response to the effects of rising relative sea level during the early Holocene (but see below). The pollen diagram indicates that *Alnus* colonised the floodplain, after which peat accumulation appears to have continued in a fen carr environment across the mid to late Holocene. The humin and humic dates from 0.84m (–0.822m OD) in

Beccles RC Core 1 are statistically consistent and indicate a date of 360–50 cal. BC (R_combine GrN-31116 and 3115) for the upper deposits, which is in agreement with the presence of Iron Age archaeology on the floodplain.

Whilst Beccles Core 1 (2007) and the chronology from the two radiocarbon-dated cores indicate that there was little significant change in the depositional regime until the later Holocene, the diatom analyses from Beccles Core 2 (2007) provide evidence for fluctuations in relative sea level. Figure 2.17 presents the variation in altitude of each sedimentary surface within Beccles Core 2 (2007), based on the interpretation of diatoms using the methodology of Vos and de Wolf (1993). The reconstruction estimates the position of the palaeoground surface relative to the level of the tide at the time of deposition, and hence provides a qualitative indicator of positive or negative sea-level tendencies. It has been assumed that, within the supratidal area, the interpreted sedimentary environment with the highest altitude relative to Mean Sea Level (MSL) is "pools within salt marshes" (primarily due to the enhanced freshwater diatom influence), followed by "salt marshes above MHW" and "salt marshes around MHW". However, establishing a robust chronology for these fluctuations has not been possible (see Chapter 6).

In general, the diatom assemblages from within the blue-grey clayey silts suggest deposition low down the tidal frame, proximal to MHW. In contrast, the diatoms within the organic-rich silts suggest deposition further up the tidal frame within pools in the salt marsh, probably closer to the Highest Astronomical Tide (HAT). Although two of the clayey-silt samples had poor diatom preservation, in general, such deposits may reflect the supratidal zone on salt marshes around MHW. Only the lower clayey silt sample (–2.83m OD) contained a diatom assemblage reflecting deposition occurring further up the tidal frame, and this may have been a consequence of the erosive contact boundary with the underlying fen peat unit. All four of the organic-rich units contained diatom assemblages suggesting deposition occurred at a higher altitude along the tidal frame, either within salt marshes above MHW or within pools on the salt marsh.

It can be concluded that the five blue-grey clayey silt units represent discrete periods of positive sea-level tendency, separated by negative sea-level tendencies during which the organic-rich silt units were deposited. The episodic reductions in tidal influence resulted in enhanced *in-situ* organic sedimentation and the deposition of diatom assemblages indicative of sedimentation within the upper limits of the palaeo-tidal frame. The stratigraphic differences between Core 1 (2007) and the other three cores are significant and suggest that the transition from freshwater to estuarine deposition during the later Holocene was located between these sampling points.

Whilst Beccles Core 2 (2007) reflects evidence for multiple fluctuations in sea level, the Core 1 (2007) sequence only appears to record the latest one. Although present in relatively low abundances, diatom frustules typical of estuarine environments imply a shift in the depositional environment in Beccles Core 1 2007 (0.90–1.00m) from a predominantly terrestrial freshwater-influenced peatland environment to a tidally influenced estuarine environment. This may correspond to a transition from peat to estuarine clays after a date of 1985±40 BP (Q-2184; 90 cal. BC–cal. AD 140) recorded at Stanley Carr (Alderton, 1983) just to the north-east of Beccles Marshes, interpreted as evidence of a marine transgression (see also Chapter 7).

Although the diatom sequence from Beccles Core 2 (2007) has not been robustly dated, the data may indicate a period of positive sea level tendency in the Waveney Valley during the later prehistoric period. The marked differences in stratigraphy between Cores 1 and 2 (2007) may indicate that the furthest limits, or the 'feather edge' of the later Holocene marine transgression in the Waveney Valley (the 'upper clay' – see Chapter 6) may be located at Beccles Marshes. These data have potential implications for the landscape context of the later prehistoric timber alignment site, which will be discussed further below (see Chapters 4 and 6).

Hengrave

The base of the Hengrave sequence was not radiocarbon dated in Phase II as the stratigraphy (Table 2.7) indicated potential for penetration and possible bioturbation by *Phragmites*. However, the Phase II dating programme indicates that the deposits at this location accumulated from the Iron Age through to the later medieval period. Although the base of the sequence is relatively high (16.8m OD) the later prehistoric date for aggradation of the valley floor is notable (see below). However, without further more detailed stratigraphic survey and analyses, the spatial variation and causes of floodplain sedimentation at this time are unclear.

Beetle assemblages from the base of the sequence indicate that initial deposition occurred in a reed fen environment, with relatively deep water, surrounded by dense, emergent vegetation. The evidence then suggests the establishment of drier conditions at the site, with muddy, seasonal pools and extensive swathes of tall reeds. This drier period however finally gave way to wetter conditions, with the return of pools of permanent, standing water on the valley floor. The sequence reflects later Holocene environmental change as the vegetation in the pollen source area was clearly associated with an open landscape with very few trees and indications of both arable and pastoral agriculture.

Although transposing the radiocarbon dates from the RC Core to the pollen diagram can only be done with some caution, it can be noted that allowing for the difference in absolute heights of the two sequences, that the date of cal. AD 570–655 (R_combine GrN-31114 and 31149), corresponds with a rise in *Plantago lanceolata* mid-way through HEN-2. The Anglo-Saxon settlement of West Stow is less than 4km upstream to the north-west of the sampling location and the valley of the River Lark (along with the River Blackbourn and Little Ouse) was apparently a focus of settlement during the early Anglo-Saxon period (Dymond and Martin, 1999). It is possible that the pollen diagram reflects local settlement and intensification of land-use from the 6th to 7th centuries AD.

Ixworth (Mickle Mere)

The pollen diagram and the Phase II radiocarbon dating programmes demonstrate that sedimentation of the valley floor of the Blackbourn at Mickle Mere began during the early Holocene (6460–6360 cal. BC, R_combine GrN-31112 and 31147). This relatively early date can be compared and contrasted with those from Beccles and Hengrave discussed above. In particular, whilst at Beccles, paludification of the Waveney valley floor (–5 to –6m OD) close to the coast had begun in the 8th–7th millennium BC, although the base of the Mickle Mere core is significantly higher (23.63m OD) peat inception also occurred in the 7th millennium BC. There is no simple linear relationship between these deposits in terms of valley floor level, distance from the coast and aggradation in connection with rising relative sea level, but it is clear that in certain locations in Suffolk, floodplains began to aggrade relatively early during the Holocene. However, the precise spatial and chronological pattern of development cannot be reconstructed on the basis of the extant data, and this highlights the complexity in terms of the environmental history of the Suffolk river valleys that is also observed in other data from the region (see Chapter 3).

The Ixworth pollen diagram demonstrates that a significant record of Holocene vegetation change is preserved at this location, providing evidence of patterns of environmental change and human activity from the prehistoric through to the Romano-British period. In particular, high values for *Tilia* demonstrate that lime was clearly a dominant component of the mid-Holocene woodland. The upper zone (IX-3) of the diagram indicates a marked and apparently sustained phase of woodland clearance. Although transposing the radiocarbon dates from the Mickle Mere RC Core must be done cautiously and allowing for the differences in stratigraphy and absolute height between the two sequences, the dates from the RC Core at 1.24m produce a combined estimate of 910–800 cal. BC (R_combine GrN-31111 and 31146); this correlates approximately with a depth of 1.13m in the pollen diagram, which may indicate that woodland clearance had begun before the later Bronze Age at this location.

It is also tempting to relate the phase of alluviation represented by the upper-most minerogenic layer (Table 2.10), dated to the Romano-British period (cal. AD 130–340, R_combine GrN-31110 and 31145), to soil erosion in response to human disturbance, perhaps associated with the Villa on the eastern edge of the valley. However, this date is somewhat earlier than that of 1290±100 BP (HAR-5936, cal. AD 580–970) previously obtained from below the upper alluvial layer at this site (Murphy and Wiltshire, 1989). This may indicate that more than episode of alluviation is recorded at the site.

2.5 Summary: the Suffolk River Valleys Project Phases I and II

As outlined in Chapter 1, the SRVP had been initially envisaged as a 'first order' resource assessment of the Suffolk River Valleys. In the event, whilst the project demonstrated the presence of *in situ* wet-preserved Holocene deposits in the selected study areas, it also resulted in new perspectives on methodological approaches to the radiocarbon dating of floodplain deposits. The anomalous radiocarbon determinations from Phase I led to the subsequent re-dating of the sequences in Phase II. This indicated that the initial set of dates was probably compromised by a combination of sampling error and the particular, somewhat poorly understood, formation processes of floodplain peats and sediments in these lowland systems.

Although these problems somewhat hindered the establishment of secure chronologies for the palaeo-environmental sequences assessed during Phase I, the subsequent re-analysis during Phase II demonstrated that provisional chronologies for deposit formation could be provided but that different fractions from these deposits did not always produce consistent age estimates. The SRVP palaeoenvironmental assessments demonstrated that although the quality of the preservation of analysed proxies varied, pollen was on the whole well-preserved. The beetle assessments produced variable results, although given the low quantities of sediment processed, these data were regarded as a restricted guide to the preservation of such material. Certainly, where demonstrated, the presence of beetle remains in such small samples implies generally good preservation in the deposits.

The project thus achieved its primary aim of demon-strating that the river valleys of the county had rich, but to date, largely untapped archaeo-environmental potential, akin to other systems in lowland England. The presence of *in situ* deposits dating from across the Holocene, also indicated the potential for the preservation of organic archaeological remains, but given the difficulties of remotely identifying buried archaeology in wetland contexts, no direct attempt was made to assess this any further. However, this high potential was subsequently and rather serendipitously illustrated during the initial phases of the SRVP in 2006, by the discovery of the wetland archaeological sites in the valley of the River Waveney at Beccles, and later at Barsham and Geldeston. These sites will be discussed in further detail in Chapters 4, 5 and 6. The timing and character of floodplain sedimentation in the river valleys also has implications for human activity during the early Holocene and for the distribution and visibility of archaeological sites during the Mesolithic and Neolithic in particular (see Chapter 7).

Radiocarbon dating of floodplain sediments: lessons from the SRVP

This work generated data and perspectives with relevance for future radiocarbon dating programmes of peat deposits. Whilst it is clear that sampling error might explain in part the anomalous radiocarbon dates obtained during Phase I of the SRVP, the rigorous programme of dating of multiple fractions of peat during Phase II illustrates that significant differences in age can be identified between short-lived *Alnus glutinosa* macrofossils (most of the submitted material were twigs, which were 1 year old at death) and corresponding humin and humic fractions (Figure 2.18).

The stratigraphic recording of the Beccles 2008 RC Core 1 (Table 2.3) indicated that *Phragmites* remains were present in the sediments immediately overlying both of the horizons in which the dating discrepancies were evident, indicating the potential for disturbance through rhizome penetration (see Chapter 6). This therefore raises the possibility that: (1) the *Alnus* fragments are intrusive and that the bulk samples are providing reliable dating measurements; or (2) the *Alnus* fragments provide an accurate chronology and the bulk sediment measurements are inaccurate. The latter hypothesis can probably be discounted due to the consistency of the humic and humin measurements (see Howard *et al.* 2009 for a detailed discussion of these data) and the preferred hypothesis is that the latter fractions provide the most robust chronology for this sequence. Very few comparative palaeoenvironmental studies, which include similar detailed multi-fraction dating of floodplain sediments, have been carried out (but see Mansell *et al.*, 2014). Multiple fraction radiocarbon determinations from a sediment sequence sampled through a palaeochannel by Gearey *et al.* (2009) also found that two *Alnus* roundwood macrofossils appeared to be too young for their stratigraphic context.

It can be hypothesised that the specific formation

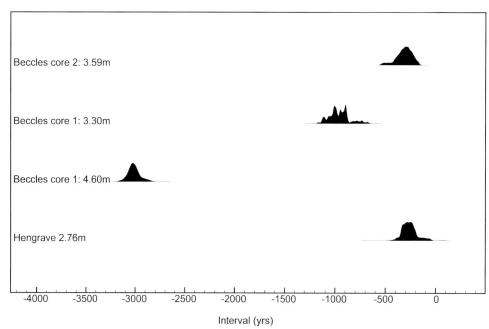

Figure 2.18: Difference in age between bulk peat samples (weighted mean humic and humin) and Alnus macrofossils (selected horizons)

processes of floodplain peatlands may be implicated, perhaps the impact of *Phragmites* root systems. *Phragmites* has the ability to develop extensive root and rhizome systems that can penetrate deep within soils (up to 1m in certain situations) and reach considerable lateral length (e.g. Moore *et al.*, 2012). These root systems can certainly damage buried organic archaeology (see Chapter 6) and *Phragmites* remains are apparent in all of the sequences investigated by the SRVP. The action of *Phragmites* root systems might lead to the downward migration of other plant remains, perhaps via down-washing through root channels that can open during periods of deeper water tables. However, this mechanism is somewhat speculative, as is the possibility of roots physically moving small fragments of other plant remains down profile.

Studies of the effects of root penetration on the movement of plant macrofossil remains down-profile in wetland contexts have produced contrasting results: Cox *et al.* (2001) found that modern birch seeds had moved down through desiccation cracks from the contemporary ground surface at the Abbots Way trackway in the Somerset Levels, whilst more recent and extensive study in the Somerset Levels did not find evidence of any such processes (Brunning, 2013). The pattern of intrusive *Alnus* macrofossils observed here and elsewhere (e.g. Gearey *et al.*, 2009) is thus notable and further work is required to test

if there is a particular problem concerning the taphonomy of alder macrofossils in fluvial environments. Other issues that may affect the homogeneity of deposits and the different organic fractions that can be isolated for radiocarbon dating include the impact of formation processes such as hydrological fluctuations on the movement of humic acids, and the mechanisms of peat accumulation under different vegetation communities (see Brock *et al.*, 2011).

In terms of establishing robust chronologies for palaeo-environmental sequences from floodplain and similar organic deposits, it can be concluded from this work that great care must be taken during sampling, sub-sampling and the selection of fractions for radiocarbon dating. Perhaps the only way to ensure a robust chronology for any given sequence is through the dating of multiple sediment fractions from selected horizons. Even under these strictures, it may well be the case that the particular formation and taphonomy of organic deposits associated with fluvial processes may sometimes preclude the establishment of neat, linear chronologies that are sought for palaeoenvironmental interpretation. Relatively little study of the taphonomy of different carbon fractions used routinely for radiocarbon dating has been undertaken and this is clearly an area, which would benefit from further investigation.

3. Palaeoenvironmental and Geoarchaeological Investigations of the Suffolk River Valleys: Birmingham Archaeo-Environmental Commercial Projects 2005–2012

With contributions from

Tom Hill, Emma Hopla, Kristina Krawiec, Emma Tetlow, Pam Grinter, David Smith, Wendy Smith, Eileen Reilly and Andy Moss

3.1 Introduction

Whilst on the whole, the study sites chosen by the SRVP were not at immediate threat from aggregate extraction, the data provided by the project was critical in terms of assisting curators at Suffolk County Council planning archaeological mitigation for subsequent developments likely to impact on the resource and for demonstrating that other river valley contexts in the county provided potential in terms of wet-preserved palaeoenvironmental and archaeological remains. This chapter outlines the results of a number of investigations from across the county, carried out as part of archaeological mitigation associated with various developments and informed in part by the results of the SRVP.

Birmingham Archaeo-Environmental (BA-E) undertook a number of palaeoenvironmental and geoarchaeological investigations in Suffolk between 2005 and 2012. These works were generally part of archaeological mitigation associated with various commercial developments carried out under the auspices of *PPG* 16 and subsequent legislative frameworks. They varied in scope and extent, but in the main consisted of stratigraphic recording of boreholes and trial trench surveys of sites and deposits associated with the river valleys of the Gipping, Stour and Lark, as well as investigations of areas along the east coast at Ipswich and Sizewell. Most of the studies, which identified deposits of palaeoenvironmental potential, subsequently included some level of assessment (typically pollen, plant macrofossil, beetles and occasionally diatoms), often but not always supported by radiocarbon dating of suitable organics. Whilst occasionally recommendations were made to clients for full analyses of those sequences that were regarded as of high potential, very few of these were ever subsequently carried through to this stage.

This chapter summarises the key results of these various studies (see Table 3.1 and Figure 3.1). With the notable exception of the multi-proxy analyses of the deposits from the Stowmarket Relief Road, the palaeoenvironmental data are often available at assessment level only, restricting the interpretative value of the studies. The various projects will be described in the following section in relation to the river valleys in which they were situated, beginning with the River Gipping, followed by the Stour and the Lark and finally those on the east coast at Ipswich and Sizewell. The chapter concludes with a summary of this work and the broad insights that it provides into patterns and processes of the Holocene evolution of these valleys within the context of geoarchaeological and palaeoenvironmental work on other lowland river systems in the United Kingdom. Unless otherwise indicated, boreholes were excavated by hand generally using an Eijkelkamp 'gouge corer and all palaeoenvironmental assessments and analyzes were carried out following the standard methodologies described in Chapter 1. Radiocarbon dates were obtained from Beta Analytic, Miami, Florida, and the Scottish Universities Environmental Research Centre (SUERC), East Kilbride (Table 3.2).

Table 3.1. Summary of palaeoenvironmental work carried out by BA-E in Suffolk. Code for study: B = Boreholes, TP= trench/ test pit, P=Pollen, PM=Plant macrofossils, Bt=Beetles, D=Diatoms, RC=Radiocarbon dating.

River/Site	Grid Ref	Study	Report Reference
Gipping			
Stowmarket Relief Road	TM052587	B, P, PM, Bt, RC	Hill, 2008
			Hopla *et al.*, 2008
		(Full analysis)	Gearey *et al.*, 2010a
Stowmarket Station Road	TM053587	B, T, P, B, PM	Gearey *et al.*, 2009
Great Blakenham	TM123496	B, P, Bt, PM, RC	Hopla *et al.*, 2010
Cedars Park	TM108530	B	Hill, 2007a
Stour			
Sudbury AFC	TL870408	B, T, P, Bt, PM, RC	Gearey, 2009
			Gearey *et al.*, 2010b
Wixoe	TL708431	B	Hopla and Krawiec, 2010
Lark			
Abbey Precinct, Bury St Edmunds	Site A TL858643	B, P, R, Bt, PM	Krawiec *et al.*, 2009
	Site B TL857643		
Eastgate Street, Bury St Edmunds	TL858645	B, T	Hill, 2007b
Rushbrooke-Nowton	TL872622	B, T	Hill, 2007c
East Coast-Ipswich			
Ipswich University/Docks/Albion Wharf	TM169440	B, T, Bt, D, RC	Hill and Tetlow, 2007
River Orwell, Ipswich Triangle	TM165441	B, T	Hill, 2007d
Ipswich Mills	TM165440	B, T	Hill, 2007e
Sizewell Belts	TM471631	B, T, P, Bt, RC	Hill and Gearey, 2008
			Hill *et al.*, 2008b

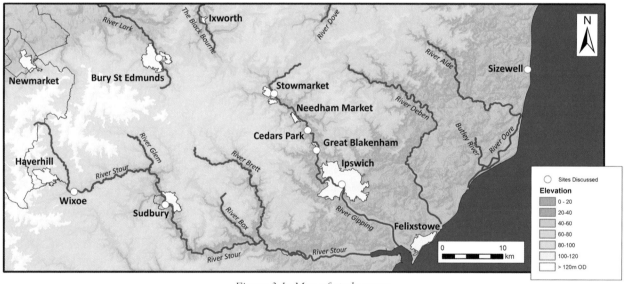

Figure 3.1: Map of study areas

3.2. The River Gipping

3.2.1 Stowmarket: Stowmarket Relief Road

The most detailed and comprehensive of all the commercial projects carried out in Suffolk by BA-E was that associated with the construction of the Stowmarket Relief Road (Figure 3.2). The results of these analyses, which provide information regarding the development of the floodplain of the River Gipping from the early to mid-Holocene, are described in detail in this section. Other smaller scale studies (see below) of the Gipping floodplain were undertaken at Station Road, some 200m south-west of the relief road site, Cedars Park, and at Great Blakenham some 5km downstream and south-west of the town.

Extensive peat deposits associated with the route of the relief road across the floodplain had been recorded in geotechnical boreholes drilled in advance of this civil engineering project. BA-E was sub-contracted by Suffolk County Council Archaeological Service to undertake a palaeoenvironmental evaluation of the sediments (Hill,

Table 3.2: Radiocarbon dates from Birmingham Archaeo-Environmental projects in Suffolk. Note: Stowmarket Relief Road – dates in italics have been derived from simple linear interpolation between radiocarbon determinations and should be regarded as tentative estimates

Depth/m	Lab Code	Date BP	Material	Calibrated date (2 σ)/estimated date
Stowmarket Relief Road				
4.10–4.11	SUERC–20656	1265±30	Peat (acid-alkali-acid)	cal. AD 670–860
4.5	–	–	–	*220 cal. BC*
4.82–4.90	Beta–267388	2810±80	Peat (acid-alkali-acid)	1210–810 cal. BC
5	–	–	–	*1090 BC*
5.50–5.55	Beta–267389	3070±70	Peat (acid-alkali-acid)	1490–1130 cal. BC
6	–	–	–	*1710 cal BC*
6.26–6.27	SUERC–20657	3570±35	Peat (acid-alkali-acid)	2030–1780 cal. BC
6.5	–	–	–	*2375 BC*
7–7.05	Beta–267391	4590±70	Peat (acid-alkali-acid)	3630–3090 cal. BC
7.5	–	–	–	*4630 BC*
8	–	–	–	*5905BC*
8.50–8.51	SUERC–20658	8160±35	Peat (acid-alkali-acid)	7300–7060 cal. BC
Great Blakenham				
4.10	Beta–281671	143.5±0.4 pMC	Peat (acid/alkali/acid)	Post-0 BP & has been reported as % of modern reference standard, indicating material was living within last 50 years ("pMC"=% modern carbon)
4.56	Beta–281672	110±40	Peat (acid/alkali/acid)	cal. AD 1670–1780 and 1800–1950
4.98	Beta–281673	1630±40	Peat (acid/alkali/acid)	cal. AD 340–540
Sudbury AFC				
Sudbury 1b Top	Beta–263580	1280±40	Peat (acid/alkali/acid)	cal. AD 660–810
Sudbury 1b Base	Beta–263579	2350±40	Peat (acid/alkali/acid)	510–380 cal. BC
Abbey, Bury St Edmunds				
2.77 –C26b	Beta–258111	1350±40	Peat (acid/alkali/acid)	cal. AD 640–710 and 750–760
3.90 –C26b	Beta–258112	2670±40	Peat (acid/alkali/acid)	900–790 cal. BC
2.71 –C27	Beta–258114	1250±40	Peat (acid/alkali/acid)	cal. AD 670–880
4.92 –C27	Beta–258113	4240±40	Wood (acid/alkali/acid)	2910–2860, 2800–2750 and 2710–2710 cal. BC
2.51 –C28	Beta–258110	890±40	Wood (acid-alkali-acid)	cal. AD 1030–1230
2.80 –C28	Beta–258115	960±40	Wood (acid-alkali-acid)	cal. AD 1010–1170
Ipswich, University				
UNIIPS–1.65	Beta–226829	350±40	Peat (acid/alkali/acid)	cal. AD 1450–1650
INIIPS–2.94	Beta–226830	370±0	Collagen extraction: with alkali	cal. AD 1440–1640
Sizewell Belts				
BAE1806 0.80	SUERC–19649	1505±25	Peat (acid/alkali/acid)	cal. AD 530–630
BAE1806 1.04	SUERC–19650	2415±30	Peat (acid/alkali/acid)	750–390 cal. BC
BAE1806 1.28	SUERC–19651	2870±30	Peat (acid/alkali/acid)	1130–930 cal. BC

Table 3.3: Stratigraphy of the Stowmarket Relief Road core

Depth/m	Description	Troels Smith (components)
0–4.0	Made ground	–
4.0–4.10	Grey organic silts	Ag. 2 Sh. 2 Dh. +
4.10–7.48	Red brown wood rich peat, wood remains increasing with depth	Sh. 2 Dl. 2 Ag. + Nig. 4 Strf.0 Elas.0 Sicc. 2
7.48–8.50m	Grey brown well humified silty peat	Sh. 2 Ag. 2 Dh. + Nig. 3 Strf.0 Elas.0 Sicc. 2
8.50m+	Grey brown saturated silty, organic sands	Gmin4 Ag + Sh + Nig. 2 Strf.0 Elas.0 Sicc. 3

2008). This work included initial sampling using a cable percussive auger (Figure 3.3), which recovered a sequence of organic deposits 8.5m thick (see Table 3.3 for stratigraphy) from a location 200m east of the current river course (Figure 3.4). Subsequent palaeoenvironmental assessments demonstrated that although pollen preservation was generally poor, there was good preservation of plant macrofossils and beetles; hence full analysis of the latter supported by radiocarbon dating was recommended (Hopla *et al.*, 2008).

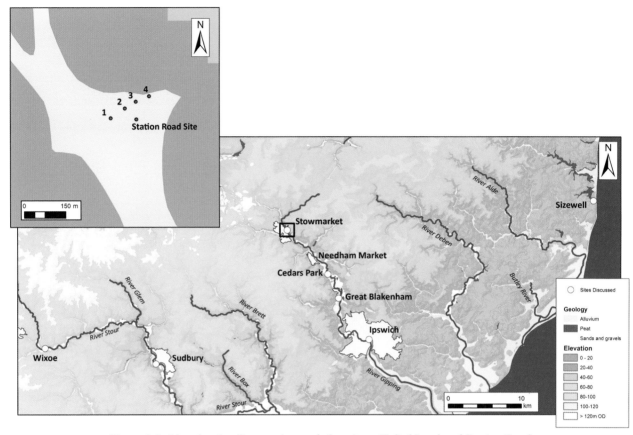

Figure 3.2: Map showing Stowmarket study locations (Relief Road and Station Road)

Figure 3.3: Cable percussive rig in operation at the Stowmarket Relief Road site

Nine core sections were bulked into 0.5m thick sections (4.0–4.5m, 4.5–5.0m, 5.0–5.5m, 5.5–6.0m, 6.0–6.5m, 6.5–7.0m, 7.0–7.5m, 7.5–8.0m and 8.0–8.50m) for full beetle and plant macrofossil analyses (Gearey *et al.*, 2010a). In addition, molluscs were found to be abundant in the basal section of the core and a sub-sample of shells was picked out for identification. Three sub-samples for radiocarbon dating (4.10m, 6.26m and 8.50m) had previously been submitted during the assessment phase of the project to SUERC (Hopla *et al.*, 2008). Table 3.2 presents all the radiocarbon dates discussed this chapter. Material from four further bulk samples were selected for a second round of radiocarbon dating (4.82m, 5.50m, 6.0m and 7.0m) (Figure 3.5); the dates presented as *circa* in the following section are derived from simple linear interpolation between the radiocarbon determinations (see Chapter 1 for a brief discussion of this radiocarbon chronology). The results of the mollusc analyses are presented in Table 3.4 and plant macrofossils in Table 3.5.

Results: analyses of beetles and plant macrofossils from Stowmarket Relief Road

SAMPLE 1: 8.5–8.0M (7300–7060 TO C. 5900 CAL. BC)
Coleoptera
This sub-sample produced a relatively small assemblage dominated by aquatic taxa. Many of the species, such as

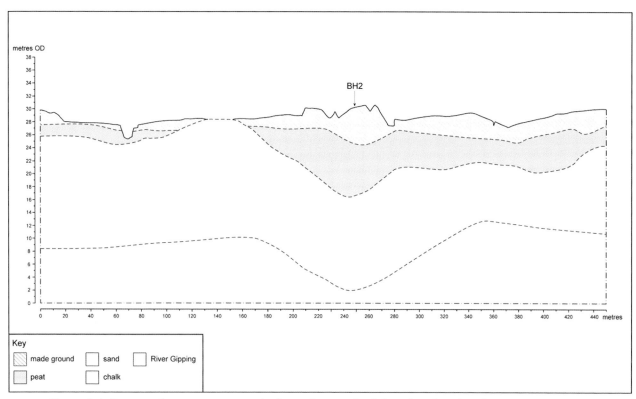

Figure 3.4: Stratigraphic transect across the River Gipping floodplain, based on data from geotechnical logs

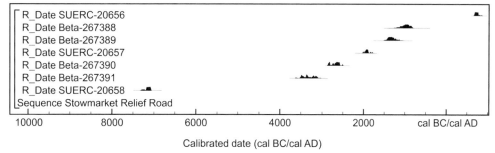

Figure 3.5: Stowmarket Relief Road calibrated radiocarbon dates

Table 3.4: Molluscs from Stowmarket Relief Road basal sample 1 (8.5–8m)

Species	Common name	No. recorded	Ecology
Bithynia tentaculata	Mud Bithynia, common Bithynia or faucet snail	61	Freshwater standing or slowly running waters.
Valvata cristata	Flat valve snail	8	Stagnant/still water
Valvata piscinalis	European stream valvata	2	Running water
Planorbis crista (or Gyraulus crista)	Nautilus ramshorn	1	Lives on freshwater plants
Segmentina complanata	Flat ram's horn snail	1	Lives in ponds and ditches, prefers calcium-rich waters
Lymnaea peregra	Wandering pond snail	1	Colonises weedy ponds, does not travel far from water, always stays in damp places.
Carychium minimum	Short-toothed Herald Snail	2	Damp conditions
Planorbis leucostoma (Anisus leucostoma)	Button ramshorn snail	1	Freshwater

Taxon	Common Name	Habitat	4.0–4.5	4.5–5.0	5.0–5.5	5.5–6.0	6.0–6.5	6.5–7.0	7.0–7.5	7.5–8.0	8.0–8.50
							Sample/depth –m				
Nymphaea alba L.	White water-lily	Still shallow water	+								+
Ceratophyllum submersum L.	Soft hornwort	Still water	+								
Urtica dioica L.	Stinging nettle	Woods waste ground					+				
Betula pendula Roth	Silver birch	Woods	+							+	
Alnus glutinosa L	Alder	By fresh water	+++	+	++	++++	+++++	+++	++	+	+
Chenopodium album L.	Fat-hen	Disturbed ground								+	
Chenopodium spp.	Goosefoots				+						
Moehringia trinervia (L) Clairv.	Three nerved sandwort	Woods and hedge banks		+							
Stellaria neglecta Weihe	Greater chickweed	Damp, shady, streams					++	+	++		
Cerastium cf fontanum Baumg	Common mouse-ear	Grassland	+								
Lychnis flos-cuculi L.	Ragged robin	Damp Marshy places	+	+			++	+			
Rumex sp.	Dock	Disturbed ground	+								
Rumex crispus L.	Curled dock	Disturbed ground		+							
Rubus fructicosus L.	Bramble	Woods, scrub					+	+			
Potentilla erecta (L) Raeusch	Tormentil	Moors, bogs, grass	+	+							
Prunus spinosa L.	Blackthorn	Hedges scrub woods				+					
Crataegus monogyna Jacq.	Hawthorn	Hedges, scrub		+							
Linum usitatissimum L.	Flax	Cultivar	+	+							
Hydrocotyle vulgaris L.	Marsh pennywort	Bogs, fens and marshes sides of lakes.			+						
Apium repens (Jacq) Lag.	Creeping marshwort	Open wet places	+								
Stachys palustris L.	Marsh woundwort	By rivers and ponds						+	+		
Lycopus europaeus. L	Gypsywort	Fens and wet fields	+	++				+	+		
Pedicularis palustris L.	Marsh lousewort	Wet grass and bogs								+	
Sambucus nigra L.	Elder	Hedges, woods					+	+	+	+	
Cirsium palustre (L) Scop.	Marsh thistle	Marshes, damp grasslands		+							
Anthemis cotula L.	Stinking chamomile	Arable, waste, rough ground	+								
Carex appropinquata Schumach	Fibrous tussock sedge	Lakes, streams marshes and fens	++++			+++++	+	+			
Carex spp. Trigonous nut	sedges		++		+		+	+	+	+	
Carex spp. Ovate nut	sedges				+						
Iris pseudacorus L.	Yellow iris	Fens, ditches, lakes		+							

Arable	Water
Woods	By water
Carr	Wet grassland
Grass	Cultivar
Disturbed	

Table 3.5 Stowmarket Relief Road macrofossil analyses, rated on a relative scale of abundance within samples from rare (+) to common (+++++) and should only be used to compare between samples with caution

the Hydraenidae family, are associated with open mud and shallower waters at the margins of a variety of wetland bodies (Hansen, 1987). The Hydrophilidae *Hydrobius fuscipes*, *Chaetarthria seminulum* and *Anacaema* sp., reflect similar habitats, the former pair are particularly associated with the well-vegetated margins of standing water (Hansen, 1987). The Dytiscid *Agabus bipustulatus* is indicative of well-vegetated, deeper water (Nilsson and Holmen, 1995). The sample also contained large numbers of the Dryopidae *Oulimnius* spp., a genus associated with well-oxygenated flowing waters, such as in the splash zone at the edges of lakes and rivers with gravel substrates (Holland, 1972).

Species associated with the wider, terrestrial environment are scarce, but the Orthoperid, *Corylophus cassidoides*, is found with decaying grasses and flood detritus on tussocky grassland (Duff, 1993). A further indictor of damp grassland is the Chrysomelid, *Plateumaris discolour*, a phytophagous species found on *Carex* sp. (sedges) and *Eriophorum* sp. (cotton grasses) (Menzies and Cox, 1996). Such habitats may have been present on the floodplain, but other indicators of drier grassland perhaps beyond the wetland edge include the Scarabaeid *Cetonia aurata* and the Curculionidae, *Gymnetron* sp. and *Phyllobius* sp. (Koch, 1992; Jessop, 1996).

Plant macrofossils and molluscs

The sub-sample produced a very small, poorly preserved flot and the seeds of only three species were recorded: *Nymphaea alba* (white water lily), *Alnus glutinosa* (alder) and *Pedicularis palustris* (marsh lousewort). White water lily requires shallow, standing water to support its leaves and flowers. The concentration of *Alnus* remains is probably too low to indicate dense local alder carr but some trees were perhaps established nearby. The mollusc assemblage (Table 3.4) is characterised by a range of taxa associated with freshwater environments and damp vegetation. The dominant species is *Bithynia tentaculata* (mud Bithynia), which is found in slowly running calcium-rich freshwater habitats. The second most abundant species is *Valvata cristata* (flat valve snail) and is typical of still / stagnant waters.

SAMPLE 2: 8.0–7.5M (C. 5900 TO C. 4630 CAL. BC)

Coleoptera

Species composition is similar to the previous sample. Aquatic taxa dominate the assemblage with relatively large numbers of the Dryopid, *Oulimnius* sp., and the Hydraenidae in slightly lower concentrations. Another indicator of fluvial environments is *Hydraena testacea*, which is associated with slow moving and standing waters (Hansen, 1987; Foster, 2000). The presence of the Chrysomelid, *Plateumaris braccata*, suggests that *Phragmites australis* (common reed) was growing nearby

(Menzies and Cox, 1996). This species can grow on damp soils as well as standing water (up to *c*. 1m deep). There is an increase in species associated with rotting organic material, a small suite of Staphylinidae, which include *Micropeplus fulvus,* and *Phylodrepa florialis*, found in drier rotting material, whilst *Anotylus rugosus* is more commonly associated with fouler rotting organics including carrion and dung (Tottenham, 1954).

Macrofossils

The flot produced poorly preserved macrofossils, but contained a wider range of plant species. The macrofossils included *Betula pendula* (silver birch), *Alnus glutinosa* (alder) and *Sambucus nigra* (elder) indicating a fen carr environment with elder and perhaps birch, although the seeds of *Betula* are readily dispersed by wind or water. The presence of *Stachys palustris* (marsh lousewort), *Lycopus europaeus* (gypsywort) and *Carex* sp. (sedge) suggest the presence of damp, open conditions.

SAMPLE 3: 7.5–7M (C. 4630 TO C. 3630–3090 CAL. BC)

Coleoptera

A marked decrease in aquatic taxa, particularly the Hydraenidae and the Hydrophilidae is apparent in this sample, although the Dryopid genus, *Oulimnius* sp. remains relatively abundant. Species associated with rotting organic material or sedge tussock and damp grassland are scarce, but two indicators of grassland do persist in the form of the Scarabaeid, *Cetonia aurata* and the Curculionid, *Alophus triguttatus*. These taxa are found in a range of habitats including pasture and floodplain (Koch, 1992) with plant species such as *Plantago* spp. (plantains*)*, *Symphytum* spp. (comfreys) and *Eupatorium* spp. (thoroughworts).

Macrofossils

This was very similar in species composition to Sample 2. The presence of *Alnus* and *Sambucus* indicates the persistence of fen carr. *Stellaria neglecta* (greater chickweed) is also recorded and is a herb that is typically found in damp places.

SAMPLE 4: 7.0–6.5M (C. 3630–3090 TO C. 2370 CAL. BC)

Coleoptera

Overall species abundance and diversity demonstrates a significant increase. Many of these species are hygrophilous taxa, which suggest relatively wet environments, but fewer appear to represent fluvial contexts. The Dryopid, *Oulimnius* sp. is much reduced, as are those species typical of slowing moving or standing water. The Orthoperid, *Corylophus cassidoides* reappears, suggesting the persistence of tussocky grassland. The Staphylinidae, *Lesteva heeri*,

Lesteva punctata and *Lathrobium brunnipes*, are associated with flood debris, particularly reed, sedge and grass litter (Koch, 1989a). Other hygrophilous species indicative of similar riparian and lentic macrophyte communities include the Carabidae *Pterostichus diligens* and *Bembidion obliquum*. Both species are typical marsh and wetland taxa, the latter found in reed, sedge and grass litter (Lindroth, 1974). *Bembidion obliquum* is indicative of sparsely vegetated, muddy substrates (Lindroth, 1974).

There is also an increase in species associated with foul, rotting organic material and dung. The Scaradbaeidae or 'dung beetle' *Geotrupes* spp. are recorded exclusively within this sample. The Geotrupidae or 'Dor beetles' are more closely associated with the dung of larger herbivores such as cows and horses (Jessop, 1986). Other indicators of accumulated dung and fouler, rotting material than recorded in the previous samples are the non-aquatic Hydrophilidae, *Cercyon impressus* and *Cryptopleurum minutum*, both of which are associated with the dung of large herbivores and with organic litter and flood detritus. The latter species and the Histerid, *Acritus nigricornis* (Duff, 1993) are also found with carrion and can be considered indicative of particularly foul, rotting material (Hansen, 1987; Duff, 1993; Kenward and Hall, 1995).

Macrofossils

This sample produced a larger flot with a similar range of taxa to the previous sample but with higher numbers of *Alnus* seeds. The impression is of the expansion of alder fen carr relative to the previous samples, but with more open, damp habitats persisting. *Rubus fructicosus* (blackberry) and *Carex appropinquata* (fibrous tussock sedge) both appear in this sample. Bramble is a hedgerow-type species often associated with disturbed ground/waste, whilst fibrous tussock sedge is often found in lakes, streams marshes and fens. This may indicate the presence of drier areas within the local environment as older tussocks may provide such habitats beneath the tree canopy (Haslam, 2003).

SAMPLE 5: 6.5–6.0M (C. 2370–C. 1710 CAL. BC)

Coleoptera

This assemblage was much smaller than the previous sample and whilst still relatively diverse, overall abundance has decreased. The fauna indicates little detectable change in the environment. Indicators of tussocky grassland and sedge/grass litter, *Corylophus cassidoides*, *L. heeri*, and *L. punctata* persist and further marsh and wetland species are recorded including the Pselaphid *Bryaxis bulbifer*, which is also found in grass tussocks and marshland (Pearce, 1957; Duff, 1993). The Chrysomelid, *P. braccata* and the Curclionid, *Notaris* sp. may suggest stands of taller reeds and grasses including *Phragmites australis*.

There is a marked decrease in the group of species found with foul rotting material whilst taxa associated with dung have disappeared completely. A small component

of the fauna perhaps hints at disturbed ground and grassland, probably beyond the floodplain edge. Many of the Curculionidae or 'weevils', are typical of grassland, meadows and pasture. This group includes *Apion* spp. more commonly found on *Rumex* spp. (docks and sorrels) (Koch, 1992) and *Sitona* spp., which feeds upon *Vicia* spp. (vetches) and *Trifolium* spp. (clovers).

Macrofossils

This sample contained large numbers of *Alnus* seeds and a range of plants also typical of fen carr and damp vegetation (*Stellaria neglecta* and *Carex* sp.) and *Lychnis flos-cuculi* (ragged robin), a herb found in floodplain grassland. A further notable record is that of *Urtica dioica* (stinging nettle), an indicator of disturbed ground unlikely to be present in a wetland without an enriched nutrient content (see below). *Rubus fruiticosus* may also indicate somewhat disturbed soils, such as woodland edge or hedgerow environments.

SAMPLE 6: 6.0–5.5M (C. 1710 CAL. BC TO C. 1490–1130 CAL. BC)

Coleoptera

This sample produced the richest and most abundant assemblage of the entire sequence. However, the overall composition has changed very little from the previous sample, with the Staphylinid group associated with tussocky grassland and a pair of Carabidae consisting of *Pterostichus nigrita* and *Pterostichus strenuus*, which are found in a variety of habitats, particularly very wet, well-vegetated environments (Lindroth, 1974, 1986). The most pronounced change is the re-emergence of an extensive aquatic assemblage, especially species associated with deeper, standing water, including the Hydrophilid *Cymbiodyta marginella* and *Hydrobius fuscipes*, and the Dytiscidae *Agabus bipustulatus* and *Haliplus* sp. (Hansen, 1987; Nilsson and Holmen, 1995).

A further Carabid, *Agonum thoreyi* and the Chrysomelid *Plateumaris sericea* are associated with tall reeds and sedges including *Typha latifolia* (reedmace), *Iris pseudoacorus* (yellow flag) and in the case of *P. sericea*, the emergent macrophyte *Nuphar* sp. (yellow water lily) (Lindroth, 1974, 1986; Menzies and Cox, 1996). A much smaller component probably reflects the dryland environment beyond the floodplain edge. Two species that may be regarded as monophagous are the Eucnemid *Melasis buprestoides*, which is particularly associated with *Fagus sylvatica* (beech), and the Scoytid *Leperisinius varius*, found on *Fraxinus excelsior* (ash) (Hyman, 1992).

Macrofossils

There is a slight decrease in numbers of *Alnus* seeds in this sample, although alder carr probably remained in the near vicinity. *Sambucus* disappears from the record suggesting this shrub is no longer part of the scrub layer. The high numbers of *C. appropinquata* may reflect the development of tussocks of sedge on the sampling site itself. *Prunus spinosa* (blackthorn) is recorded, indicating the presence of this shrub, which is typical of undergrowth or woodland margin.

SAMPLE 7: 5.5–5.0M (C. 1490–1130 TO C. 1090 CAL. BC)

Coleoptera

Species abundance and overall diversity declines in this sample, especially amongst the aquatic species and those of rotting organic material such as flood debris. Small numbers of Hydreanidae and Dytisicidae remain, as does a single indicator of rotting material in the form of a Scarabaeid of the *Aphodius* family. A range of species typical of damp, tussocky grassland are recorded, namely the Staphylinidae *L. punctata* and *L. heeri*, the Orthoperid *Corylophous cassidoides* and the Carabid *Pterostichus nigrita*. Indicators of taller reeds also decline and the Chrysomelidae recorded in previous samples are absent, with species associated with this type of vegetation restricted to *A. thoreyi*.

Macrofossils

The range of plant remains is similar to Sample 6, with evidence for the persistence of *Alnus* fen carr and damp, open environments (*Carex* sp. and *Lychnis flos-cuculi*). The aquatic *Hydrocotyle vulgaris* (Marsh pennywort) is also recorded.

SAMPLE 8: 5.0–4.5M (C. 1090 TO C. 220 CAL. BC)

Coleoptera

Aquatic taxa are slightly more abundant in this sample and include the larger Hydrophilidae, *C. orbiculare* and *H. fuscipes*, as well as the smaller species *C. seminulum* and *Anacaema bipustulatus*. Species of rotting material also increase, including a further pair of Hydrophilidae, *Cercyon sternalis* and *Cercyon analis*, and the Staphylinidae *Carpelimus bilineatus* and *Rugilus* sp. The latter species is associated with a variety of rotting material including drier hay/straw like material and reed litter (Koch, 1989b).

The assemblage reflecting the wider environment also demonstrates a subtle shift. Species of damp grassland and sedge tussock have disappeared and been replaced by those typical of drier grassland such as the Scarabaeid *Cetonia aurata*, the larvae of which are found in rotting material and the adult commonly amongst the flowers of the Apiaceae (carrot family) (Jessop, 1986). The numbers of Curculionidae (*Apion* sp., *Sitona* sp., *Hypera* sp. and *Gymnetron* sp.) all increase markedly. The preference of *Apion* sp. and *Sitona* sp. for nitrophilous forbs has already been noted, whilst *Hypera* spp. is found on a variety of grassland plants including *Trifolium* sp., *Medicago* sp. (medick / burcolver), *Rumex* sp., *Lathyrus* sp. (sweet pea). *Gymnetron* sp. is associated with *Plantago* sp., *Veronica* sp.

(speedwells) and *Linaria* sp. (toadflaxes) (Hyman, 1992; Koch, 1992; Bullock, 1993).

Macrofossils

There is evidence for a range of habitats in this sample. Lower numbers of *Alnus* seeds are recorded, possibly indicating a local decrease in fen carr, whilst *C. appropinquata* is well represented, demonstrating the local persistence of tussocky sedge. Herbs typical of open fen such as *Lycopus europaeus* (gypsywort), *Potentilla erecta* (tormentil) and *Cirsium palustre* (marsh thistle) remain present and *Iris pseudocarus* (yellow iris) is also recorded. There is an indication of disturbed ground in the form of *Rumex crispus* (curled dock) and of scrub/hedge by *Crataegus monogyna* (hawthorn).

Most notably, seeds of *Linum usitatissimum* (flax) are present in this sample. This plant is an introduced species and indicates that its cultivation and/or processing were taking place on the floodplain. Flax is a shallow-rooted plant and requires ample moisture during early stages of development (Percival, 1918; Renfew, 1973) and is hence often cultivated on alluvial soils (see below).

SAMPLE 9: 4.5–4.0M (C. 220 CAL. BC TO CAL. AD C. 670–860)

Coleoptera

The assemblage from the final sample again displays an increase in abundance and diversity, especially in species, which are associated with drier, rotting material. This group contains sclera, which could not be identified to species level but include the Rhizophagid *Rhizophagus* sp., the Cryptophagid *Atomaria*, and the Lathridiidae *Enicmus minutus* and *Corticaria* sp. Whilst several species of this group are associated with drier flood debris, they may also be indicative of anthropogenic environments (Hall and Kenward, 1990; Kenward and Hall, 1995) in the near vicinity of the sampling site. The component of the assemblage found with foul, rotting organic material also changes somewhat with the Staphylinidae *Oxytelus tetracarinatus* and *Platystethus arenarius* replacing the Hydrophilidae, which were found in the previous samples. The implications of this will be discussed in greater detail below.

There is an increase in aquatic and hygrophilous species with relatively large numbers of the Hydraenidae family recorded. The Hydrophilidae *C. Orbiculare*, *H. fuscipes* and *C. marginella* are found in shallower water at the well-vegetated margins of a variety of wetland bodies (Hansen, 1987). The monophage *P. braccatare* is recorded, indicating the proximity of *Phragmites australis*. A further species associated with emergent vegetation is *Prasocuris phellandrii*, a monophage found on *Oenanthe aquatica* (fine leaved water dropwort) (Bullock, 1993). Species of damp, tussocky grassland re-emerge, such as the Orthoperid *C. cassidoides*, and the Staphylinid *L. heeri*. Taxa of drier grassland such as *Sitona* sp. and *Apion* sp. remain and two individuals of the former genus were identified to species level: *Sitona suturalis* is found with *Vicia* spp. and *Lathyrus pratense* and *Sitona puncticollis* with *Lotus* spp. (bird's foot trefoil), *Trifolium* spp. and *Vicia* spp. (Koch, 1992).

Macrofossils

The final sub-sample produced the largest plant species list for the sequence. An increase in *Alnus* implies some re-expansion in fen carr whilst the re-appearance of *Betula*, albeit in low quantities, may suggest the presence of birch as local scrub/woodland. The impression of increased woodland cover is reinforced by the record of *Moehringia trinervia* (three nerved sandwort), a herb that grows in shady woodland environments.

The range of taxa includes those found in the previous samples (*Lychnis flos-cuculi*, *Lycopus europaeus* and *Potentilla*) and several other species typical of wet floodplains including *Apium repens* (creeping marshwort) and the aquatic herb *Ceratophyllum submersum* (soft hornwort). The presence of *Linum usitatissimum* again implies cultivation/processing of flax. Cultivated land may also be indicated by the record of *Anthemis cotula* (stinking chamomile), a weed associated with waste ground and arable habitats.

Discussion

The stratigraphic profile (see Figure 3.4) indicates that the organic sediments fill a buried channel, which may have originated sub-glacially. Elsewhere along the Gipping, this channel is infilled with a variety of unconsolidated sediments of Middle and Late Pleistocene age (Woodland, 1970; Rose *et al.* 1980). The channel was probably active during the earlier Holocene, but the basal radiocarbon date indicates that organic sediment accumulation commenced around 8160±35 BP (SUERC-20658; 7200–7060 cal. BC). This date is associated with the silty peat (7.48–8.50m) overlying basal sands (Table 3.3) and reflecting increasingly sluggish flow of water at the sampling location and aggradation of the channel as vegetation colonised the sampling site. Linear interpolation between the basal radiocarbon date and that from 7.0–7.05m (4590±70 BP; Beta-267391; 3630–3090 cal. BC) indicates that the transition from organic silt to peat accumulation and hence the eventual infilling of the palaeochannel occurred *c.* 4630 cal. BC.

The palaeoenvironmental record reflects the evolution of the depositional regime between 8.5m (8160±35 BP (SUERC-20658; 7200–7060 cal. BC) and 7.5m (*c.* 4630 cal. BC). The beetle fauna from these samples are dominated by aquatic taxa with the presence of large numbers of 'riffle beetles' *Oulimnius* sp., suggesting frequent influxes of flowing water, which most probably introduced the silt component in the basal peat. The presence of sparse remains of *Nymphea alba* in the macrofossil record are further evidence of open water, although the low concentrations of identifiable plant material somewhat restricts interpretation

of these data. The molluscs from the basal sample (Table 3.4) include species found in stagnant/still water, indicative of the conditions associated with much reduced flow and accumulation of peat.

The nature of many lowland British rivers changed during the early Holocene, from unstable, braided, multi-channel systems to meandering and anastomosing ones with increasing channel stability facilitating the subsequent expansion of extensive floodplain wetlands (e.g. see Brown and Keough, 1993; Howard and Macklin, 1999). This process appears to be reflected in the proxies, with species of Coleoptera, indicative of open, standing water increasing in Sample 2 (7.5–8.0m). By this point, *c.* 5905–4630 cal. BC, there is also less evidence from the insect remains for relatively high-energy fluvial conditions. This presumably reflects the accumulation of peat in what was by this point an inactive channel, which was cut-off from the main river system, other than during flood events. However, although species associated with open water were reduced as peat accumulation progressed, the taxon *Oulimnius* sp. remains dominant in the sample from 7.5–7.0m, between *c.* 4630 cal. BC and *c.* 4590±70 BP (Beta-267391; 3630–3090 cal. BC). This might imply that although sedimentation at the site had shifted from within a fluvial to semi-terrestrial environment, the location was subject to occasional influxes of flowing water from a nearby active channel.

The accumulation of peat in a drier floodplain environment is reflected in the fauna from Samples 3–5 (7.0–6.0m, 4590±70 BP; Beta-267391; 3630–3090 to *c.* 1710 cal. BC), with a marked decline in hygrophilous taxa suggesting further isolation from fluvial influence. The range of beetles associated with grasses and reeds including *Phragmites australis* alongside others found with flood debris may instead reflect a seasonally flooded environment. This impression of a context increasingly marginal to fluvial influence may be reinforced by the record of *Bembidion obliquum* in Sample 5 (6.5–7.0m), a species often found at the periphery of water bodies (Lindroth, 1974).

However, Sample 6 (6.0–5.5m) (3070±30 BP; Beta-267839; *c.* 1710 to *c.* 1490–1130 cal. BC) reflects a further change in the depositional environment with evidence for a shift to wetter conditions. Aquatic taxa including species indicative of deep, standing water and others associated with wetland plants are recorded. The macrofossil record is dominated by *Carex approprinquata* indicating the dominance of tussocky sedge locally, although no true aquatic plants are recorded. Pools and puddles may develop between the tussocks of this species during periods of raised water-tables (Haslam, 2003), perhaps accounting for the presence of beetles associated with standing water.

There is a subsequent decline in species abundance and diversity in Sample 7 (5.0–5.5m, *c.* 1490–1130 to 1090 cal. BC) and the fauna would appear to indicate slightly drier conditions with tussocky grassland persisting. This is followed by evidence for wetter environments in Sample 8 (5.0–4.5m, *c.* 1090–*c.* 220 cal. BC), which appear to be maintained into Sample 9 (4.5–4.0m, *c.* 220 cal. BC–*c.* cal.

AD 670–880) alongside indications of shallow open water. This final sample cuts across stratigraphic boundaries with the well-humified peat overlain at a depth of 4.10m by organic-rich silts. It seems likely that the beetles indicative of aquatic habitats are largely associated with the deposition of this silt layer. Such open water environments are also reflected by presence of *Ceratophyllum submersum* in the plant macrofossil record.

There are thus notable differences between the hydrological conditions apparent in the lower samples (Samples 1–3; 7300–7060 to 3630–3090 cal. BC) compared to those of the upper part of the sequence (Samples 6–9; *c.* 1710 cal. BC to *c.* cal. AD 670–860). In the latter group of samples, species associated with flowing water are absent and the aquatic assemblage is dominated by species of still or standing waters, many of which are found at the margins of running water and in muddy, ephemeral pools. This would indicate that this second wetter phase during the mid-later 2nd millennium BC is unlikely to be associated directly with reactivation or movement of a channel close to the site, but rather with a general rise in local ground-water tables.

Wetland vegetation change

The Coleopteran samples from Stowmarket provide evidence for changes in fluvial conditions and floodplain evolution during the Holocene. The taxa within samples from 8.5–7.0m are characteristic of fast flowing water and strongly indicate deposition in a higher-energy regime, whilst those from Samples 6.0–4.5m reflect slower moving and standing waters. Coleoptera found on emergent and aquatic vegetation are virtually absent in the lower samples but become more prevalent in the upper samples (6m+), all of which contained taxa characteristic of standing water. A further suite of coleoptera associated with aquatic vegetation such as *Nuphar* sp., *Oenanthe aquatica* and taller reeds such as *Typha* spp. and *Phragmites australis* can also be identified in these upper samples. These herbaceous taxa are typical of standing water and silty substrates, conditions not favoured by the Elmid ('riffle' beetles) family that are abundant in Sample 1. The data therefore demonstrate the significant change in fluvial conditions from the early to the later Holocene, a pattern observed in other British catchments (see Smith and Howard, 2004).

However, whilst the analyses appear to provide good evidence of the evolution of the fluvial system, there are interpretative issues associated with reconstructing the wider floodplain environment from the palaeoentomological data. There are problems associated with extrapolating the extent of *Alnus* on the wider floodplain from the macrofossil data, especially in the absence of detailed pollen evidence (see Bunting *et al.*, 2005), but the impression is that fen carr was significantly close to the sampling site for much of the time-frame represented by the sequence. The pollen assessment of this sequence indicated that *Alnus* was abundant on and around the sampling site, especially in the basal deposits (7.7–8.5m) where it was generally better preserved (see Hopla *et al.,* 2008), although these data are insufficiently detailed to draw firm conclusions.

However, the relative abundance of *Alnus* macrofossils indicates that this tree might have been present from early in the Holocene, with seeds recorded in Sample 1 from a date of 8160±35 BP (SUERC-20658; 7200–7060 cal. BC). The representation of *Alnus* peaks in Sample 6.0–6.5m (*c.* 1710–2375 cal. BC), after which a gradual decline in abundance is recorded. The general decrease in wood sub-fossils in the stratigraphy probably also reflects this process, although there is macrofossil evidence that *Alnus* expanded at the close of the sequence (Sample 9, 4.5–4.0m, 220 cal. BC to *c.* cal. AD 670–860).

The identification of *Alnus* fen carr using palaeoentomological data is problematic for two main reasons (Girling, 1985; Robinson, 1993a, b; Smith *et al.*, 2000; Smith and Whitehouse 2005). Firstly, a relatively limited number of beetle taxa (14) are closely associated with *Alnus* in comparison to other trees (e.g. *Quercus* – 93; Bullock, 1993). The second relates to the lack of modern entomological knowledge of *Alnus* dominated habitats. Establishing the presence of alder carr at other wetland sites has also proved problematic (see Girling, 1985; Robinson, 1993; Smith *et al.*, 2000). A site that compares well with Stowmarket is Goldcliff East in the Gwent Levels (south Wales) where the presence of alder carr was indicated by the waterlogged plant and sub-fossil wood remains, but where no evidence for this tree was found in the palaeoentomological record, which was dominated by beetles indicative of grass and sedge tussock vegetation (Tetlow, 2003; 2007a, b).

Dryland vegetation: woodland

There is little evidence in either the beetle or macrofossil record for the nature of the dryland woodland beyond the wetland edge. The available palynological evidence from Suffolk (see Chapter 2) indicates that the mid-Holocene terrestrial vegetation consisted of dense mixed *Tilia-Corylus-Quercus-Ulmus* (lime-hazel-oak-elm) woodland. However, the precise structure of this woodland is unclear; *Pinus sylvestris* (Scots' pine) and *Betula* probably remained important components of the vegetation on thinner and unstable soils. Such contexts probably included certain areas of floodplain such as that of the River Gipping. The only beetle evidence for woodland is found in Sample 6 (see below) where *Melasis buprestoides*, which is particularly associated with *Fagus sylvatica* (beech), and *Leperisinius varius*, which is associated with *Fraxinus excelsior* (ash) (Hyman, 1992) are recorded. *Fagus sylvatica* is recorded only sporadically and in very low quantities in Holocene pollen diagrams from Suffolk (see Chapter 2).

Anthropogenic activity: grassland and pastoral habitats

There are indications in the plant and Coleoptera data for the presence of grazing animals on or near the sampling site during the Neolithic-early Bronze Age, with 'dung' and 'dor' beetles first recorded in Sample 4 (7.0–6.5m, *c.* 3630–3090 to 2370 cal. BC). This suggests grazing by wild and/or domesticated animals, although dung beetles are ready fliers, hence the presence of this species may not be an unequivocal indicator of *in situ* dung or of grazing animals on the site itself. The indicators of foul rotting material might suggest the accumulation of dung and other foetid deposits, but evidence for such material is present throughout the sequence and may equally reflect the partial decay of plant material becoming incorporated into the peat system.

Further perhaps somewhat equivocal evidence for anthropogenic impact is apparent in Sample 5 (6.5–6.0m, *c.* 2370–1710 cal. BC). Dung beetles are absent and reappear as only a single record in Sample 7 (5.5–5.0m). However, the insect taxa in Sample 5 include the Curculionidae or 'weevils' such as the Apionidae and *Sitona* spp., which suggest species-rich grassland including *Trifolium*, *Vicia* and *Rumex*. The record of *Uritca diocia* also implies disturbed, possibly ruderal environments, as this species is associated with nitrogen rich habitats. Haslam (2003: 203) stated that: "... over four years of careful study *Urtica dioica* was never seen, in undisturbed fen". The evidence thus indicates the expansion of grassy, pastoral environments during the early Bronze Age. It seems highly likely that the sequence thus reflects the first identifiable impact of settlement and farming on the local environment at this time.

The increase in *Alnus* in the macrofossil record in Sample 5 would seem to be at odds with the evidence for possible human activity in the wider environment. It is possible that the presence of 'dung' beetles in Sample 4 might reflect grazing of parts of the floodplain itself, whilst during this later period, pastoral activity moved onto the dryland fringes allowing *Alnus* to regenerate. Interpretation is hindered by taphonomic factors; it is possible that the growth of alder carr on the sampling site may have acted to physically 'screen out' the representation of the dryland fauna in a similar manner in which the dryland pollen signal can be excluded (e.g. see Bunting *et al.*, 2005). In addition, it is not immediately clear what the precise implications of the relative concentration of plant macrofossil remains are for the spatial structure of the local palaeovegetation.

Beetles in Samples 6 and 7 (5.5–4.0m) provided less evidence for the character of the dryland vegetation, but there is an increase in Sample 8 (*c.* 1090–220 cal. BC) of beetles reflecting grassland habitats including *Trifolium*, *Plantago* and *Rumex*. These plants are regarded as 'anthropogenic indicators' (Behre, 1981) and the suite of associated beetles may imply increased grazing activities and expansion of grassland locally during the late Bronze Age / early Iron Age. The plant macrofossil record also demonstrates a reduction in *Alnus* in Samples 6 to 8, perhaps reflecting anthropogenic clearance of the fen carr between *c.* 1490–1130 and *c.* 220 cal. BC. This provides further indications that the later prehistoric period saw

a general increase in the exploitation of what may be described as 'marginal' environments such as floodplains, which may be related to general increased pressure on the land resource and/or other social/environmental factors (see Chapter 6).

Evidence for prehistoric human activity and flax cultivation/processing

Direct evidence for human activity during the later Bronze Age/Iron Age is also present in the form of *Linum usitatissimum* in the macrofossil record (Sample 8; *c.* 1090–220 cal. BC). Whilst it seems unlikely that flax was being grown on the floodplain itself, 'retting' of this crop in pools/ponds might have been taking place locally. It can be noted that flax grows well in alluvial soils and it is possible that the crop was being cultivated on such contexts on the floodplain margins. In this case, it is possible that the plant remains represent material re-deposited on the floodplain during periods of erosion from the slopes around the site. It is also possible that some of the other plant macrofossils (e.g. *Anthemis cotula*) may have arrived on the sampling site with the flax crop (*cf.* Latalowa, 1998) or with re-worked sediment. It is unclear whether wider significance can be attached to these relatively early records for flax in the east of England (see Chapter 6). There is archaeological evidence for human activity in the close vicinity during the Iron Age, in the form of settlement with possible round house structures, some 800m to the east of the sampling site (Rolfe, 2007).

The final Sample 9 (4.0–4.5m, *c.* 220 cal. BC to *c.* cal. AD 670–860) covers the period from the Iron Age into the early medieval and contains further evidence for human impact and activity. *L. usitatissimum* is again present, reflecting continued processing/cultivation of this crop in the close vicinity. There is also evidence from Staunch Meadow, Brandon, Suffolk and Buckenham Mere, Norfolk, that flax was being processed and/or cultivated during the Anglo-Saxon period (Godwin, 1968; Murphy, 1982). A small component of the beetle fauna in the final sample are associated with relatively dry rotting organic material and form part of the 'House Fauna' (Kenward and Hall, 1995). This group is commonly associated with unheated earthen-floored dwellings and wooden or wattle and daub structures, and is also associated with relatively dry 'hay-like' material in the early stages of decay (Hall and Kenward, 1990; Kenward and Hall, 1995).

This may reflect some form of human habitation nearby, or the occasional dumping or deposition of quantities of domestic waste on the floodplain. There are two further possibilities for the source of this fauna: the first is that these species were incorporated in material dumped from a hayrick or similar store of hay or straw; the second is that they are from very dry, grassy flood deposits. The absence of dung beetles and other grazing indicators would suggest the former is unlikely, hence the most plausible origin for this assemblage is domestic waste, which may have been

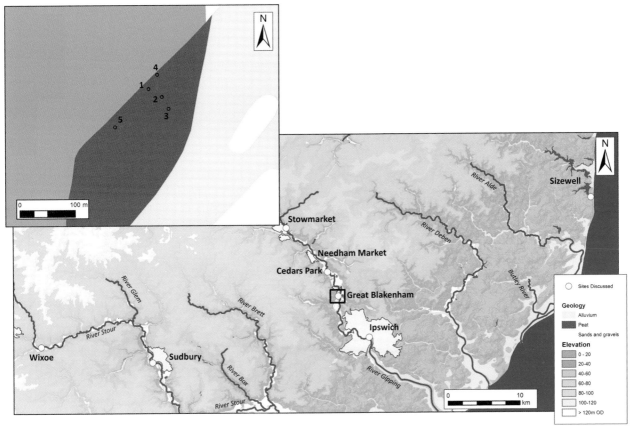

Figure 3.6: Great Blakenham study site

washed downstream and/or re-deposited during floods, preserved as 'trash-line' debris.

3.2.2 Stowmarket: Station Road

A second commercial project was carried out by BA-E (Gearey *et al.*, 2009b) in the centre of Stowmarket, at Station Road (Figure 3.2; Table 3.1) immediately to the east of the River Gipping and around 200m to the south-west of the Relief Road site described above. Five trial trenches were excavated across this site in advance of re-development. The stratigraphy in Trench 3 was recorded as:

0–0.50m: Made ground
0–50–0.90m: Grey-orange mottled clay silt
0.90–1.20m: Orange-yellow coarse gravel rich sand
1.20–1.50m: Brown, well-humified peaty silt
1.50 + m: Coarse, sandy gravel

The stratigraphy across the site was fairly uniform and suggested a significant amount of disturbance at this location, with a pronounced brick-filled cut though the clay silt unit. A core taken from adjacent to Trench 3 using a windowless sampler displayed a similar stratigraphy to that recorded from the section in Trench 3. The sequence of deposits indicates a peaty silt (1.20–1.50m) overlain by alluvium (0.50–1.20m). This site lies just to the north of

the Stowmarket Relief Road stratigraphic profile (Figure 3.4) and the relatively shallow depth of organic deposits indicates that it is located on the western edge of the deeper extent of peat observed in the relief road boreholes.

A total of seven sub-samples were taken for pollen assessment from the alluvium and peaty silt unit. Two bulk samples (Sample 1: 1.20–1.35m and Sample 2: 1.35–1.50m) were taken from the unit of brown humified peaty silt and a single bulk sample of the alluvium (Sample 3: 0.50–0.90m) was taken for beetle and plant macrofossil assessment. Whilst all three bulk samples contained organic remains including twigs, wood and other detritus, only Sample 3 contained any identifiable plant remains, including *Rubus fructicosus* agg., *Sambus nigra*, *Rumex* sp., *Prunus domestica* (wild plum) and *Carex* sp.. Pollen concentrations and preservation was very poor for all seven samples and only one sample (1.05m) yielded sufficient pollen for an assessment level count. This was dominated by *Alnus glutinosa*, with a few other tree species including *Quercus*, *Corylus* and *Pinus sylvestris*. Given the poor quality of the preservation, no radiocarbon dates were obtained for this sequence; the generally poor preservation of the palaeoenvironmental record and relatively shallow depth of organic deposits contrasts somewhat with that at the previous site.

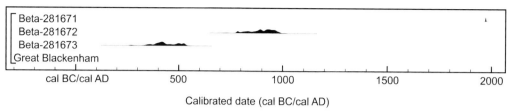

Figure 3.7: Great Blakenham calibrated radiocarbon dates

3.2.3 Great Blakenham

BA-E was contracted by Entec UK Ltd to provide a palaeoenvironmental survey of the Suffolk County Council Highway's Depot Site in Great Blakenham, some 10km to the south-east of Stowmarket and *c.* 0.2km west of the contemporary River Gipping (Hopla *et al.*, 2010) (Table 3.1; Figure 3.6). Five cores were drilled across an area 120m² using a windowless sampler. The general stratigraphic sequence consisted of sands and gravels at the base, between 5–6m depth, overlain by peat and organic-rich clay layers varying in thickness from 0.30–0.90m. The *in situ* deposits were sealed beneath approximately 4m of 'made ground'. Prior to construction of the Highway's Depot, the area was water meadow, but its development resulted in the stripping and backfilling of the site. Palaeoenvironmental assessments including pollen, plant macrofossils and beetles were carried out on samples from three of the cores (Cores 2, 4 and 5), with three radiocarbon dates also obtained from Core 4 (Table 3.2; Figure 3.7).

Core 2

The stratigraphy of Core 2 was recorded as:

> 0–4.58m: Made ground
> 4.58–5.20m: Dark brown, well-humified, woody peat
> 5.20–5.33m: Dark grey, clayey sand
> 5.33–5.80m: Sand

Four sub-samples were taken from the woody peat of Core 2 (4.58m, 4.74m, 4.90m and 5.06m depths) but all produced extremely low concentrations of pollen. From the few grains that were recorded Poaceae appears in all samples along with Cyperaceae, which is present in all samples other than at 5.06m. *Centaurea cyanus* (cornflower) in Sample 4.58m is typical of arable land, the presence of which is confirmed by the record of cereal grains (4.74m and 4.90m). It is difficult to infer the nature of the landscape confidently due to the low concentrations of pollen, but open disturbed arable land is implied.

The two bulk samples from the woody peat of Core 2 (4.58–4.89m and 4.89–5.20m) produced very limited and eroded insect faunas. The beetles recovered were not very specific in terms of interpretation beyond the *Enochrus* and *Hydroporus* species indicating the presence of slow-flowing or still waters (Hansen, 1986; Nilsson and Holmen, 1995). This interpretation is supported by the small weevil

Leiosoma deflexum, which is associated with *Caltha palustris* (Marsh marigold), and *Tanysphyrus lemnae*, which is associated with *Lemna* spp. (duck weed). The two plant macrofossil samples from Core 2 were dominated by seeds of *Menyanthes trifoliata* (bog bean), with limited quantities of other plant taxa. Bog bean frequently occurs in wet places (marshes, bogs, fens and watersides) and often occurs on peats or gley soils (Hewett, 1964: 726; Stace, 2010: 677); typically, it grows in patches, but it can form stands on the edge of water bodies (Hewett, 1964: 729). The plant macrofossil and beetle data therefore imply open, probably fairly tranquil aquatic environments, perhaps typical of a floodplain backswamp.

Core 4

The stratigraphy of Core 4, located 60m north of Core 2, was recorded as:

> 0–4.10m: Made ground
> 4.10–4.30m: Dark brown, well-humified peat
> 4.30–4.34m: Angular sandy gravel
> 4.34–4.46m: Grey-blue clay
> 4.46–4.62m: Dark brown, well-humified peat
> 4.62–4.76m: Grey clay (erosive upper contact)
> 4.76–5.0m: Black, slightly sandy, very well-humified peat (core aborted due to recovery difficulties associated with the water table)

Six sub-samples were taken for pollen assessment from Core 4 (4.11m, 4.26m, 4.42m, 4.58m, 4.74m and 4.90m). Three bulk samples for radiocarbon dating were also taken from this core from the organic units at 4.10m, 4.56m and 4.98m (Table 3.2). The date of 1630±40 BP (Beta-281673; cal. AD 340–540) from the basal peat at 4.98m indicates accumulation at this location from the end of the Romano-British period/ early Anglo Saxon period. However, the date of 110±40 BP (Beta-281672; cal. AD 1670–1780, cal. AD 1800–1950 and cal. AD 1950–1960) from 4.56m suggests that the peat unit between 4.46–4.62m dates to the post-medieval or perhaps even later, indicating the presence of a significant hiatus in accumulation or, more probably, the removal of older material by the erosive event indicated by the grey clay layer (4.62–4.76m). Given the fact that the uppermost determination (4.10m) yielded a modern radiocarbon age, the chronology for Core 4 provided by these dates may not be regarded as robustly secure.

The pollen samples all produced very low counts. Herbaceous pollen dominated and included Poaceae, Cyperaceae, *Plantago lanceolata* (ribwort plantain), Caryophyllaceae (pink family), *Potentilla*, *Rumex*-type (docks) and *Ranunculus*-type (buttercups), Apiaceae (carrot family), *Filipendula* (meadowsweet), Chenopodiaceae (fat hen family), *Secale cereale* (Rye), *Rumex*-type and *Centaurea cyanus*. Trees and shrubs were present at very low values of <5%, mainly *Corylus avellana*-type, *Quercus*, *Alnus glutinosa* and *Pinus sylvestris* (Scots' pine). The pollen implies largely open grassy meadow with damp banksides illustrated by the presence of the carrot family, meadowsweet and the pink family. Arable land is also suggested by the occurrence of rye and weeds such as cornflower.

The four bulk samples from Core 4 (4.10–4.30m, 4.34–4.62m, 4.62–4.76m and 4.76–5.00m) produced very small and poorly preserved beetle faunas. The beetles recovered are not very ecologically diagnostic and given the poor preservation any interpretation must be regarded as tentative. However, there are a number of indicators for slow-flowing or stagnant water conditions such as the *Haliplus* species, the Hydrophilids *Coelostoma orbiculare* and *Laccobius* spp. and the Helodidae species (Hansen, 1986).

Sample 4.62–4.76m contained a single individual of *Donacia vulgaris*, a reed beetle associated with a range of waterside plants and *Prasocuris phellandrii,* which is associated with Apiaceae. The only other taxa of any significance are the *Aphodius* and *Onthophagus* dung beetles, which were found throughout the samples and may indicate the presence of grazing animals or grassland in the vicinity of the sampling site.

The four plant macrofossil samples from Core 4 produced varying results. The upper two units (4.10–4.30m and 4.34–4.62m) were dominated by bog bean and rush seeds, with lower quantities of other plants including *Rununculus* spp., *Urtica dioica*, *Persicaria* spp. (knotweed), *Rumex* spp. and *Carex* spp. Again this suggests a waterside/fen habitat, as was evident from the Core 2 samples. The third sample (4.62–4.76m) was dominated by well-preserved *Rumex* spp. seeds, still fully encased in their perianth, with *Urtica dioica*, *Stellaria* spp. (stichwort) and *Carduus* spp./*Cirsium* spp. (thistle) also noted. Although rush and sedge seeds were recovered from this deposit, they were not particularly abundant and certainly there is no suggestion from the plant macrofossils that there was standing or flowing water in the vicinity.

The lower-most sample (4.76–5.00m) was dominated by *Juncus* spp. (rush) seeds, and small numbers of a range of plants typical of meadow/marsh environments were also recovered including *Ranunculus* spp., *Urtica dioica*, *Sambucus nigra*, *Chenopodium* spp., *Galeopsis* spp. (hemp nettle), *Mentha* spp. (mint), *Bidens cernua* (nodding bur-marigold), *Polygonum* spp. (knotgrass), *Persicaria* spp., possible *Stellaria cf. palustris* (marsh stitchwort) and *Carex* spp. The presence of elder and common nettle

in this deposit may provide evidence for nitrogen-rich soils, perhaps associated with grazing, as *Aphodius* and *Onthophagus* dung beetles were recorded in this sample.

Core 5

The stratigraphy of Core 5, 90m west of Core 3 and on the western edge of the study area, was recorded as:

> 0–5.48m: Made ground
> 5.48–5.66m: Dark brown, well-humified peat
> 5.66–5.68m: Sand
> 5.68–5.87m: Dark brown, well-humified peat
> 5.87–5.90m: Sand
> 5.90–5.98m: Dark brown, well-humified peat
> 5.98–6.00m: Sand

Four sub-samples were taken for pollen assessment from the peat units (5.48m, 5.64m, 5.80m and 5.95m depths). All produced low pollen counts apart from that at 5.64m, which produced high concentrations and allowed an assessment count to be obtained. High percentages (over 80%) of *Cannabis*-type (hemp) in this sample almost certainly reflect the 'retting' of hemp (see Gearey *et al.,* 2005; Schofield and Waller, 2005), on or very close to the sampling site. Retting of hemp is strongly associated with the medieval period when this crop was grown for fibre, particularly for canvas and rope (Edwards and Whittington, 1990).

A single bulk sample (5.48–6.00m) from the peat in Core 5 was assessed for plant macrofossils and beetles. The sample was dominated by *Menyanthes trifoliata* and *Juncus* spp., suggesting that the sediment accumulated at the edge of a water body or possibly in shallow water. Low numbers but a relatively wide range of plant taxa were recovered including: *Alnus glutinosa*, *Brassica nigra* (black mustard), *Silene* sp. (campion), *Papaver rhoeas/dubium* (common/long-headed poppy), *Sambucus nigra*, *Thlaspi arvense* (field penny-cress), *Chenopodium* spp., *Lycopus europaeus*, *Polygonum* spp. and *Persicaria* spp., *Mentha* spp., *Bidens cernua* (nodding bur-marigold), *Carex* cf. *diandra* (lesser tussock-sedge), *Carex* spp., *Carduus* spp./ *Cirsium* spp. and *Epilobium* spp. (willowherb). Most of these taxa also suggest meadow and/or waterside habitats. The single sample from Core 5 produced a very small, highly fragmentary fauna of beetles of which only the weevil *Notaris acridulus*, a species associated with the waterside plant *Glyceria* (reed grass), might be regarded as diagnostic.

Discussion: Great Blakenham

The stratigraphic survey at Great Blakenham demonstrated the presence of deposits of palaeoenvironmental potential associated with the floodplain of the River Gipping, now sealed beneath a substantial thickness of 'made ground' (nearly 5m). The three cores selected

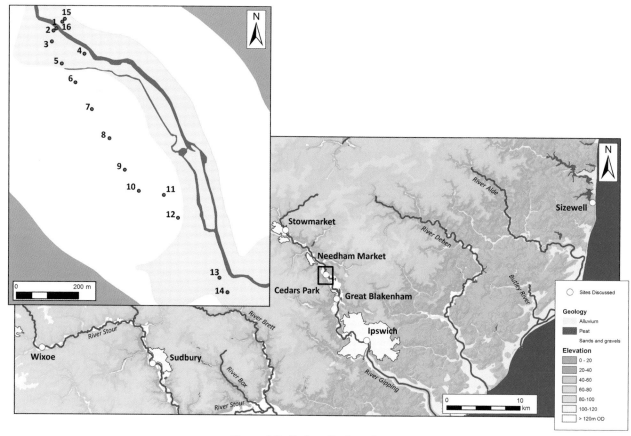

Figure 3.8: Cedars Park study area

for palaeoenvironmental assessment each demonstrate three discrete periods of peat accumulation, separated by episodes of fluvial sedimentation and probable erosion. The radiocarbon dates from Core 4 (Table 3.2) indicate that peat accumulation began at this location at the end of the Romano-British/early Anglo Saxon period. The middle peat unit might date to the post-medieval period, although the top of the sequence produced a modern age estimate, indicating contamination within the upper peat deposits. The end of peat accumulation remains undated and the chronology for the sequence must be considered as tentative.

The plant macrofossil assessment demonstrated good preservation of this material but both pollen and beetles were present in low concentrations. The available data illustrate similar environments represented by the peat layers in each core, with accumulation taking place in a waterlogged, floodplain environment with areas of slow-flowing or still waters and open grassy meadows, near or on the sampling site. The available pollen record provides tentative evidence for arable activity on the adjacent dryland, with the occurrence of cereal pollen, rye and cornflower in Cores 2 and 4. The layers of silt, clay and sand, which separate the periods of peat accumulation, demonstrate episodes of fluvial activity associated with flooding of the River Gipping or alternatively with periods of landscape instability and inwash of eroded material from the adjacent dryland areas.

Figure 3.9: The River Gipping at Cedars Park, looking north from adjacent to the location of Borehole 1

There is evidence for use of the floodplain for hemp retting, although the abundance of *Cannabis*-type pollen in Core 5 does not directly concur with the plant macrofossil data from the corresponding peat layer. However, palaeoenvironmental work elsewhere has shown that significant representation of *Cannabis*-type pollen can occur without *Cannabis sativa* (hemp) plant macrofossils or with only low quantities of hemp seed (Gearey *et al.*,

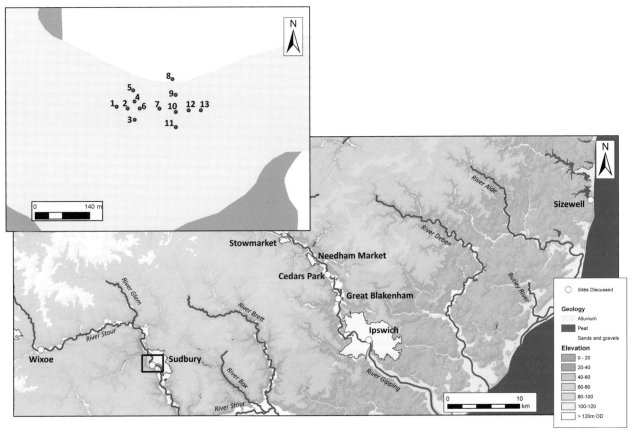

Figure 3.10: Map of Sudbury AFC study area

Figure 3. 11: Sudbury AFC Trench 1b under excavation. The current course of the River Stour is behind the line of trees in the background

2005). In particular hemp 'retting' (processing) usually requires that the seeds were 'beaten off' the plant (e.g. Gearey *et al.* 2005: 218, quoting Thomas Tusser, 1580, *Five Hundred Points of Good Husbandry*, (ed. W. Mavor, London, 1812), September, verse 24.). Indeed, hemp seeds may have been intentionally saved for next year's crop seed or, since they are extremely nutritious, they may have been put to alternative use, especially as bird feed.

3.2.4 Cedars Park

Geoarchaeological survey was carried out (Hill, 2007a) along the route of a proposed pipeline between Creeting St Mary and Baylham Pumping Station, situated within the central Gipping Valley, immediately north of Ipswich (Figure 3.8; Table 3.1). Sixteen boreholes were drilled along a 1.25km transect running approximately north-west to south-east and parallel to the river. These boreholes indicated considerable variation within the valley floor stratigraphy with boreholes closest to the current channel (Figure 3.9) *c.* 3.0m deep and demonstrating significant palaeoenvironmental potential. The stratigraphy of BH 1 typifies the palaeoenvironmental potential of these deposits:

0–0.30m: Topsoil
0.30–0.50m: Medium grey-brown, organic rich silt
0.50–1.05m: Medium brown, clayey silt
1.05–1.42m: Light brown, iron mottled clayey silt
1.42–1.65m: Dark brown, organic-rich clayey silt
1.65–2.02m: Light grey-brown, clayey silt
2.02–2.50m: Medium dark brown, organic-rich clayey
  silt
2.50–2.62m: Dark brown, well-humified peat
2.62–3.04m: Dark brown, well-humified silty peat
3.04–3.10m: Dark brown, very well-humified peat
3.10m+: Sands and gravels

Down by the river

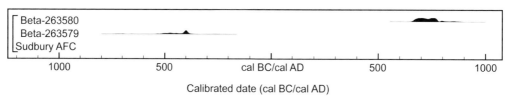

Calibrated date (cal BC/cal AD)

Figure 3.12: Sudbury AFC calibrated radiocarbon dates

Despite recommendations, no palaeoenvironmental assessments or radiocarbon dating was carried out at this site. The well-humified peat units towards the base of the sequence (2.50–3.10m) probably represent an early-mid Holocene fen carr environment on the valley floor, similar to that recorded in other river valley sequences in Suffolk (this chapter and Chapter 2). The overlying layers of silt and organic clay silt indicate increased fluvial influence, perhaps reflecting the effects of rising water tables due to changes in relative sea-level, climate and perhaps human activity during the mid-late Holocene. The organic deposits are shallower in boreholes further away from the river channel, with medium brown sand and orange-brown sand and gravel recorded. These probably represent mid to late Pleistocene terrace deposits.

3.3 The River Stour

3.3.1 Sudbury AFC, Sudbury

BA-E was subcontracted by AF Howland Associates to undertake recording and palaeoenvironmental assessment at Sudbury AFC, Suffolk (Figure 3.10; Table 3.1), in advance of re-development works (Gearey, 2009). The site is located around 0.25km west of the current course of the River Stour, at which point the floodplain is *c.* 0.6km wide. A series of test pits and trial trenches were excavated using a tracked excavator (Figure 3.11) and cores were extracted from the base of the trenches.

Palaeoenvironmental assessment focussed on samples recovered from Trenches 1a and 1b (Gearey *et al.*, 2010b). The stratigraphy of Trench 1a was recorded as:

    0–0.60m: Made ground
    0.60–1.00m: Orange-brown, silty clay
    1.00–1.20m: Blue-grey, silty clay
    1.20–3.20m: Brown, well-humified silty peat with
        monocotyledonous remains
    3.20–3.30m: Grey, sandy silt

The stratigraphy of the Trench 1b sequence was recorded as:

    0–0.80m: Made ground
    0.80–0.94m: Grey-black silt
    0.94–2.00m: Brown, well-humified silty peat

Palaeoenvironmental Assessments

Eight sub-samples from Trench 1a were assessed for pollen and three bulk samples for plant macrofossil and beetles from Trench 1b (Sample A: 0.80–1.00m, Sample D: 1.40–1.60m and Sample F: 1.80–2.00m). Two samples from the base and top of the organic deposits in Trench 1b were submitted for radiocarbon dating (Table 3.2; Figure 3.12) and produced estimates of 2350±40 BP (Beta-263579; 510–380 cal. BC) and 1280±40 BP (Beta-263580; cal. AD 660–810) respectively, indicating sediment accumulation from the Iron Age until the early Medieval period.

RESULTS: POLLEN

The results of the pollen assessment of the Trench 1a samples are presented as a percentage pollen diagram (Figure 3.13) that has been tentatively divided into three zones (SUD-1 to SUD-3). The basal zone (SUD-1) suggests an open Poaceae and Cyperaceae dominated environment, with other herb species present including *Filipendula*, *Potentilla* and *Galium*-type typical of wetland environments. The high values for *Sparganium* indicates open water on or very near to the sampling site. The range of trees and shrubs probably reflects the presence of fen carr vegetation with *Alnus* and *Tilia* dominated woodland beyond the floodplain edge.

The middle zone (SUD-2) is characterised by higher values for *Alnus*, but with Poaceae and Cyperaceae consistently recorded. The impression is of an expansion in alder carr on the floodplain around the sampling site. The concomitant decline in trees and shrubs at this time are probably initially associated as much with these values being suppressed by the rise in *Alnus*. However, there is some suggestion that human activity might have been responsible for the reduction in woodland. A low peak in *Plantago lanceolata*, *Centaurea nigra* (ruderal knapweeds) and Lactuceae (dandelions etc.) at 1.35m suggests the presence of open, grassy areas on the drier soils, which may be associated with the clearance of woodland. The steady rise in *Pteridium aquilinum* (bracken) might also reflect the spread of open habitats on better-drained soils beyond the floodplain edge.

The uppermost zone (SUD-3) is dominated by Cyperaceae, almost certainly related to the expansion of sedge fen on and around the sampling site at the expense of the *Alder* carr. This was perhaps connected to increased local wetness, which may also be apparent in the small increase in *Sparganium* towards the top of the zone. It is likely that the disappearance of *Tilia* and decline of other trees and shrubs in this zone is partly a result of the increased representation of local pollen at the expense of

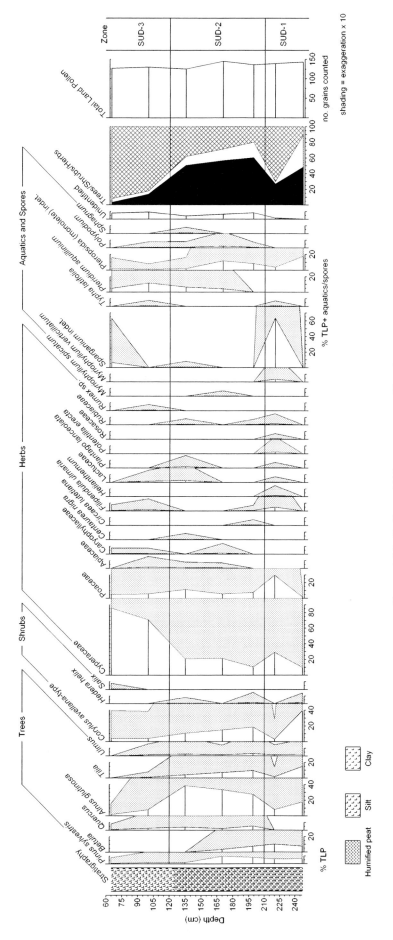

Figure 3.13: Sudbury AFC percentage pollen diagram

vegetation growing in the wider landscape. The impact of human activity and the clearance of woodland for farming/ settlement is also a possibility, but there are no significant increases in herbs such as *P. lanceolata,* which generally accompany anthropogenic impacts in pollen diagrams.

PLANT MACROFOSSIL AND BEETLE ASSESSMENTS

The three sub-samples all contained broadly similar plant macrofossil remains indicative of wet or damp environments, consisting mainly of seeds and hard nuts with leaves and other plant material and detritus absent from the flot. *Carex* remains were abundant in all the samples suggesting that the deposits had accumulated in a sedge fen. Other species recorded included *Lycopus europaeus, Alnus glutinosa* and *Bidens cernua,* all of which are typical of fen carr environments. There were no species present that directly indicated any human activity in the near vicinity of the sampling site. Taxa that imply disturbed ground including *Rumex* and *Galeopsis tetrahit* (common hemp nettle) were recorded (Samples D and F), but these plants probably indicate the presence of naturally disturbed areas (e.g. eroding river banks).

All three samples also produced large workable assemblages of beetles. Preservation was excellent, with all body segments well-represented, allowing for preliminary and even full identification of some species. Species diversity was also high suggesting mixed trophic conditions in the local environment. Good preservation of insect remains is normally a result of basic-neutral to slightly acidic water quality (Robinson, 2002).

The species- and numerically-rich insect assemblages present a clear picture of the environment. Beetles such as *Plateumaris ?braccata, Plateumaris* spp., *Limnobaris t-album/dolorosa* present in Sample F, from the base of the peat deposit, suggests standing water with a rich plant community of reeds, rushes and sedges (Cox, 2007). Muddy ground and generally wet ground conditions are indicated by many of the Staphylinid beetles recorded as well as species like *Dryops* spp. and *Chaetarthria seminulum.* Other beetles, such as *Dorytomus* spp., *Anoplus plantaris/roboris* and *Curculio* spp., indicate the presence of carr woodland with trees such as willow and alder (Hyman, 1992). Birch and oak may have also been present in the surrounding landscape; *Clambus* spp., *Carpelimus? elongatus* and *Othius* spp., which are recorded at this level, are generally found in damp wood litter (Lott, 2003).

Sample D (0.60–0.80m) has a similar ecological profile but has an even more diverse beetle assemblage. This is due in part to a diverse decaying vegetation/litter fauna as well as a variety of dung beetles. The dung beetles may indicate the presence of grazing animals, but may also reflect the presence of putrefying plant matter. Additional woodland indicators (?*Phyllobius* spp., *Rhamphus* sp.) are recorded, suggesting continued presence of carr woodland. The water beetle fauna suggests standing and stagnant water rather

than fresh or moving water.

The uppermost sample (Sample A; 0–0.20m) had reduced species and numerical richness but a similar ecological profile to those discussed above. Many of the same standing water, wetland plant and carr woodland indicators are present, but the decaying vegetation/litter fauna is much less species-rich. However, one interesting species is recorded at this level only: *Hydrochus* spp. is a generally rare water beetle genus, which is today confined to shallow water and reed litter in fens and marshes in eastern and southern Britain (Foster, 2000). This suggests that while the species diversity was somewhat reduced at this level the same general environmental conditions prevailed.

Many water beetles are recorded throughout the profile but almost all indicate stagnant and standing water rather than flowing or fresh water (habitats indicated by members of the Dysticidae, Hydraenidae, Hydrophilidae and Dryopidae families). However, very few of the water beetles are suggestive of eutrophic conditions at any point in the profile (as might be expected in the transition from fen to raised mire, for example), which suggests that some groundwater or freshwater nutrient input was maintained, reflecting the influence of run-off from the adjacent higher ground. The uppermost deposit of organic silt might have been the result of flooding but this is not clear from the insect assemblages.

There were no synanthropic (i.e. human-dependent) elements or indicators of arable/cultivated ground in any of the three beetle assemblages. The woodland indicators are similar throughout the profile with no indication of a reduction in tree cover that could be attributed to human activity (although the current sampling resolution may be insufficient to identify this). Dung beetles are commonly encountered in Sample D, with a smaller number indicated in Samples A and F. This suggests the presence of grazing animals but whether they were domesticated or wild is not clear.

Summary: Sudbury AFC

The radiocarbon dates from Trench 1b demonstrate that organic sediment accumulation began around 2350±40 BP (Beta-263579; 510–380 cal. BC). The palaeoenvironmental assessments demonstrate these accumulated in a fen carr environment on the floodplain of the river. The main channel of the Stour was probably some way to the east of the sampling site for much of the period of sediment accumulation since both the beetle and plant records demonstrate sedge-alder fen typical of a floodplain backswamp with standing water but no persistent evidence for open, flowing water. The pollen record confirms the local presence of sedge, other wetland taxa during the period of peat accumulation, and also supports the plant macrofossil evidence for the local presence of alder, indications of which are absent from the beetle record (see discussion regarding this issue in Section 2.1.1). The pollen data may also indicate that other trees such as oak

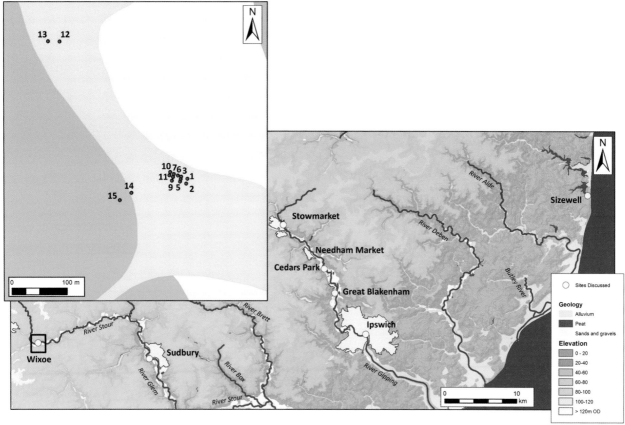

Figure 3.14: Wixoe study area

and birch were growing as part of the floodplain vegetation.

The pollen record suggests that a phase of alder carr dominance (SUD-1 and 2) was followed by its demise and replacement by sedge fen (SUD-3), also marked by a stratigraphic change from peat to blue-grey silty clay in Trench 1a (1.20m). No radiocarbon dates are available for the pollen sequence from Trench 1a, but this may correlate on stratigraphic grounds with the grey-black silt (0.94m) layer in Trench 1b. The absence of radiocarbon dates from Trench 1a hinders more detailed interpretation, but this change is dated to 1280±40 BP (Beta-263580; cal. AD 660–810), the early Medieval period, in Trench 1b. The precise mechanism(s) behind this change are unclear, but the data imply rising local water tables demonstrated by an increase in the silt content in the sediment, perhaps as a result of the migration of a channel of the River Stour closer to the western edge of the floodplain, and/or increased run-off from adjacent dryland slopes.

The plant macrofossil and beetle records very much reflect the local environment during peat formation and do not indicate any human interference or activity close to the sampling site, whilst the pollen record sheds some light on the character of the wider landscape. It would appear that lime-dominated woodland was present beyond the floodplain until SUD-3. Despite the decline of trees and shrubs apparent in the upper two zones, the role of human communities is somewhat unclear, with little sustained

palynological evidence for the expansion of open, ruderal habitats that might be expected to accompany the clearance of woodland. This may be explained in part by the relatively low pollen counts used at assessment level and perhaps also by the poor representation of herbaceous taxa growing at distance from the sampling site.

3.3.2 Wixoe

In March 2010 BA-E were commissioned (Hopla and Krawiec, 2010) to carry out a palaeoenvironmental assessment of deposits within the area of the proposed Kirby-Wixoe water pipeline close to the pumping station at Wixoe, immediately to the west of the River Stour (Figure 3.14; Table 3.1). The borehole survey identified deposits of palaeoenvironmental potential immediately to the west of the current channel, with the stratigraphy recorded as:

> 0–0.10m: Topsoil
> 0.10–1.10m: Stiff yellow clay
> 1.10–1.35m: Blue-grey silty clay
> 1.35–2.35m: Well-humified silty peat, with occasional mollusc fragments
> 2.35–2.60m: Grey, mollusc-rich sand, with rootlets and wood fragments.

The 1st Edition Ordnance Survey mapping (c. AD 1880) indicates a parish boundary in this area and together

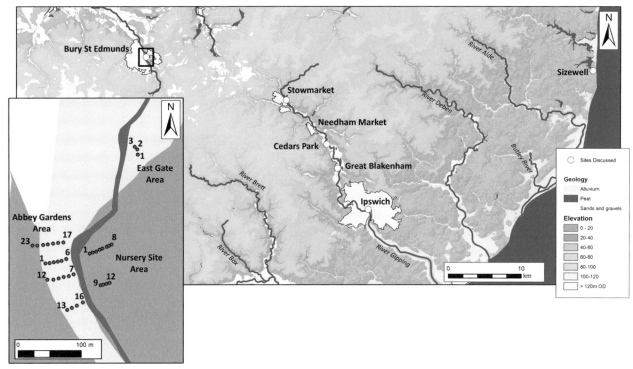

Figure 3.15: Bury St Edmunds study area

with the character of the deposits, it is suggested that a former river channel was encountered. The historic map evidence suggests that the final infilling of this channel must post-date the establishment of the boundary in the Post-Medieval period. Despite recommendations for further palaeoenvironmental assessment, no other work was carried out at this site.

3.4 The River Lark

3.4.1 Bury St Edmunds: The Abbey Precinct

In March 2009 BA-E were commissioned (Krawiec *et al.*, 2009) to undertake a borehole survey of two sites within the precinct of Bury St. Edmunds Abbey, Suffolk, on the floodplain of the River Lark (Figure 3.15; Table 3.1). The upstanding remains of the Abbey date to its foundation in the 11th–12th century AD. Two locations were investigated using a cable percussive borehole rig (Figure 3.16): Site A was located to the east of the river, at a former nursery just outside the main abbey wall where the remains of greenhouse structures were still visible. Site B was located on the western bank of the River Lark within the lawn of the abbey gardens, where the floodplain slopes gently down towards the modern course of the river.

Site A

The borehole survey at Site A involved the excavation of 12 cores in two transects *c.* 40m long and perpendicular

Figure 3.16: Windowless sampler in operation at Site B within the grounds of Bury St Edmunds Abbey

to the river. The deposits were characterised by a thick layer of 'made ground' containing fragments of brick, coal and gravel within a sandy clay matrix. This overlay a deposit of light grey-brown silty clay, which may be the partially disturbed or re-worked remnants of the alluvium overlying the natural gravels. No organic sediments of palaeoenvironmental potential were identified, which may be explained in part by reference to Thomas Warren's map of AD 1747, indicating a vineyard at this location and hence a well-drained area since at least the 18th Century (Figure 3.17).

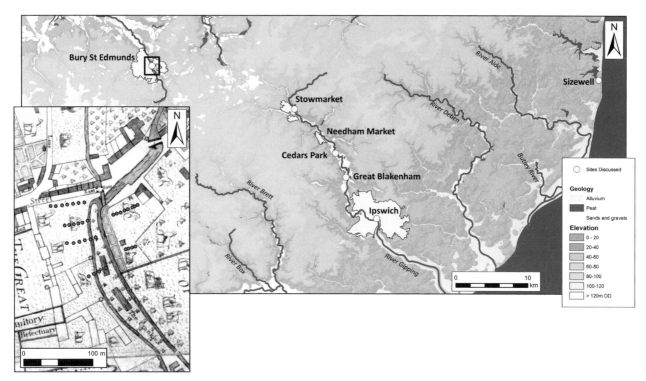

Figure 3.17: Location of boreholes in relation to Warren's Map of Bury St Edmunds Abbey (AD 1747)

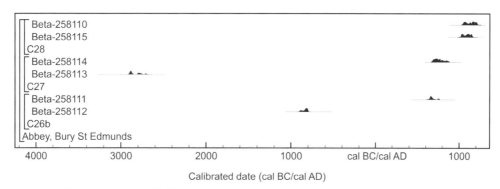

Figure 3.18: Bury St Edmunds Abbey sequence calibrated radiocarbon dates

Site B

The borehole survey at Site B involved the excavation of 23 cores in four transects *c.* 60m long and perpendicular to the river. Two of the cores at Site B were excavated through features marked on Warren's map: a channel-cut or leat (Core 6b) and a feature marked as a 'fishpond' (Core 27). During the Medieval period fishponds were established to provide an easy source of fresh fish for the dining table. The pond may have been fed with freshwater by the leat discussed above, which appears to run alongside it.

PALAEOENVIRONMENTAL ASSESSMENTS AND RADIOCARBON DATING

Palaeoenvironmental assessments and radiocarbon dating focussed on five cores from Area B. A total of 26 subsamples

were assessed for pollen from: Cores 24, 25, 26b, 27 and 28. However, pollen concentrations in samples 3.58m, 3.68m and 3.78m from Core 25; samples 2.76m and 3.61m from Core 26b and 2.56m, 4.72m and 4.84m from Core 27 were very low and full assessment counts were not achievable. A total of 6 sub-samples were submitted for radiocarbon dating (Table 3.2; Figure 3.18): three samples of sub-fossil wood (*Quercus* sp.), two from Core 28 and one from Core 27. Three bulk sediment samples were also submitted, one from Core 27 and two from Core 26b.

ARTEFACTS AND OTHER MATERIAL

The boreholes also contained anthropogenic material in the form of animal bone, tile, metal and pottery, which mostly dated from the Medieval period. A distinct horizon up to 0.40m thick overlay most of Site B, most probably an occupation layer related to the abbey buildings, which extend across this area. In addition, animal bone was also recovered from the basal gravels in Cores 25 and 28 and this may suggest some re-working of these deposits by fluvial or human agencies. Drilling of Core 26 was halted due to the presence of a large fibrous piece of wood at 1.60m, which may well indicate the presence of timber structures associated with the abbey or at the very least a burial environment that is conducive to the preservation of organic archaeological materials as well as palaeoenvironmental remains. Ten fragments of animal bone were recovered from the cores at site B, much of which was from fowl and game birds with a few fragments of cattle bone. Large *Buccinium undatum* (whelk) shells were also present in Cores 9, 21 and 22.

CORE 6B

The stratigraphy of Core 6b was recorded as:

> 0–0.60m: Topsoil
> 0.60–1.00m: Grey-brown, sandy silt with brick fragments, mortar and shell
> 1.00–2.00m: Yellow-grey, silty clay with occasional wood fragments
> 2.00–2.76m: Grey, sandy silt
> 2.76–3.00m: Well-humified, black silty peat
> 3.00–3.60m: Grey, sandy silt
> 3.60–3.96m: Well-humified, black silty peat
> 3.96–4.00m: Gravel

It seems likely that the deposits between 0.60m and 2.76m represent the fill of the leat. However, the basal units (2.76–3.96m) of intercalated peats and sandy silts indicate the presence of *in situ* sediments associated with the earlier development of the floodplain (see discussion below).

CORE 24

The stratigraphy of Core 24 was recorded as:

> 0–0.49m: Topsoil
> 0.49–1.00m: Mid-brown, sandy silty clay with mortar, shell and brick fragments
> 1.00–1.20m: Not recovered
> 1.20–2.00m: Yellow-brown, silty clay
> 2.00–2.45m: Yellow-grey, sandy silt with large pebbles to base
> 2.45–2.70m: Brown sandy silt, increasingly organic with depth
> 2.70–3.00m: Mottled black-brown, organic silt, occasional rootlets and small pebbles
> 3.00–3.62m: Brown gravel-rich sand
> 3.62–3.87m: Black organic silt with occasional rootlets
> 3.87–4.00m: Gravel

The pollen assessments focussed on the organic deposits with six samples analysed from between 2.70–2.90m and 3.62–3.86m. The results are presented as a pollen diagram (Figure 3.19). The base of the diagram is dominated by herbaceous pollen (*c.* 90%). Poaceae dominates at over 40% with *Cerealia*-type (oats, wheat) recorded at 20% and *Centaurea cyanus* (cornflower) and Cyperaceae over 5%. Other herbs including *Filipendula*, *Helleborus* (stinking hellebore) and *Secale cereale* rise from trace values up to and over 5% at 3.56 m. Other herbs are scarce but include Apiaceae, *Cirsium*-type, Lactuceae, *Plantago lanceolata* and Rosaceae (rose family). Trees and shrubs are rare and include *Quercus, Betula, Corylus-avellana*-type and a few grains of *Tilia, Ulmus* and *Salix*.

The basal segment of the diagram (between 3.86–3.62m) therefore reflects an open, grassy landscape with little woodland cover locally. It is likely that some of the grasses might be *Phragmites* (common reed) associated with wetter areas on the floodplain, particularly with the indication of still to moderate flowing water suggested by the presence of the aquatic *Sparganium* (bur-reed). Tall herbs such as *Filipendula* and Apiaceae are indicative of open fen/meadow vegetation, probably on the damp soils around the sampling site. High values of anthropogenic indicators (*sensu* Behre, 1981) are recorded, especially of arable cultivation: *Cerealia*-type, *Secale cereale* and *Centaurea cyanus* (a weed of arable fields).

No samples were taken from the sands and gravels between 3.62m and 3.00m. These minerogenic sediments indicate deposition under relatively high-energy fluvial conditions and a hiatus in organic sedimentation. The pollen diagram recommences at 2.90m with little change in the pollen assemblage. Herbaceous pollen continues to dominate, largely Poaceae and *Cerealia*-type. Trees and shrubs remain scarce with a decline in *Betula, Ulmus* and *Tilia* but an increase in occasional grains of *Pinus sylvestris*, *Alnus* and *Fraxinus excelsior*. The environment in the upper segment of the diagram thus remained similar to that at the base with slight fluctuations in the herb spectra.

CORE 25

The stratigraphy of Core 25 was recorded as:

> 0–0.69m: Topsoil
> 0.69–1.00m: Gritty, brown silty clay with mortar and shell fragments
> 1.00–1.68m: Yellow-brown silty clay, calcareous with depth
> 1.68–2.00m: Grey-brown silty sand with flint clasts
> 2.00–2.58m: Coarse sand
> 2.58–3.78m: Well-humified silty peat
> 3.78–3.80m: Brown, silty sand
> 3.80–4.00m: Grey, sand and gravel

Four samples from the humified silty peat (2.58–3.78m) were submitted for pollen assessment, but only one (2.93m depth) contained a sufficient concentration of pollen for a palaeoenvironmental assessment. Cyperaceae dominated this sample (54%) with Poaceae and Lactuceae also present, indicating a damp, open, grassy landscape.

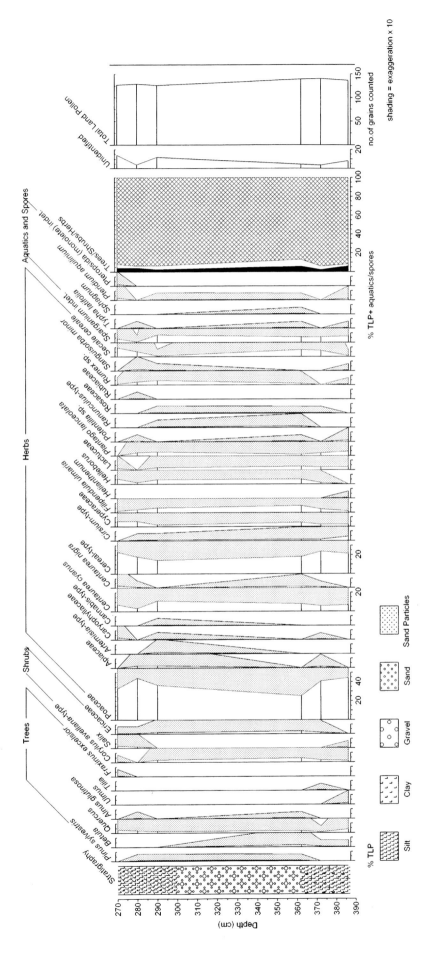

Figure 3.19: Bury St Edmunds Abbey Core 24 percentage pollen diagram

CORE *26B*

The stratigraphy of Core 26b was recorded as:

0–0.58m: Topsoil

0.58–1.00m: Grey-brown, sandy silty clay with brick fragments, mortar and shell.

1.00–1.67m: Yellow-grey, silty clay

1.67–2.00m: Grey, silt clay with flints and occasional wood fragments

2.00–2.76m: Grey, sandy silt

2.76–3.00m: Well-humified, black silty peat

3.00–3.60m: Grey, sandy silt

3.60–3.96m: Well-humified, black silty peat

3.96–4.00m: Gravel

A radiocarbon sample from the basal well-humified peat unit at 3.90m produced a date of 2670±40 BP (Beta-258112; 900–790 cal. BC) indicative of the later Bronze Age. Five samples were submitted for pollen assessment from the humified peat units and those from 2.94m, 3.81m and 3.97m contained sufficient concentrations of pollen for a reliable count. The two lower-most samples were dominated by herbaceous pollen largely consisting of Cyperaceae and Poaceae, with rare grains of Lactuceae, *Filipendula, Galium*-type and *Plantago lanceolata.* The implied environment was apparently fairly open probably with sedges growing locally on the floodplain. Some of the grasses may be associated with wetland vegetation (e.g. *Phragmites*, common reed), but the presence of *Plantago lanceolata* and Lactuceae also indicate open grassy meadow-like areas on the dryland beyond the floodplain.

No samples were taken from the inorganic sandy silt deposits between 3.00m and 3.60m. The top of the humified silty peat at 2.77m was dated to 1350±40 BP (Beta-258111; cal. AD 640–710 to cal. AD 750–760), the early Anglo-Saxon period. The pollen record recommences at 2.94m, with the spectrum indicating a similar environment to the basal samples, largely dominated by Cyperaceae and Poaceae with few other herbs, trees or shrubs. The associated sample from this depth contained a few grains of Cyperaceae and Lactuceae, but the count was too low to permit a reliable environmental assessment.

CORE *27*

The stratigraphy of Core 27 was recorded as:

0–0.30m: Topsoil

0.30–0.80m: Brown silty, sandy clay with fragments of mortar and charcoal

0.80–1.40m: Yellow, sandy gravel

1.40–1.64m: Grey, sandy silt

1.64–1.90m: Grey, gravelly sand

1.90–3.00m: Brown, organic silt

3.00–3.60m: Gravelly silt, increasingly calcareous with depth

3.60–4.00m: Grey-black, well-humified, silty peat

4.00–4.28m: Grey, sandy silt

4.28–4.85m: Well-humified, silty peat, calcareous with depth

4.85–5.00m: Grey sand with wood fragments

The base of Core 27 at 4.92m dated to 4240±40 BP (Beta-258113; 2910–2860 cal. BC, 2800–2750 cal. BC, 2710–2710 cal. BC), the later Neolithic. Eight samples from the organic deposits between 2.56m and 4.84m were submitted for pollen assessment (avoiding the grey sandy silt between 4.00–4.28m). However the pollen diagram (Figure 3.20) does not commence until 4.28m due to low pollen concentrations in the basal samples of the well-humified silty peat. Herbaceous pollen dominates between 4.28m and 3.70m (*c.* 90%) mainly consisting of Cyperaceae, Poaceae and Lactuceae. Other herbs are rare, but include occasional grains of *Cirsium*-type, *Filipendula*, Apiaceae, *Cerealia*-type, *Helleborus* and *Ranunculus*-type. The impression is again of an open, pastoral landscape with herb communities typical of damp meadow vegetation. Increases in arable pollen types including *Secale cereale* and *Cerealia*-type are recorded above 3.70m, suggesting arable cultivation and/or cereal processing in the close vicinity of the sampling site.

Other than *Corylus* and *Quercus*, which reach values up to 10%, all other trees and shrubs are scarce. The record is probably heavily dominated by the local pollen signal with sedges and other aquatic vegetation growing close to or on the sampling site. Discerning changes at a greater spatial distance from the current site data is difficult, but it seems likely that some oak-hazel scrub/woodland was present in the wider landscape. No samples were taken from the gravelly silt unit between 3.70m and 2.95m. When the pollen record recommences at 2.94m the implied environment is similar to that apparent towards the base, an open landscape with grasses/sedges and evidence for pastoral vegetation as well as arable cultivation. The top of the sequence at 2.71m is dated to 1250±40 BP (Beta-258114; cal. AD 670–880), the later Anglo-Saxon period.

CORE *28*

The stratigraphy of Core 28 was recorded as:

0–0.46m: Topsoil

0.46–1.00m: Light brown, silty clay with mortar, brick fragments and shells

1.00–2.36m: Yellow-brown, silty clay, calcareous with depth

2.36–2.70m: Mottled black-brown silt with humified plant remains at 2.45m and a fragment of roof-tile (*c.* 13th–15th century AD)

2.70–3.00m: Black-grey, sandy gravel. Fragments of domestic fowl bones (tibiotarsus and tarso-metatarsus) between 2.77m and 2.88m. Wood fragments at 2.80m.

Pollen assessment focussed on the brown-black silts (2.36–2.70m) and all three samples (2.36m, 2.54m and 2.70m) provided sufficient counts for palaeoenvironmental

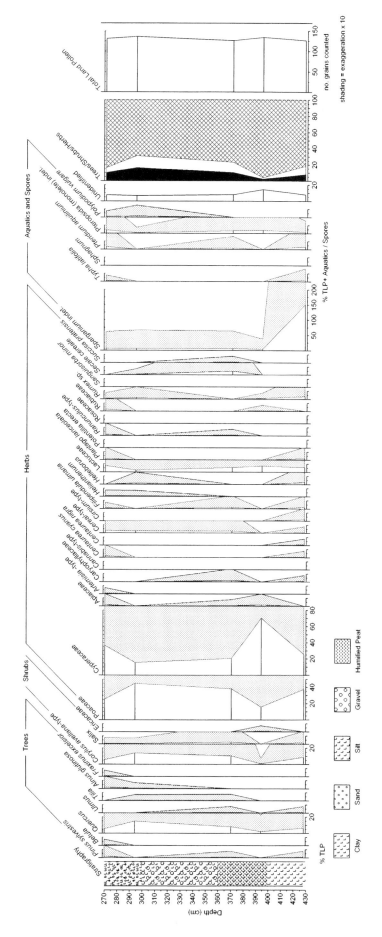

Figure 3.20: Core 27 ('Fishpond') percentage pollen diagram

assessment. A sample of wood from just below the silts at 2.80m produced a radiocarbon date of 960±40 BP (Beta-258115; cal. AD 1010–1170), the later Medieval period. Poaceae and *Cerealia*-type pollen dominate the sample from the base of this silt. Cereal increases to values up to 45% at 2.54m, at a date of 890±40 BP (Beta-258110; cal. AD 1030–1230). Other herbs recorded include *Secale, Centaurea cyanus, Rumex, Plantago lanceolata, Helleborus*, Cypercaeae and Apiaceae. The upper sample is dominated by a similar herb spectrum to the lower samples. Pollen of trees and shrubs are scarce with only occasional grains of *Corylus, Quercus, Salix* and *Pinus* recorded within all three samples. These pollen spectra are strongly suggestive of an open agricultural landscape. The suite of taxa indicates cereal cultivation/processing in the immediate vicinity of the site and the presence of open pastoral vegetation communities. It would appear that there was very little tree or shrub cover present at this time.

Bury St Edmunds Abbey Summary

It would appear that a palimpsest of deposits is preserved on the floodplain adjacent to the Abbey on the floodplain of the River Lark. The earliest dated deposits are at the base of Core 27, indicating peat formation from the later Neolithic at 4240±40 BP (Beta-258113; 2910–2860 cal. BC, 2800–2750 cal. BC, 2710–2710 cal. BC). The basal peat unit in Core 26b produced a younger estimate of 2670±40 BP (Beta-258112; 900–790 cal. BC). The pollen sample associated with the latter date implies open and perhaps anthropogenically disturbed vegetation at this time. The current data are insufficient to reconstruct a detailed chronological and spatial history of the study area and it is clear that none of the sequences represent continuous deposition, but human activity associated with the Abbey has directly affected the suite of deposits present on the site.

The date from the top of the humified peat unit in Core 26b of 1350±40 BP (Beta-258111; cal. AD 640–710 to 750–760), the early Anglo-Saxon period, is close to the date of the foundation of the monastery at the site. Likewise, the two radiocarbon dates from the basal silts in Core 28 produced age estimates of 960±40 BP (Beta-258115; cal. AD 1010–1170) and 890±40 BP (Beta-258110; cal. AD 1030–1230), implying these deposits could well be associated with the foundation of the Cistercian Abbey in AD 1020. The pollen spectra from these sediments suggest an agricultural landscape, with very high values for cereals including rye. Cereal pollen is poorly dispersed and tends to be significantly under represented, even in the immediate vicinity of crops (e.g. Brun *et al.,* 2007) and these relatively high values must therefore indicate the presence of arable land (wheat/oat and rye), probably immediately adjacent to the sampling site. Alternatively, it is possible that cereal processing was being carried out locally since this activity can enhance pollen dispersal (e.g. Hall, 1988). The presence of bones of domestic fowl towards the base of the core and a fragment of roof-tile dating to the 13th–15th century AD

from 2.45m demonstrate that these deposits incorporate archaeological material and cereal pollen might have been entering the deposits alongside domestic waste from the abbey being dumped or washed onto the marshy ground at the edge of the river.

3.4.2 Bury St Edmunds, Eastgate Street

An archaeological evaluation of this site also in Bury St Edmunds (Figure 3.15; Table 3.1), immediately to the east of the River Lark, was carried out prior to re-development (Hill, 2007b). A single trial trench, approximately 18 m in length and varying in depth from 0.30m to 1.70m, was excavated across the site and four cores were extracted, at *c.* 5m intervals through the trench base. Core 4 was positioned at the northern end of the trench within the deepest section closest to the river and the stratigraphy was recorded as follows:

> 0–1.70m: Made ground
> 1.70–1.98m: Yellow-brown, clayey silts with chalk clasts
> 1.98–2.70m: Grey-brown, pebbly sand with organic mottling
> 2.70–2.92m: Dark grey-brown, organic pebbly silt and sand
> 2.92–3.35m: Dark brown, very well-humified sandy peat
> 3.35–3.55m: Dark brown, very well-humified sandy peat
> 3.55 +m: Sand and gravel

The upper clayey silts and pebbly sand (1.70–2.92m) are interpreted as fluvial deposits associated with the adjacent River Lark, prior to its embankment and confinement to its current channel. The basal humified peat indicates either a wider floodplain deposit similar to those recorded at the Abbey site (above) or one, which has accumulated at the base of a discrete palaeochannel. However, despite recommendations for palaeoenvironmental assessments, no further work was carried out at this site.

3.4.3 Rushbrooke-Nowton

Archaeological mitigation works were carried out (Hill, 2007c) in connection with an Anglian Water pipeline between Rushbrooke and Nowton (Table 3.1). During the desk-based assessment and subsequent site walk-over, the majority of the proposed pipeline route was found to cut through probable colluvial deposits. Therefore, a programme of coring and test pitting was commissioned, which concentrated on the western section of the pipeline corridor, immediately west of the River Lark, on an area of floodplain approximately 40m wide. The sedimentary sequence at the deepest point cored in the centre of this corridor comprised:

> 0–0.70m: Light brown, sandy clay-silt with iron mottling

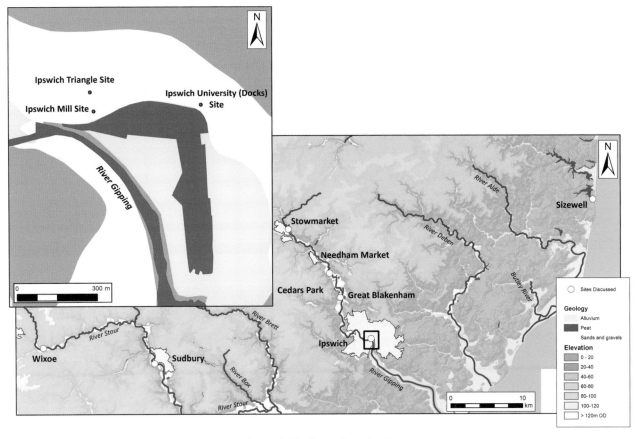

Figure 3.21: Ipswich study sites

0.70–0.82m: Light grey-brown, gravel-rich silty sand
0.82–0.97m: Light yellow-brown, gravel-rich sand
0.97–1.10m: Light grey-brown, sandy gravel grading
　　　　　 into coarse sands and gravels with depth.

No organic deposits suitable for palaeoenvironmental assessment were identified during this work and no further work was carried out.

3.5 The east coast of Suffolk

3.5.1 Ipswich Docks (Albion Wharf)

Deposits of palaeoenvironmental potential were identified during ground investigations at a proposed development next to the Ipswich Docks (Figure 3.21; Table 3.1). Two trenches were excavated and boreholes drilled within the trenches; samples were recovered for palaeoenvironmental assessment and radiocarbon dating (Hill and Tetlow, 2007).

Made ground across the site varied in thickness from 1.60m in Trench 1 and 2.10m in Trench 2. Below the 'made ground' in Trench 1, dark brown-black, organic pebbly sands were recorded at *c.* 1.60m. An auger core taken from the centre of Trench 1 (see Figure 3.22) established that this unit continued to a depth of *c.* 2.98m and included organic material, bone and shell fragments (including some

Figure 3.22: Trench 1 Ipswich docks (Albion Wharf) site facing east. The boreholes are visible in the foreground

identifiable as oyster). A leg bone of the common goose (*Anser anser*) was recovered at 2.94m (David Brown, Birmingham Archaeology, *pers. comm.*). From 2.98m to *c.* 4.31m, light grey, occasionally pebbly and mottled silts and clays were encountered. Below this unit, grey sands were recorded from 4.31m to 4.36m.

The second trench contained 'made ground' to a depth

Table 3.6: Summary of stratigraphy and palaeoenvironmental analyses at Ipswich Docks (Albion Wharf)

Depth (m)	m (OD)	Stratigraphy	Beetle analysis (bulk samples)	Diatom analysis	Radiocarbon sample
0.00–1.60	3.35–1.75	Made ground	–	–	–
1.60–2.98	1.75–0.37	Dark brown organic sand with occasional gravel, shell fragments, wood, bone	1.60–2.05m (1.75–1.30m OD)		1.65m (1.70m OD)
			2.05–2.50m (1.30–0.85m OD)		
			2.50–2.98m (0.85–0.37m OD)	2.97m (0.38m OD)	2.94m (0.41m OD)
2.98–3.73	0.37 to –0.38	Light grey clayey silt with occasional pebble & organic mottling	–	2.99m (0.36m OD)	–
				3.65m (–0.30m OD)	
3.73–4.31	–0.38 to –0.96	Light grey silty clay with organic mottling		4.30m (–0.95m OD)	
4.31–4.36	–0.96 to –1.01	Grey-brown sand	–	–	–

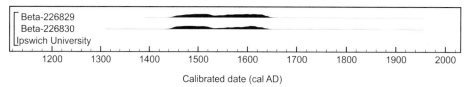

Figure 3.23: Ipswich Docks (University site) sequence calibrated radiocarbon dates

of *c.* 2.10m. Organic sands, similar to those in Trench 1, were recorded to a depth of 2.89m with occasional shell fragments and small pebbles. This unit was underlain by light grey silts and clays to 4.05m with occasional plant remains and thin (<1cm) sand horizons. Sands were once again located below the silts and clays to a depth of 4.12m.

Three bulk samples were taken from Trench 1 for beetle assessment and four samples analysed for diatoms (Table 3.6). Two further samples were taken from the top and base of the organic deposit for radiocarbon dating (Table 3.2; Figure 3.23). The samples from the top and base of the unit on fragments of bone and sub-fossil wood respectively produced dates (Table 3.2) of 370±40 BP (Beta-226830; cal. AD 1440–1640 and 350±40 BP (Beta-226829; cal. AD 1450–1650), which are statistically inseparable. This may indicate a relatively rapid period of sediment accumulation; alternatively, given the sand-rich nature of the sediment, one or both of the samples may have been reworked by fluvial processes. However, the dates suggest that the organic-rich sand was probably deposited during the late Medieval/early post-Medieval periods.

Beetle analysis

All three samples contained well-preserved insect remains. Species abundance and diversity were also found to be good, particularly within the basal assemblage of the organic-rich sand (2.50–2.98m). Smaller, more restricted assemblages were recovered from depths of 2.05–2.50m and 1.60–2.05m.

The sample from 2.50–2.98m contained a diverse and well-preserved assemblage. Direct evidence of the vegetation in the local environment is restricted to the basal sample and is limited to specimens of the Curculionid family, *Sitona* spp. This family of weevils is associated with a variety of plants commonly found in both meadows and disturbed ground, including *Vicia* spp., *Trifolium* spp. and *Lotus* spp. (Koch, 1992). Scarabaeidae or 'dung' beetles were also recovered from this sample. However, although dung beetles commonly indicate grazing, this does not seem likely when taking into account the full beetle assemblage encountered (see below).

The sample also contained a suite of synanthropic taxa including the Colydiid, *Aglennus brunneus*, the Endomychid, *Mycetaea hirta,* the Ptinid, *Ptinus fur*, and the common woodworm, the Anobiid, *Anobium punctatum*. All these taxa form part of the so-called 'House Fauna' (Hall and Kenward, 1990; Kenward and Hall, 1995; Kenward and Hall, 1997) and are associated with accumulations of foul and rotting material. Such taxa have also been recovered in the archaeological record from deposits of urban waste, rubbish and squalid flooring (e.g. Kenward and Hall, 1995).

The sample from 2.05–2.50m produced a restricted but nonetheless well-preserved beetle assemblage. Indicators of dung such as *Aphodius* spp. or *Geotrupes* spp. are absent and have been replaced by species such as the Scarabaeid, *Oxyomus sylvestris*, which indicates accumulations of rotting manure and vegetation and not fresh dung in pasture or meadowland (Koch, 1989; Jessop, 1996). Whilst several indicators of diseased wood were also recovered from all three samples, lignacious and saproxylic taxa are particularly prolific in this sample. For example the

Anobid *Xyletinus* spp. is commonly found on powdery, decaying oak and elm (Hyman, 1992). In addition, the Scolytid *Leperisinus* spp. is generally found on dead ash, whilst the Tenebrionid *Hypophloeus* spp. is a family found on a variety of decaying wood. These species are not associated with living trees and instead are more often found with dead, diseased or rotting wood. It therefore seems unlikely that they are derived from nearby woodland from which timber has been used for construction or firewood, for example. The upper sample from 1.60–2.05m also produced a restricted but well-preserved assemblage. The Scarabaeids or 'dung beetles' reappear in this sample, whilst the Staphylinid *Oxytelus rugosus* was recorded, a species associated with dung and accumulations of rotting, organic material (Tottenham, 1954).

Diatom analysis

Diatoms were found in all four samples, with high species abundance and diversity throughout. The majority of species were either 'polyhalobous' or 'mesohalobous' specimens, which require predominantly marine and brackish waters (salinity ranging from over 30 g l^{-1} to 0.2 g l^{-1} respectively) for optimal frustule growth. The diatom sample taken from 4.30m (–0.95m OD) towards the base of the silty clay was dominated by the planktonic polyhalobous species *Paralia sulcata*, with the mesohalobous benthic species *Diploneis didyma*, *Nitzschia punctata* and *Nitzschia navicularis* also recorded. The diatoms *Rhophalodia gibberula* and *Cocconeis placentula* ('oligohalobian indifferent' species), requiring predominantly freshwater environmental conditions to survive are also present, although in lower abundances.

At 3.65m (–0.30m OD), within the clayey silts, *Paralia sulcata* continues to dominate again supported by *Diploneis didyma*, *Nitzschia punctata* and *Nitzschia navicularis*. The mesohalobous species *Achnanthes brevipes* is also present. There is an increase in abundance of species typical of freshwater depositional conditions, including the oligohalobian indifferent species *Rhophalodia gibberula* and *Synedra capitata*. The 'oligohalobian halophilous' species *Epithemia turgida*, although present in low numbers, is restricted to freshwater environments and is not tolerant of brackish and marine waters.

The remaining two samples were taken from the top of the clayey silt unit (2.99m; 0.36m OD) and from the base of the overlying organic-rich sand (2.97m; 0.38m OD). Similar species were again encountered, with *Paralia sulcata* dominating and *Diploneis didyma*, *Nitzschia punctata* and *Nitzschia navicularis* contributing. The mesohalobian species *Campylodiscus echeneis*, *Achnanthes brevipes* and *Diploneis interrupta* were also present. Although the diatom assemblages were broadly similar within the two samples, there was an overall subtle increase in the influence of species requiring freshwater-dominated conditions within the overlying organic-rich sands (in evidence through the presence of *Cocconeis placentula* and *Hantzschia amphioxys*). Diatom preservation was found to be poorer within the organic-rich sand, with frustule disarticulation commonly hindering species identification. This probably reflects the higher energy depositional environment of this sand.

The diatom assessment has identified that estuarine conditions were responsible for the deposition of the basal clays and silts that underlie the organic-rich sand unit. This is further supported by the relative proximity of the site to the Ipswich Docks and the tidally-influenced River Orwell, and perhaps by the presence of a leg bone fragment of *Anser anser* toward the base of the organic-rich sand (common geese are frequently found in estuarine lowlands). Frustule preservation was good and species abundance and diversity high. The fine-grained nature of the sediment, combined with the diatom species encountered, suggests deposition occurred predominantly on upper tidal flats and lower saltmarsh.

The overall dominance of *Paralia sulcata* throughout the samples indicates tidal inundation dominated the depositional environment, enabling the accumulation of the marine planktonic diatom species. Although the planktonic nature of the species can sometimes result in its over-representation within diatom assemblages, the abundance of *Paralia sulcata* may in fact indicate that the site was located within a tidal inlet of the River Orwell (Vos and de Wolf, 1988).

There are subtle fluctuations in the influence of freshwater diatom species within the assemblages, which could be inferred as a possible indicator of changes in the influence of relative sea-level on lowland coastal evolution. The basal silty clay assemblage for example (4.30m) contains less freshwater-influenced species than the diatoms present within the overlying clayey silts at 3.65m. The diatom assemblage from 2.99m, in turn, contains fewer freshwater species than that at 3.65m. Therefore, whilst tidally-controlled sedimentation is likely to have dominated the depositional environment, variations in freshwater influence, probably in response to variations in the influence of sea-level or palaeo-landsurface elevation, can be inferred.

The final diatom assemblage sampled from the base of the organic-rich sand (2.97m), contained lower species abundances with frustule disarticulation common. The sharp lower unit boundary of the organic-rich silt combined with the dominance of marine diatom species within the underlying clayey silt, suggests an erosive episode occurred prior to sedimentation of the organic-rich sand. The diatoms within the organic-rich sand however continue to be dominated by *Paralia sulcata*, which therefore suggests episodic tidal submergence continued, at least during the initial onset of sedimentation. The presence of aerophilous species such as *Diploneis interrupta* and *Hantzschia amphioxys*, indicates that deposition occurred higher up the tidal-frame than previously due to the need for prolonged periods of tidal emergence for these species to survive.

3.5.2 River Orwell (Ipswich Triangle West)

Archaeological investigations were undertaken by BA-E (Hill, 2007d) at Ipswich Triangle West, proximal to Ipswich Docks and the River Orwell (Figure 3.21; Table 3.1). Two large trenches were excavated across the site: one running north-south along the western boundary of the site and one running east-west in the centre of the site. Deposits containing organic remains were identified under 'made ground' from a depth of *c.* 0.90m. Coring within Trench 1 revealed a thin organic silt *c.* 0.30m thick below the 'made ground'. This deposit capped horizons of orange-brown sand, silty sand and sands and gravels of varying thickness. Highly fragmented shells were common in the sand-rich horizons, which were recorded to a depth of *c.* 1.50m. In Trench 2, grey-brown sand and gravel was recorded below the 'made ground'.

A core excavated close to the foundations of a 14th century building on the site revealed 0.65m of dark brown silt, underlain by well-sorted, light brown silty sand and fine sand resting on a basal unit of sand and gravel. The low organic content of the deposits precluded sampling for palaeoenvironmental assessment or radiocarbon dating. From analogy with other sites within the region, it is suggested that the basal sands and gravels are likely to date to the Late Devensian or Early Holocene period, and that the overlying finer-grained deposits are associated with a former channel of the River Orwell, which is recorded in historical documents as flowing across the site in the 14th century AD (Hill, 2007d).

3.5.3. Ipswich Mills

Trial trenches were excavated by BA-E (Hill, 2007e) at the site of the former Ipswich Mills (Figure 3.21; Table 3.1). Of these, the first trench, running approximately east-west through the site, identified *c.* 0.60m of peat, possibly infilling a palaeochannel. The peat was underlain by grey-brown organic-rich sands and gravels, in turn, resting upon grey sands and gravels. In the northern trench face, a thin (*c.* 5cm) grey sandy silt unit was present within the grey sands and gravels, and contained preserved rootlets and organic matter. Four auger cores were drilled through the floor of the main trench to record the underlying sedimentary sequence.

The general stratigraphy comprised an orange-brown sand and gravel unit. The sands were coarse, and the gravels were medium to coarse, consisting of predominantly quartz and flint, with occasional sandstone; all were angular or sub-rounded. A core taken towards the centre of the trench identified a grey sandy silt unit underlying the sands and gravels. This was similar in character to the thin sandy silt unit exposed on the northern trench face. A second trench to the south of the site, also running east-west, revealed a wooden structure interpreted as a revetment, providing possible evidence for attempted coastal reclamation. A dark brown fill containing abundant shell, bone, wood and flint

fragments overlay the wooden structure and were in turn, capped by *c.* 0.30m of grey-brown, iron mottled clayey silts.

The sequence of deposits suggests fluvial deposition and a possible palaeochannel, with the coarse sands and gravels indicating higher-energy conditions during the Late Devensian period followed by channel accretion and peat formation in response to relative sea-level rise in the early Holocene. To the south of the site, the clayey silt unit capping the fill deposit is reminiscent of estuarine deposits found elsewhere across the Suffolk coastal lowlands (e.g. see Chapter 2). However, despite the clear potential of these deposits and recommendations for further analyses, no palaeoenvironmental assessments or radiocarbon dating were carried out at this site.

3.5.4 Sizewell: Sizewell Belts

This site is located on the North Sea coast immediately south of Sizewell Power Station and in the area of coastal wetlands and Site of Special Scientific Interest known as the Sizewell Belts (Figure 3.24; Table 3.1). Deposits of palaeoenvironmental potential were discovered during ground investigations along a proposed cable route for the Leiston Sub-station. BA-E was sub-contracted by Suffolk County Council Archaeological Service to undertake a coring survey along the cable route followed by targeted trial trenching and window sampling for palaeoenvironmental assessment and dating (Hill and Gearey, 2008; Hill *et al.*, 2008b).

A total of 25 cores were excavated across the site. Below the modern plough soil, dark brown sand with varying organic content was encountered to a depth of *c.* 0.70m. Orange-brown sand underlay the dark brown sand to a depth of up to *c.* 2.20m (core 3). Gravel content varied considerably but showed an overall increase with depth through the orange-brown sand. Towards the centre of the study area, a peat unit was interbedded between the dark brown sand and the basal orange-brown sand. There was a distinct increase in the thickness of this peat unit towards a tributary stream flowing into the Sizewell Belts to the east. Trial trenching subsequently undertaken by SCCAS confirmed the presence of coarse sand deposits across the site.

Due to the depth at which organic deposits were encountered during manual coring (up to 2m) below coarse sands, sampling was undertaken using a 'window sampler' to recover sufficient material for palaeoenvironmental assessment (Core 23). A *c.* 0.60m thick organic unit within Trench 30 (Figure 3.25) was sampled for pollen and beetles. This sequence was recorded as:

> 0–0.50m: Plough soil
> 0.54–0.76m: Dark brown, slightly organic sand
> 0.76–0.80m: Medium brown, iron mottled sand
> 0.80–1.04m: Dark brown, well-humified peat
> 1.04–1.28m: Dark brown, well-humified peat with monocotyledonous remains

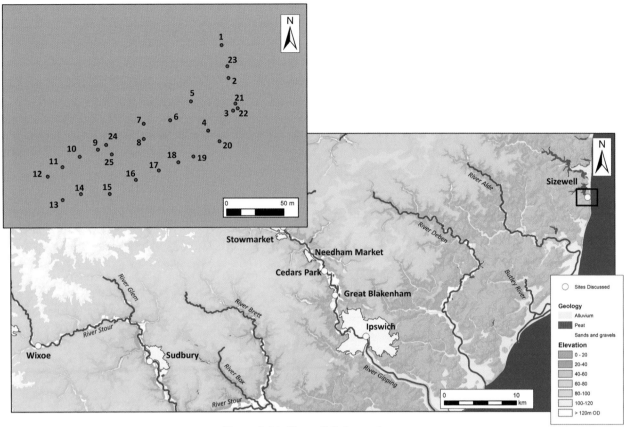

Figure 3.24: Sizewell Belts study area

1.28–1.36m: Dark brown, sandy peat
1.36–1.45m: Medium brown, organic gravelly sand

The palaeoenvironmental assessments focussed on the organic-rich deposits. Samples for pollen analysis were taken at 0.08m intervals through the peaty units (0.72m, 0.80m, 0.88m, 0.96m, 1.04m, 1.12m, 1.20m, 1.28m and 1.36m). Three bulk samples were processed and assessed for beetles: 0.80m–0.99m, 0.99m–1.18m and 1.18m–1.36m. Three samples (Table 3.2) were submitted for radiocarbon dating from the top (0.80m), middle (1.04m) and bottom (1.28m) of the sequence (Figure 3.26).

Radiocarbon dating results

The basal sample (1.28m) indicates that the onset of organic accumulation occurred around 2870±30 BP (SUERC-19651; 1130–930 cal. BC), the later Bronze Age. The middle sample (1.04m depth) was dated to 2415±30

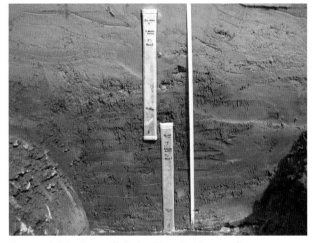

Figure 3.25: Sizewell Belts Trench 30 west-facing section, showing monolith tins (0.50m long) in position for sampling. The transition between the overlying sands and the sandy peat is clear around 0.80m

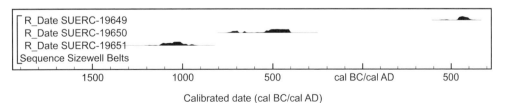

Figure 3.26: Sizewell Belts sequence calibrated radiocarbon dates

BP (SUERC-1650; 750–390 cal. BC) the later Bronze Age to Iron Age. The upper sample (0.80m) dates the cessation of organic accumulation and a shift to the deposition of the upper coarse sands after 1505±25 BP (SUERC 19649; cal. AD 440–630), the early medieval period.

Diatom assessment

Diatom assessments were carried out to assess the potential for these proxies to provide information regarding the role of changes in relative sea-level on sediment formation processes. A total of nine sub-samples were taken from the organic unit for diatom assessment from the same depths as those assessed for pollen; they were prepared following the standard procedure described by Plater *et al.* (2000). However, no diatoms were present in the samples.

Pollen assessments

The majority of the pollen samples contained well-preserved pollen although samples from 0.80m and 1.36m produced low pollen counts. Preservation was good, but percentages of broken and crumpled grains were relatively high. In addition, high numbers of pre-Quaternary spores (PQS) were also noted. Although there was no clear relationship between the abundance of PQS and stratigraphic changes, the presence of these spores suggests some re-worked material derived from local geological sources has been incorporated into the sediment. This is perhaps not surprising considering the presence of sand and silt within the organics, demonstrating the in-wash of inorganic material during peat accumulation.

The results are presented as a pollen diagram (Figure 3.27). *Alnus* is well represented in the basal sample with only occasional grains of *Tilia* and *Pinus sylvestris*. *Corylus avellana*-type dominates the shrub taxa with *Calluna vulgaris* (heather) also recorded. The diagram shows a relatively rapid decline in *Alnus* above the base at 1.27m but shrubs including *Corylus avellana*-type and *Calluna vulgaris* maintain values of up to 40%. Herb taxa are well represented across the diagram with Poaceae, Lactuceae undiff., *Plantago lanceolata,* Ranunculaceae undiff. (buttercups), *Rumex* and Chenopodiaceae all recorded. *Cerealia*-type increases to <5% around 0.97m, at which point rises in *Calluna* and Lactuceae and concomitant reductions in *Alnus* are observed.

The impression is of an open, grassy landscape but with hazel scrub and heathland persisting locally across the period of time represented by the diagram. Following an initial fall in alder at the base of the diagram, percentages of this tree are sufficient to indicate that some scattered alder remained on the damper soils, presumably around the edges of the woodland. The comparatively high values for herbs including ribwort plantain and dandelions give the impression of a pastoral, meadow-like environment in the close proximity of the site. The presence of cereal pollen within the sequence may reflect arable cultivation in the close proximity of the site, but this pollen type can include wild grasses specifically *Glyceria fluitans*.

Beetle assessments

The three faunas were fairly similar and imply that slow flowing or stagnant water was present, suggested by the range of water beetles recovered. Taxa typical of aquatic environments include *Noterus* and *Agabus* 'diving' beetles and the *Ochthebius* and *Hydreana* species of Hydraenidae (Hansen, 1986; Nilsson and Holmen, 1995). A similar shallow and waterlogged environment is also suggested by species of Hydrophilidae recovered, such as *Coelostoma orbiculare* and *Chaetarthria seminulum* (Hansen, 1986). The plant feeding (phytophage) beetles recovered also suggest that a range of waterside plants were close to the site. This is suggested by the presence of *Notaris* and *Limnobaris,* weevils that are normally associated with rushes, reeds and other emergent vegetation (Koch, 1992). *Tanysphyrus lemnae,* recovered from the basal sample, reflects *Lemna* spp. in the open areas of water. All of the three samples recovered contained the remains of several individuals of *Aphodius* and *Geotrupes* 'dung' beetles. These taxa are normally associated with areas of grazing and open pasture. This type of environment is also suggested by the recovery of 'the garden chaffer' *Phyllopertha horticola,* which is commonly associated with old grassland and pasture (Jessop, 1986).

Sizewell Belts: Discussion

The variation observed in the recorded sediment profiles (the intercalation of organic-rich sands with herbaceous peats) and sharp bed contacts suggest variation in depositional energy conditions and possible alternating episodes of erosion and deposition at Sizewell Belts. Given the proximity of the sampling site to the coast, it is possible that the sediments accumulated in an estuarine context, although the lack of more extensive stratigraphic data rather hampers understanding of the extent of any such system, whilst the absence of diatoms prevents the identification of the influence of relative sea-level on the sedimentary archive. Whilst the presence of saltmarsh may be indicated through low levels of Chenopodiaceae in the pollen record, this herb type includes taxa from a range of other environments including arable land.

The basal deposits consisted of gravel-rich sand, indicating deposition in a relatively high-energy fluvial environment. The subsequent shift to the accumulation of peat from around 2870±30 BP (SUERC-19651; 1130 930 cal. BC), the later Bronze Age, suggests a change in the depositional regime to a lower-energy system, which the beetle fauna implies was a fairly sluggish watercourse, with no faunal evidence for faster flowing water (e.g. Smith and Howard, 2004). The beetles also indicate emergent and aquatic vegetation including rushes, reeds and duckweed, although relatively few aquatic plants are

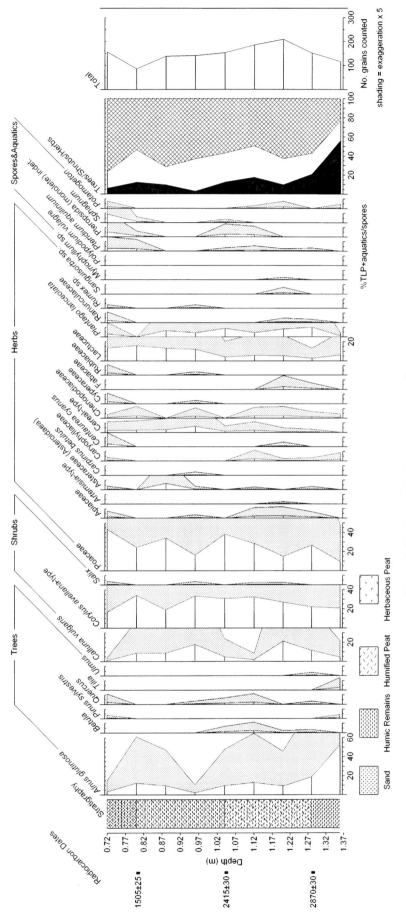

Figure 3.27: Sizewell Belts percentage pollen diagram

recorded in the pollen data. In terms of the wider, dryland areas around the sampling site, the overall absence of beetle species associated with woodland suggests a largely cleared landscape with indicators for grazing animals and/ or pasture also present.

This environmental reconstruction is supported in part by the palynological assessment, which indicates that few woody taxa other than hazel and scattered alder were present in the wider landscape. More extensive populations of alder seem to have been present near the site at the opening of the pollen diagram, but these appear to have contracted somewhat, probably as a result of the impacts of human activity, which increases through the sequence (see below). Hazel was probably growing on the drier areas beyond the sampling site but scrub/woodland was either restricted to denser stands in specific parts of the landscape or was scattered with an open under-storey. In particular, the presence of heather is an indication of the local sandy soils, which must have favoured the development of scrubby heathland. Herbs including wild grasses, ribwort plantain, buttercups and dandelions are all typical of meadow/pastoral vegetation, which was probably created and/or maintained by the grazing animals suggested by the beetles. The record of *Cerealia*-type pollen may also indicate local arable cultivation.

Both pollen and beetle records therefore indicate an expanse of slow flowing water within an open, pastoral landscape, with possible arable cultivation and only limited areas of scrubland suggested by the pollen. Although the grazing of wild animals cannot be discounted, given the palynological indications of pasture, it seems probable that the presence of domestic animals from the later Bronze Age onwards was responsible for the open environments evidenced at Sizewell. Such pastoral activity seems to have continued through the Iron Age and early medieval periods, suggesting that this area might have been a focus of farming/settlement activity for much of the later Holocene.

The available palaeoenvironmental data indicate few identifiable changes in the local environment during this time period. A rise in herbs and reduction in total tree and shrub values in the middle part of the diagram (0.97m) may reflect some intensification in pastoral farming not long after the date of 2415±30 BP (SUERC-1650; 750–390 cal. BC), or perhaps in the Iron Age. The persistence of hazel in the pollen record is notable in the light of the evidence for this continuous agricultural pressure on the environment, possibly reflecting the management of local woodland resources (see Chapter 6). The cessation of peat accumulation and hence the pollen record, and the deposition of coarse sands above 0.76 m, suggests the impact of increased fluvial influence on the sampling site after 1505±25 BP (SUERC-19649; cal. AD 440–630), the early medieval period. This may reflect local processes, such as increased deposition of alluvial material associated with soil erosion from agricultural activity. By this point, the pollen record indicates that the local area had probably been under pastoral and possibly arable land-use for maybe

1000 years. It is also possible that hydrological changes resulting from climatic and sea-level change may be implicated in the changes recorded at the Sizewell Belts (see below).

3.6 Discussion: palaeoenvironmental and geoarchaeological evidence from commercial projects in the Suffolk river valleys

Whilst the level of analytical detail provided by the commercial projects outlined in this chapter restricts comprehensive conclusions regarding landscape evolution, the results demonstrate the largely untapped rich research potential of the river valleys in Suffolk and also provide 'snapshots' into the timing, pattern and process of fluvial development, human activity and landscape change during the Holocene. However, it is often difficult to assess the broader significance of the site specific data, as the work was restricted to study areas, which were defined by the limit and extent of the various developments concerned, rather than a research-based approach, which would look to take a more problem-oriented angle to understanding the depth, extent and character of deposits across individual floodplains.

This section will provide a brief overview of the projects described above, beginning with the results of the most detailed study, the multi-proxy investigation of the deposits at the Stowmarket Relief Road site, summarised in Table 3.7. The full analyses of beetle and plant macrofossils from Stowmarket have produced a detailed record of environmental changes associated with the development of the River Gipping and its surrounding landscape during the Holocene. These data represent the first such coherent data for Suffolk, with few comparable modern studies currently available, though the work of Rose *et al.* (1980) at Sproughton provides a valuable contextual framework, especially for the Lateglacial period.

The nature of many lowland British rivers changed during the early Holocene, from unstable, braided, multi-channel systems to meandering and anastomosing ones with increasing channel stability facilitating the subsequent expansion of extensive floodplain wetlands (Brown and Keough, 1993; Howard and Macklin, 1999). The spatial and chronological development of systems is likely to have been highly complex and is difficult to reconstruct in any detail without extensive open areas of excavation and multi-proxy studies (see French and Pryor, 2005). Channel aggradation at Stowmarket commenced relatively early in the Holocene, with the accumulation of silty peat as water flow became more sluggish from around 7200–7060 cal. BC. The accumulation of increasingly organic sediments and the eventual infilling of the palaeochannel took place *c.* 4630 cal. BC. The beetle fauna suggest a series of phases, probably reflecting local catchment processes as well as allogenic 'forcing' mechanisms such as changes in relative sea-level and perhaps human activity, although

Table 3.7: Summary of environmental changes in the Stowmarket sequence

Approx Age	Site hydrology	Floodplain vegetation	Terrestrial vegetation
AD765	Floodplain peat, rising watertables and flooding	*Phragmites* Ruderal habitats, flax retting Some expansion in *Alnus* fen carr?	Open landscape/pastoral habitats Patchy woodland?
220 BC	Floodplain peat, possible expansion in wetter areas	Sedge fen with wet grassland Flax retting	Increasingly open landscape? Grassland/pastoral habitats
1090 BC	Floodplain peat	*Alnus* carr, damp open environments Tussocky grassland	?
1310 BC	Floodplain peat accumulation, rising watertables and expansion in areas of standing water	*Alnus* carr but reduced extent. *Carex* and *Phragmites,* aquatic/emergent vegetation expanding	Woodland/woodland edge with *Fagus* and *Fraxinus*
1710 BC	Floodplain peat accumulation *Seasonal flooding*	*Alnus* fen carr *Phragmites* beds and wet grassland and disturbed contexts	Woodland? Grassland/meadow
2370 BC	Floodplain peat accumulation *Seasonal flooding*	*Alnus* fen carr	Woodland? Grazed/disturbed areas?
3360 BC	Backswamp peat accumulation, *frequent flooding*	*Alnus* fen carr Sedge/damp grassland	Mixed woodland? Some open grassland/grazed areas
4630 BC	*Flowing water* but increasing ponding and peat accumulation	*Alnus* fen carr Tussocky grassland, *Carex* and *Phragmites*	Mixed woodland?
5900 BC		Damp tussocky grassland	Mixed woodland?
c. **7180 BC**	*Flowing water* – shallow aggrading channel	?expanding *Alnus*	Some open grassland (wetland edge?)

there is no direct evidence of the latter. The first stage evident at Stowmarket was characterised by the infilling of a palaeochannel, which was initially characterised by rapidly flowing water (*c.* 7180–3360 cal. BC). This was followed by a period of perhaps greater tranquillity in terms of the fluvial regime, with evidence for the infilling of the channel, slower moving/standing water and the steady accumulation of peat in a floodplain/backswamp environment (*c.* 3360–710 cal. BC). A final phase of increased local wetness and rising water tables is then inferred (*c.* 1710 cal. BC–cal. AD 765). The chronology of these phases should be regarded as approximate given the thickness of the sample depths analysed. A period of increased wetness has long been recognised during the early Bronze Age across Britain (e.g. Tooley, 1982) and appears to be recorded, for example, in the Humber Estuary *c.* 1800 cal. BC (Van de Noort and Fletcher, 1998), the Somerset Levels and the Severn Estuary from around *c.* 2000 cal. BC (Haslett *et al.*, 1998). A deteriorating climate, coupled with rising sea-levels at the end of the 'climatic optimum' is thought to be the catalyst for this period of change (e.g. see Macklin *et al.*, 2009) (see also Chapters 2 and 7 for further discussion of changes in sea-level and human activity during the later prehistoric period).

The Coleoptera demonstrate a series of changes in the local environment, but the evidence for a generally open environment conflicts somewhat with the plant macrofossil data, which indicates alder carr. This is likely to be a reflection of the taphonomic issues associated with identifying *Alnus* using sub-fossil insect remains. This illustrates the importance of a multi-proxy approach; it is unfortunate that the pollen was poorly preserved in the sampled deposit since these data would have provided further comparative information regarding changes in the wider environment (e.g. see Brayshay and Dinnin, 1994). It can also be noted that the subtle evidence for hydrological changes provided by the beetle analyses is generally not apparent in the lithostratigraphy, demonstrating the value of such data for identifying subtle changes in the depositional environment.

Despite the interpretative problems associated with plant and beetle data, the Stowmarket analyses provide potential indications of prehistoric human activity in the Gipping Valley. The appearance of 'dung beetles' in Sample 4 (*c.* 3360–2370 cal. BC) indicates the presence of grazing animals during the Neolithic/Bronze Age, although it is unclear if these were domesticated or wild. Clearer evidence for open, pastoral habitats possibly associated with human activity during the Bronze Age is recorded in Sample 5 (2370–1710 cal. BC). Direct indications of anthropogenic activity are apparent in Sample 8 (1090–220 cal. BC) with the presence of *Linum usitatissimum* in the macrofossil record and associated insect evidence for pastoral vegetation. Cultivation and/or processing of flax in the close vicinity of the sampling site can be inferred during the later Bronze Age/Iron Age. It can be noted that there is archaeological evidence for human activity close to the sampling site during the latter period, with an Iron Age settlement (SKT018) and associated field systems located some 800m to the east (Rolfe, 2007).

The proxy evidence for human activity is maintained into the final Sample 9, which cuts across the later prehistoric as well as early Medieval periods. A small but distinctive assemblage of beetles (characterised as the 'House Fauna'; Hall and Kenward, 1990; Kenward and Hall, 1995) was recovered from this sample. The significance of this assemblage is ambiguous but it probably implies human habitation and/or the dumping of domestic waste nearby, or into the river channel, which appears to have re-activated during this later period. The impression of significant anthropogenic activity on the floodplain is clear in both insect and plant macrofossil records. A Roman villa site (SKT018) was built over the Iron Age settlement described above. It seems very likely that the palaeoenvironmental evidence for human impact at the close of the sequence relates to settlement of the area during the later Holocene. Unfortunately, the chronological resolution of the upper sample (4–4.5m) covers the period from the Iron Age through to the early medieval (220 cal. BC to *c*. cal. AD 670–860) but it is clear that this later period saw significant impact on the floodplain environment.

The sampling site is also less than 100m south-east of Thorney Hall, the mid–late Saxon settlement, which was the precursor to the post-Conquest settlement of Stowmarket (SKT012). The valley fill is characterised by thick peats, which suggest that the course of the River Gipping has not changed significantly in this reach since the early Holocene, a feature of the valley floor also noted at Sproughton (Rose *et al.*, 1980) and in the lower Waveney Valley (see Chapter 2 and 7). The name 'Thorney' includes the Anglo-Saxon word for an island or islet (Rolfe, 2007); the stratigraphic transect demonstrates such an 'island' in the floodplain peats to the west of the sampling site. Whilst no further stratigraphic data are available, it seems likely that the Anglo-Saxon settlement was located on this feature, which extended to the north of the recorded transect, effectively forming an 'island' with the river to the west and floodplain marshland to the east. The identification of the 'House Fauna' discussed above may indicate the close proximity of human habitation or possibly the dumping/re-deposition of domestic waste on marginal, seasonally flooded land beyond the settlement itself.

The deposition of the organic silts that cap the peats suggest wetter conditions on the floodplain after cal. AD 670–860, which were perhaps also related to the effects of local human activity (see below). The Stowmarket Relief Road sequence contrasts with the evidence from nearby Station Road, where the deposits on the edge of the current channel of the River Gipping were revealed to be less than

2.5m thick with poor preservation of palaeoenvironmental proxies. Although it is clear that sediments at the latter location have been heavily disturbed and truncated by later human activity associated with the development of Stowmarket, the basal gravels are clearly much higher in this location. As discussed above, this appears to be related to significant variation in the morphology of these basal deposits across the floodplain, perhaps related to the existence of a series of buried floodplain terraces. Pollen preservation was poor in the organic sediments at Station Road, but plant macrofossil and beetles were well-preserved. This illustrates both the significant variation in sediment depth and character in floodplain contexts and demonstrates that sites must always be assessed on their own merits; the quality of preservation of palaeoenvironmental remains at one location may not necessarily be a reliable indication of preservation conditions at an adjacent site. It is unclear whether this relates to particular conditions at the time of sediment deposition, or post-depositional factors such as fluctuations in groundwater associated with drainage for example (see also Chapter 6).

Further downstream at Great Blakenham, the floodplain deposits have also been heavily disturbed by later development, but the study demonstrates the accumulation of floodplain peat from the later Romano-British period. The pollen and related palaeoenvironmental data indicate largely open grassy meadows with damp bankside vegetation and arable land, the latter suggested by the occurrence of cornflower and rye pollen. The retting of hemp is also indicated during this later period and is thus broadly comparable to the evidence from the Stowmarket Relief Road site for the economic exploitation of floodplain environments by water-based activities. The investigations at Cedars Park did not result in any radiocarbon dates or palaeoenvironmental data but again demonstrate the presence of organic deposits with potential for the preservation of palaeoenvironmental information on the floodplain of the River Gipping.

The assessments at Sudbury AFC have provided an insight into environments on the floodplain of the River Stour during the later Holocene, with the radiocarbon dates from Test Pit 1b demonstrating the accumulation of peat within an alder fen carr community from the Iron Age through to the Medieval period. No radiocarbon dates were obtained for the pollen diagram from Test Pit 1a, but it would appear on the basis of the biostratigraphy to correspond to the later Holocene, perhaps the Later Bronze Age to Iron Age. It can also be noted that the transition from floodplain peat to fluvial sediment at this site was dated to 1280±40 BP (Beta-263580; cal. AD 660–810) and hence it is close in date to a similar transition (cal. AD 670–860) apparent in the Stowmarket Relief Road sequence, although the chronology for the latter is rather imprecise. A shift from peat to the deposition of coarse sand is also recorded in the Sizewell Belts sequence (see above), although this is at a slightly earlier date of 1505±25 BP (SUERC 19649; cal. AD 440–630).

It has been hypothesised that increased soil erosion resulting from intensified agricultural production seems to have led to accelerated rates of overbank floodplain sedimentation during the later Holocene (*c.* cal. AD 950) across many British catchments (Macklin *et al.* 2009). At Sudbury, it may be that an event of this form resulted in the loss of the fen carr vegetation, as the fen deposits that had been accumulating since the prehistoric period were sealed beneath alluvium from the 7th–9th centuries AD. It is not known whether this was a relatively localised event, or if increased alluviation as a result of anthropogenic activity resulted in similar changes across wider areas of Suffolk during this period. Further research is required to investigate the spatial and chronological pattern of alluviation in Suffolk and to link this to changes implied by the archaeological and historical records.

The three investigations along the River Lark also indicate significant variation in both the depth and palaeoenvironmental potential of deposits in this valley. The studies at Eastgate Street demonstrated that floodplain peats survived *in situ*, but no further work was carried out; hence the age and palaeoenvironmental potential of these deposits are unknown. The floodplain at Rushbrooke-Nowton was relatively narrow and demonstrated the presence of shallow inorganic alluvial and colluvial deposits, perhaps derived from processes dating to the early Holocene, but no organic remains were recorded and the chronology of landscape development remains to be established.

The investigations at the Abbey site in Bury St Edmunds showed the presence of an intriguing complex of organic deposits containing clear evidence of past human activity on the narrow floodplain within the confines of the Abbey. Although the eastern floodplain (Abbey Site A) preserved no deposits of palaeoenvironmental potential, the western area (Abbey Site B) was characterised by deposits dating from the Neolithic through to the late Medieval period, including both natural and apparently archaeological contexts. In places (Cores 26–27) it is clear that *in situ* organic deposits relating to processes of floodplain aggradation during prehistory survive, preserving palaeoenvironmental information relating to these earlier landscapes. The shallower organics of Core 27 date to the Anglo-Saxon period, but it is unlikely that the sequence reflects continuous accumulation from the Neolithic. Fluvial activity, the erosion and in-wash of material from the dry-land and human activity, or a combination of these factors, have probably all affected the continuity of the palaeoenvironmental record.

The pollen from the Abbey cores was generally well-preserved, although some samples produced only low concentrations. It is notable that the spectra are generally very similar and tend to be dominated by herbaceous taxa, notably sedges and grasses. It is probable that the high percentages of Cyperaceae and taxa such as *Sparganium* indicate a highly localised pollen signal, dominated by plants growing on and around the sampling site. It would

appear that the vegetation at this site was open sedge fen, rather than the dense alder carr attested in other river valley environments in Suffolk during the mid-Holocene (see above and Chapter 2). The possible role of different processes and influences during prehistory, including the potential impact of human activity at this location, are unclear on the basis of the available data.

However, the high percentages of *Cerealia*-type pollen and *Secale cereale* recorded during the Anglo-Saxon and Medieval periods strongly suggest that cereal cultivation and/or processing must have been taking place in the very close vicinity of the sampling site. The other possibility is that these high percentages of *Cerealia*-type pollen and other indicators of cultivation were derived from secondary sources, such as the dumping of food waste or crop processing remains, perhaps representing midden deposits next to the river. It is clear from the range of archaeological material, including animal bone, recovered from the cores that a variety of such taphonomic pathways might be represented in the pollen record. The radiocarbon dates demonstrate that certain of these organic deposits date to the period of the foundation of the Abbey in the 11th century AD and there is a strong possibility that organic archaeological remains associated with this and perhaps earlier human activity in Bury St Edmunds, are preserved *in situ* at this site.

The sites investigated in Ipswich also provide some discrete 'snapshots' into the environment of this area during the later Holocene, although establishing the wider context or significance of these data requires further work. Archaeological investigations at Ipswich Triangle West have suggested that settlement commenced on the site in the 14th century AD and slowly expanded eastwards. Historical records also indicate that a river channel or tributary of the River Orwell flowed approximately north-south through the eastern margin of this site, with settlement developing along the banks of this channel. The assessment of the deposits encountered at Ipswich Triangle West broadly supports this hypothesis with deposits of evident fluvial origin. In Trench 1, orange-brown sand and gravelly sand horizons were commonly encountered below the thin organic silt layer. The overall well-sorted nature of the sand deposits, combined with the presence of disarticulated shell fragments, suggests a fluvially-derived origin. In Trench 2, grey-brown sands with varying gravel content were encountered.

Different phases of fluvial activity were probably responsible for the accumulation of the deposits in Trench 1 and Trench 2, with the orange-brown sands and gravels of Trench 1 (present across the western margin of the site) deposited during an earlier period of fluvial activity, possibly during the Late Devensian or early Holocene. In contrast, the grey-brown, well-sorted sands and gravels are likely to relate to the palaeochannel feature recorded in historical records. The channel was probably located proximal to the 14th century AD buildings, but migrated eastwards over time. The thin, dark brown organic clayey silt layers across much of the central and western area probably reflects accumulation in a floodplain environment, possibly coinciding with human occupation during the 14th century AD.

The analyses of the deposits at Ipswich Docks (Albion Wharf site) suggest the accumulation of silts within an estuarine context with subsequent deposition of organic-rich sand occurred from a date of 370±40 BP (Beta-226830; cal. AD 1440–1640) with a notable and distinctive range of beetles associated with this unit. The insect fauna from 2.50–2.98m suggest a relatively restricted and specific range of environments, closely associated with human habitation and activity, and might reflect the dumping of housing waste on the sampling site. Further evidence, in the form of dung beetles and other taxa associated with accumulations of rotting waste, may also indicate the presence of stabling detritus. It is therefore possible that the organic-rich sand deposit represents a combination of both types of material. The basal sample may reflect an episode of increased human activity at the site, perhaps the construction of a small homestead or farm in close proximity, followed by a period of abandonment. This is supported by the declining 'House Fauna' component in the upper two assemblages. Whilst dung beetles associated with fresh dung are absent from the middle sample, indicators persist for decaying manure and dung heaps. In the upper sample, indicators of fresh dung return, which perhaps indicates that animals were once again kept in the close vicinity of the sampling site.

Whilst it cannot be discounted that the deposits are some form of ditch fill, the relatively well-sorted nature of the sands implies accumulation in an environment with steady depositional energy. In addition, there was a general absence of artefacts within the unit during initial trial trenching (Mark Sommers, *pers. comm.*). The dominance of sand along with very well-humified organic remains, occasional bone, shell and gravel components, could reflect sediment deposition in a fluvial system, possibly within a small tributary stream. Alternatively, the organic-rich sand unit may have accumulated within a 'man-made' drainage channel. What is clear is that the feature was taking water flow, whether as part of a minor tributary system or an artificial drainage channel. The feature's proximity to an area of human occupation explains the incorporation, whether deliberate dumping or in-wash of waste material, of beetle assemblages indicative of settlement, agricultural activity and eventual site abandonment.

The coring survey, palaeoenvironmental assessments and radiocarbon dating at Sizewell provides evidence of landscapes during the later prehistoric through to the early Anglo-Saxon period on the coastal fringe of Suffolk. The organic-rich deposits represent a shallow valley mire or a palaeochannel that began accumulating from the Late Bronze Age or early Iron Age. The beetle fauna suggest that this body of water, contained rich aquatic vegetation with the overall absence of species associated with woodland implying a cleared landscape beyond the wetland areas, with some indicators for pasture in the area present. This is supported by the palynological assessment, in which tree species are restricted to the basal sample, with alder carr growing on the damper soils. The overall dominance of hazel, grasses and heather are likely to be a reflection of the dominant vegetation on drier soils. In addition, herbs including wild grasses, ribwort plantain, buttercups and dandelions are all typical of meadow/pastoral vegetation. The range of herbs present therefore supports the evidence for pastoral farming as indicated by the presence of dung beetles. Some of the taxa recorded however, such as ribwort plantain, dandelions and (to a lesser extent) sorrels, may reflect the presence of these plants as field edge weeds. This adds weight to the evidence for cultivation in close proximity to the site reflected through the presence of cereal pollen within the sequence. Diatom assessments could not identify whether relative sea-level influenced the development of the depositional archive. The presence of saltmarsh conditions close to the site may be supported through the presence of low levels of fat hen in the pollen record.

4. Archaeological Excavations and Analyses of a Late Prehistoric Timber Alignment: The Beccles Project (2006–2012)

With

Michael Bamforth, Kristina Krawiec, Eamonn Baldwin, Chris Gaffney, Emma Hopla, Peter Marshall, Abby Mynett, David Smith, Wendy Smith, Ian Tyers, Cathy Tester and Sarah Percival

4.1 Introduction

As outlined in Chapter 1, in 2006–2012, archaeological excavations and associated investigations were carried out at a site directly north of the town of Beccles in the lower Waveney Valley (Figure 4.1). The site was discovered during the course of soke dyke excavation as part of Environment Agency funded flood alleviation measures that were being carried out across Broadland; a process which subsequently revealed two additional sites within the region (see Chapter 5).

The first season of excavation at Beccles was undertaken in the summer of 2006 under *PPG* 16 and in partnership with SCCAS, alongside the programme of coring and associated palaeoenvironmental assessment carried out as part of the SRVP outlined in Chapter 2. A second season of excavation was carried out in summer 2007 in the form of an undergraduate training excavation run under the auspices of the Institute of Archaeology and Antiquity (IAA), University of Birmingham. The English Heritage funded project at Beccles began in 2009 with a phase of survey, subsequent excavation, stake-excavation analyses and a two-year programme of hydrological monitoring (see Chapter 1 for further details regarding project organisation). This chapter describes the results of these excavations and associated research at Beccles.

The study area

Beccles is located in the lower reach of the River Waveney on the 'marshes' to the south of the river, which were reclaimed in the medieval period. Hodskinson's Map of Suffolk (Dymond and Martin, 1999) show that Beccles Marshes area was un-drained common land in AD 1783, but that by AD 1838 the area had been ditched and was under management (Ordnance Survey 1st Edition). The canalisation of the Waveney triggered widespread reclamation of remaining wetland and riverside common land up the valley. The soils are recorded as deep fen peats and silts of the Mendham Series, with underlying alluvial deposits of gravels and sands of the Newport Series that form small sandy islands and ridges along the southern side of the river (British Geological Survey Sheet 176: Lowestoft). Currently, the marshes along the river are mainly rough pastureland.

4.2 Summary of the excavations at Beccles in 2006 (BCC-043) and 2007 (BA1472)

The results of the two seasons of excavation in 2006–2007 at Beccles will be briefly summarised in this section (see also Gearey *et al.,* 2011), as these data defined the approach taken by the subsequent English Heritage funded study at this site. The results of all phases of excavation, including palaeoenvironmental, geoarchaeological, radiocarbon and

Down by the river

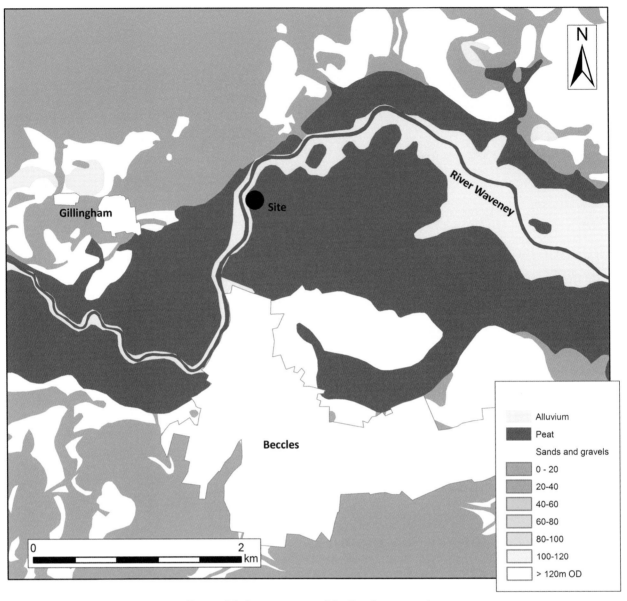

Figure 4.1: Location map of the Beccles excavations

dendrochronological analyses will be integrated in Chapter 7. The soke dyke excavations through the floodplain peats at Beccles had initially removed several large *Quercus* (oak) stakes with worked pencil point ends and other fragments of archaeological wood. The excavations in 2006 concentrated on a trench (Trench 1; Figure 4.2 and Figure 4.3) some 16m long and 5m wide, defined by the footprint of disturbance by the soke dyke excavation. A 20 × 5m strip directly to the north (Trench 2) was also cleaned to the top of the archaeology, indicating that the monument continued in this area, although individual features were not excavated. A third area (5 × 5m) was excavated directly to the south of Trench 1 (Trench 3), although no features were identified. Survey of the newly profiled soke dyke revealed a number of additional stakes and 'stake-sockets', indicating that the archaeology continued beneath the undisturbed area of the floodplain to the south-south-east.

The projected alignment indicated by this first season of excavation in 2006 provided the location for a second season of excavation in 2007. These excavations concentrating on a primary trench (Trench 4, Figure 4.4) which exposed an area of 17 × 9m in a position 55m to the south-south-east of the 2006 excavation's Trench 1. An additional trench was excavated (Trench 5) directly to the east of the 2006 Trench 1 to examine a possible extension of a trackway feature identified in 2006, although no continuation was identified.

From across the two seasons of excavation, the tops of large upright wooden stakes were identified *c.* 0.70m below the current ground surface in Trenches 1, 2 and 4, in addition to exposures within the dyke. These upright wooden stakes provided the basis for estimating the potential continuation of the structure to the south-south-east (Figure 4.5) Following the identification of the tops

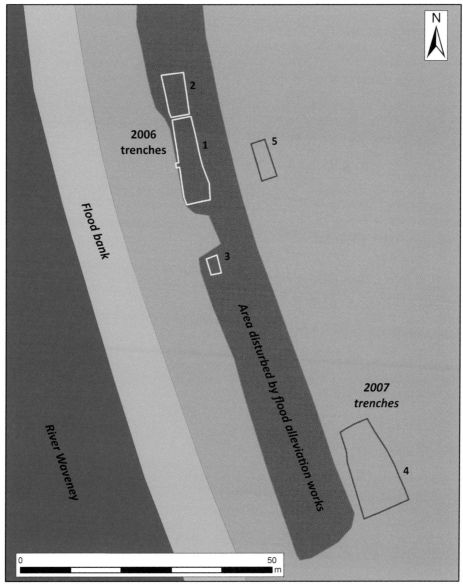

Figure 4.2: Location of the 2006 and 2007 trenches at Beccles

of these stakes, Trench 1 (in 2006) and Trench 4 (in 2007) were excavated by removing successive 0.10m spits manually to allow hand planning. In addition, two open sections 1m wide were excavated in Trench 1 to an additional depth of 0.4m on an east-west orientation across the alignment of the stakes and three such sections were excavated in Trench 4. Abundant wood remains including timber, roundwood and wood working debris were found within the peat deposits and concentrated within the alignment to a maximum depth of 1.10m below the current ground surface (see below). *In situ* coppice stools and roots were also recorded, demonstrating the growth of trees on the floodplain. Four of these were sampled within Trench 1 and identified as *Alnus glutinosa* (alder).

The two seasons of excavation recorded a total of 67 upright *Quercus* stakes and two *Alnus* stakes aligned north-west to south-east over a total distance of 95m. The

stakes formed three discrete rows spanning 3–4m wide and were generally single, but in places were in pairs and in one instance a group of three. The 26 sampled stakes survived in the round and varied in length between 0.61–1.96m and in diameter from 0.14–0.26m, representing a relatively uniform size of raw material. As the tops of the oak stakes survived to a broadly similar level in the peat, length of survival was dictated by depth of insertion in antiquity as opposed to original timber length. The stakes were generally formed of straight-stemmed timbers with central piths, even diameters and few side branches. Although the majority of these features could be explained by trees growing vertically in relatively dense woodland, the tendency for the proximal/butt ends of the stakes to curve slightly, as is often seen where coppice stems meet the stool (Rackham, 1977), raises the possibility that these timbers were derived from long-lived or overgrown

Figure 4.3: Plan of trenches 1 and 2 at Beccles

N

Stakes
Archaeological roundwood
Wooden planks
Natural roots
Drain

0   5
                      m

Figure 4.4: Plan of Trench 4 from the 2007 excavations at Beccles

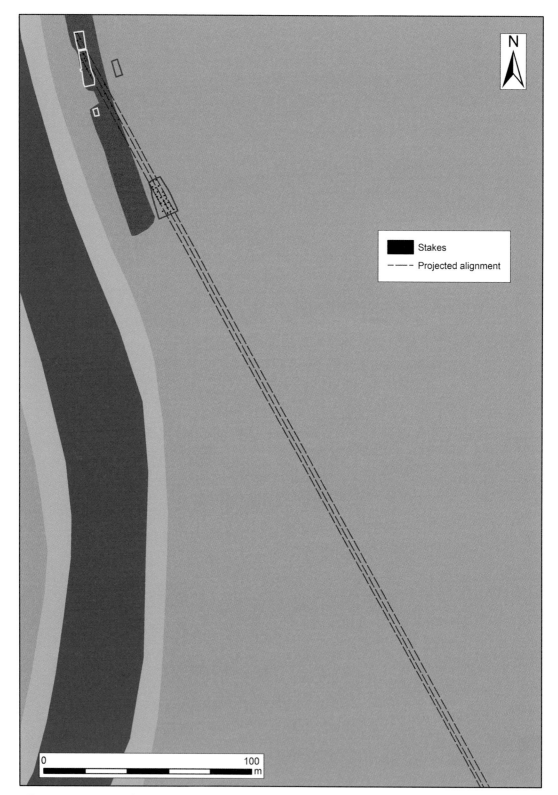

Figure 4.5: Projected continuation of the timber alignment observed in the 2006 and 2007 excavations

coppice. Alternatively, the trees may all have been growing on a bank or slope.

Nine of the recorded stakes had either intact or broken cross-halving lap joints at a level of between −1.15m OD and −1.94m OD, and two of these jointed timbers also had small notches cut into them. The small notches seem to describe the woodworker starting to cut a halving lap joint, then deciding that the position was wrong, abandoning the work (leaving a notch) and then cutting out a halving lap on a different section of the timber. Three of these notched stakes in Trench 4 had *in situ* lateral wooden cross bars, each of which had been worked to a square cross section.

A concentration of coppiced *Alnus* rods was recorded, on an east–west alignment, at right-angles to the main timber alignment in the south-western segment of Trench 1, and continuing under the baulk of the western edge of the trench. The positioning of the rods suggests they may have originally formed a discrete bundle, with three driven stakes; two of split *Quercus*, and one of *Fraxinus* (ash) found in close association and possibly used to secure it in place. This feature can be interpreted as a short trackway (Brushwood Structure 06), perhaps designed to bridge a patch of wetter peat, but this did not continue to the east of the principal timber alignment (Trench 5). Three unmatched tool signatures and a single tool mark were recorded, suggesting that a minimum of four tools were involved in harvesting and construction. Two samples for radiocarbon dating were taken from this feature (see below).

A second brushwood structure (Brushwood Structure 07) was located in the north-western end of Trench 4, again at right angles to the main timber alignment and consisted of seven lengths of coppiced roundwood (four *Quercus* and three *Alnus*), which had been pegged into place using short roundwood stakes with trimmed ends. Two samples for radiocarbon dating were taken from this feature (see below). In close association with this bundle was a tangentially faced, small *Quercus* plank (L: 0.69, W: 0.21, T: 0.05m) with a small, square, naturally occurring hole in one end, into which a tangentially aligned *Fraxinus* peg (L; 0.205, W: 0.41, T: 0.038m) had been inserted to secure the plank in place. Although heavily disturbed and in poorer condition than the bulk of the material recovered from the site, the pegged plank and the coppiced bundle may have formed some kind of *ad-hoc* working platform/trackway.

4.3 The Beccles Project (2006–2012): understanding, contextualising and managing a later Iron Age wetland site

The results of the two seasons of excavation therefore demonstrated that a substantial monument in the form of a triple alignment of oak stakes and associated features was preserved in the floodplain peats at Beccles. The data indicated that the structure continued for an unknown distance to the south-east with initial dendrochronological analyses (see below) suggesting a later Iron Age date for the oak timbers. These earlier investigations formed the basis for a subsequent English Heritage funded project designed to investigate this site; the aims and structure of which have been outlined in Chapter 1. Building upon the results from these two phases of excavation, a programme of survey was undertaken comprising airborne remote sensing, borehole survey and deposit modelling, and geophysical survey. This survey phase was aimed at addressing the first aim of the project, which was to investigate the efficacy of novel, non-intrusive geophysical techniques in the identification of

peatland archaeological sites (see Chapter 1). An approach combining airborne remote sensing, deposit modelling and geophysical survey was therefore devised. The results from this work fed into the subsequent phases of work including excavation.

4.3.1 Methods

Airborne remote sensing, borehole excavation and deposit modelling

Environment Agency LiDAR data for the Beccles area was available and was interrogated to identify any topographic variations or anomalies on the floodplain, which may have had significance for the site, for example, the presence of discrete islands within the floodplain which might have implications for the orientation of the alignment. The LiDAR data was analysed within a GIS environment where it could be integrated with other datasets from the project. A borehole survey was carried out along and around the projected alignment of the site in the form of a grid of cores (e.g. Chapman and Gearey, 2003, 2013) to facilitate three-dimensional modelling of the pre-peat topography and the overlying floodplain deposits. It was intended that the results from this could be used to inform the positioning of archaeological trenches.

Geophysical survey

The geophysical survey component of the project had two principal aims. Firstly, it was aimed at investigating the projected alignment and any features identified through the airborne remote sensing and borehole modelling. Secondly, it provided the opportunity to test a novel method of geophysics for applications within wetland environments where traditional methods have been of limited value (Coles and Coles, 1996). In general, this can be considered a problem related to a lack of contrast between the target and the surrounding ground. Using a variety of techniques (magnetometry, earth resistance, ground-penetrating radar (GPR), electrical imaging, and induced polarisation,) it was hoped that the project could investigate the efficacy of both traditional and novel non-intrusive geophysical techniques in the identification of wetland sites.

The geophysical survey focused on three areas (Figure 4.6). The first area, Geophysical Survey Area A, was positioned adjacent to and overlapping the area of the southern-most trench from the 2007 excavations. This provided the potential for comparison between the geophysical datasets and the positions of known archaeology observed previously to provide calibration. The second and third survey areas (B and C) were positioned over the projected alignment of the archaeological structure in order to establish whether addition features could be identified on the basis of observations within Geophysical Survey Area A. In all three areas, magnetometry and

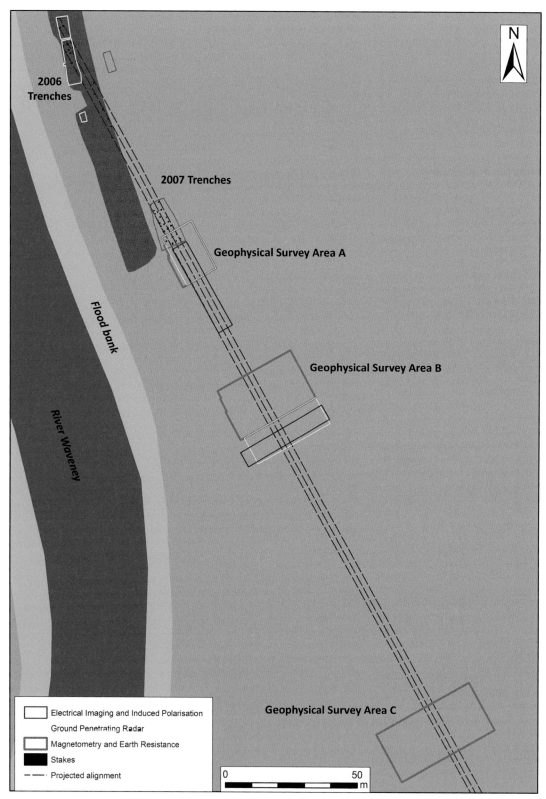

Figure 4.6: Location of the areas surveyed using terrestrial geophysics techniques showing where different methods were used

earth resistance were carried out over the same areas. GPR survey was carried out over the same area as these techniques in Geophysical Area A, and adjacent to the southern side of Geophysical Survey Area B. Electrical Imaging and Induced Polarisation data capture were carried out both along the projected alignment (in Area A) and across the alignment (in Area B) in case of any potential deviations in the alignment further to the south.

The magnetometry survey was carried out using fluxgate technology in gradiometer mode. The fluxgate gradiometer indirectly measures changes in magnetic susceptibility and also detects features exhibiting remnant magnetisation. The instrument contains two fluxgate sensors. The upper sensor mainly detects variations in the Earth's magnetic field due to geology and secular variation, while the lower sensor detects variations due to geology, secular variations and variations due to buried features. When the upper reading is subtracted from the lower reading, only the variations due to subsurface features remain. For the sensors to work properly both must be correctly balanced and held as near as vertical as possible. Further details of this standard geophysical technique are provided by Scollar *et al.* (1990), Clark (1996) and Aspinall *et al.* (2008).

Fluxgate gradiometer surveys are most effective when attempting to identify areas or zones of high magnetic enhancement, such as burnt areas or cut features such as ditches and pits. However many other types of features produce measurable magnetic responses. The majority of the magnetic data was collected using a Geoscan FM instrument, and some additional data were collected using the Foerster Ferrex system (Area B). The data in all of the areas were collected along 0.5m transects sampled at 0.25m intervals for the Geoscan and 0.1m for the Foerster. The Geoscan data were subject to de-spike, zero mean traverse, low pass filter and interpolated to a 0.25 × 0.25m raster. The Foerster data have been subject to zero mean traverse and visualised in Surfer. No de-staggering was undertaken on any of the magnetic data-sets.

Earth Resistance survey involves passing an electric current through the ground between two current electrodes and measuring the electrical potential between two other 'potential' electrodes. From this information the earth resistance can be measured and the apparent resistivity of the ground can be calculated. Earth Resistance mainly depends on the moisture of investigated ground. As a result, the moisture of the volume of earth that is measured and the porosity of buried features within that volume, contribute to the value. Areas of low porosity (low moisture) produce high resistance values. Conversely, high porosity materials produce lower than average resistance. Extended discussions of this standard technique can be found in Scollar *et al.* (1990) and Linford (2006).

There are many variations for the layout of the four probes and the most common for archaeological prospecting is the Twin Probe. The Twin Probe involves one current and one potential electrode fixed in the ground (the 'remote probes'), and another pair mounted on a moveable frame (the 'mobile probes'). Three areas were subject to Twin Probe survey. A Geoscan RM15 with a MPX15 multiplexer was used to collect the measurements. Using the MPX15 it is possible to collect data at two probe separations (0.5m and 1.0m). This effectively allows exploration at different depths, with the 1.0m separation prospecting to a greater depth (Walker, 2000). The 1.0m data were collected on a 1 × 1m grid while the 0.5m data were mapped at 0.5 ×

1m. The data were minimally processed; the processing included de-spiking, low pass filter and interpolation to a common 0.25 × 0.25m raster.

It has been suggested at other sites that GPR may have value within wetland environments (Clarke *et al.*, 1999). Ground-Penetrating Radar is an active geophysical technique involving the transmission of electromagnetic (radio) pulses from a transmitter antenna moved across the ground surface. When the pulse reaches an interface between different materials, some of the energy is reflected back to a receiving antenna whilst some travels further into the ground and is reflected from a deeper subsurface discontinuity (Conyers, 2004). The amplitude of the returned pulse is dependent on the velocity of the radar wave as it passes through a material. The relative dialectric permittivity (RDP) is a measure of the ability of a material to conduct the radar wave and will vary depending on the composition, porosity and moisture content of the material. The travel times of each pulse are recorded and allow an approximate depth measurement to be made by assuming a dialectric constant value, although these depths should only be considered as estimations unless accompanied by ground-truthing (David *et al.*, 2008).

The GPR data were collected with a SIR3000 GPR system manufactured by Geophysical Survey Systems Inc. (GSSI). The survey was carried out using 200MHz and 400MHz antennae to provide depth penetration and resolution of results in the attempt to locate the timber alignment. A calibrated survey wheel was employed for the data collection to ensure that transect lengths were accurately recorded. Radar scans were recorded along traverses 0.5m apart, using survey lines for guidance. Traverses were orientated north-south and east-west across the proposed survey target (projected line of the timber alignment), and were collected uni-directionally (parallel method) to ensure that staggering between traverses was reduced. The sample interval was set to record 512 samples per scan and 100 scans per metre. The range setting was set to 40 nanoseconds (ns) on the 400 MHz antenna and 50 ns on the 200 MHz providing a maximum estimated depth of *c.* 2m, although it should be noted that this is an estimated depth based on an assumed dialectric value of 12.

The processing of the radar data was carried out in Radan 6.5 software. The raw traverse (.dzt) files were initially loaded into Radan for a preliminary examination prior to any processing or combining of files. The processing techniques to be applied to the datasets were first tested on several of the profiles individually until suitable parameters were obtained. A macro was created using these processing functions and applied to all of the files within the project. The processing included a time-zero correction, an FIR filter for horizontal background removal and a 2D constant velocity migration. Following processing, the individual profiles were then combined together to form a single Radan 3D file, which could subsequently be viewed as a 3-dimensional cube, allowing both plan (time-slice) and profile views of the data at varying depths. Selected time-slices were exported from Radan and converted into ASCII format before being geo-referenced to the National Grid co-ordinates (OSBG36) in a GIS environment.

The Electrical Imaging (EI) data were collected along a profile of 72 electrodes using a Syscal Pro 10 Channel Resistivity and IP system (Isis Instruments). A pseudo-section was created by expanding the probe separation of a Dipole-Dipole array around successive points, thereby increasing the depth of measurement. This method is an extension of earth resistance noted above and the same expectations and limitations are common. In this case, however, resistance is measured at an assumed depth for each point and this facilitates the calculation of an electrical resistivity pseudo-section, which can be improved via iterative inversion to a model data-set.

The bibliography for environmental use of EI is very large and the theory, use and processing of this data are very well summarised by Loke (2004). Archaeological applications are not as prevalent, but typical uses can be found in Neighbour *et al.* (2001) and Astin *et al.* (2007). In these two cases topographic corrections were applied; at Beccles the ground is essentially flat and no topographic corrections have been applied. The data was collected at the same time as the IP measurements and the processing is common, and linked within the inversion process.

In addition to the techniques outlined above, the principal new technique applied to the site was Spectral Induced Polarisation (SIP) (Schleifer *et al.,* 2002). Induced Polarisation (IP) is based on the recognition of potential difference that exists after current has been injected into the ground and switched off. The voltage that is induced gradually decays to zero and it is this curve that is of interest for IP measurements. There are a number of possible causes of the polarisation. Classically the technique has been used for locating metal ores or slag deposits (e.g. Meyer *et al.,* 2007), but more understated affects can be identified that result from common minerals such as those found in clay. In this case the interface of the materials is important to the propagation of the effect.

Aspinall and Lynam (1970) discussed the potential of SIP, but at the time it was a technique that had rarely been used for archaeological prospecting (David *et al.,* 2008). In the English Heritage guidelines (David, 1995) IP was dismissed as non-viable in an evaluation exercise but its efficacy has since been re-assessed (English Heritage, 2008). Important research by Schleifer *et al.* (2002) describes 'spectral' IP in the frequency-domain; in effect this is a broadband approach where the variation is 'swept' through many channels. Weller and Bauerochse (2013) have also recently experimented with the utility of SIP for identifying wooden archaeological remains in peatlands.

There are two ways to measure IP: frequency or time-domain. For archaeological purposes the original time-domain work was undertaken by Aspinall and Lynam (1970) and while that indicated some value, there was little momentum in its application. In recent years, interest while still marginal, has broadened to include

Figure 4.7: Spectral Induced Polarisation survey in progress

prospecting for wooden material within wet or waterlogged environments. The work by Schleifer and colleagues (e.g. Schleifer *et al.,* 2002), working in the frequency domain, sparked some interest in the archaeological literature, although time domain measurement systems were also apparently indicating similar success (e.g. Finzi-Contini, 2001; Losito *et al.,* 2001). It is believed that the cellular structure of wood is the factor that activates low level IP where the cell walls act as membranes for ions that create an increased 'chargeability' which can be measured by both IP systems. In context of this work the important driver here is that IP measurements may be able to identify artefacts or constructions that are made of material that is traditionally difficult to identify by geophysical means and within environments that are similarly challenging.

Frequency-domain measurements are difficult to undertake and there are no suppliers of equipment that is suitable for the production of pseudo-sections in the UK. For this work a 72-probe Syscal Pro instrument was used to acquire both resistivity and IP data. This is a time-domain IP (chargeability) measurement system. It has the ability to measure the decay curve by sweeping down it in defined segments. The chargeability is reported in mV/V. The data were collected in a pseudo-3D mode in two areas i.e. along parallel traverses where the probe separation is varied to create a vertical (pseudo) section (Figure 4.7). The data were captured along 0.5m spaced parallel lines with 0.5 m electrode separation in the majority of the lines, except for Line 1 Area 1 where the probes were separated by 0.25m. The dipole-dipole configuration was used as it often produces good responses to vertical discontinuities such as may be expected from upright timber stakes (Loke, 2004).

Data collection was informed by discussions with Jenny Upwood from Geomatrix-Earth Science Ltd and via the Syscal Pro manufacturer (Iris). There was additionally some trial and error when on site to establish the most appropriate settings on the instrument for this project. In order to produce reliable IP signals with small electrode spacing a 2 second pulse was injected into the ground, with

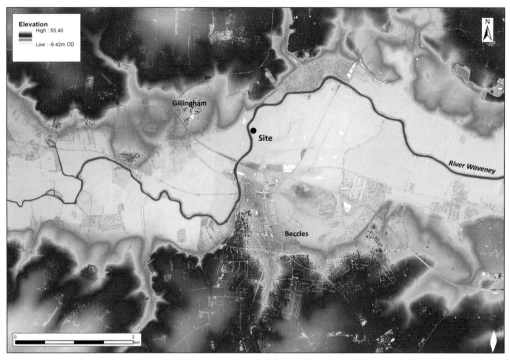

Figure 4.8: LiDAR data (provided by The Environment Agency)

the IP curve 'swept' in a semi logarithmic fashion after a delay of 40ms. Twenty IP windows were measured to define the decay curve. A stack range was set at 3–8 and a quality factor of 3% was chosen to assure data quality. While these settings should be sufficient to establish reliable IP within the first metre or so, the need for greater depth required the distance between the current and potential pairs to be doubled at the larger depths. This has the effect of increasing the signal strength at greater depths. Once the optimum set up had been achieved a 'sequence' for data collecting was created using Electre Pro and uploaded to Syscal Pro meter.

The end of each survey line was accurately set out using the project's GPS, and the 72 probes were placed along each line with a probe spacing of 0.25m for line 1 and 0.5m for the remaining lines. The probes were hammered into position since the top 10cm of the ground was extremely dry; therefore, a probe check was undertaken prior to each measurement sequence. An external 12V battery was attached to the resistivity meter and the resistivity and IP measurements were automatically collected. The resistivity meter provided an estimated time for each measurement sequence, usually about 100 minutes. However, this part of the process was the most problematic as battery failure caused many re-measurements.

Once collected the data were transferred to a laptop using Prosys II Software. This software was used to initially view the data, and to eradicate poor readings defined via the automatic filtering option. Data were subsequently saved in Res2DINV format in both raw and filtered versions. The data were inverted using RES2DINV and viewed as individual sections through the ground. Additionally, the data from each area were collated in RES2DINV and

imported into the RES3DINV software. In the latter a 3D inversion was undertaken and depth slices were produced for both areas. Additionally, the 3D information was exported as a cube into 'Slicer-Dicer' for visualisation and analysis. The combination of techniques therefore provided the opportunity to explore the potential of both the more traditional and the more novel techniques within wetland environments. The different types of landuse (with Areas A and B being within improved pasture, and Area C being within an area of unimproved pasture) provided additional variations for comparison.

4.3.2 Results of the survey phase

This section summarises the results of the initial, survey phase of the project, which addressed Aim 1 of the project (see above). There were three components to this initial stage; assessment of airborne remote sensing data, geophysical survey and borehole excavation/deposit modelling.

Airborne Remote Sensing: LiDAR and aerial photography

LiDAR datasets covering the study area were provided by the Environment Agency at a $2 \times 2m$ surface resolution in ASCII format. Tiles were surfaced, merged and analysed using ESRI ArcGIS software. A comprehensive variety of surface analysis techniques were applied to the datasets in order to highlight subtle details, including surface lighting, slope and aspect, and selective vertical bracketing. These analyses (Figure 4.8) did not identify any archaeological features nor do the data show any evidence of past floodplain development (e.g. palaeochannels) or highlight any previously unidentified topographic anomalies such as gravel islands.

Borehole excavation and deposit modelling

Following the analysis of airborne data, the second element of the survey phase examined the three-dimensional context of the burial environment to the south of the 2006 and 2007 trenches through the excavation of a grid of boreholes. The projected alignment of the site as established by the 2006–2007 excavations provided a baseline that was oriented using differential GPS (see Figure 4.5). The central alignment was set out at 20m intervals to the south of the Trench 4. The grid was extended by 40m to both the east and west of the central alignment, covering a total maximum area of 400m x 80m. The overall grid thus extended from the edge of the River Waveney to the north, to the field adjacent to the allotment gardens to the south. This provided a broad sample of the area around the alignment from wetland to dryland edge. The southern extent of the grid marks the current extent of surviving peat deposits and may also approximately correspond with the floodplain edge during later prehistory (see below).

A total of 86 boreholes were excavated over this grid across the floodplain and up to the edge of dry land to the south. The boreholes were excavated primarily at 20m intervals, although higher resolution coring was undertaken in areas displaying local variations in basal topography where the intervals between boreholes were reduced (minimum of 7m). Higher distances between boreholes occurred in areas of modern obstructions (e.g. the modern track). Depths of boreholes ranged from 0.40m to 4.65m below the current land surface. The grid provided three-dimensional surface positions for the boreholes, which ranged from –0.82m OD to –0.01m OD. The stratigraphy of the cores was recorded but demonstrated little variation across the study area (see below).

Basal elevations, defined by the transition between the organic peat and the underlying inorganic deposits (sand and gravels), were calculated for each of the boreholes by subtracting depth from the surface elevations provided by the GPS survey. Across the whole of the survey area, basal elevations ranged from –5.09m OD to –0.41m OD, providing a mean basal elevation of 2.62m OD. The basal topography was modelled three-dimensionally using GIS to provide a continuous surface. Standard techniques were used to generate this 3D surface to eliminate the generation of spurious 'artefacts' in the data (Chapman and Cheetham, 2002; Chapman and Gearey, 2003; Chapman, 2006). Cell resolution for this surface was generated at 0.5m. The resulting model (Figure 4.9) shows the morphology of the pre-peat land surface with the projected edge of the floodplain during the Iron Age, based upon the elevation of dated archaeological features and levels from the excavations in 2006 and 2007.

Geophysics results

This section presents the results of these geophysical surveys, which comprised Magnetometry, Earth Resistance, Ground-Penetrating Radar, Electrical Imaging and Induced Polarisation (Figure 4.6). The data from the magnetometry surveys of Geophysical Survey Areas A, B and C revealed some large-scale variation across the site. Within Area A, the majority of features reflected small-scale magnetic anomalies resulting from ferrous type material. Towards the southern edge of Area A, adjacent to the centre of the projected alignment, were a series of possible pits or cut features, although it is possible that rotted wood may be the cause (see Fassbinder, 1990, 1993, for the mechanism and the results from Stanton Drew as a practical example, David *et al.*, 2004). In Area B, the magnetic background was significantly greater than in Area A with additional evidence for ferrous debris near the edge of the current field. The level of background noise makes it virtually impossible to identify any low level anomalies. In Area C, the responses and patterning of features in the data are typical of natural soil variation.

The Earth Resistance surveys within the three areas produced similar results to those from the magnetometry surveys. In general the values from the Twin Probe were very low, for the most part less than 10 ohms. However, the expectation of the Earth Resistance data was not to identify individual wooden stakes, but to identify trends of moisture variation that may indicate the alignment. Within Area A, the survey identified the edge of the 2007 trench in both the 1m and 0.5m data. There is a significant correlation between the two ER data-sets from Area 1, which may be expected in relatively homogenous deposits. There are individual high readings in the 0.5m data, but as they are isolated readings they are unlikely to be significant. High pass filtering of the data revealed differences between the two datasets for Area A, although the major discrepancy was a broad low resistance band in the 1m data that is at 45° to the presumed alignment of the stakes and therefore not thought to be associated with the site.

Both the 1m and 0.5m datasets from Area B revealed a band of high resistance at the eastern edge and it is assumed that the origin is pedological rather than archaeological. There are however some anomalies in the 0.5m data indicating a clear boundary almost running through the whole length of Area B. It is a coherent low resistance anomaly that may be flanked by a resistive 'lip' and a second similar anomaly can be seen at right angles to it. It is presumed that these anomalies indicate former field divisions, possibly ditches, and the general change in Earth Resistance levels either side of the main boundary suggests differing moisture regimes within different fields. Evidence for these changes within the deeper 1m data is scant and it must be assumed that the origins of anomalies are relatively shallow, and there are no indications of the timber alignment.

Within Geophysical Survey Area C, there was a reasonable amount of concordance between the two

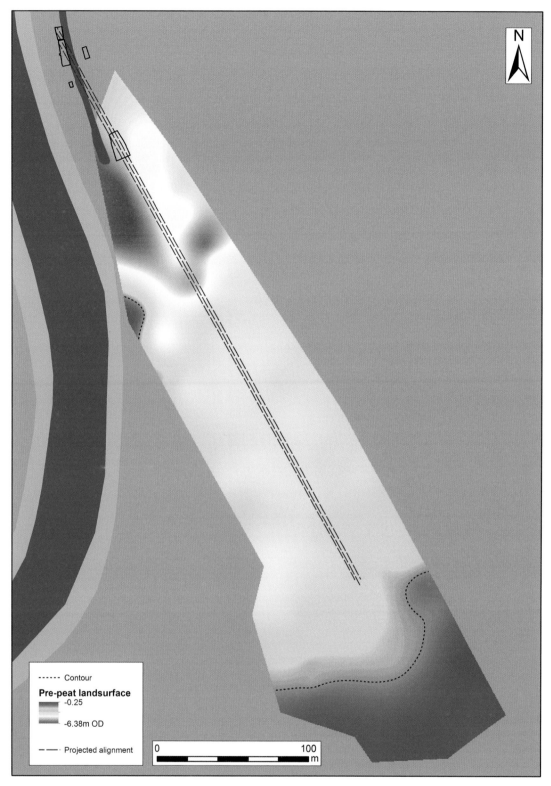

Figure 4.9: Pre-peat land surface modelled from borehole data. The projected alignment from 2006–2007 excavations is plotted at the top of the surveyed area, and the edge of the later prehistoric floodplain marked by the contour

ER data-sets. There was a general trend towards higher resistance toward the eastern edge of Area C. However, there is also an amorphous spread of resistive material in the 1m data, to the west of the presumed centre line of the timber alignment. It is assumed that this is likely to be pedological in origin. Again, there was no evidence for the timber alignment in either ER data-sets from this area.

The GPR survey focused on Geophysical Survey Areas

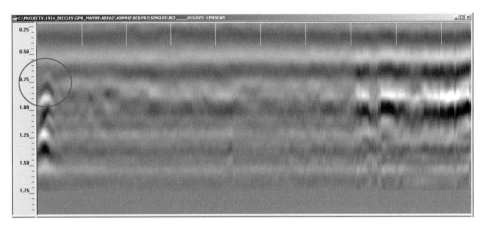

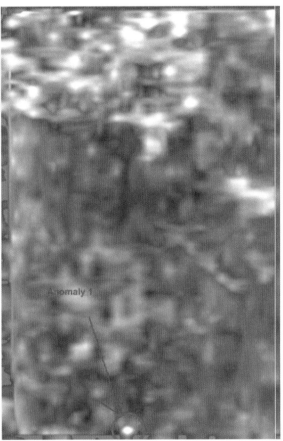

Figure 4.10: GPR results from Geophysical Area A showing a low amplitude response visible in both section and plan

A and B. Within Area A, the two GPR datasets have produced very few coherent anomalies. The 400MHz results were particularly featureless, even in the zone over the 2007 trench. However, the deeper penetrating (but poorer resolution) 200MHz antenna appears to map reasonably effectively the disturbance of the trench. Also there is some correlation between the position of the stakes revealed by the 2007 excavation and anomalies within the data. One single response of interest, but outside of the trench, was identified both in section and in plan (Figure 4.10). This low amplitude response was the only really distinct hyperbola in any of the GPR datasets, although the position of the response is unsatisfactory as it as at the edge of the survey.

Hyperbolas are the result of localised small features and it is hard to identify what sort of natural feature would be at this depth but it can be observed that the response is roughly on the centre line of the timber alignment.

Within Area B, the results were also relatively featureless, except for the eastern edge of the survey, which is the same area in which a significant increase in magnetic noise was identified. Within the 200MHz data, at a depth of approximately 0.75m, this feature correlated with a response in the 0.5 separation Twin Probe Earth Resistance data. Comparison with the Ordnance Survey 1st Edition (1:2500 scale) mapping revealed that the features identified in the geophysical results reflect a buried ditch that was present

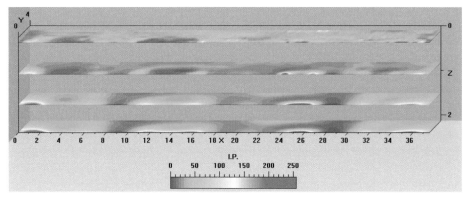

Area A Induced Polarisation. View from east

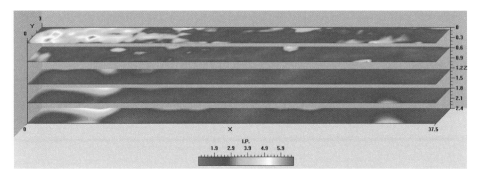

Area B. Induced Polarisation. View from north

Figure 4.11: Induced Polarisation results from Geophysical Survey Areas A and B

in the late 19th century, a continuation of which was also possibly observed in the Earth Resistance data. A single anomaly was identified just to the east of the centre line in both the 200MHz and 400MHz datasets, adjacent to the disturbed zone at the eastern edge of Area B. However, a small trial trench was excavated over this area and revealed the response to be natural (see Section 4.5 below).

Two areas were surveyed using Electrical Imaging (and replicated for Induced Polarisation – see Figure 4.6). Within Area A, the survey extended southwards from the area covered by the other techniques along the projected alignment of the site. Depth slices were generated at approximately 0.5m, 1.0m and 1.5m. The 0.5m surface was dominated by small, high resistance anomalies, presumably reflecting the changing nature of the near surface soil moisture content, although there was one coherent anomaly approximately 14m from the south of the 2007 trench edge. The other two depths show less background noise, although the edges of the survey appear to contain many individual high readings. However, within the central part of the survey can be seen a zone of low resistivity values that may be significant. There also appears to be similar weaker anomalies along the central line. While these results appear to endorse the potential for wet 'pockets' at depth, some caution must be recorded as the resolution at 1.5m is significantly less than at 0.5m.

Within Area B, the near surface results from the Electrical

Imaging again exhibited high and varied resistivity values. Three small high resistance anomalies have been identified at 0.5m depth. The 1.0m and 1.5m depth slices show some low resistivity patterning similar to that observed in Area A. As expected, the greater resolution is within the 1.0m data and the interpretation is that relatively damp zones have been mapped. These zones do not correlate with the high resistance anomalies seen in the 0.5m data. A deep 2m slice indicated a band of high resistance on the eastern side of Area B, which can also be partly identified at shallower depths. Comparison with the Ordnance Survey First Edition (1:2500 scale) mapping revealed that this is likely to reflect a buried 19th century ditch. It is probable that the infill of this ditch has produced the high resistivity zone at the eastern edge of the survey.

The Induced Polarisation data from Area A provides little in the way of coherent anomalous values. The majority of the anomalies were at the edge of the survey and these appear to 'ring' through the whole of the investigation depth. However, between 10m and 15m from the southern edge of the IP survey area were some positive anomalies that lie on the central alignment of the stakes (Figure 4.11). However, these are very small changes and given the depth the link to individual stakes is tenuous.

As with the Electrical Imaging data from Area B, the Induced Polarisation results revealed the most obvious anomalies were at depth on the eastern side of the survey

(Figure 4.11). The positive chargeability response is consistent with the type of response found by Aspinall and Lynam (1970) over a buried ditch. The near surface 0.5m results show a patchwork of small amplitude responses that have no clear patterning. Investigation of the 1.0m and 1.5m slices reveal few clear anomalies. However, within the central part of the survey a series of very slightly elevated responses were identified, which might represent possible anomalies within the suspected alignment.

Overall, the five different geophysical techniques used on the site aimed to explore the challenge of prospection within wetlands, and particularly in relation to identifying targets that are small and randomly positioned, at depth and displaying very little contrast with the peat that surrounds them. Despite these challenges, the results have demonstrated certain successes. Various anomalies were identified by Earth Resistance, Electrical Imaging and Induced Polarisation, which corresponded to features visible on late 19th century Ordnance Survey mapping. In addition, other possible features were identified in the GPR and Magnetometry datasets. There is some indication, particularly from the Induced Polarisation data, of variations associated with the projected triple timber alignment, which required ground-truthing. However, there was nothing to indicate that any of the techniques applied to the site would be able to establish the presence or absence of a previously unknown site with any certainty.

4.4 Excavations and analyses

The airborne remote sensing did not identify any features or anomalies to inform subsequent phases of fieldwork. However, the deposit model (Figure 4.9) identified two main features: firstly, a possible 'embayment' in the morphology of the basal gravels, which may be associated with a Late-glacial/early Holocene course of the River Waveney. This feature is beneath a maximum of c. 6m of floodplain peat, the base of which dates to the early Holocene (see Chapter 3), and is hence well below Iron Age levels. It is unlikely that this had any significance in terms of the later prehistoric landscape, and the peat across the study area shows very little variation that might be related to differences in formation processes (see also Chapter 3). However, extrapolation of the elevation of the ground surface during the Iron Age (based on previous excavations) permitted the identification of the southern floodplain edge in later prehistory. This indicates the maximum extent of the peat deposits and hence the hypothetical maximum extent of the timber alignment (assuming no deviation in the projected alignment).

The five different geophysical techniques were inconclusive in terms of identifying the timber alignment, although subsequent excavation demonstrated that many of the grids were located off the alignment itself (see below). The most pronounced anomaly was identified using GPR in Area 1 with a further highly tentative anomaly in Area 2. These data were thus regarded as of little direct

application in terms of planning further excavation at the site. In practice, it became evident that the orientation of the structure was not entirely straight, meaning that several of the geophysics grids were not positioned over the archaeology.

Trench array

A total of six trenches was excavated (Figures 4.12) at the site. Since the remote sensing and geophysical methods failed to provide any information regarding the possible orientation of the alignment, the locations of these trenches was based on linear projections of the structure from one location to the next. Excavation and sampling methodologies are outlined in Chapter 1.

Site stratigraphy, palaeoenvironmental and archaeological wood analyses and chronology

Previous investigations had established the depth and character of the floodplain deposits and indicated that there was rather little variation in the stratigraphy of the sediments associated with the main phase of activity during the later prehistoric period (see Chapter 2 and above; also Gearey *et al.*, 2011). In general, the peat deposits associated with the archaeological sequences described in this chapter were recorded as red-brown, moderately humified herbaceous peat with abundant monocotyledonous and wood remains (natural as well as archaeological). These peats were often slightly silty with rare lenses of grey sand and small fragments of natural flint. There was little variation in the stratigraphy of the deposits across the excavated trenches and hence no further discussion of site stratigraphy is provided for each individual trench. The upper peats that sealed the archaeology were in general desiccated due to the depth of the water table across the study area (see Chapter 6) and capped by a layer of dry, grey-orange, mottled silty clay of variable thickness (0.30–0.60m) from which the floodplain top soil was derived.

Palaeoenvironmental assessment and analyses focused on pollen, plant macrofossils and Coleoptera. This sampling phase was tied closely to the soil chemistry analyses and water table monitoring to permit the physical sediment characteristics to be related to the quality of preservation of the environmental proxies (Chapter 6). Palaeoenvironmental analyses of these three proxies focused on two sequences in the form of monolith and bulk samples from Trench 1 (0.30–1.10m) and Trench 4 (0.60–1.0m). Seven bulk samples were taken from the north facing section of Trench 1 and five bulk samples from the southern face of Trench 4. Sediment samples were also collected for geochemical analyses (see below). Sampling of archaeological wood followed the methodology outlined in Chapter 1. Dendrochronology and radiocarbon dating provided the site chronology and phasing discussed below (see also Chapter 1).

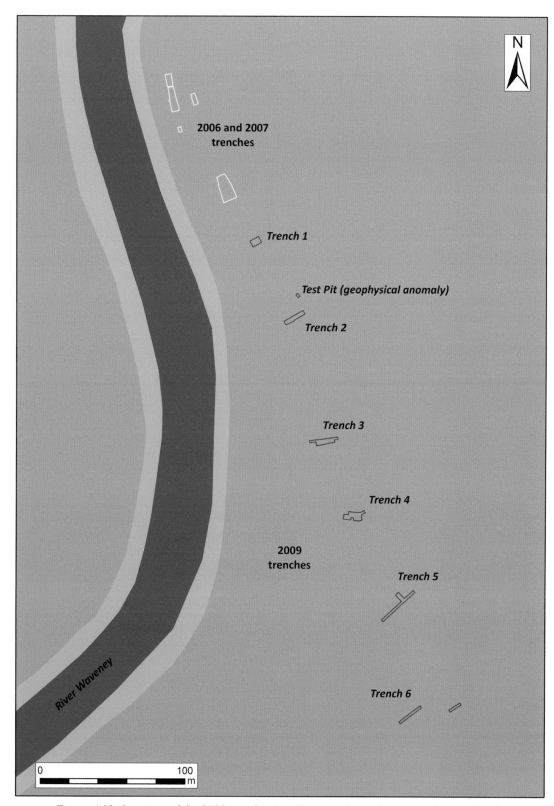

Figure 4.12: Location of the 2009 trenches in relation to the earlier excavations at Beccles

Condition assessment of timber, soil chemistry and water table modelling

The condition assessment studies aimed to produce a picture of the physical and chemical characteristics of the archaeological wood (Panter and Spriggs, 1996). This was to formulate an understanding of the history of the structure, both pre- and stake-deposition; and establish a profile of the chemical and physico-chemical make-up of the wood,

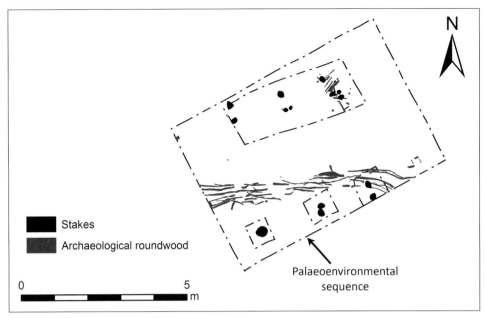

Figure 4.13: Plan of Trench 1 (2009)

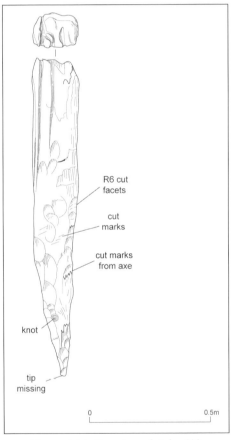

Figure 4.14: Drawing of stake 612

thereby establishing a 'baseline' condition of the current state of preservation of the structure.

Soil samples were collected and analysed for the principal redox sensitive parameters (sulphate, sulphide,

nitrate, nitride and ammonia) as well as for pH and organic matter content (through Loss on Ignition tests) to provide baseline data on the nature of the burial environment, indicating whether conditions were reducing (and therefore suitable for *in situ* preservation of organic material) or oxidising (aggressive towards organic preservation). This work was intended to complement the subsequent ground water monitoring programme, also discussed in Chapter 6. Following the establishment of the extent and character of the archaeological remains through excavation, a network of piezometers was installed to permit fluctuations in the ground water table at the site to be modelled. Subsequent monitoring of ground water levels was undertaken at intervals of 2 weeks over a period of two years (see Chapter 1). The data from the ground water monitoring was subsequently modelled within a GIS environment to investigate relationships with the archaeo-environmental record (e.g. Chapman and Cheetham, 2002; Van de Noort *et al.*, 2002); these results are discussed in Chapter 6.

4.5 Results from 2009 excavations at Beccles

Trench 1

Trench 1 (Figure 4.13) measured 6.80 × 4.80m and the top of the archaeology was encountered at –1.02m OD. The uppermost archaeological feature was a cluster of roundwood orientated north-west to south-east (770–860) and not wholly perpendicular to the timber alignment. This was divided into two layers (1 and 2) for the purposes of sub-sampling, and was recorded and sub-sampled for species ID, ring counting and radiocarbon dating. This feature, which was interpreted as a trackway, was in poor condition as it was located predominantly in the drier upper

Figure 4.15: Stake 1062 with horizontal inserted into halving lap joint. Stake 1134 bottom left had been sampled for dendrochronology.

Figure 4.16: Stake packing around stake 1062 (before 1134 had been sampled for dendrochronology)

peat of the floodplain. When the upper portion was lifted (layer 1) it was found to overlie one of the central upright stakes (853). Unambiguous stratigraphic relationships between different components of the site were rare and this represents one of only two examples where structures overlie the tops of the stakes, providing information regarding aspects of monument form and phasing (see below, also Trench 4). Three samples of wood from this trackway were subsequently submitted for radiocarbon dating (SUERC-32931, 32935 and 32936).

After the initial cleaning and recording of the trackway a section was excavated to include two rows of stakes (603, 604, 608, 612, 613, 729, 730 and 733) at the north end of the trench (Figure 4.14). This section was also excavated in three 0.10m spits and the wood debris was recorded as in Trench 1. The debris in this trench was much sparser and contained more horizontal rod-like pieces than other trenches (e.g. 736 and 840). Trench 1 also contained six upright stakes representing two rows of the alignment. One

triple group of stakes in a single cluster (612, 613 and 744) was extracted for analysis.

Once the roundwood feature described above had been lifted and sampled, the three southern-most stakes (882, 1014, 1044, 1053 and 1062) were box-sectioned. These box-sections revealed a complex series of small upright stakes and horizontal timbers, some of which were inserted into notches in the upright stakes (stakes 1062, 1044 and 882, Figure 4.15). This relationship between the notches and horizontal timbers was similar to that identified in the 2007 excavations (see above). The upright stake (1062) also had two half-split pieces of *Quercus* wedged in at angles around it (Figure 4.16) possibly to support or 'pack' the stake in its upright position. A number of roundwood rods and squared-up stakes of unclear function were located around this stake, although one of which (1147) appeared to peg down a large piece of felling debris (1138).

Trench 2

Trench 2 (14.93 × 2.78m; Figure 4.17) was oriented north-east to south-west across the projected timber alignment, as derived from the results of earlier excavations. However, the alignment deviated from the projection and the first archaeological features were encountered 10m to the west of the estimated position. The final trench measured 14.93 × 2.78m and the top of the archaeology was reached at –1.02m OD. An initial surface collection of wood debris was carried out over the whole trench. A section (measuring 3 × 1.50m) was then excavated across the alignment to sample the wood debris, which was removed in three 0.10m spits. The debris field became less dense with depth and towards the base of the section consisted solely of large pieces of degraded bark and compressed roundwood (1210–1214, Figure 4.18 marked by yellow tags).

Within the section three upright stakes (600, 601 and 602) were identified. Stakes 600 and 602 displayed notches (halving lap joints, Figure 4.18) similar to those identified in the 2006/2007 excavations. There were no horizontal timbers associated with the notches as was observed in the case of the Trench 2 stakes (see below). Other material recorded in this trench included a horizontal, north-south orientated tree trunk 652 (to the north of stake 600). This displayed evidence of working at one end and due to its size only the worked end was recovered with the remaining trunk left *in situ*. Two clusters of un-abraded sherds of pottery, including the rim and base of vessels, were found to the south of stake 600.

Trench 3

Trench 3 (Figure 4.19) was located 78m to the south of Trench 2 and was positioned across the revised alignment derived from the excavations of Trenches 1 and 2 (see above). This trench measured 19.45 × 3.65m and the archaeology was encountered at –1.10m OD. A dense field of wooden debris and six upright stakes (958, 959, 960, 961,

Figure 4.17: Plan of Trench 2 (2009)

Figure 4.18 Stakes and debris field at the northern end of Trench 2 (2009), showing the positions of halving lap joints in Stakes 600 and 602, indicated by white arrows

962 and 963) were revealed, representing two complete rows of the timber alignment. Two small box sections were excavated to facilitate sampling of the uprights. Only the upper most levels of the archaeology were recorded and selectively sub-sampled.

Several highly degraded horizontal timbers were present amongst the dense debris field, including one east-west orientated timber, which appeared to overlie a north-south orientated beam (Figure 4.20: 1175 and 1176). Two other large horizontal timbers were also recorded to the east (1174) and west (1172) of the outer stakes of the alignment and were sub-sampled for analysis; again due to their size, a small amount was removed and the remainder of the timber was left *in situ*. A total of fifty sherds of pottery were recovered from this trench, found in a discrete scatter to the east of the alignment.

Trench 4

Trench 4 (Figure 4.21) was located 50m to the south-east of Trench 3 across the revised projection of the alignment derived from Trenches 1 to 3 (see above). This trench measured 11 × 6.27m and the archaeology was encountered at –1.072m OD. A single row of three clusters of upright stakes (1215 1220 1221, 1216 1217 1222 and 1218 1245 1246) was identified and each stake cluster was box-sectioned. The alignment had been truncated by a north-east to south-west orientated ditch infilled by a grey, silt-clay deposit. The ditch terminated in a butt-end to the

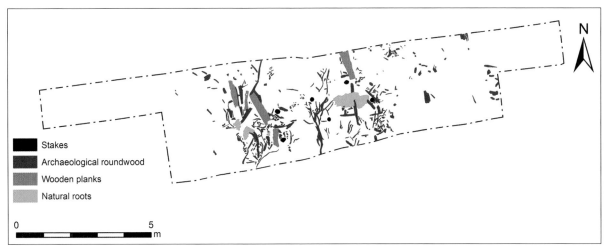

Figure 4.19: Plan of Trench 3 (2009)

north of stake cluster (1215–1220) and had also disturbed the stakes in the ground. The main feature in this trench was an arrangement of 17 large wooden 'beams' aligned north-west to south-east (Figure 4.22). The beams varied in length (0.63–1.94m) and state of preservation, and had been truncated by the ditch described previously.

This feature also displayed a stratigraphic relationship with the upright stakes, as one of the beams (1219) appeared to have overlain the top of a stake (1222, Figure 4.23). These beams contrast with the sections of ground level structures identified in other trenches, (i.e. Trench 2 see above and excavations in 2006/2007). Samples of the beams were taken for radiocarbon dating (OxA-23863). A small area was sub-sampled for debris that was taken as a bulk sample. The remainder of the wood debris was left *in situ*. A single sherd of pottery similar in form and fabric to that from Trench 3 was also recovered.

Figure 4.20: Possible collapsed and degraded plank overlying horizontal beam

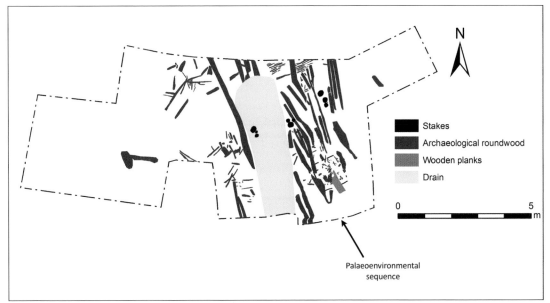

Figure 4.21: Plan of Trench 4 (2009)

Figure 4.22: Trench 4 beams looking south (with later ditch-cut to the right)

Figure 4.23: Beam (below scale bar) overlying stake 1222

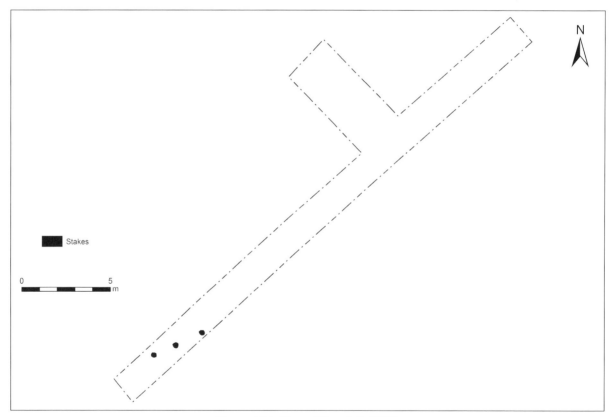

Figure 4.24: Plan of Trench 5 (2009)

Trench 5

Trench 5 (Figure 4.24) was positioned 67m to the south-east of Trench 4 and was positioned across the alignment as projected from the previous trench; although again the archaeology was located to the west of this point demonstrating the unpredictability of the alignment over distance. The trench measured 30m x 1.80m and the archaeology was encountered at –1.10m OD. The alignment was represented by three upright stakes (1184, 1185, 1186; Figure 4.25), of which one (1185) was extracted. This trench was recorded in plan and photographed, but no sections were excavated and for the most part the archaeology was left *in situ*. Isolated scatters of woodworking debris were recorded 10m to the east of the alignment; this was noted as unusual since the debris fields in the previous trenches were rarely located more than a few metres from the stakes.

Trench 6

Trench 6 (Figure 4.26) was positioned 68m to the south-west of Trench 5 and measured 18.41 × 1.80m and the archaeology was encountered at –0.97m OD. This trench was excavated in order to locate the terminus of the alignment. The peat in this trench was shallow (0.70m) and the highly degraded tips of three upright stakes (Figure 4.27, stakes 1248, 1249 and 1250) were recovered.

Figure 4.25: Heavily truncated remains of the alignment in Trench 5

Otherwise this trench was devoid of any debris or natural wood. This trench falls close to the southern terminus of the monument and it is clear that peat wastage has significantly affected the preservation of the archaeology at this floodplain-dryland interface.

Test pit

A test pit measuring 1.5 × 2.6m and 0.90m deep was excavated by machine (see Figure 4.12 for location) to ground truth an anomaly identified by geophysical survey (see above). In the southern limit of the test pit a silt infilled cut *c*. 1.2m wide was identified, which seemed to represent the butt end of a post-medieval field drain and was similar in character to those identified in other trenches (e.g. Trench 4). Although these features are not marked on the 1st edition Ordnance Survey 25in County Series mapping, they probably relate to the post-medieval drainage of the floodplain. No other archaeological material was recovered from this test pit.

4.6 Post-excavation analyses

This section describes the post-excavation study that included analysis of the archaeological wood, palaeoenvironmental assessments and analyses, dendrochronological and radiocarbon dating. A number of small finds including pottery and flint were also recovered during the excavations and these are described below.

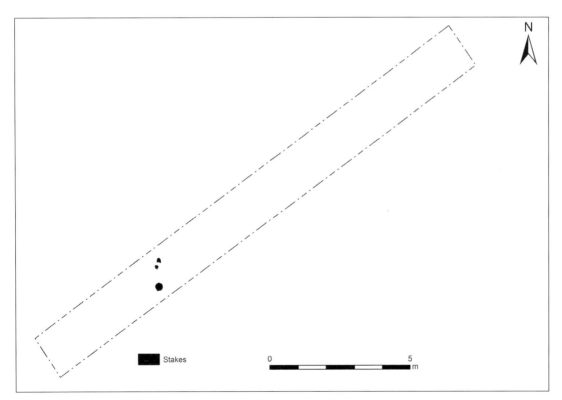

Figure 4.26: Plan of Trench 6 (2009)

Figure 4.27: Surviving tips of alignment stakes in Trench 6

Archaeological wood analyses

The following section presents the analyses of the archaeological wood assemblages by trench. The excavation produced a relatively large assemblage of six hundred and seventy-three wood records. Several of these represent bulk collections of wood chips, bark and roundwood, not all of which were fully recorded, as well as a significant quantity of timber and woodworking debris (Tables 4.1 and 4.2). Thirty-three of the items assigned as timber were the upright stakes of the alignment. The four artefacts were: a peg, a possible rope runner and two dowels that may have formed handles of some sort (Figure 4.28, see below).

Trench 1 (2009)

TRENCH 1 (2009) ARTEFACTS

A single artefact was recovered from Trench 1, an ovoid dowel 993 (200 × 35 × 30mm), which scored a 4 for condition and had been hewn from oak heartwood. One end was cross cut with a slightly worn, convex profile, probably representing the butt end of the broken handle of an unknown tool.

TRENCH 1 (2009) TIMBERS

Fourteen upright stakes were recorded in Trench 1 forming two rows of the alignment. Several of these stakes had one or more vertical stakes inserted adjacent to them, possibly to support or 'pack' the stake. Upright stake 603 was supported by roundwood stake 1056 and timber debris stake 1070. Upright stake 1062 was supported by timber stakes 1151, 1151/2, 1061/2 and timber debris stakes 1136, 1062/2 and 1147/2. Upright stake 1134 was supported by roundwood stakes 1135 and 1147/3. A final two items recovered from this trench were classed as timber: 1094, a radial quarter split stake; and 750, an unconverted *Quercus* (oak) stake. One sample of debris was submitted from this trench for radiocarbon dating (OxA-23831; see below).

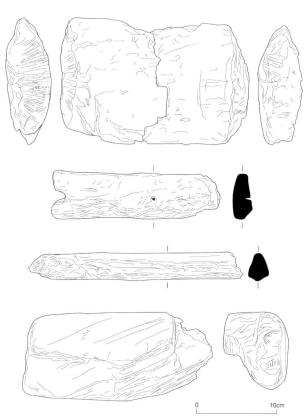

Figure 4.28: Artefacts and timber debris (from top: 1137, 1077, 708. Object 039 is included here but was recovered from Trench 1 of the 2006 excavations)

Table 4.1: Frequency of wood records

Trench	Wood records
1	266
2	319
3	14
4	66
5	5
6	3
Total	673

Table 4.2: Frequencies of wood categories within assemblage

Category	Frequency	% assemblage	Additional records representing bulk collections
Unassigned	4	0.6	–
Artefact	4	0.6	–
Bark	7	1.1	5
Debris	58	9.1	1
Root	47	7.4	2
Roundwood	224	35.5	9
Timber	62	9.8	–
Timber debris	90	14.2	–
Wood chips	138	21.8	22
Total	634	100.0	39

Brushwood structure (Trench 1 2009)

A discrete structure in Trench 1 was identified and interpreted as a brushwood trackway (Figure 4.29). The trackway was formed of two distinct layers of roundwood aligned west-north-west to east-south-east and hence almost perpendicular to the axis of the triple-stake row. The feature was approximately 0.8m wide and although its full extent could not be identified as it extended beyond the limits of the trench, a 6.25m length was exposed and recorded (Figure 4.13). Lying stratigraphically above the decayed top of upright stake 853, the date of construction of this feature therefore represents a *terminus post quem* for the decay of any above ground portion of the upright stakes at this location (see below). The upper section of the structure appears to have been divided into three discrete 'bundles' of roundwood that are discussed separately below (Layer 1A, 1B and 1C). A further layer of roundwood was located below these distinct bundles (Layer 2). Three samples of roundwood from separate sections of this feature were submitted for radiocarbon dating (SUERC-32931 (860), SUERC-32935 (773) and SUERC-32936 (797) (see below).

Figure 4.29: Brushwood trackway identified in Trench 1 (2009)

The condition of the material forming the trackway ranged from poor to good, with the majority of the material described as being in a moderate condition. This reflects the location of the structure in the upper, drier parts of the peat deposits, just below the preservation horizon for waterlogged wood (see Chapter 6). The majority of samples were well enough preserved to be identified to species, to count growth rings and to record any evidence of woodworking. Sub-samples for microscopic analysis were recovered from the proximal ends of the stems. The following section describes the results from the excavations of the structure stratigraphically, from the upper layer (1A) down to the lower layer (2).

Layer 1A

The western section of the structure consisted of twenty-three pieces of roundwood; all samples in a suitable condition for microscopic analysis were identified as alder (*Alnus glutinosa* – 21 items) (Table 4.3). The roundwood varied in length from 150–1720mm and in diameter from 15–56mm. Ring counts were recovered from 15 items, with ages ranging from 4 to 9 years of growth. The season of felling was apparent for 13 items; 12 were felled in winter and one in spring. Fifteen items were noted as having the straight, even stems with central piths, devoid of side-branches that may be indicative of coppiced material (Rackham, 1977). Three items had been trimmed at one end from one direction to form a chisel point and one item was radially half split.

Layer 1B

The central section consisted of nineteen pieces of roundwood; all samples in a suitable condition for microscopic analysis were identified as alder (*Alnus glutinosa* – 15 items) (Table 4.3). The roundwood varied in length from 120–1486mm and in diameter from 13.5–74mm. Ring counts were recovered from 15 items, with ages ranging from 5 to 14 years of growth. The season of felling was apparent for 15 items; 12 were felled in winter and three in spring. Fourteen items were noted as having the straight, even stems with central piths, devoid of side-branches that may be indicative of coppiced material (Rackham, 1977). Eight items had been trimmed at one end from one direction to form a chisel point.

Table 4.3: Trench 1 brushwood trackway wood analyses data

Layer	Frequency	Length (mm)	Diameter (mm)	Growth rings	Frequency winter felled	Frequency spring felled	Frequency morphological coppicing evidence	Frequency trimmed end
Layer 1a	N=23	150–1720	15–56	4–9	12	1	15	3
Layer 1b	N=19	120–1486	13.5–74	5–14	12	3	14	8
Layer 1c	N=21	121–1380	13–55	4–13	9	3	17	8
Layer 2	N=36	101–939	10–91.5	2–12	17	10	31	4
TOTAL	N=99				50	17	77	23

Layer 1C

The central section consisted of 21 pieces of roundwood; all samples in a suitable condition for microscopic analysis were identified as *Alnus glutinosa* (13 items) (Table 4.3). The roundwood varied in length from 121–1380mm and in diameter from 13–55mm. Ring counts were recovered from 13 items, with ages ranging from 4 to 13 years of growth. The season of felling was apparent for 12 items; nine were felled in winter and three in spring. Seventeen items were noted as having the straight, even stems with central piths, devoid of side-branches that may be indicative of coppiced material (Rackham, 1977). Eight items had been trimmed at one end from one direction to form a chisel point.

Layer 2

This group lay beneath parts 1A, 1B and 1C, extending for the same length and in the same direction as the three upper groups. Layer 2 consisted of 36 pieces of roundwood; all samples in a suitable condition for microscopic analysis were identified as *Alnus glutinosa* (29 items) (Table 4.3). The roundwood varied in length from 101–939mm and in diameter from 10–91.5mm. Ring counts were recovered from 29 items, with ages ranging from 2 to 12 years of growth. The season of felling was apparent for 27 items: 17 were felled in winter and ten in spring. Thirty-one items were noted as having the straight, even stems with central piths, devoid of side-branches that may be indicative of coppiced material (Rackham, 1977). Four items had been trimmed at one end from one direction to form a chisel point. A vertical, alder heartwood, tangentially cleft peg was recovered from this layer. The peg measured 155 × 39 × 21mm and had been trimmed at the lower end from one direction to form a tapered point.

DISCUSSION: TRENCH 1 BRUSHWOOD STRUCTURE 09

All material that was identifiable was alder (78%), which is known to coppice well and also preserves well in wet environments (Gale and Cutler, 2000; Rackham, 2001). Alder carr was certainly present on the floodplain during the later prehistoric period (see Chapter 2 and below) and it seems probable that this wood was sourced locally. There are numerous other examples of its use in prehistoric trackways (Meddens and Beasley, 1990; Crockett *et. al.*, 2002; Taylor, 2010: 79). There are also other examples from prehistory of roundwood bundles being utilised to build trackways across wetlands. A Bronze Age example from Rainham, Essex, was constructed from overlapping bundles of coppiced alder (Meddens and Beasley, 1990). Another Bronze Age trackway from Barking, London, was formed of bundles of brushwood held in place by occasional vertical stakes (Meddens, 1996). Perhaps the best-known example is the Neolithic Honeygore track from the Somerset Levels, formed of bundles of birch roundwood, secured in places by wooden stakes (Coles *et al.*, 1985).

The presence of (often proximal) ends trimmed from one direction (often with a single blow) may represent either trimming to length or the primary harvesting of roundwood from woodland. Although it seems common sense that the roundwood was carried to the site in the bundles recorded during the excavation, the tempting hypothesis that each the bundles of layer 1 represent a single harvesting event does not hold true. Although there is a bias towards winter felled stems within each analytical unit and across the assemblage (50% in total), spring felled stems are also identified within each analytical unit. This suggests that neither the discrete bundles of Layer 1, nor the material forming Layer 2, were harvested at a single moment in time. However, there is good morphological evidence to suggest that the roundwood stems from which the trackway was constructed may have been derived from woodland management in the form of coppicing. Although no coppice heels were encountered, 77% of the material was noted as having the straight, even stems with central pith and a low prevalence of side branches often indicative of coppicing (Rackham, 1977).

As discussed elsewhere, it is difficult to disentangle possible felling and woodland management strategies from archaeological wood data (Out *et. al.*, 2013). Despite the prevalence of material within the archaeological record that from a morphological perspective appears to be coppiced, disentangling the signals that would arise from different woodland management techniques (including coppicing with or without defined periodic cycles) and different felling strategies (i.e. clear-felling or draw felling) often proves elusive.

In terms of diameter, the material is relatively tightly grouped with 84% falling between 10mm–39mm, suggesting that draw felling may have been used (selecting material for harvesting by diameter) (Figure 4.30). Interestingly, 96% of the material falls within the 10–60mm zone described by Taylor (2003, figure 3.34: 47) as being the 'norm' for coppiced prehistoric roundwood. Although there are peaks in the growth ring data at 4, 5 and 8 years, the distribution is too diffuse to support any hypothesis of coppicing utilising a periodic cycle (Figure 4.31). The distribution is similarly diffuse when diameter and growth are plotted together (Figure 4.32), again providing no evidence for coppicing on a defined periodic rotation.

It seems likely that the roundwood stems were harvested utilising draw felling and it is tempting to suggest that the wood was sourced locally given the evidence for alder carr on the floodplain (see below, also Chapter 2). Although the morphological evidence suggests the material may have originated from managed coppiced woodland, the growth ring data provides no evidence for defined periodic harvesting cycles. The presence of both winter and spring harvested stems in each of the analytical units suggests that the material was brought from a store of wood. The lower part of the structure (Layer 2) seems to be formed of a continuous layer of roundwood stems with at least one retaining peg present, whereas the upper Layer 1 (A, B and C) was constructed from discrete bundles of roundwood.

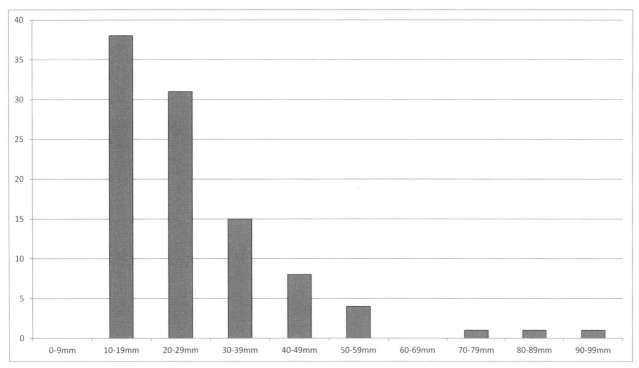

Figure 4.30: Trench 1 brushwood structure – wood diameter counts

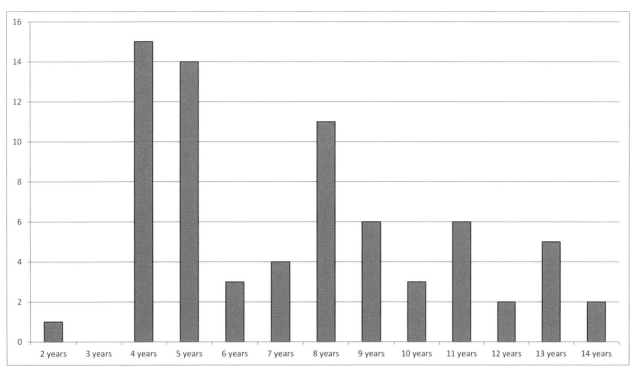

Figure 4.31: Roundwood ring counts from Trench 1 brushwood structure (N = 72)

Trench 2 (2009)

TRENCH 2 (2009) ARTEFACTS

Three artefacts were recovered from the debris scatter. Item 708, a rough dowel (269 × 34 × 29mm) scored a 4

for condition (Figure 4.33) and was fashioned from slow grown, oak heartwood and is a radial 1/8 conversion that had been hewn roughly circular. One end had been trimmed from one direction. This item may represent the broken handle of an unknown item.

Down by the river

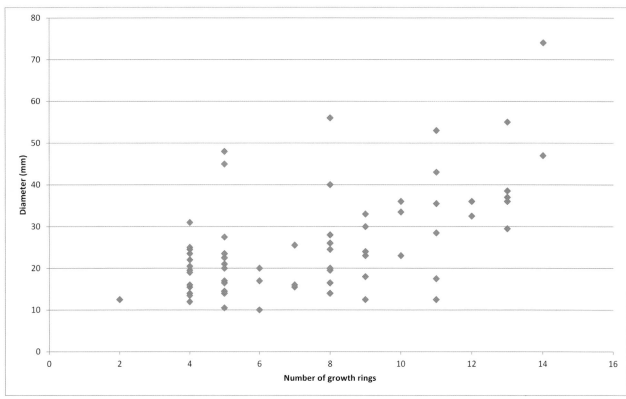

Figure 4.32: Diameter of roundwood plotted against growth rings

Figure 4.33: 708 Dowel (Scale in cm)

Figure 4.34: 1077 Rope runner? (scale in cm)

Tapered, square peg 932 (320 × 75 × 70mm) scored a 3 for condition. It has been fashioned from oak heartwood with the thick end cross-cut. Although the item's surface describes evidence of use-wear, the original function is unknown.

Artefact 1077 (220 × 55 × 25mm) scored a 4 for condition (Figure 4.34). Formed of oak heartwood, it is a radially aligned fragment, broken in antiquity across a centrally aligned circular hole, with a diameter of 20mm. The item appears similar in form to examples of medieval rope runners.

Three stakes of the alignment and three horizontal timbers were present in this trench. Immediately to the south of the stakes, a large unconverted timber 1210 (3120mm in length with a heavily compressed diameter of 260 × 30mm) lay across the full axis of the alignment with one end trimmed from one direction. This item retained its bark and scored a 2 for condition. Timber 622 (670 × 120 × 120mm) had been converted into a boxed heart from *Quercus* sapwood and heartwood and scored a 3 for condition. Three faces had been split, with the fourth face displaying evidence of hewing. One end had been cross cut and the other trimmed from one direction. Timber 652 (3310 × 275 × 160mm) was a radial quarter split, with the proximal end displaying a complete felling scar. Tool marks recorded from the two faces of the felling scar suggest that two distinct tools were used during the felling process (side A 49:3mm and 41:4mm, side B 54:1mm). A sample was taken from this timber for radiocarbon dating (OxA-23832).

Trench 3

The material in this trench was generally in a poor to moderate condition, with a high degree of compression damage. Six single upright stakes of the triple row, representing two complete chords across the alignment, as well as an extensive debris scatter were recorded but no sections were excavated. A number of horizontal timbers were evident: Timber 1174 (1110 × 230 × 160mm) had been radially half split and trimmed at one end from one direction and lay split face up, aligned with the axis of the triple stake row, to the east of the eastern stake row and extending into the northern baulk. This item is reminiscent of the beams seen in Trench 4 (below). Another beam, unconverted timber 1176 (1640mm long with a diameter of 90mm) lay to the south of and in line with timber 1174. Timber 1176 (930 × 480 × 50mm) lay below extensively degraded timber 1175. The majority of the sapwood was degraded with little of the heartwood remaining.

Timber 1172 lay to the west of the triple stake row, aligned along its axis and represents a possible beam, as recorded in Trench 4. It is a radial half, lying converted face up. It is unclear whether this is a cultural conversion or the result of degradation and decay. One end was cross cut. Three samples from these timbers were submitted for radiocarbon dating: two samples of the outer rings of Timber 1172 (OxA-23828 and 23829), and a single sample of the outer rings of Timber 1174 (OxA-23830) (see below).

Trench 4

This trench displayed evidence of multiple phases of activity. The most recent phase was a linear cut, orientated north-north-west to south-south-east, which extended 5.1m into the trench from the southern baulk and was some 2m wide, terminating in a butt-end to north, which has been interpreted as a drainage ditch. All three rows of the timber alignment were present, arranged in three clusters of three (west: 1215, 1220 and 1221; central: 1216, 1217 and 1222; east: 1218, 1245 and 1246) and identified as *Quercus* in the round with no bark remaining. Five of these stakes were extracted and recorded: all had been trimmed at their lower ends to a tapered point and varied in length between 185–1190mm with diameters from 170–280mm. In the eastern cluster, a smaller radially cleft piece of *Quercus*, 1247 (560 × 80 × 58mm) had been inserted vertically down the eastern side of upright 1245. The western-most cluster was severely truncated by the ditch described above. A debris field of roots, roundwood and wood chips was also present, although somewhat less dense than observed in the trenches further to the north.

A total of 25 horizontal timbers (beams) were recorded in this trench and were parallel to the timber alignment extending across its full width (*c.* 4m). There was also a direct stratigraphic relationship between the beams and the uprights of the timber alignment – beam 1219 overlay stake 1222. There was a high degree of variation in the size of the material, with the beams varying in length between 425–4090mm and in diameter between *c.* 70–300mm. The diameter was approximate as a high degree of horizontal compression was prevalent within the assemblage. The relatively poor condition of this group of timbers might relate directly to the shallower depth of the archaeological deposits at this location (see Chapter 6).

Beams 1191, 1195 and 1202 have been identified as *Quercus* (oak) and the other twenty beams as *Alnus* (alder). No clear spatial patterning of species was noted. Of the 25 beams, ten have one or more side branches with a maximum of four side branches overall. In the majority of cases, tool facets were present where the side branches had been trimmed away. The beams were derived from wood that was generally short-lived and fast-grown. The majority of the material (19 items) was in the round and only two items, 1198 and 1223, were positively identified as having been converted via splitting. The north end of beam 1198 was radially half split, fading out 0.6m along the length of the timber and was laid split face down. Beam 1223 was radially half split and although the converted face lay upwards in the ground, it was covered by another beam. As the converted surfaces were highly degraded it was not possible to ascertain whether the material had been converted by cultural or natural processes, or a combination of the two.

Evidence for anthropogenic modification of the beams was present in the form of both tool facets and marks. Six of the beams had been trimmed to length, including one item (1189) that had been trimmed at both ends. Seven of the beams (including two that were also trimmed to length) displayed evidence of the removal of one or more side branches, but only two of the beams (1189 and 1196) had a recordable tool mark. A sample was taken from one of the beams (1190) for radiocarbon dating (OxA-23863) (see below).

For the most part the beams respected the upright stakes, suggesting they were placed after the stakes were inserted. However, beam 1219 was recorded as overlying upright stake 1222 (Figure 4.35), which appears to indicate that the stake had rotted-off to this level prior to the placing of this beam on the overlying ground surface. This may lend further weight to the hypothesis that the clusters of stakes identified in some locations represent an initial construction phase with a subsequent phase or phases of repair.

Alternatively, it is possible that the apparent relationship between beam and stake resulted from disturbance to one or both at some point following construction, perhaps associated with truncation by the later ditch. Despite the poor preservation of the beams, there is still strong evidence for anthropogenic modification in the form of both splitting and trimming to length. Similarly, their position and orientation in and around the uprights of the timber alignment are suggestive of careful and deliberate placement, broadly oriented parallel to the axis of the timber alignment. The relationship of beam 1219 overlying stake 1222 may hint that this stake had rotted off before the beam was placed suggesting a phase of construction/repair. The beams are not particularly tightly packed but may have functioned as a section of raised walkway or perhaps platform.

Figure 4.35: Close-up of beam overlying stake 1222

TRENCH 4 SONDAGES

During the excavation of the 1m sample areas in Trench 4 all the material encountered was recorded as one of three categories: 1231 (roundwood), 1232 (wood chips/debris) and 1233 (bark). Roundwood 1231 contained thirty-four fragments that were recorded as an assemblage. All items (diameters varying between 15–95mm) scored a 4 for condition and had their bark, sapwood and heartwood present. No woodworking evidence was noted. A single piece of roundwood (d: 32mm) displayed woodworking evidence (1231/2) in the form of a trimmed end.

Thirteen pieces of debris were recovered and individually recorded: 1232/1 to 1232/9, 1233/2, 1233/3, and 1233/4 and 1233/6. Nine of these were identified as *Quercus*, one *Fraxinus excelsior* and the remaining were unidentified. Of the 13 items, eight were wood chips, three were debris and two were timber debris. Five of the wood chips were radially aligned, two tangentially aligned and one was derived from a piece of roundwood.

Trench 5

A single stake (1184) (435mm in length, maximum diameter of 110mm), which possibly corresponds to the western-most row of the triple alignment, was recorded in this trench. Only the lower tip of this stake survived, worked in the round and trimmed from all directions to a tapered point. Four isolated items were recovered from some 10m to the west of this stake: two pieces of roundwood (1186 and 1188) and two pieces of timber debris (1185 and 1187). These items are unusual on the site in that they occur at some

distance from the triple stake row, but it is unclear if they are contemporary with the timber alignment.

Trench 6

The tip of an upright stake (59 × 230mm) (1248) and two timber debris stakes were recovered from this trench. The two timber debris stakes were hard and fibrous, which may indicate that they represent a later phase of activity, but no radiocarbon dates are available to test this hypothesis.

4.6.1 Small finds: pottery, burnt flint

A combined total of two hundred and forty two sherds of pottery weighing 1097g were collected from forty-five contexts/find spots during the 2006, 2007 and 2009 excavations. The quantities by period are summarised in Table 4.4. The assemblage was analysed using the Prehistoric Ceramic Research Group Guidelines for Analysis and Publication (PCRG, 2009). The total assemblage was studied and a full catalogue prepared. The sherds were examined using a binocular microscope (×10 magnification) and were divided into fabric groups defined on the basis of inclusion types. Fabric codes were prefixed by a letter code representing the main inclusion

Table 4.4: Pottery by period from Beccles

Period	No	Wt/g
Prehistoric	230	686
Roman	11	407
Post medieval	1	4
Total	242	1097

Table 4.5: Prehistoric pottery quantities by excavation year and trench

Year	Trench	No	Wt/g
2007		40	129
2009	2	139	418
	3	50	133
	4	1	6
2009 Total		*190*	*557*
Total prehistoric pottery		*230*	*686*

Table 4.6: Prehistoric pottery fabric quantities

Fabric	Description	No	% No	Wt/g	% Wt
Q1	Common well-sorted quartz sand, some larger rounded quartz pieces.	173	75.2	580	84.5
Q2	Common well-sorted quartz sand with common mica shreds	57	24.8	106	15.5
Total		*230*	*100.0*	*686*	*100.0*

Table 4.7: Vessel types by (rim) count

Vessel type	Total
Angle shouldered jar with concave neck	1
Fine jar	1
Jar with medium upright neck	1
Jar/ bowl with everted neck	1
Shouldered jar	1
Jar with short upright neck	1
Uncertain	2
Total vessels	*8*

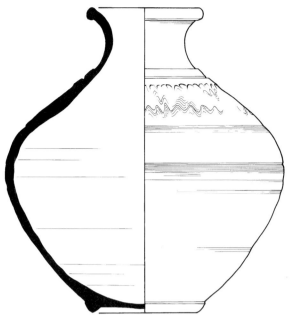

Figure 4.36: Roman vessel of the form represented by pottery recovered in 2006 (BCC-043)

recorded (Q representing quartz). Vessel form and form element were recorded. The sherds were counted and weighed to the nearest whole gram. Decoration, surface treatment and abrasion were also noted.

Prehistoric pottery (2007 and 2009)

A total of 230 later Iron Age sherds weighing 686g were collected during excavations in 2007 and 2009. The quantities are shown in Table 4.5.

The condition of the assemblage varies, with just under a third of the sherds being abraded or heavily abraded. The mean sherd weight for the assemblage is low, at just 3.2g for the 2007 excavations and 2.9g for the 2009 season. The small sherd size and high fragmentation is compatible with the redeposited nature of the assemblage. All of the pottery is made in sandy fabrics, which are typical in later Iron Age assemblages. The fabric descriptions and quantities are shown in Table 4.6.

Sandy fabrics are a common component of later Iron Age assemblages in the region such as those at West Stow (Martin, 1990: 65) and Burgh (Martin, 1988b: 34). The micaceous fabric, Q2, is also likely to be of local origin, utilising the same clay sources along the Waveney Valley, which were subsequently exploited for pottery production

in the Romano-British and Medieval periods. In common with many northern East Anglian sites, no chaff tempered (Martin, 1990: 65) or grog-tempered fabrics are present (Thompson, 1982).

All of the pottery is hand-made and includes rims from a total of eight vessels, all domestic jars/bowls. The vessels' types and rim counts are summarised in Table 4.7. They have distinct shoulders below a concave or up-right neck and rounded rim, similar to 'S' profile vessels from phase II at West Stow (Martin, 1990: fig. 47). One vessel has a pinched out cordon emphasising the shoulder, similar to examples from Burgh (Martin, 1988b: fig. 24, 160). The majority of the sherds have smoothed surfaces, although one had scratched surface treatment (also recorded at Burgh; Martin, 1988: fig. 19, 22 and 23); otherwise the pottery is undecorated.

The pottery was recovered from scatters dispersed across the timber alignment. The largest individual assemblage was collected during the 2009 excavations from Trench 2 (Table 4.5), in the form of several discrete clusters and including the remains of seven vessels. Pieces of one vessel, a distinctive jar with concave neck, were found in three locations across Trench 1 (Find spots 2001, 2022 and 2025), suggesting that the vessels may have come to the site as complete or semi-complete pots and been dispersed stake-breakage. The small size of the sherds is compatible with material that had worked down between the wooden elements making up the trackway and suggests that they had been subjected to some stake-deposition attrition perhaps due to trampling. No joining sherds from the same vessel were found in more than one trench, but the vessel forms are analogous, indicating that the pottery in all trenches was used and deposited at a similar time.

Table 4.8: Flint catalogue (2006 and 2007)

Context	Type	No.	Notes
2006			
1005	flake	1	Retouched flake, small grey & squat
2007			
SF1	core	2	Two small irregular multiplatform flake cores with several incipient cones of percussion
SF1	flake	1	Thick flake with hinge fracture & small amount of crude edge retouch. 66% cortex on dorsal face

Roman pottery (2006)

A substantial proportion (eleven sherds weighing 407g) of a single Roman vessel, a narrow mouthed bottle or flask (Figure 4.36) were collected from two find spots (1003 and 1004) during the 2006 excavation. Two more pieces of the same vessel were unstratified (0001) in the southern end of the trench. The vessel is made in the black-surfaced variant (GMB) of the grey coarse-ware fabric group made from micaceous clay sources available in the Waveney Valley. Micaceous wares are always a major component of Roman coarseware assemblages in the northern part of the county. It has a fine uniform sandy texture with few other inclusions apart from abundant mica throughout and the surface is soft and powdery due to adverse stake-depositional conditions.

The vessel was small to medium-sized, 180mm high with a rim diameter of 68mm and a true footring base 70mm in diameter, with a bulged cordon at the base of its neck, and was decorated with bands of incised lines. The first zone, just below the cordon, contained two horizontal bands of irregular wavy lines followed by bands of horizontal lines at uneven intervals down the wall of the vessel. The form is similar to *Camulodunum* form *Cam* 231a that is described as fully-Romanised (Hawkes and Hull, 1947) and it probably belongs to the mid or late 1st to early 2nd century AD.

Flint (2006 and 2007) and burnt flint (2007)

Four fragments of worked flint weighing 72g were collected from the 2006 and 2007 trenches. All of the flint is dark grey or black and unpatinated. Cortex, when present, is creamy off-white. The material was classified by type and additional descriptive comments were made as necessary (Table 4.8).

Two struck flakes and two crude and simple flake cores were identified. The presence of cores suggests that knapping was carried out in the vicinity. The flint is later prehistoric, Bronze Age or Iron Age and possibly contemporary with the associated later Iron Age pottery. Thirteen fragments of burnt flint 'pot-boiler' debris were recovered from the surface during the 2007 excavation. The flint is blue-grey to white and fire-crackled; a cluster of five fragments from Find spot 1 and single fragments

from Find spots 2 – 7 were recorded. Although un-datable in itself, all of it was found in association with later Iron Age pottery.

4.6.2 Site chronology and phasing
Radiocarbon dating
Whilst the oak timbers of the alignment were suitable for dendrochronological dating, there was a range of other archaeological wood recovered from the site, which could only be dated using radiocarbon methods. The subsequent dating programme was designed to investigate hypotheses regarding the possible phasing of the site, and in particular the discrete structural elements that had been identified in several of the trenches (see above). These data also include samples that were submitted as part of the 2006, and 2007 excavations. A total of 15 radiocarbon dates were obtained from archaeological material. Five samples were submitted to the Oxford Radiocarbon Accelerator Unit (ORAU), with one of the samples (Trench 3, 2009; BA1952 – 1172) measured twice as part of the laboratories internal quality assurance procedures (see Chapter 1). The results and associated calibrations, relating the radiocarbon measurements directly to calendar dates, are given in Table 4.9 and Figure 4.37. The ranges quoted in italics are *posterior density estimates* derived from mathematical modelling of archaeological problems (see below).

Dendrochronological dating: the stakes of the alignment

The following discussion incorporates the dendrochronological dating results of material from all three phases of excavation combining the data into a single narrative. A total of 86 timbers were sampled for dendrochronological assessment and analysis, of which 79 were identified as *Quercus* and were generally unconverted timbers, usually 150–270mm in diameter and from the 2006 (BCC-043) and 2007 material (BA1472) (see Gearey *et al.,* 2011) mostly complete with sapwood and bark present. The 2009 timbers were less intact presumably due to differences in the preservation environment (see Chapter 7). Forty of the samples were assessed to be of no potential dendrochronological value due to their lack of rings, aberrant anatomical characteristics or other issues. Thirty-nine samples were selected for analysis, including eight with 35–50 rings but complete sapwood and bark, and three from the 2009 (BA1952) excavations that should have contained suitable long sequences but instead contained two measureable series either side of an unknown number of rings in an irresolvable narrow growth band. The details of these analysed timbers are provided in Tables 4.10–4.12, using composite data where multiple radii were measured.

These thirty-nine samples were prepared for analysis, measured, any multiple radii synchronised and combined to form sample composite series and then compared with each other; fifteen of the samples were found to cross-match each other (Tables 4.13–4.15). The cross-matched data was combined to create a single composite data-set, which was then compared with prehistoric, Roman, and early medieval tree-ring data from throughout England and Wales. The composite sequence was found to cross-match against late Iron Age data from the longer-lived and strongest Roman chronologies from London, along with some weaker Roman material from elsewhere. This process provided consistent calendar dates for this sequence; a summary of the results for the 15 component samples of the composite sequence are provided in Tables 4.13–4.15, and Figure 4.38.

This initial analysis dates the rings present in the datable samples. The correct interpretation of those dates relies upon the character of the final rings in the samples. If a sample ends in the heartwood of the original tree, a *terminus*

post quem (tpq) for the felling of the tree is indicated by the date of the last ring plus the addition of an estimated number of sapwood rings missing. This *tpq* may be many decades prior to the real felling date. Where some of the sapwood or the heartwood/sapwood boundary survives on the sample, a felling date range can be calculated using the maximum and minimum number of sapwood rings likely to have been present based on figures derived from Roman, medieval and modern oaks from England and Wales. If bark-edge survives then a felling date can be directly utilised from the date of the last surviving ring.

The season of felling can also be determined by examining the completeness or otherwise of the terminal ring lying directly under the bark. Complete material can be divided into 3 major categories; 'early spring' where only the initial cells of the new growth have begun, this

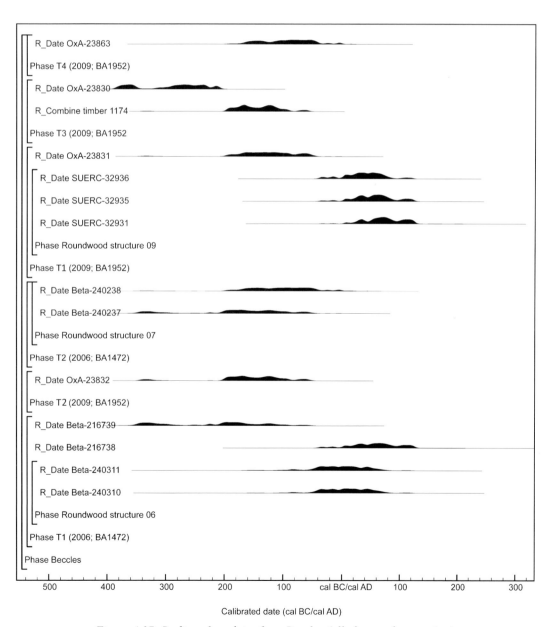

Figure 4.37: Radiocarbon dates from Beccles (all phases of excavation)

Down by the river

Table 4.9: Radiocarbon dates from Beccles (all phases of excavation)

Laboratory Code	Sample and context	Material	δ¹³C (‰)	Radiocarbon age (BP)	Calibrated date (95% confidence)
Trench 1(2006)					
Beta-240310	Brushwood track 06 – coppiced rod S1	Wood,	−30.1	2000±40	90 cal. BC–cal. AD 90
Beta-240311	Brushwood track 06 – coppiced rod S2	Wood	−29.2	1990±40	100 cal. BC–cal. AD 80
Beta-216738	Chisel point	Wood	−30.0	1940±40	40 cal. BC–cal. AD 120
Beta-216739	Upright stake	Wood; bark edge	−27.0	2150±40	360–50 cal. BC
Trench 2 (2007)					
Beta-240327	Brushwood track 07 – coppiced rod S3	Wood	−25.8	2130±40	360–40 cal. BC
Beta-240328	Brushwood track 07 – coppiced rod S4	Wood	−29.2	2080±40	210 cal. BC–cal. AD 10
Trench 1 (2009)					
SUERC-32931	860: cluster of roundwood oriented W–E and interpreted as a brushwood trackway	*Alnus glutinosa;* 9 years old	−29.4	1930±30	cal. AD 1–130
SUERC-32935	773: cluster of roundwood oriented NW–SE and interpreted as a brushwood trackway	*Alnus glutinosa;* 8 years old	−29.6	1945±30	20 cal. BC–cal. AD 130
SUERC-32936	797: cluster of roundwood oriented W-E and interpreted as a brushwood trackway	*Alnus glutinosa;* 11 years old	−30.4	1960±30	40 cal. BC–cal. AD 130
OxA-23831	1105: located NE of three upright stakes (612, 613, and 744)	*Alnus glutinosa;* outer rings	−26.0	2104±29	210–40 cal. BC
Trench 2 (2009)					
OxA-23832	652: one of a cluster of wooden beams aligned NE–SW	*Alnus glutinosa;* outer rings	−27.7	2124±28	350–50 cal. BC
Trench 3 (2009)					
OxA-23828	1172: one of several degraded horizontal timbers associated with six upright stakes of the triple-stake alignment	*Alnus glutinosa;* outer rings	−27.7	2118±25	–
OxA-23829	1172: one of several degraded horizontal timbers associated with six upright stakes of the triple-stake alignment	*Alnus glutinosa;* outer rings	−27.0	2120±25	–
Weighted mean 1172	T'=0.0; v=1; T'(5%)=3.8			2119±18	200–55 cal. BC
OxA-23830	1174: one of several degraded horizontal timbers associated with six upright stakes of the triple-stake alignment	*Alnus glutinosa;* outer rings	−26.9	2241±26	400–200 cal. BC
Trench 4 (2009)					
OxA-23863	1190: from a cluster of large wooden beams aligned NW–SE presenting a structural relationship with the upright stakes of the triple-stake alignment	*Alnus glutinosa;* outer rings	−27.1	2072±30	180 cal. BC–cal. AD 10

is equivalent to a period in March/April when the oaks begin leaf-bud formation, 'later spring/summer' where the early wood is complete but the late wood is evidently incomplete, is equivalent to May-through-September of a normal year, and 'winter' where the latewood is complete and this is roughly equivalent to September-to-March (of the following year) since the tree is dormant throughout this period and there is no additional growth put on the trunk. Figure 4.38 and Tables 4.10–4.12 include the interpreted date of each of the datable samples. These dates do not necessarily indicate the date of the structure from which the samples were derived since these timbers may be reused or represent repairs to the structure.

The tree-ring analysis of this material yielded a short but robust tree-ring sequence. The site composite sequence was found to strongly match the inner part of many of the 1st century AD Roman reference chronologies where these were made from 200–400 year old oaks (Table 4.16). This cross-matching indicated a 1st century BC date for this group of timbers with the composite sequence dated to 157–76 BC inclusive. A total of 12 of the dated samples are complete to bark-edge allowing these to be given precise felling dates. One of the other dated sequences was derived from an exclusively heartwood sample, BCC-043 0013, enabling this to be given a *terminus post quem* date, whilst both 605 and 882 were complete to the onset

Table 4.10: Details of the 15 measured oak dendrochronological samples from Beccles site BCC-043 (2006)

Sample	Size (mm)	Rings	Sap	Date of measured sequence	Interpreted result
2	?	58	14+Bw	undated	–
3	?	67	21+Bs	142–76 BC	75 BC spring
4	?	63	18+Bs	138–76 BC	75 BC spring
5	?	71	23+Bs	146–76 BC	75 BC spring
0011	265 × 255	51	14+Bw	undated	–
0013	255 × 230	43	-	135–93 BC	after 83BC
0014	200 × 190	43	20+Bw	undated	–
0041	150 × 150	41	14+Bw	undated	–
0047	235 × 230	54	19+Bw	undated	–
0057	250 × 250	56	11+Bs	undated	–
0058	240 × 230	49	15+Bs	124–76 BC	75 BC spring
0061	190 × 190	50	13+Bw	undated	–
0118	145 × 145	60	23+Bw	undated	–
0184	170 × 170	43	17+Bw	undated	–
0204	260 × 250	68	26+Bs	143–76 BC	75 BC spring

Key for Tables 4.10–4.12: In the sap column B = bark-edge season indeterminate; Bw = bark-edge winter felled; Bs = bark-edge with incomplete start of additional ring, indicating a timber felled early in the following spring. H/S indicates sequence ends at heartwood/sapwood boundary. The value in italics in BA1472 254 sap column indicates the number of counted but un-measurable rings.

NB. Three timbers from BA1952 with a narrow band of growth rings and series ending in bark-edge were measured as inner & outer sections in an attempt to identify their felling dates. Despite this experiment none of this material proved datable, the number of rings in these bands is thus unknown and given as ?

Table 4.11: Details of the 13 measured oak dendrochronological samples from Beccles site BA1472 (2007)

Sample	Size (mm)	Rings	Sap	Date of measured sequence	Interpreted result
250	165 × 165	40	15+Bw	undated	–
251	170 × 165	66	19+B	undated	–
254	210 × 210	46	13+*8*	undated	–
255	200 × 200	66	20+Bs	141–76 BC	75 BC spring
256	220 × 210	51	20+Bw	undated	–
257	220 × 220	57	30+Bs	132–76 BC	75 BC spring
258	270 × 270	61	12+Bs	136–76 BC	75 BC spring
260	220 × 220	51	15+B	undated	–
261	170 × 160	52	28+Bw	undated	–
268	195 × 195	82	43+Bs	157–76 BC	75 BC spring
270	200 × 200	43	11	undated	–
527	195 × 180	35	15+Bs	110–76 BC	75 BC spring
543	210 × 210	60	30+Bs	135–76 BC	75 BC spring

Table 4.12: Details of the 11 measured oak dendrochronological samples from Beccles site BA1952 (2009)

Sample	Size (mm)	Rings	Sap	Date of measured sequence	Interpreted result
600	245 × 230	36	–	undated	–
601	250 × 230	43	–	undated	–
603	240 × 240	49	4	undated	–
605	165 × 165	49	H/S	139BC–91 BC	81–45 BC
612	170 × 120	35+?+23	23+Bw	undated	–
613	210 × 210	68	35+Bs	143BC–76 BC	75BC spring
730	160 × 160	37+?+21	20+Bs	undated	–
733	230 × 180	39	2	undated	–
882	190 × 190	35	H/S	144BC–110 BC	100–64 BC
959	180 × 180	40+?+32	+Bw	undated	–
961	140 × 140	53	13	undated	–

of sapwood allowing these to be assigned felling date ranges. The felling date of all 12 of the datable timbers complete to bark-edge was identified as having occurred in the early spring of 75 BC, since each timber includes the preliminary cells of the growth ring for that year. These partial rings do not form part of the measured tree-ring sequences because they are incomplete growth rings and would distort the data. The other three dated samples all

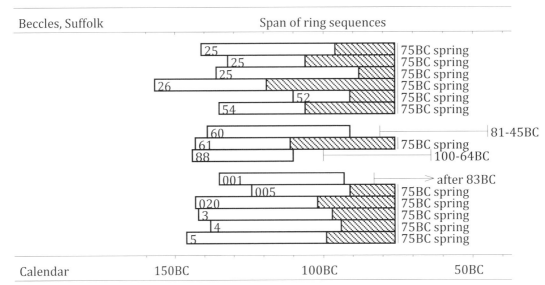

Figure 4.38: Bar diagram showing the absolute dating positions of the 15 dated tree-ring sequences. The interpreted felling dates are also shown. Key: White bars are oak heartwood, hatched bars are oak sapwood

Table 4.13: The t values (Baillie and Pilcher, 1973) between the individual series from the 12 dated timbers from Beccles sites BCC-043 & BA1472. – t-value less than 3.0. The high correlation between samples 0204 and 3 (highlighted in bold) may indicate these were derived from the same timber, or that two different timbers may have been derived from the same tree. These 12 were combined into a site master sequence, subsequently used during the analysis of the 2009 material

	257	258	268	527	543	0013	0058	0204	3	4	5
255	7.49	6.16	–	–	3.09	–	6.46	–	–	–	3.02
257		9.15	–	3.24	3.52	–	5.18	–	–	–	5.29
258			–	3.48	4.03	–	5.02	3.16	–	3.60	4.67
268				–	–	3.02	3.24	5.09	3.76	3.51	3.64
527					3.26	–	3.53	–	–	3.38	–
543						3.03	3.86	3.36	–	4.57	4.50
0013							–	3.70	3.65	–	3.14
0058								3.34	–	4.92	3.28
0204									13.27	5.26	3.54
3										3.39	3.09
4											–

Table 4.14: The t values (Baillie and Pilcher, 1973) between the individual series from the three dated timbers from Beccles site BA1952 and the site master from the analysis of the 2006/7 material. These were combined with the 2006/7 material to form the new site master sequence

	605	613	882
Beccles 2006/7	4.16	5.06	8.21

Table 4.15: The t values (Baillie and Pilcher, 1973) between the individual series from the 3 dated timbers from Beccles site BA1952. – t-value less than 3.0. These were combined with the 2006/7 material to form the new site master sequence

	613	882
605	8.59	–
613		–

Table 4.16: Showing example t values (Baillie and Pilcher,1973) between the 15 timber composite sequence from Beccles sites BCC-043 (2006), BA1472 (2007) and final phase (2009) and oak reference data

	Beccles T15 157–76 BC
London, 11–11A Pudding Lane (Hillam, 1986)	7.17
London, 12 Throgmorton Ave (Tyers, 2008)	6.61
London, 39–46 King William St (Tyers, 1995)	5.91
London, 1 Poultry (Tyers, 2000)	5.73
London, 72–80 Cheapside (Tyers, 1992)	5.66
Kent, Dover Town Wall Street (Nayling, 2001)	4.87
Norfolk, Snettisham Bypass (Hillam, 1991)	4.56

appear likely to have been felled at the same time, but in the absence of sapwood this cannot be proven precisely.

The dated material comprises three samples from the initial sample group (BCC-043 3, 4 and 5), three samples from the 2006 excavation (samples 0013, 0058 and 0204, two of which are shown on Figure 4.39), six from the 2007

excavation (sample 255, 257, 258, 268, 527 and 543, all shown on Figure 4.40), and three from the excavations described above, these latter all from Trench 2 (2009). The results demonstrate that material felled at precisely the same time is present along a significant length of the alignment. Unfortunately this does not definitively provide

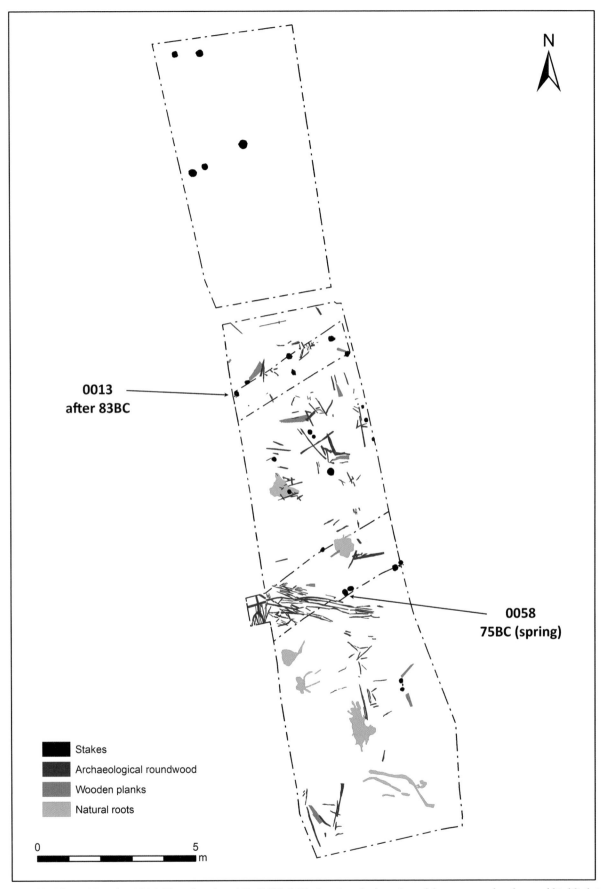

Figure 4.39: Plan of Beccles 2006 (Trenches 1 and 2) (BCC-043) showing the location of the excavated stakes and highlighting the two dated samples. Dated samples 3, 4, 5 and 204 were derived from the soke dyke to the south of these trenches

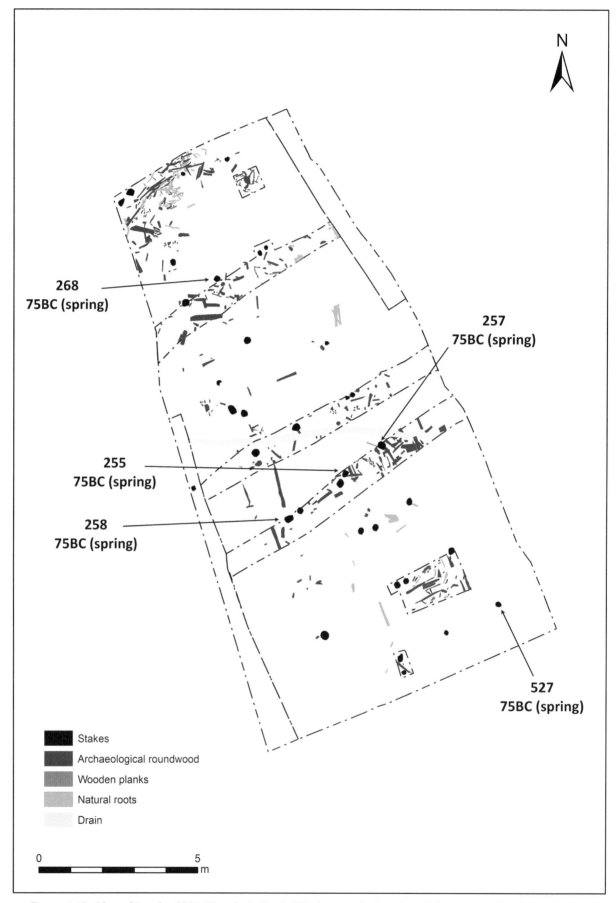

Figure 4.40: Plan of Beccles 2007 (Trench 4) (BA-1472) showing the location of the excavated and dated stakes

a date for the entire known length of the alignment, since the dated material from the 2009 excavation is confined to the northern-most trench, which is closest to the 2006, and 2007 trenches. From 2006, 2007 and Trench 2 (2009) the analysis has identified that timbers felled at the same date are present in all three lines of stakes, and in one instance from 2007 there are three stakes definitely of the same date in different lines but within the same row. In two locations within Trench 4 (2007) and another in Trench 2 (2009) it is also evident that where there are single stakes, as opposed to clusters, the single stake dates from 75 BC (2007 samples 257 and 527, Trench 2 Sample 613). This makes it highly likely that the original construction event used material felled in 75BC.

Further phases of construction or repair activity may be 'hidden' within the undated material. The 38% success rate is on the low side when compared to typical assemblages of structural oak timbers from Roman and Medieval sites (where 60–80% is typical), and is also low compared to that from the only other comparable Iron-age structure at Fiskerton, Lincolnshire (~56%). Short sequences naturally have a lower chance of reliable and conclusive cross-matching.

The Fiskerton timbers were also dominated by short-lived, unconverted oak timbers used as vertical piles, arranged in clusters and rows. However, superstructure planks recovered from this excavation provided 100–150 year tree-ring sequences with which to anchor the rest of the material. A total of eighty-five out of one hundred and fifty stakes or piles were analysed from Fiskerton and these dated samples complete to bark-edge form twenty different felling groups over a 116 year period, with one group containing sixteen samples and two other groups including the earliest containing eight and seven samples. It is likely that additional repairs have not yet been identified from the analysis because of the use of unsuitable material, or the spatially localised nature of some repairs, or that repairs occurred beyond the robust part of the tree-ring sequence so far produced for the site (Field and Parker Pearson, 2003; Tyers, 2002).

In contrast 39 samples from Beccles have been analysed, only 15 of which have produced dendrochronological dates. These have proven thus far to represent only one felling phase. At present there is no evidence for the frequent major repairs at 5–7 year intervals found at Fiskerton, but the Beccles 75 BC felling group is larger than all but one of the individual felling events at the former site, despite analysis of an assemblage of samples less than 30% of the size of that from Fiskerton.

Radiocarbon dating: phasing

The two timbers from Trench 3 (2009, see above) identified outside the edge of the timber alignment were radiocarbon dated to test the hypothesis that these were contemporary with the alignment and hence possibly deliberate structural elements. The two measurements on timber 1772, from the western outside edge of the alignment are statistically consistent (T'=0.0; v=1; T'(5%)=3.8; Ward and Wilson, 1978) and a weighted mean was calculated prior to calibration (1172; 2119±18 BP). The calibrated range for this large timber (200–55 cal. BC; 95% confidence) contains the date of 75 BC, suggesting it could have been part of the same felling event. However, the large timber 1174 from the eastern outside edge of the alignment is, on the basis of the radiocarbon date (OxA-23830; 400–200 cal. BC; 95% confidence), unlikely to have been associated with the timber alignment, unless it was a re-used timber.

One of the alder beams (1190) was dated from the cluster of large wooden beams in Trench 4 (see above), which appeared to present a structural relationship as one of the beams (1219) may have overlain the top of stake-1222 of the alignment. The calibrated range for timber 1190 (OxA-23863; 180 cal. BC–cal. AD 10; 95% confidence) contains the date of 75 BC suggesting this material might have been part of the same felling event. This could imply that stakes of the alignment in this part of the site at least, did not actually protrude far above the contemporary ground surface and may have been overlain by a platform, although it is possible that the observed relationship relates to disturbance to the site during the excavation of a later drainage ditch, which cuts through the site. This will be discussed further below (see Chapter 7).

BRUSHWOOD STRUCTURES

Three features interpreted as short sections of brushwood trackway were identified in Trenches 1 and 4 (2006 and 2007; see above). Two samples (Beta-240310 and Beta-240311) of wood (unidentified coppiced rods) from brushwood structure 06 produced statistically consistent results (T'=0.3; v=1; T'(5%)=3.8; Ward and Wilson, 1978). A second brushwood structure (brushwood structure 07) was identified at the north-western end of Trench 4 (2007; BA1472), again at right-angles to the main timber alignment. This feature consisted of eight lengths of roundwood (four *Quercus* and three *Alnus*), also displaying evidence of coppicing and pegged into place using short roundwood stakes. Two samples (Beta-240327 and Beta-240328) (unidentified coppiced rods) from this structure are also statistically consistent (T'=0.0; v=1; T'(5%)=3.8). Three samples (797, SUERC-32936; 860, SUERC-32931; and 773, SUERC-32935) were dated from the Trench 1 (2009) brushwood structure (brushwood structure 09, see above). This structure overlay one of the central upright stakes (853), although elsewhere it appeared to group around and thus respect the timber alignment. The three measurements are statistically consistent (T'=0.5; v=2; T'(5%)=6.0; Ward and Wilson, 1978) and could therefore be of the same actual age.

Interpretation

The seven measurements from the three brushwood structures are not statistically consistent (T'=24.9; v=6;

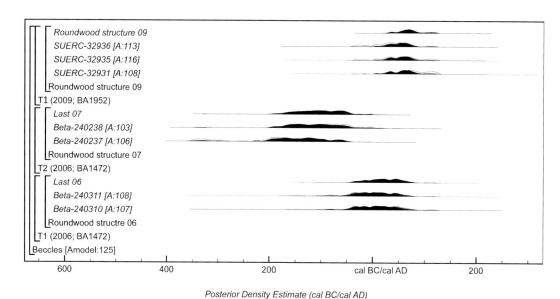

Figure 4.41: Probability distributions of dates from the three brushwood trackways. Each distribution represents the relative probability that an event occurs at a particular time. For each radiocarbon date, two distributions have been plotted: one in outline which is the result of simple radiocarbon calibration, and a solid one based on the chronological model used. The other distributions correspond to aspects of the model. For example, the distribution 'Last 06 is the posterior density estimate for the construction of brushwood trackway 06. The boundaries used in the models have not been plotted. The large square brackets down the left-hand side of the diagram and the OxCal keywords define the overall model exactly

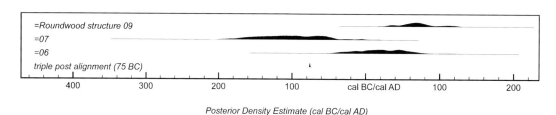

Figure 4.42: Probability distributions of dates relating to the construction of trackways and the timber alignment. The estimates are derived from the model shown in Figure 4.21

T'(5%)=12.6; Ward and Wilson, 1978) and these structures are therefore not all of the same date. However, employing a Bayesian approach to chronological modelling (see Chapter 1) (Figure 4.41) which assumes the samples represent three separate phases of activity, the subsequent model (Figure 4.42) shows good agreement (Amodel=126%) with the radiocarbon dates and provides estimates for the construction of:

1. Brushwood structure 06: *50 cal. BC–cal. AD 85 (95% probability; Last 06)* and probably *20 cal. BC–cal. AD 60 (68% probability)*.

2. Brushwood structure 07: *195–5 cal. BC (95% probability; Last 07)* and probably *150–50 cal. BC (68% probability)*.

3. Brushwood structure 09: *cal. AD 25–125 (95% probability; Last 09)* and probably *cal. AD 30–90 (68% probability)*.

Thus brushwood structures 06 and 09 are both therefore

later (>99% probability) than the timber alignment, while the radiocarbon evidence suggest brushwood structure 07 could potentially be earlier (70% probability). Brushwood structure 09 presented a clear stratigraphic relationship with the timber alignment, overlying the tops of the stakes in Trench 1 (2009). This indicates that the above ground section of the stakes in this part of the site at least, had rotted off and collapsed by the 1st–2nd century AD, suggesting a maximum life of 100–200 years. Such questions concerning the longevity of the structure are discussed further in Chapter 7.

THE DEBRIS FIELD

Two samples of wood from the debris field (OxA-23831 – Trench 2 and OxA-23832 – Trench 1 are statistically consistent (T'=0.2; T' (5%)=3.8; v=1; Ward and Wilson, 1978) and could therefore be of the same actual age. A sample of a worked wood chisel point (Beta-216738; 1940±40 BP) from Trench 1 (2006) is later (40 cal. BC–

cal. AD 120; 95% confidence) than the construction of the triple timber alignment.

4.6.3 On-site palaeoenvironmental analyses

On-site sampling for palaeoenvironmental analyses focused on Trenches 1 and 4 (2009). Sampling for pollen analysis was carried out using monolith sequences extracted from the open trench section faces (see Figures 4.13 and 4.21), and in line with the central stakes of the timber alignment, with corresponding bulk samples collected in 0.10m spits for plant macrofossil and beetle analyses from adjacent to the monoliths. The sampling strategy was also aligned with the geochemical sampling and water table monitoring (see Chapter 7) to allow an integrated approach to assessing variation in the state of preservation of the archaeo-environmental records (*cf.* Panter, 2009). The preservation of the pollen, plant macrofossil and beetle records was hence also quantified but these data will be discussed separately in Chapter 7.

Methods: plant macrofossils and beetles

Initially, 13, one litre sub-samples (0.10m thickness: seven samples from Trench 1; six samples from Trench 4) were assessed for plant macrofossils and beetles. In Trench 1, samples were taken from between 0.30m and 1.00m depth (Samples 1–7), although Samples 1 and 2 (0.30–0.50m depth) did not display sufficient preservation for plant macrofossil analysis. In Trench 4, samples were taken from between 0.50m and 1.10m depth (Samples 1–6), although Sample 1 (0.50–0.60m depth) did not present sufficient preservation for either plant macrofossil or insect analysis, and Sample 6 (1.00–1.10m depth) was not analysed for plant macrofossils.

The stratigraphy of both sequences was described as dark brown, herbaceous silty peat, with abundant monocotyledonous and wood remains. Due to the problems with the peat samples from Beccles identified during the SRVP (see Chapter 2), no further samples for radiocarbon dating were obtained from the on-site palaeoenvironmental sequences, but a relative chronology can be established through the relationship of the samples to the archaeological deposits in the form of the level of the 'debris field' representing the later Iron Age land surface (see above) and also the results of the second round of radiocarbon dating from the SRVP (Chapter 2).

Plant macrofossil and beetle sample processing were carried out using standard techniques for each 0.10m lens of sediment (see Chapter 1; Kenward *et al.*, 1980). The heavy residues were retained in water but were not analysed. In general, the residues contained larger fragments of wood with a few fragments of common reed (*Phragmites australis* (Cav.) Trin ex Steud. in Trench 1 Samples 3, 5 and 7). One fragment of worked wood was noted in Sample 6 from Trench 1. In all cases the flot from one litre of sediment was fully sorted for waterlogged plant macrofossils. However, in the case of Trench 4, Sample 2, rush (*Juncus* spp.) seeds were superabundant and it would have been prohibitively time consuming to count all of these remains. Hence, a 100 ml sub-sample of flot was fully sorted for rush seeds and this score was factored up to arrive at an estimated total of rush seeds for the entire flot.

Pollen analyses

Sub-samples for analysis were extracted at 0.04m intervals from the monolith sequences (0.35–1.10m: Trench 1 and 0.60–0.93m: Trench 4) and prepared following standard techniques (see Chapter 1). At least 300 total land pollen grains (TLP) excluding aquatics and spores were counted for each sample. The results are presented in the form of pollen diagrams (Figures 4.43–4.46). All percentage figures are of Total Land Pollen (TLP) unless otherwise specified.

Results: plant macrofossils

Table 4.17 presents the list of waterlogged plant macrofossils recovered in all nine samples analysed from Trenches 1 and 4. The assemblages from both trenches are broadly similar, with the upper deposits (Trench 1 Samples 3–6 and Trench 4 Samples 2–4) dominated by macrofossils of alder (*Alnus glutinsa* (L.) Gaertn.), common nettle (*Urtica dioica* L.), gypsywort (*Lycopus europaeus* L.), mint (*Mentha* spp.) and rush (*Juncus* spp.). The two lower deposits (Trench 1, Sample 7 and Trench 4, Sample 5) also have substantial numbers of macrofossils from this suite of alder carr/valley fen woodland plants, but there is an increase in the quantity of meadow/creeping/bulbous buttercup (*Ranunculus acris* L./*repens* L./*bulbosus* L..) achenes and grass (Poaceae) caryopses.

The higher numbers of indeterminate grasses (Poaceae) and meadow/creeping/bulbous buttercup in the lower deposits of Trenches 1 and 4 are notable and worthy of further consideration.

The upper deposits in both sequences (Trench 1 Samples 3–6 and Trench 4 Samples 2–4) are dominated by a relatively limited suite of plant remains. Alder (*Alnus glutinosa* (L.) Gaertn.), common nettle (*Urtica dioica* L.), gypsywort (*Lycopus europaeus* L.), mint (*Mentha* spp.) and rush (*Juncus* spp.) account for 61–97% of all identifications made in these samples. Today, this suite of plants commonly occurs together in carr and valley fen woodlands; nettle is often associated with alder carr (e.g. Rodwell, 1991). This component is also present in the lower samples from Trench 1 (Sample 7) and Trench 4 (Sample 5) although higher numbers of medium-sized grass (Poaceae) caryopses and meadow/creeping/bulbous buttercup (*Ranunculus acris* L./*repens* L./*bulbosus* L.) achenes are recorded.

Overall grasses form a relatively minor part of the plant macrofossil record. It was not possible to identify the majority of grass caryopsyes to either genus or species level, and those in the size range clearly lacked

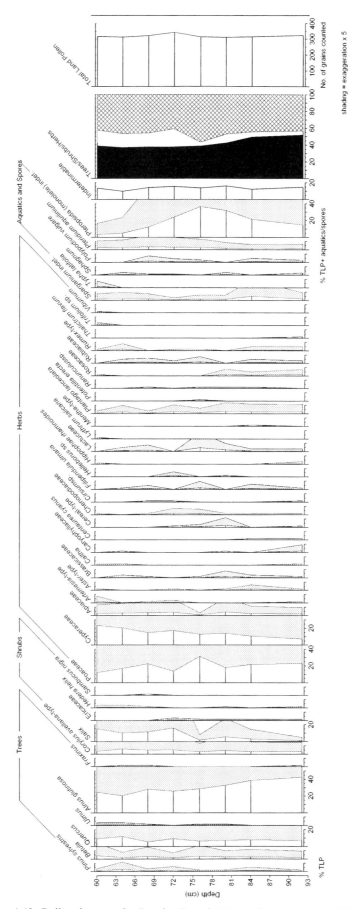

Figure 4.43: Pollen diagram for Beccles Trench 1 (top of sequence at –0.90m OD)

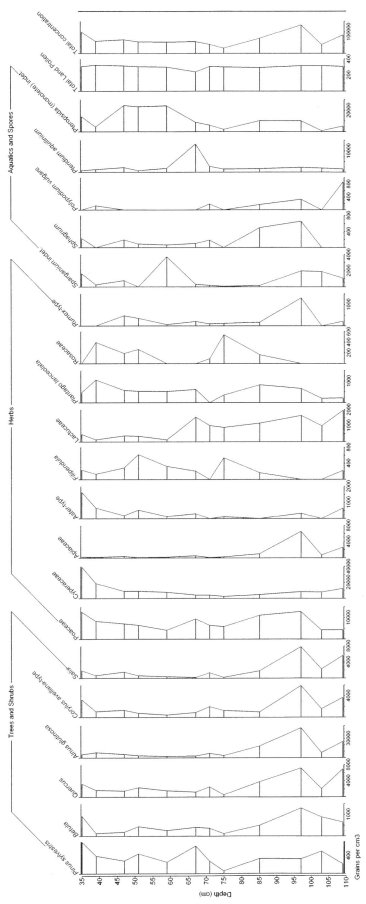

Figure 4.44: Pollen concentration for Beccles Trench 1 (top of sequence at –0.90m OD)

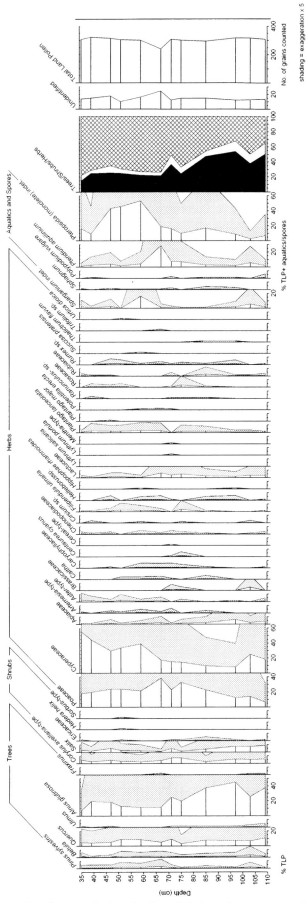

Figure 4.45: Pollen diagram for Beccles Trench 4 (top of sequence at –0.43m OD)

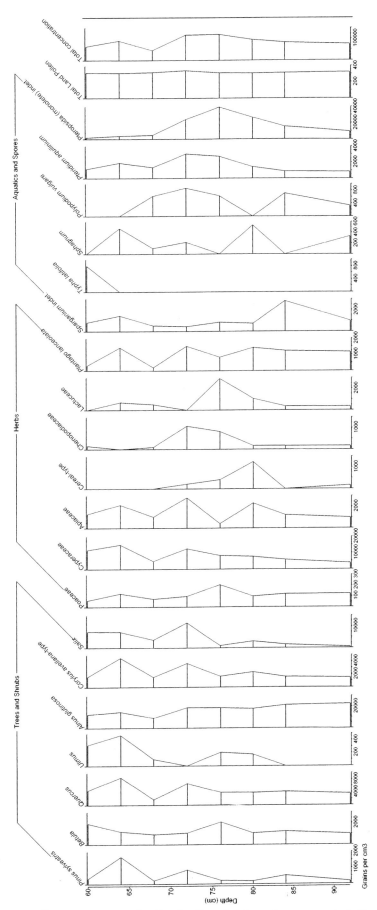

Figure 4.46: Pollen concentration for Beccles Trench 4 (top of sequence at –0.43m OD)

Table 4.17: Plant macrofossil analyses results from Beccles Trenches 1 and 4

Habitat Key: V = various, T = Typical, Aq = aquatic, As = acidic soil, B = bogs, C = cultivated ground, D = damp ground, DW = damp woodland, F = fens, G = grassland, Gb = bare ground, Hg = hedgerows, M = marshes, N = nitrogen rich soils, O = Open ground, R = rough ground, Sf = slow flowing water; Wb = woodland borders, Wg = waste ground, Wo = woodland, Wp = waste places and Ws = waterside.

Rush (Juncus spp.) seeds were superabundant in Sample 2 from Trench 4. It would have been too time-consuming to count all of the rush seeds, so a 100ml sub-sample was fully sorted for rush seeds and this score was factored up for all 550ml of wet flot.

Trench	1	1	1	1	1	4	4	4	4		
Depth (m)	0.50–0.60	0.60–0.70	0.70–0.80	0.80–0.90	0.90–1.00	0.60–0.70	0.70–0.80	0.80–0.90	0.90–1.00		
Sample	3	4	5	6	7	2	3	4	5		
Sample Volume (L)	1 L	1 L	1 L	1 L	1 L	1 L	1 L	1 L	1 L		
Latin Binomial										Habitat(s)	English Common Name
Ranunculus acris L./ repens L./ bulbosus L.	4	2	16	37	86	2	–	3	9	V – TG	meadow/ creeping/ bulbous buttercup
cf. Ranunculus acris L./ repens L./ bulbosus L. - fragment	–	–	–	–	–	–	–	1	–	V – TG	possible meadow/ creeping/ bulbous buttercup
Ranunculus sceleratus L.	2	3	1	–	–	–	–	–	–	M Ws	celery-leaved buttercup
Ranunculus subgenus RANUNCULUS	2	3	1	–	–	–	–	–	–	–	buttercup
Ranunculus subgenus BATRACHIUM (DC.) A. Gray	2	8	6	1	–	5	–	3	–	TAq	crowfoot
Aphanes arvensis L./ australis Rydb.	–	4	1	–	–	–	–	1	–	C Gb	parsley-piert/ slender parsley-piert
Rubus section Rubus	10	2	1	–	–	–	–	1	–	V	indeterminate blackberry/ raspberry
Filipendula ulmaria (L.) Maxim.	–	1	–	1	–	3	–	–	–	D Wp	meadowsweet
cf. Filipendula ulmaria (L.) Maxim.	1	–	–	–	–	–	–	–	–	D Wp	possible meadowsweet
Potentilla sp.	1	–	–	–	–	–	–	–	–	–	cinquefoil
Urtica dioica L.	17	20	31	21	15	200	64	67	11	V – TN	common nettle
Alnus glutinosa (L.) Gaertn.	3	19	90	48	89	24	10	19	–	DW Ws	alder
Alnus glutinosa (L.) Gaertn. - cone fragment	–	–	5	5	5	–	1	–	14	DW Ws	alder
cf. Alnus glutinosa (L.) Gaertn.	–	–	–	–	–	–	–	1	–	DW Ws	possible alder
Viola sp.	–	1	–	–	–	–	–	–	–	V	violet
Epilobium spp.	1	1	–	–	–	7	7	2	1	–	willowherb
cf. Raphanus raphanistrum L. - capsule fragment	1	–	–	–	–	–	–	–	–	C R Wp	wild radish
BRASSICACEAE - unidentified (compressed, winged seed ca. 1mm)	2	–	–	–	–	–	–	–	–	–	Mustard Family
BRASSICACEAE - unidentified capsule fragment	–	1	–	–	–	–	1	–	–	–	Mustard Family
Persicaria hydropiper (L.) Delarbre	2	1	–	–	–	3	–	3	–	D Ws	water-pepper
Persicaria sp.	1	1	–	–	–	–	–	–	–	–	knotweed
Persicaria spp./ Polygonum spp. - indeterminate seed coat fragment	–	1	–	–	–	–	–	–	–	–	
Polygonum cf. aviculare L.	–	4	–	–	–	1	–	1	–	O	possible knotgrass
cf. Polygonum aviculare L. - seed coat fragment	–	1	–	–	–	–	1	–	–	O	tentative knotgrass
Rumex cf. hydrolapathum Huds.	–	–	1	–	–	–	–	–	–	Ws M	possible water dock
Rumex spp.	1	2	–	1	–	1	1	–	–	–	dock
Moehringia trinervia (L.) Clairv.	–	–	–	–	–	3	–	–	–	Wo Hg	three-nerved sandwort
Stellaria cf. alsine Grimm	10	–	2	1	7	9	1	1	–	Ws D As	bog stitchwort
Stellaria spp.	–	5	1	2	2	–	4	2	–	–	stitchwort
Cerastium spp.	1	–	–	–	–	–	–	–	–	–	mouse-ear

Latin Binomial	English Common Name	Habitat(s)	Trench 1 / 0.50–0.60 / Sample 3 / 1L	Trench 1 / 0.60–0.70 / Sample 4 / 1L	Trench 1 / 0.70–0.80 / Sample 5 / 1L	Trench 1 / 0.80–0.90 / Sample 6 / 1L	Trench 1 / 0.90–1.00 / Sample 7 / 1L	Trench 4 / 0.60–0.70 / Sample 2 / 1L	Trench 4 / 0.70–0.80 / Sample 3 / 1L	Trench 4 / 0.80–0.90 / Sample 4 / 1L	Trench 4 / 0.90–1.00 / Sample 5 / 1L
cf. Spergularia spp.	possible sea-spurrey	–	–	–	–	–	–	–	4	2	–
Silene flos-cuculi (L.) Clairv.	ragged-robin	M D	1	1	8	–	–	1	1	1	1
Silene sp.	campion	–	–	1	–	–	–	–	–	–	–
CARYOPHYLLACEAE - unidentified (Sagina spp. type)	Pink Family (pearlwort type)	–	–	6	–	–	–	6	–	–	–
CARYOPHYLLACEAE / CHENOPODIACEAE - indeterminate	Pink Family / Goosefoot Family	–	1	–	–	–	–	–	–	–	–
Chenopodium spp.	goosefoot	–	5	2	1	–	–	4	–	9	–
Galium cf. aparine L.	cleaver	–	–	–	6	–	8	–	–	2	–
Solanum cf. dulcamara L.	bittersweet	Hg F Wo Ws	–	–	–	1	2	3	4	4	–
Plantago major L.	greater plantain	O C G	–	–	–	–	–	1	1	–	–
Callitriche sp.	water-starwort	Aq	–	–	–	–	–	1	1	–	–
Stachys sp. - type	woundwort type	–	–	–	–	–	1	–	–	–	–
Lycopus europaeus L.	gypsywort	F D Ws	10	6	3	2	–	2	3	3	13
Mentha spp.	mint	–	12	10	53	67	76	20	7	22	13
Chaerophyllum temulum L.	rough chervil	G Hg Wb	–	–	1	–	–	4	5	9	17
cf. Chaerophyllum temulum L. - internal structure	probable rough chervil	G Hg Wb	–	–	–	1	2	–	3	3	–
Carduus spp. / Cirsium spp.	thistle	–	3	–	3	1	1	6	–	3	1
Cirsium spp. - type (<2mm)	thistle	–	4	3	–	–	–	–	1	–	–
Bidens cernua L.	nodding bur-marigold	Ws M	3	2	–	–	–	–	–	–	–
Eupatorium cannabinum L.	hemp-agrimony	D Ws	3	2	9	–	–	11	20	14	12
Sambucus nigra L.	elder	Hg Wg R TN	–	–	–	–	–	–	–	1	–
Dipsacus fullonum L.	wild teasel	Wb Ws Wg	–	–	–	–	–	1	–	–	–
cf. Hedera helix L.	common ivy	V	1	–	–	–	–	–	–	–	–
Hydrocotyle vulgaris L.	marsh pennywort	B F M Ws	–	–	2	1	–	–	–	–	–
Apium nodiflorum (L.) Lag.	fool's water-cress	Aq Ws	2	1	6	9	31	–	–	–	–
Apium spp. - internal structure	marshwort	–	–	3	2	2	–	3	–	–	2
APIACEAE - indeterminate internal structure (1.5 - 2mm x 1.5 - 2mm)	Carrot Family	–	–	4	2	–	–	6	1	2	2
APIACEAE - indeterminate internal structure (1.5mm x 0.75 mm)	Carrot Family	–	–	–	–	–	–	–	2	–	–
Lemna sp.	duckweed	Aq	–	1	–	–	1	–	–	–	–
Sagittaria sagittifolia L./ Alisma spp. - indeterminate internal structure	arrowhead/ water-plantain	Aq Sf	1	–	–	–	–	1	2	3	2
Alisma cf. plantago-aquatica L.	water-plantain	Aq Sf	3	2	–	–	–	6	4	4	1
Iris pseudacorus L.	yellow iris	D F Ws	–	–	1	–	–	–	–	–	–
Sparganium erectum L.	branched bur-reed	Aq Ws	–	–	–	–	1	–	1	–	–
Juncus spp.	rush	TD TWs	ca. 200	202	26	3	1	4983*	378	63	26
Carex spp. - 3-sided	sedge	TD TWs	4	14	6	2	5	36	6	19	3
cf. Glyceria maxima (Hartm.) Holmb.	possible reed sweet-grass	Aq Ws	–	–	2	–	–	1	–	–	–

Latin Binomial	English Common Name	Habitat(s)	1 / 0.50–0.60 / 3 / 1 L	1 / 0.60–0.70 / 4 / 1 L	1 / 0.70–0.80 / 5 / 1 L	1 / 0.80–0.90 / 6 / 1 L	1 / 0.90–1.00 / 7 / 1 L	4 / 0.60–0.70 / 2 / 1 L	4 / 0.70–0.80 / 3 / 1 L	4 / 0.80–0.90 / 4 / 1 L	4 / 0.90–1.00 / 5 / 1 L
Trench											
Depth (m)											
Sample											
Sample Volume (L)											
Unidentified - medium bud (1 - 2mm)	–	–	3	–	7	11	–	3	–	1	–
Unidentified - bud-scar	–	–	5	–	–	–	7	–	–	12	10
Unidentified - capsule fragment	–	–	–	–	–	–	1	–	–	–	–
Unidentified	–	–	1	1	1	1	1	–	–	–	–
TOTAL COUNT			347	364	326	227	371	5369	530	283	187
TOTAL TAXA			32	33	36	23	20	31	26	29	20
Total *Alnus, Urtica, Lycopus, Mentha & Juncus*			242	257	203	141	181	5229	459	174	63
Proportion *Alnus, Urtica, Lycopus, Mentha & Juncus*			69.74%	70.60%	62.27%	62.11%	48.79%	97.39%	86.60%	61.48%	33.69%
Other Remains											
Charophyte	green algae	Aq	1	–	–	–	–	3	1	–	–

the distinctive 'barb' (the style) at the apical end of reed sweet-grass (*Glyceria maxima* (Hartm.) Holmb. As a result, these grasses could not be attributed to a specific habitat although the dominant flora is clearly that of alder carr. The meadow/ creeping/bulbous buttercup achenes are typical of grassland habitats, but members of this group also occur in alder carr (swamp carr) and valley fen woodland environments (e.g. Rodwell, 1991: 87 and 99). The full analysis of the insect fauna (see below) suggests limited areas of grasses on the site, with restricted evidence for grazing, possibly at some distance from the sampling site, and/or wild animals rather than managed herds.

Several tall herbs recovered in this assemblage are typical of the *Phragmites australis* (Cav.) Trin. ex Steud. sub-community of alder carr (Rodwell 1991: 82), such as common nettle (*Urtica dioica* L.), meadowsweet (*Filipendula ulmaria* (L.) Maxim.), hemp-agrimony (*Eupatorium cannabium* L.), yellow iris (*Iris pseudacorus* L.), marsh thistle (*Cirsium palustre* (L.) Scop.) and occasionally gypsywort (*Lycopus europaeus* L.). The plant macrofossil evidence therefore implies that fen carr woodland was locally dominant during the accumulation of these peat deposits. There does appear to be higher levels of grass (Poaceae) caryopses in samples from Trenches 1 (0.60–0.70m) and 4 (0.90–1.00m). These were primarily medium-sized caryopses, which could not be identified, even to genus level and therefore lack habitat data. The other plant taxa recovered in these samples are still in keeping with alder fen carr; therefore, these samples may suggest more grassy watersides or limited areas of meadow in the vicinity; possibly marking the transition from damp (possibly seasonally drying out) to continuously waterlogged conditions.

Results: beetles

The majority of the insect remains present are beetles (Coleoptera), with very few individuals of true bugs (Hemiptera) and caddis flies (Tricoptera) present. A list of the insects recovered is presented in Table 4.18. The nomenclature for Coleoptera (beetles) follows that of Lucht (1987). Column 12 in Table 4.18 lists the host plants for the phytophage species of beetle that were recovered and are predominantly derived from Koch (1989, 1992). The plant taxonomy follows that of Stace (2010). In order to aid interpretation, where possible, taxa have been assigned to ecological groupings. The Coleoptera follow a simplified version of the scheme suggested by Robinson (1981, 1983). The affiliation of each beetle species to a particular ecological grouping is coded in the second column, the meaning of each ecological code is explained in the key at the base of Table 4.18. The occurrence of each of the ecological groupings is expressed as a percentage in Table 4.19 and in Figure 4.47. The pasture/grassland, dung and woodland/ timber beetle species are calculated as percentages of the number of terrestrial species, as opposed to the whole fauna.

Table 4.18. The insect remains from Beccles Trenches 1 and 4

Ecological codes a = aquatic; ws = waterside; l= tree, woodland and leaf feeders; df = animal dung and similar deposits; p = pasture and grassland

Trench		Trench 1								Trench 4				
Depth (m)	Ecological code	0.90–1.00	0.80–0.90	0.70–0.80	0.60–0.70	0.50–0.60	0.40–0.50	0.30–0.40	Trackway	1.00–1.10	0.90–1.00	0.80–0.90	0.70–0.80	0.60–0.70
Sample		7	6	5	4	3	2	1		6	5	4	3	2
HEMIPTERA														
Family, genus and spp. Indet.		–	–	–	–	–	–	–	1	1	–	–	–	–
COLEOPTERA														
Carabidae														
Carabus spp.		–	–	–	–	–	–	–	–	–	–	–	–	–
Elaphrus uliginosus F.	ws	1	–	–	–	–	–	–	–	1	–	–	–	1
Clivina fossor (L.)		–	–	–	1	–	–	–	–	1	–	–	–	1
Dyschirius globosus (Hbst.)		1	2	–	–	–	–	–	–	3	–	–	–	1
Trechus secalis (Payk.)	ws	–	–	–	–	–	–	–	–	–	1	–	1	–
Trechus. rubens (F.)		–	–	1	–	–	1	–	–	–	–	–	–	–
Bembidion guttula (F.)		–	1	1	–	–	–	–	–	–	–	–	–	–
Bembidion doris (Panz.)		–	–	–	–	–	–	–	–	3	–	–	–	–
Bembidion spp.		1	–	1	–	–	–	–	–	2	–	–	–	–
Bradycellus spp.		–	–	–	–	–	–	–	–	–	–	–	1	–
Pterostichus strenuus (Panz.)	ws	–	–	–	–	1	–	–	–	1	–	–	–	–
Pterostichus nigrita (Payk.)	ws	–	–	–	–	–	–	–	1	1	–	–	1	2
Pterostichus minor (Gyll.)	ws	1	1	–	1	–	–	–	2	3	–	–	3	3
Pterostichus melanarius (Ill.)		–	–	–	–	–	1	1	–	–	–	–	–	–
Pterostichus spp.		–	–	3	–	2	1	–	–	–	2	–	–	–
Agonum thoreyi Dej.	ws	–	1	–	–	–	1	–	–	–	–	1	–	–
Agonum sp.		–	–	1	–	–	–	–	–	–	1	1	–	–
Platynus assimilis (Payk.)		–	–	–	–	–	–	–	1	–	–	–	–	–
Amara spp.		–	–	1	–	1	1	–	–	1	–	–	–	–
Dromius longiceps Dej.		–	–	–	–	1	–	–	–	–	–	–	–	–
Dromius spp.		–	–	–	–	–	1	–	–	–	–	–	–	–
Dytiscidae														
Hydroporus melanarius Sturm.	a	–	–	–	–	–	–	–	–	–	–	–	–	1
Hydroporus spp.	a	–	1	–	–	–	–	–	1	–	–	–	–	–
Agabus bipustulatus (L.)	a	1	–	–	–	–	–	–	–	1	–	–	–	–
Agabus spp	a	–	–	–	1	–	–	–	–	–	1	–	–	–
Gyrinidae														
Gyrinus spp.	a	–	–	–	–	–	1	–	–	–	–	–	–	–

Note (Agonum thoreyi Dej.): Mainly associated with Phragmites australis (Cav.) Trin. ex Steud. (Common reed)

Trench		*Trench 1*							*Trackway*	*Trench 4*				
Depth (m) / Ecological code		0.90–1.00	0.80–0.90	0.70–0.80	0.60–0.70	0.50–0.60	0.40–0.50	0.30–0.40		1.00–1.10	0.90–1.00	0.80–0.90	0.70–0.80	0.60–0.70
Sample		7	6	5	4	3	2	1		6	5	4	3	2
Hydraenidae														
Hydraena testacea Curt.	a	–	–	–	–	2	3	–	1	–	–	–	–	–
Hydraena riparia Kug.	a	–	–	–	–	1	1	–	1	–	–	–	–	–
Hydraena spp.	a	3	4	7	6	6	8	–	7	3	5	1	1	3
Ochthebius minimus (F.)	a	1	–	–	–	1	–	1	–	2	–	1	1	–
Ochthebius spp.	a	3	5	3	3	4	3	–	4	2	8	1	3	–
Limnebius spp.	a	–	–	–	–	–	–	–	1	–	–	–	–	–
Hydrochus spp.	a	–	–	–	–	–	–	–	–	1	–	–	–	–
Helophorus spp.	a	1	1	–	–	2	–	–	–	–	1	–	–	–
Hydrophilidae														
Coelostoma orbiculare (F.)	a	–	1	–	1	–	–	–	1	1	–	–	1	3
Cercyon tristis (Ill.)	ws	–	–	–	–	–	–	–	–	–	–	–	–	2
Cercyon sternalis Shp.	ws	7	12	5	–	–	–	–	–	11	4	1	–	3
Cercyon analis (Payk.)	df	1	1	–	–	–	–	1	–	–	–	1	–	–
Megasternum boletophagum (Marsh.)		2	2	1	1	–	2	–	–	1	1	–	–	–
Hydrobius fuscipes (L.)	a	–	–	1	1	1	–	–	1	1	–	–	1	3
Laccobius bipunctatus (F.)	a	–	–	–	–	–	–	–	2	–	1	1	–	–
Laccobius spp.	a	1	1	3	–	1	–	–	–	–	–	–	–	1
Enochrus spp.	a	–	–	–	–	–	1	–	–	–	–	–	–	1
Cymbiodyta marginella (F.)	a	–	–	–	–	–	–	–	–	–	–	–	–	1
Chaetarthria seminulum (Hbst.)	a	2	–	1	–	2	–	–	1	–	1	–	1	2
Silphidae														
Thanatophilus rugosus (L.)	df	–	–	–	–	–	–	–	1	–	–	–	1	–
Phosphuga atrata (L.)	df	–	–	–	–	1	1	–	1	–	–	–	1	–
Silpha tristis Ill.	df	–	–	–	–	–	–	–	1	1	–	–	–	–
Liodidae														
Agathidium spp.		–	–	–	–	1	1	–	–	–	–	–	–	–
Clamdidae														
Clambus spp.		–	1	–	–	–	–	–	1	–	–	–	–	–
Orthoperidae														
Corylophus cassidoides (Marsh.)	ws	–	1	9	2	3	3	1	1	–	–	–	–	1
Orthoperus spp.		–	–	–	–	–	–	–	–	–	1	–	1	–
Ptiliidae														
Ptiliidae Genus & spp. indet.		2	1	1	1	–	–	–	–	1	–	–	1	–
Staphylinidae														
Micropeplus staphylinoides (Marsh.)		–	–	1	–	–	–	–	–	–	–	–	–	–
Micropeplus spp.		1	–	–	–	–	–	–	–	–	–	–	–	–
Proteinus ovalis Steph.		–	–	–	–	–	–	–	–	2	–	–	–	–

Trench		Trench 1									Trench 4				
Depth (m)	Eco-logical code	0.90–1.00	0.80–0.90	0.70–0.80	0.60–0.70	0.50–0.60	0.40–0.50	0.30–0.40	Trackway	1.00–1.10	0.90–1.00	0.80–0.90	0.70–0.80	0.60–0.70
Sample		7	6	5	4	3	2	1		6	5	4	3	2
Eusphalerum sp.	–	–	–	–	–	–	1	1	–	–	–	–	–	–
Omalium spp.	–	–	1	–	–	–	1	–	1	1	2	2	–	–
Olophrum spp.	–	1	1	–	–	2	1	–	1	1	2	2	1	–
Acidota crenata (F.)	–	–	1	–	–	–	1	–	–	1	–	–	1	–
Lesteva heeri Fauv.	–	–	–	6	–	–	–	–	–	–	–	–	–	–
Lesteva longelytrata (Goeze)	ws	–	–	–	2	2	–	–	2	1	2	–	2	–
Lesteva spp.	ws	–	–	–	2	2	3	–	2	1	–	–	2	3
Trogophloeus ?corticinus (Grav.)	–	1	1	–	–	–	–	–	–	1	–	–	–	–
Trogophloeus spp.	–	–	1	–	2	2	1	–	–	1	–	–	–	–
Oxytelus rugosus (F.)	–	1	3	3	1	–	1	–	–	2	–	–	1	–
Oxytelus sculpturatus Grav.	–	–	–	–	–	–	–	–	–	–	–	–	–	–
Platystethus cornutus (Grav.)	ws	1	–	–	–	–	–	–	–	1	–	–	–	–
Platystethus nitens Sahlb.	ws	–	–	–	–	–	–	–	–	1	–	–	–	–
Stenus spp.	–	8	5	–	2	1	3	–	5	3	3	1	1	3
Paederus spp.	–	–	–	–	–	–	1	–	–	–	1	–	–	–
Stilicus orbiculatus (Payk.)	–	1	1	2	–	2	1	–	1	3	1	1	–	2
Lathrobium spp.	–	1	1	2	–	2	1	–	1	3	1	1	–	2
Gyrohypnus fracticornis (Müll.)	–	–	–	–	–	–	–	–	2	–	1	–	1	–
Xantholinus spp.	–	1	–	1	–	–	–	–	1	1	1	–	–	–
Gabrius spp.	–	1	–	–	–	–	1	–	–	1	–	–	–	–
Philonthus spp.	–	1	1	–	–	–	–	–	1	1	–	–	–	–
Philonthus spp.	–	–	–	–	–	–	–	–	–	–	–	–	–	–
Tachyporus spp.	–	–	–	–	–	–	–	–	–	1	–	–	–	1
Tachinus rufipes (Geer.)	–	2	1	–	–	–	1	–	1	1	–	–	1	–
Tachinus spp.	–	–	–	–	–	–	–	–	–	–	–	–	–	–
Aleocharinidae Genus & spp.	–	–	–	–	–	–	–	–	–	–	–	–	–	–
Indet.	–	–	–	–	–	–	–	–	–	–	–	–	–	–
Pselaphidae														
Bryaxis spp.	–	–	1	1	–	–	1	–	–	–	–	–	–	–
Rybaxis spp.	–	–	1	1	–	1	1	–	1	–	–	–	–	–
Brachygluta spp.	–	–	–	2	–	1	1	–	–	–	–	–	–	–
Elateridae														
Agriotes spp.	p	–	–	–	–	–	–	–	1	1	–	–	–	–
Ctenicera cuprea (F.)	p	–	–	–	–	–	–	–	1	–	–	–	–	–
Selatosomus spp.	p	–	–	–	1	–	–	–	–	–	–	–	–	–
Athous haemorrhoidalis (F.)	p	–	–	1	1	–	–	–	–	–	–	–	–	–
Cantharidae														
Cantharis spp.	p	–	1	–	–	–	–	–	–	–	–	–	–	–
Eucnemidae														
Melasis buprestoides (L.)	1	–	1	–	–	–	–	–	–	–	–	1	–	–
Xylophilus corticalis (Payk.)	1	–	–	–	–	–	–	–	–	–	–	–	1	–
Helodidae														
Helodidae Gen. & spp. Indet.	a	–	2	3	–	1	1	–	1	2	1	–	–	–

	Eco-logical code	Trench 1							Trackway	Trench 4				
Depth (m)		0.30–0.40	0.40–0.50	0.50–0.60	0.60–0.70	0.70–0.80	0.80–0.90	0.90–1.00		0.60–0.70	0.70–0.80	0.80–0.90	0.90–1.00	1.00–1.10
Sample		1	2	3	4	5	6	7		2	3	4	5	6
Dryopidae														
Dryops spp.	a	–	–	–	–	–	–	1	1	3	–	–	–	1
Nitidulidae														
Meligethes spp.		–	1	–	1	–	–	2	–	–	–	1	–	–
Rhizophagidae														
Rhizophagus spp.	1	–	–	–	–	1	–	1	–	–	–	–	–	–
Cryptophagidae														
Cryptophagus spp.		–	–	–	1	1	1	1	–	–	–	–	–	1
Atomaria spp.	1	–	–	1	1	1	–	1	–	–	–	–	–	–
Phalacridae														
Phalacrus corruscus (Panz.)	ws	–	–	–	–	1	–	–	–	–	–	–	–	1
Lathridiidae														
Enicmus minutus (Group)		–	–	–	–	–	–	–	1	–	1	–	–	–
Corticaria/corticarina spp.		–	–	–	–	–	–	–	–	–	1	–	–	–
Colydiidae														
Cerylon sp.	1	–	–	–	–	–	2	–	–	–	2	–	–	–
Coccinellidae														
Thea vigintiduopunctata (L.)	1	–	–	–	–	–	–	1	–	–	–	–	–	–
Lyctidae														
Lyctus linearis (Goeze)	1	–	–	–	–	2	–	–	–	–	–	–	–	–
Elateridae														
Agriotes spp.	P	–	–	–	–	1	–	–	–	–	–	–	–	1
Ctenicera cuprea (F.)	P	–	–	–	–	–	–	–	1	–	1	–	–	–
Selatosomus spp.	P	–	–	–	1	–	–	–	1	–	–	–	–	–
Athous haemorrhoidalis (F.)	P	–	–	–	–	1	–	–	–	1	–	–	–	–
Anobiidae														
Anobium punctatum (Geer)	1	–	–	–	2	–	–	–	–	–	1	–	–	1
Grynobius planus (F.)	1	–	–	–	–	–	–	–	–	–	1	–	1	1
Ptinidae														
Ptinus fur (L.)		1	–	–	–	–	–	–	–	–	–	–	–	–
Scarabaeidae														
Geotrupes spp.	df	–	–	–	–	1	1	–	–	–	–	–	–	–
Onthophagus spp.	df	–	–	–	–	–	–	–	–	–	–	–	–	1
Aphodius coenosus (Panz.)	df	–	–	–	–	–	–	–	–	–	–	1	–	–
Aphodius contaminattus (Hbst.)	df	–	–	–	1	–	–	–	–	–	–	1	–	–

Trench			Trench 1							Trackway	Trench 4					
Depth (m)	Ecological code	0.90–1.00	0.80–0.90	0.70–0.80	0.60–0.70	0.50–0.60	0.40–0.50	0.30–0.40	Trackway	1.00–1.10	0.90–1.00	0.80–0.90	0.70–0.80	0.60–0.70	
Sample		7	6	5	4	3	2	1		6	5	4	3	2	
Aphodius sphacelatus (Panz.) or A. prodromus (Brahm)	df	–	2	8	–	–	–	–	–	–	1	–	4	–	
Aphodius lapponum Gyll.	df	–	–	–	–	–	–	–	–	1	–	–	–	–	usually in coniferous woodland
Aphodius fimetarius (L.)	df	–	–	–	1	3	2	–	–	–	–	–	–	–	
Aphodius spp.	df	1	–	–	–	–	–	–	–	1	–	–	–	2	
Phyllopertha horticola (L.)	p	1	1	–	–	–	–	–	–	–	–	–	–	1	
Lucanidae															
Sinodendron cylindricum (L.)		1	–	–	–	–	–	–	–	–	1	–	–	–	
Cerambycidae															
Leptura ?sanguinolenta L.		1	–	–	–	–	–	–	–	–	–	–	–	–	
Aromia moschata (L.)		1	–	–	–	–	–	–	–	–	–	–	–	–	usually on Salix spp. (willow)
Chyrsomelidae															
Donacia clavipes F	ws	–	–	–	–	–	–	–	–	–	1	–	1	–	Schoenoplectus lactustris (L.) Palla (Common Club Rush)
Donacia simplex F.	ws	–	–	–	–	–	–	–	–	–	3	–	1	–	Range of water reeds & rushes
Donacia spp.	ws	–	–	–	1	–	–	–	–	–	–	–	–	–	
Plateumaris braccata (Scop.)	ws	–	–	–	–	2	3	1	4	–	2	1	–	2	Phragmites australis (Cav.) Trin. ex Steud. (commonreed)
Plateumaris sericea (L.)		–	–	1	–	–	–	–	–	–	–	–	–	–	Usually on Carex spp. (sedges)
Lema spp.	p	1	–	–	–	–	–	–	–	–	–	–	–	–	Cirsium species often (thistles)
Phaedon spp.	p	1	1	1	–	–	2	–	–	–	–	1	–	–	
Hydrothassa marginella (L.)	ws	1	1	–	–	–	1	–	–	–	–	–	–	–	Often Caltha palustris L. (Marsh marigold)
Prasocuris phellandrii (L.)	ws	2	2	1	–	1	–	–	1	1	–	–	–	1	On aquatic Apiacae (Umbellifers)
Agelastica alni (L.)		–	–	–	–	–	1	–	–	–	–	–	–	–	on Alnus spp. (alder)
Phyllotreta spp.		1	1	–	–	–	1	–	–	–	–	–	–	–	
Haltica spp.		1	1	–	–	–	–	–	–	–	–	–	–	–	
Chaetocnema spp.		1	1	–	–	1	–	–	–	–	–	–	1	–	
Scolytidae															
Scolytus rugulosus (Müll.)		–	–	–	–	–	1	–	–	–	–	–	–	–	
Phloeophthorus rhododactylus (Marsh.)		–	–	–	–	–	–	–	–	1	–	–	–	–	Often on Cytisus species (Brooms)
Dryocoetes villosus (F.)		–	–	2	–	–	–	–	–	–	–	–	–	–	

Trench	Eco-logical code	Trench 1							Trackway	Trench 4					
Depth (m)		0.90–1.00	0.80–0.90	0.70–0.80	0.60–0.70	0.50–0.60	0.40–0.50	0.30–0.40		1.00–1.10	0.90–1.00	0.80–0.90	0.70–0.80	0.60–0.70	
Sample		7	6	5	4	3	2	1		6	5	4	3	2	
Curculionidae															
Apion spp.	p	–	–	–	–	–	1	–	1	1	–	–	–	3	
Phyllobius sp.	p	3	–	–	–	–	1	–	1	1	–	–	–	–	
Sitona spp.	p	–	1	1	–	–	–	–	–	–	–	–	–	–	
Rhyncolus spp.	l	–	–	–	–	–	–	–	–	1	–	–	–	–	
Bagous spp.	ws	–	2	–	–	–	–	–	–	1	–	–	1	1	
Tanysphyrus lemnae (Payk.)	ws	–	1	–	–	–	–	–	–	1	–	–	1	–	*Lemna* spp. (Duckweed)
Notaris acridulus (L.)	ws	–	1	1	1	–	–	–	1	5	1	1	1	2	Often on *Glyceria maxima* (Hartm.) Holmb. (reed sweet-grass) and other *Glyceria* species (sweet-grasses)
Thryogenes spp.	ws	2	–	–	–	1	1	1	2	–	–	–	–	–	Often on *Scirpus* spp. (rush)
Curclio spp.	l	1	–	2	–	–	–	–	–	–	–	–	–	–	
Leiosoma deflexum (Panz.)	ws	–	–	–	–	–	–	–	–	–	–	–	–	–	*Caltha palustris* L. (Marsh marigold)
Limnobaris pilistriata (Steph.)	ws	–	–	–	–	–	–	–	1	–	–	–	–	–	*Juncaceae* and *Cyperaceae* (rushes)
Eubrychius velutus (Beck)	a	–	–	–	–	–	1	–	–	–	–	–	–	–	*Myriophyllum* spp. (Water-milfoils)
Ceutorhynchus spp.	p	1	1	–	–	–	–	–	–	1	–	–	–	–	
Cidnorhinus quadrimaculatus (L.)	p	–	–	–	–	–	–	–	–	1	–	–	1	–	*Urtica dioica* L. (stinging nettle)
Mecinus pyraster (Hbst.)	p	–	–	–	–	–	–	–	–	1	1	–	–	–	*Plantago lanceolata* L. (plantain)
Gymnetron labile (Hbst.)	p	–	–	1	–	–	–	–	–	–	–	–	–	–	*Plantago lanceolata* L. (plantain)
Gymnetron spp.	p	–	1	–	–	–	–	–	–	–	–	–	–	–	*Plantago lanceolata* L. (plantain)

4. Archaeological Excavations and Analyses of a Late Prehistoric Timber Alignment

Table 4.19: The proportions of the ecological groups and related statistics for the insects from Beccles Trenches 1 and 4

Depth (m)	Trench 1								Trench 4				
	0.90–1.00	0.80–0.90	0.70–0.80	0.60–0.70	0.50–0.60	0.40–0.50	0.30–0.40	Trackway	1.00–1.10	0.90–1.00	0.80–0.90	0.70–0.80	0.60–0.70
Sample number	7	6	5	4	3	2	1		6	5	4	3	2
Total number of individuals	70	73	84	33	47	61	6	57	79	48	18	42	52
Total number of species	44	42	39	22	27	39	6	36	48	26	17	31	27
% aquatic (a)	18.6%	20.5%	21.4%	36.4%	44.7%	31.1%	16.7%	38.6%	15.2%	37.5%	16.7%	16.7%	32.7%
% waterside (ws)	21.4%	28.8%	22.6%	21.2%	12.8%	13.1%	33.3%	24.6%	35.4%	27.1%	16.7%	33.3%	38.5%
% woodland / terrestrial (l)	9.5%	8.1%	10.6%	14.3%	0.0%	8.8%	0.0%	0.0%	7.7%	11.8%	8.3%	19.0%	0.0%
% pasture / terrestrial (p)	16.7%	16.2%	8.5%	7.1%	0.0%	8.8%	0.0%	9.5%	15.4%	5.9%	8.3%	4.8%	33.3%
% dung-foul / terrestrial (df)	2.4%	10.8%	19.1%	14.3%	20.0%	8.8%	0.0%	4.8%	7.7%	5.9%	16.7%	28.6%	13.3%

TRENCH *1*

The insect faunas from Trench 1 are composed almost entirely of beetles primarily associated with fresh water and marsh habitats. Aquatic taxa and beetles associated with watersides and marsh plants (ecological groups 'a' and 'ws') account for between 40–60% of the insect faunas recovered. The water beetles recovered are indicative of slow-flowing or even stagnant waters. *Hydraena testacea, Ochthebius minimus, Coelostoma orbiculare, Cercyon sternalis* and *Laccobius bipunctatus* and *Chaetarthria seminulum* (Hansen 1986) are typical of such aquatic and waterside conditions. The 'ground beetles' *Elaphrus uliginosus* and *Platynus assimilis* are usually associated with wet, soft ground in marshes and fens (Lindroth, 1975), as are many of the *Dryops* and Helodidae species.

A range of 'reed beetles', 'leaf beetles' and weevils, recovered throughout the section, are associated with waterside vegetation. The Chyrsomelidae *Plateumaris braccata* is associated with common reed (*Phragmites australis* (Cav.) Trin. ex Steud.), *Hydrothassa marginella* with marsh marigold (*Caltha palustris* L.) and *Prasocuris phellandrii* with various waterside hog weeds (Apiaceae). The weevils *Notaris acridulus* and *Thyrogenes* spp, are associated with reed sweet-grass (*Glyceria maxima* (Hartm.) Holmb.) and rushes (*Juncus* spp.) whilst the small weevil *Eubrychius velutus* is associated with water mill-foils (*Myriophyllum* spp.).

Insects indicative of timber and trees occur in the basal sample (0.90–1.00m depth), which appears to pre-date the main phase of archaeological activity. They account for 10% of the terrestrial fauna recovered (Table 4.19 and Figure 4.47). The two species of 'longhorn beetles' recovered, *Aromia moschata* and *Leptura ?sanguinolenta* are associated with willow (*Salix* spp.) and pine (*Pinus* spp.) respectively. The *Phyllobius* and *Curculio* weevils are associated with tree leaf and nuts (Koch, 1992). The sample from 0.40m–0.50m depth contained a single individual of the 'leaf beetle' *Agelastica alni,* which is directly associated with alder (*Alnus* spp.). A restricted proportion of the insect faunas recovered indicate open pasture and grazing, such as the small numbers of *Aphodius* dung beetles recovered and a single individual of *Phyllopertha horticola* 'the garden chaffer'; as is discussed below, these probably do not indicate grazing in the immediate area of the sampling site and may have flown in (or been blown in) from terrestrial environments.

TRENCH *4*

This sequence is similar to that from Trench 1, with the majority of the insect fauna recovered being aquatic or associated with watersides and reed beds. Ecological groupings 'a' and 'ws' account for between 33% and 72% of the insect faunas recovered (Table 4.19 and Figure 4.47). Many of the water beetles, such as *Hydraena* spp., *Ochthebius spp., Cercyon sternalis, Laccobius* spp. and *Chaetarthria seminulum,* are associated with slow flowing

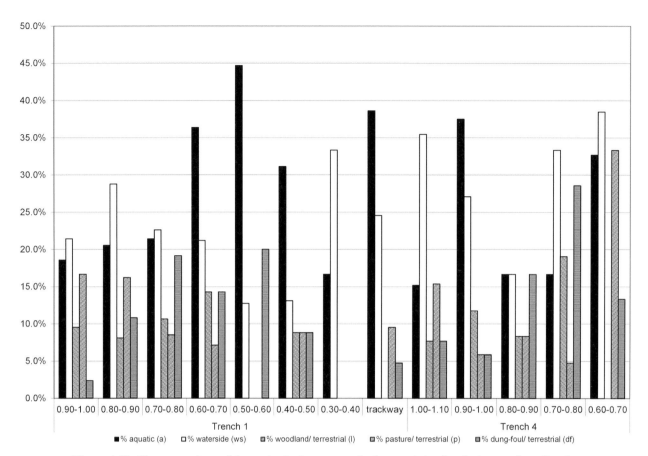

Figure 4.47: The proportions of the ecological groups and other statistics for the insects from Beccles

or stagnant waters. *Hydroporus melanarius* is usually associated with acid waters in pools and fens (Nilsson and Holmen, 1995). Many of the Carabidae 'ground beetles' such as *Elaphrus uliginosus, Trechus secalis, Pterostichus nigrita* and *P. minor* are usually found in wet watersides and fenlands (Lindroth, 1974).

The floodplain around Trench 4 also appears to have supported a mix of tall waterside vegetation. *Plateumaris braccata*, which is associated with water reed, occurs throughout the section. *Donacia clavipes* is associated with common club rush (*Schoenoplectus lactustris* (L.) Palla) and *Notaris acridulus* with reed sweet-grass and both occur throughout the sequence. *Hydrothassa marginella* and *Prasocuris phellandrii* also suggest that marsh marigold and aquatic hog weeds were present. There is a suggestion that stinging nettle (*Urtica dioica* L.) was growing nearby, since this is the food plant of the weevil *Cidnorhinus quadrimaculatus,* which was recovered in the upper two samples.

A number of species associated with dead and decaying wood were recovered from the lower two samples, including *Melasis buprestoides, c.f. Xylophilus corticalis, Cerylon spp., Grynobius planus* and *Sinodendron cylindricum.* It is possible that these species arrived on the site in the timber used in the construction of the timber alignment and represent the subsequent decay of this material, and/

or perhaps more likely, they reflect the local presence of alder carr (as evidenced by the plant macrofossil and pollen analyses). As with Trench 1, there is limited evidence for grazing animals in the area, indicated by the small fauna of 'dung beetles' recovered such as *Aphodius coenosus, A. contaminatus* and *A. sphacelatus/prodromus*. However, it is difficult to establish if animals were grazing locally or if these beetles have flown in from distant pasture. Certainly, *Aphodius* spp. have a significant flight potential and commonly enter the record from some distance away from their origin (Kenward, 1975, 1978).

SPECIES OF BIOLOGICAL IMPORTANCE

A single elytron of a Eucnemidae was recovered from 0.80–0.90m in Trench 4, which was not one of the usual ranges of Eucnemids recovered from the archaeoentomological record. No similar form could be found in the Gorham Collection of British Coleoptera at Birmingham University or the Hope Collection at the Oxford Museum. However, the detailed photographs of *Xylophilus corticalis* (Payk.) by H. Polacek (2000–2009) in the gallery section of the Koleopterologie.de website very closely resemble this specimen. However, without an actual specimen to compare to the archaeological material, identification has to remain provisional.

Xylophilus corticalis is a reasonably common, though patchily distributed, species in northern and eastern Europe where it is often encountered in white rot in decaying timber and in a range of trees (Mannerkoski *et al.,* 2009). However, it is not part of the present British fauna and has never been recorded in this country. A large number of species, which today appear to be 'extinct' in Britain, have now been recovered from the archaeological record of Britain (e.g. Buckland and Dinnin, 1993; Smith and Whitehouse, 2005; Whitehouse and Smith, 2010). Many of these, like *X. corticalis*, are associated with dead wood, which was more prevalent in early-mid Holocene woodlands.

Results: pollen analyses

TRENCH 1 (FIGURES 4.43 AND 4.44)

The basal segment of the percentage pollen diagram (Figure 4.43) is dominated by tree and shrub pollen (up to 70% at 0.97m) that largely consists of *Alnus glutinosa* (alder). *Quercus* (oak), *Corylus avellana*-type (most probably hazel but can include *Myrica gale*) and *Salix* (willow) are recorded at up to 10%. Other trees and shrubs are rare and include *Pinus sylvestris* (Scots' pine), *Betula* (birch), *Ulmus* (elm), *Fraxinus* (ash) and Ericaceae (heather family) all recorded at trace values. The general floodplain environment at this time was dominated by alder carr and stands of willow with sedges and grasses (most likely *Phragmites,* the common reed) would also have been associated with this wetland environment.

However, trees and shrubs begin to decline around 0.85m whilst herbaceous pollen increases, predominantly Poaceae (wild grasses) (25–40%) and Cyperaceae (10–25%). A wide spectra of other herbs are present at low values suggesting habitats ranging from damp ground, fen, grassy meadow and disturbed ground including Lactuceae (dandelions), Apiaceae (the carrot family) and *Plantago lanceolata* (ribwort plantain).

The upper segment of the diagram (0.65–0.35m) is dominated by herbaceous pollen, which largely consists of Cyperaceae at values up to 55% by 0.35m. Poaceae maintains consistent values *c.* 25% throughout this section but all other herbs remain at low values. *Alnus* has declined to <20% along with a slight reduction in *Salix*, implying a thinning out of the local fen carr and expansion of sedge fen on and around the sampling site. The record is heavily dominated by this local pollen signal and it is difficult to discern or characterise changes beyond the wetland edge. It would appear that *Quercus* continued to be the main component of the dryland woodland with low percentages of *Pinus, Betula* and *Corylus* suggesting that these taxa were present if not dominant. The near continuous curve for *P. lanceolata* indicates open, grassy areas on the drier soils but the precise structure of the vegetation beyond the floodplain edge is not clearly resolved in these data. The enhanced values for highly resistant spores such as Pteropsida above 0.65m may also indicate that the record

has been affected by differential preservation (discussed further below, Chapter 6).

TRENCH 4 (FIGURES 4.45 AND 4.46)

Arboreal and herbaceous pollen are equally well represented throughout the percentage diagram (Figure 4.45, with the majority of the taxa maintaining remarkably consistent values. The main arboreal species present are *Alnus, Quercus* and *Salix* with the latter expanding from 0.75m up to 20%. *Pinus* and *Betula* maintain low but consistent values (<5%) along with occasional grains of *Ulmus, Fraxinus*, Ericaeae, *Hedera helix* (ivy) and *Sambucus*-type (elder). Herbaceaous pollen is dominated by Poaceae and Cyperaceae with a wide range of other herbs present at low values including Lactuceae, *Filipendula* (meadowsweet), Caryophyllaceae (the pink family), *Plantago lanceolata* and Rosaceae (the rose family).

The general landscape illustrated throughout the pollen diagram was similar to Trench 1. Alder and willow fen carr were clearly growing on the floodplain, but this was apparently of a fairly open structure, with sedges, grasses and a variety of wetland herbs such as meadowsweet and species of the carrot and pink family also growing close by. This local vegetation probably dominates the pollen record with mixed oak woodland growing on the dryland soils. Percentages of other trees and shrubs are very low and the continuous record of *P. lanceolata* again indicates the presence of open, grassy areas. Although taphonomic issues complicate interpretation, it is possible that the wider landscape was fairly open.

Summary: palaeoenvironmental analyses

No radiocarbon dates are available for the on-site palaeoenvironmental sequences but it is clear on stratigraphic grounds (see below) that both cover approximately the same period of later prehistoric landscape development and incorporate the later Iron Age phases of activity on the floodplain itself, when the timber alignment was constructed. The overall picture is similar in both pollen diagrams, with the floodplain initially dominated by alder and willow fen carr and associated evidence for herbaceous fen vegetation including sedges and probably wetland grasses such as *Phragmites.* The presence of the latter genus is confirmed by the plant macrofossil analyses, with large amounts of this recorded throughout both sequences. The macrofossil record also demonstrates the local presence of *Juncus*; this genus tends to be 'invisible' in the pollen record. The Coleoptera in the associated samples are also typical of fen, freshwater and reed habitats, but demonstrate the importance of woody fen vegetation on the floodplain, especially towards the base of both sequences.

The Trench 1 sequence appears to show a more pronounced opening up of the fen carr and expansion of sedges in particular above 0.65m, which is not clearly resolved in the Trench 4 diagram; the main change in the latter is an increase in *Salix* above 0.72m. This may reflect a degree of spatial variation in the floodplain vegetation, but further comment is not possible in the absence of an independent chronology for both sequences. The pollen diagrams are characterised by relatively low percentages of other tree or shrub taxa, with oak the best represented at a maximum of little over 10%. This probably reflects the localised pollen source area for floodplain peat deposits accumulating within a fen carr, with plants growing on and close to the sampling site dominating the record. The macrofossil analyses confirm the presence of fen vegetation on and around the sampling site, although these data appear to be indicative of highly localised vegetation.

There is no clear indication in these data for the opening up of the alder fen suggested by the Trench 1 pollen diagram; in fact, the plant remains actually reflect an increase in grasses and other herbs down the sequence, rather than up the sequence, as in the pollen diagram from Trench 1. Rather the opposite is also implied by the Coleopteran analyses, with beetles indicative of dead and decaying wood recorded towards the base of both sequences implying the presence of trees such as alder and willow very close to the sampling site. This may be attributed to taphonomic differences between the records, with the pollen and Coleoptera probably resolving changes across a wider spatial area compared to the plant macrofossil remains. Overall, the later prehistoric floodplain at Beccles was clearly dominated by an alder fen carr (*sensu* Rodwell, 1991: 91–101), also common on other mid Holocene floodplains in Suffolk (see Chapter 3) and lowland Britain in general. The understorey consisted of tall herbs and wetland grasses. It can be observed is no direct evidence in the palaeoenvironmental records for the drier conditions that the state of preservation of the archaeological material implies (see above, also Chapter 6).

The wider dryland landscape beyond the floodplain may have been largely de-forested by this time with evidence for human impact on the lime-oak-hazel dominated woodland of the lower Waveney Valley from perhaps the Bronze Age (see Chapter 3). Certainly the record of ribwort plantain, dandelions and bracken, suggest open grassland habitats on the dryland soils within the pollen catchment. Although the Trench 4 sequence is closer to the contemporary dryland edge than Trench 1, there are no marked differences in total tree and shrub percentages, which might reflect this spatial gradient. There are a few indications of disturbed habitats in the form of 'dung' beetles that perhaps reflect grazed areas beyond the floodplain edge, but on the whole the data are insufficient to resolve the structure of the vegetation beyond the floodplain edge in any detail.

The palaeoenvironmental data therefore indicate that the timber alignment was constructed across an alder fen carr dominated floodplain. The evidence for increasingly open conditions in the beetle and pollen records coincides with the main phase of activity during the Iron Age, as reflected by the presence of worked wood debris within the peat, suggesting that the clearance of some of the alder at least

was coincident with the construction of the alignment in the later Iron Age and can therefore probably be attributed to deliberate human clearance. It is also tempting to link the palynological and Coleopteran evidence for the demise of the fen carr cover with the occasional use of alder timbers in the alignment and presence of *in situ* stools of alder identified during the excavations.

It can be noted that there is no clear evidence in the pollen record for the impact of the felling of what must have been a significant area of oak woodland for timber or indeed of the clearance of alder carr on the floodplain itself; although given that this might have been an event in a single year, then the signal of this may well fall between the sampling intervals of the pollen record. The morphological evidence that the stakes of the alignment may have been derived from coppiced woodland (see above) also implies that the woodland resources may have been managed during the later prehistoric period. The significance of the palaeoenvironmental and geoarchaeological data will be considered alongside the archaeological record in further detail in Chapter 7.

4.7 Summary: Beccles – a later Iron Age timber alignment

The excavations and associated analyses undertaken on Beccles Marshes between 2006 and 2012 revealed a triple-alignment of stakes extending for nearly 500m from the contemporary dryland edge to the southern edge of the River Waveney, the channel of which was probably in a position very close to its current course. The alignment was relatively straight but does show slight variation (Figure 4.48). The palaeoenvironmental record indicates that the later prehistoric floodplain was dominated by alder fen carr with reed swamp. This environment would have been waterlogged and thus probably treacherous to access on foot for much of the year, but there would have been seasonal fluctuation in the water table with both drier and wetter periods indicated. Periods of flooding probably account for the presence of the occasional lenses of sand recorded in the peat. Conversely, the preservation of the archaeological wood and perhaps also certain of the palaeoenvironmental proxies (see Chapter 6) indicates a period of locally relatively dry conditions, at or shortly after the time the monument was constructed in the later Iron Age.

The pollen evidence suggests that the wider dryland landscape was at least partially open with indications of deciduous woodland but significant areas of grassland and pasture. The alder fen on the floodplain must have been partially cleared at least to facilitate the construction of the site; this is indicated by the presence in several of the trenches of tree/shrub bowls that appeared to have been chopped through. The final completed form of the monument is a matter of some speculation (see below, Chapter 7) and whilst it can be assumed that the stakes of

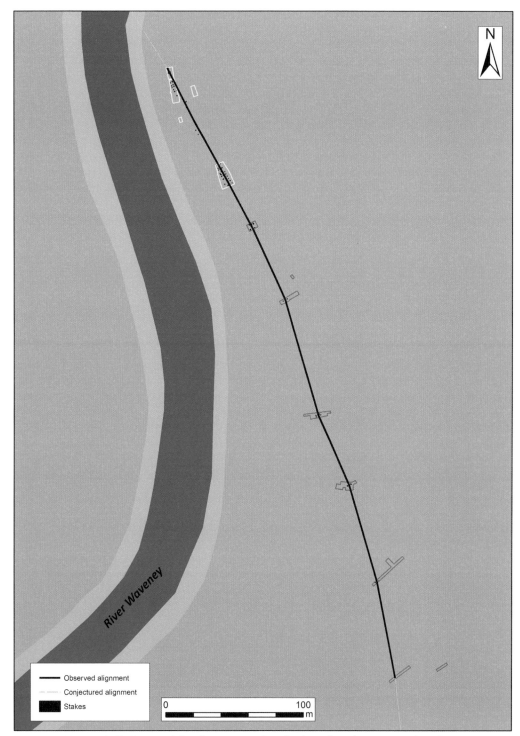

Figure 4.48: Route of the alignment at Beccles based on the excavated evidence

the alignment protruded above the contemporary floodplain ground level, the precise height of protrusion is unknown and can only be estimated based on the surviving depth below the contemporary landsurface of preserved stakes (see Chapter 7). Dendrochronology demonstrates that the alignment was constructed using timber felled in the spring of 75 BC (12 samples), the late Iron Age.

The identification of a series of horizontal wooden beams in Trench 4 indicates the presence of a ground level structure that may have been a platform or short section of trackway perhaps across a particularly wet part of the floodplain. Radiocarbon dating shows that this was also built during the later Iron Age. The relationship between this feature and the surviving tops of the vertical stakes of the alignment could not be definitively established. Other evidence from the site includes the scatters of wood from the debris field, which relates in the most part to wood working activities during the insertion of the stakes, although the identification of wood from species other than oak or alder raises further questions concerning the origin of this material. Few finds or artefacts were recovered, other than occasional Iron Age pottery, some flints and several small wooden items.

The radiocarbon analyses imply some chronological depth and possible phases of construction during the Iron Age: the brushwood structures 06 and 09 were both probably later (>99% probability) than the main alignment in 75 BC, whilst brushwood structure 07 could potentially have been earlier (70% probability). Brushwood structure 06 and 09 both seem to have led from the alignment towards the river, at the northern end of the structure, and were probably trackways designed to cross especially wet areas of the floodplain and to aid access to and from the river. The former was probably built during the late Iron Age or early Romano-British period, whilst the latter was constructed during the Romano-British period in the 1st–2nd centuries AD. It seems likely that by this time, the stakes of the alignment had rotted off at ground level, as this brushwood trackway appears to have been situated over the top of a rotted off stake. Potential evidence of repair might also be reflected by the clustering of two or three stakes in several locations, which could indicate replacements for rotted timbers. It is tempting to suggest that the repair phases also date to the Romano-British period but no absolute dates are available to confirm this hypothesis. Sherds of a single Roman vessel were also discovered.

Many of the upright stakes had halving lap joints cut into them, several of which contained horizontal timbers. The relatively flimsy nature of the horizontal pieces and the lack of any clear pattern in terms of elevation or orientation of the halving laps, indicates that they were used for the insertion of the stakes and perhaps to support the positioning of the stakes in the soft ground. The arrangement of the stakes in transverse rows across the axis of the alignment may lend some support to the hypothesis that a superstructure could have been present, such as a raised platform or walkway. If one accepts the hypotheses that the multiple stake 'clusters' represent replacements for rotted stakes, this would surely have been a very awkward procedure to carry out if a superstructure 'tied' the stakes together. No evidence of the collapsed upper sections of the stakes or indeed any structure that they might have supported was identified during the excavations. This may relate to the locally dry conditions that seem to have affected the state of the preservation of the surviving archaeological remains, although it is also possible that seasonal flooding could have washed away any wood that was lying on the surface of the floodplain. Other than the halving lap joints recorded from the upright stakes, no other timbers with any evidence of joints were recovered. Anecdotal evidence concerning the 'life' of stakes inserted into waterlogged soils, suggests a potentially very short lifespan for the initial Iron Age phase of the alignment, perhaps as short as 20–30 years (see Chapter 7). It is rather unclear therefore what the appearance of the monument was by the time of the later Romano-British activity on the site.

5. Archaeological Excavations and Analyses of other Late Prehistoric Timber Alignments in the Waveney Valley: Excavations at Barsham (2007) and Geldeston (2011)

With contributions from
Kristina Krawiec, Michael Bamforth, Catherine Griffiths,
Tom Hill, Kelly Smith, Ian Tyers and Heather Wallis

5.1 Introduction

Following the discovery of the Beccles site in 2006, the continuing soke dyke excavation as part of the Environment Agency funded flood alleviation measures (see Chapter 1) led to the identification of two further sites on the floodplain of the River Waveney. The first was discovered in 2007 on Barsham Marshes, approximately 3km upstream of the site at Beccles. Three years later, a third site was discovered just to the south of the village of Geldeston and approximately 300m to the north of the Barsham site across the River Waveney (Figure 5.1). Both the Beccles and Barsham sites are situated on the floodplain on the southern side of the Waveney, hence just within Suffolk, whilst that at Geldeston is on the north side of the river in Norfolk. Like Beccles Marshes, these areas were reclaimed in the Medieval period, shifting from un-drained common land in the late 18th century to an improved, drained landscape by the early 19th Century, as depicted on the Ordnance Survey first edition mapping of the region.

Excavations at Barsham were carried out in a single season in partnership with SCCAS in summer 2007 and have previously been reported in Krawiec *et al.* (2011). Initial excavations of the site at Geldeston were carried out by Heather Wallis in 2010, and were followed by excavations carried out as a University of Birmingham undergraduate training excavation in 2011. This chapter presents a summary of these excavations and associated analyses at both sites. The sediments are recorded as deep fen peats and silts of the Mendham Series, with underlying riverine deposits of gravels and sands of the Newport Series that form small sandy islands and ridges along the southern side of the River Waveney (British Geological Survey Sheet 176: Lowestoft). At the time of excavation, the land use across both study areas was pasture.

5.2 Excavations at Barsham (2007)

5.2.1 Introduction

The area of disturbance by soke dyke re-profiling (a maximum exposure of approximately 70 × 11m) immediately to the south of the River Waveney that initially exposed archaeological remains defined the subsequent extent of the archaeological work, with no excavations outside of this area. Archaeological methods followed those described in Chapter 1. Re-machining and hand cleaning of the disturbed area identified a series of *in situ* upright stakes on a north-north-east to south-south-west alignment, some 30m long and 4m wide (Figures 5.2 and Figure 5.3). Two sections across the predominant alignment of this structure were excavated by hand to a maximum depth of 0.40m. Twenty-nine *Quercus* stakes were extracted and samples submitted for dendrochronological analysis. A series of borehole transects were excavated at 5m intervals

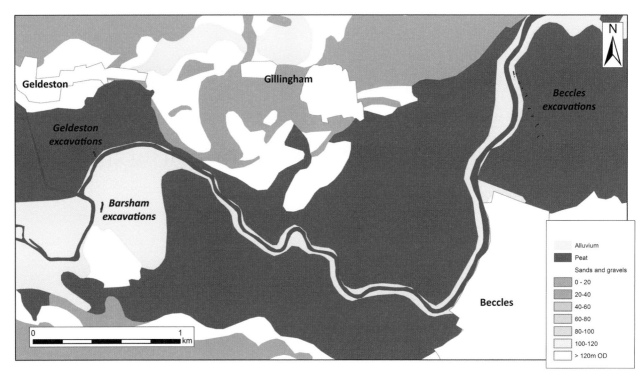

Figure 5.1: Location of the Barsham and Geldeston sites in relation to Beccles in the lower Waveney Valley. For trench plans see Chapter 4 (for the Beccles excavations) and Figure 5.2 (for Barsham) and Figure 5.9 (for Geldeston)

immediately to the west of the excavation (Figure 5.2). A monolith sequence (for pollen and diatom assessments) was recovered and a series of six bulk samples (for plant macrofossil and insect assessments) collected adjacent to the monolith from the exposed section at the eastern edge of the trench (Figure 5.2).

5.2.2 Results

Excavation

The excavation identified 29 earthfast, driven *Quercus* stakes (see Figure 5.2) arranged in three roughly parallel rows with four double clusters of stakes: (28)/(04), (08)/(29), (30)/(19), (22)/(26). The tops of these stakes (elevations of between 0.13m OD and –0.80m OD) indicated that these had rotted through at some point in antiquity. The alignment extended outside the excavated area to the north and south and thus neither terminus of the structure has been identified. A gravel spur located approximately 90m to the south-south-west, assuming no deviation, may mark the southern landfall, whilst to the north the site appears to extend tangentially towards the River Waveney.

The structure was perhaps built in a single phase, although the grouping of double clusters of stakes may represent the replacement of a broken or rotted timber and thus hint at more than one phase of construction or repair. The stakes were driven in and through black organic silts

with their upper degraded tops approximately coincident with a thin horizon of humified peat (see below). The site was constructed in shallow water at the edge of a palaeochannel of the River Waveney. As at Beccles, it is clear that the course of the river has not moved significantly in this reach during the mid-late Holocene, but prior to embankment it may have been somewhat wider at this location.

The stakes (Figure 5.4) were fashioned from moderate to good quality converted and unconverted timbers, some of which may have been obtained from coppiced woodland. The ends of the stakes had been trimmed to a point with axes and a range of conversion methods were recorded (Table 5.1), probably reflecting different sizes of raw material and perhaps also the personal preference of the woodworker. The tool marks, recorded using a profile gauge, represent a minimum of three to eight different tools, and if as Brennand and Taylor (2003) have suggested, a tool may be representative of an individual woodworker, then at least this many people might have been involved in woodworking activities. Although none of the measurements were identical, several of the curvature ratios were very similar and could represent the same tool (Table 5.2). The marks from timbers (03) and (07) have a difference in curvature ratio of only 0.09%, whilst those from (01) and (09) have a difference of 0.05%. In both cases, these values may represent the same tool leaving a complete and then a partial mark. The tool marks recorded from (05) were located next to and in line with each other.

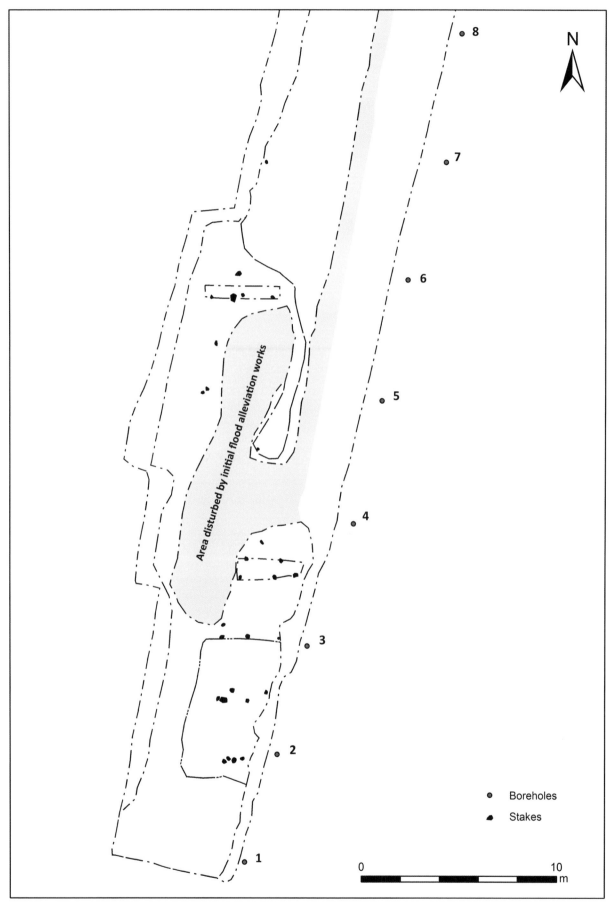

Figure 5.2: Plan of the excavations at Barsham showing position of boreholes

Figure 5.3: Barsham excavations looking north towards the river

Table 5.1: Barsham timber conversions

Conversion	Frequency	% of timber assemblage
Unconverted	14	46.67
Radial 1/2 split	2	6.67
Radial 1/3 split or less	10	33.33
Boxed or partially boxed heart	4	13.33
Total	*30*	*100*

Table 5.2: Barsham tool mark curvature ratios

Timber	Toolmark	Curvature index %
(01)	48:7	14.58
(02)	Partial 45:1	2.22
(03)	Partial 27:2	7.41
(04)	Partial 48:3	6.25
(05)	43:5	11.63
(05)	41:4	9.76
(07)	40:3	7.5
(09)	41:6	14.63
(11)	38:5	13.16
(17)	Partial 28:3	10.71
(22)	Partial 27:1	3.70

Dendrochronology

Dendrochronological analyses were carried out following the methodology outlined in Chapter 1; the results are presented in Table 5.3, and a summary of the results for the 6 component samples of the composite sequence is provided in Figure 5.5. The data can be cross-matched against late Iron-age data from the longer-lived Roman chronologies of London, the Midlands and East Anglia and dated to 170–11 BC inclusive. A total of three of the dated samples retained sapwood whilst the other three dated sequences were derived from exclusively heartwood samples. Where several timbers are dated from a single structure but none retain bark-edge, then an estimated date for the structure can be derived from combining the individual estimated felling date ranges. The felling date ranges calculated for the three samples with sapwood are:

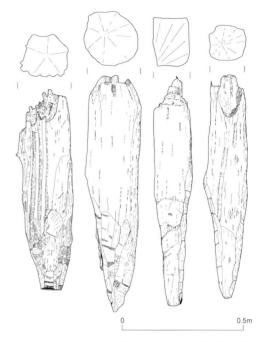

Figure 5.4: Drawings of the Barsham stakes (05, 07, 08 and 12)

20 BC–AD 8 (W21), 11 BC–AD 30 (W14) and 8 BC–AD 37 (W3). If this material is from a single event, which is not certain, the combination of these estimated ranges would yield a suggested construction (or repair?) date of 8 BC–AD 8 for this group.

Stratigraphic and palaeoenvironmental analyses

The auger survey revealed that the floodplain deposits varied in thickness from *c.* 0.95m to *c.* 1.90m to the east of the Trench, with basal elevations of between –0.75m OD and –1.70m OD, and pinched out towards the gravel outcrop to the south of the excavation. The basal gravels were overlain by olive-grey silty sand (Unit 1) (Figure 5.6), which were sealed by grey-brown silts and clays of varying organic content up to 0.40m thick (Unit 2). An orange-brown silt unit with abundant rootlets and occasional organic detritus (Unit 3) overlay these silts and clays. Above this, a humified dark brown peat with abundant herbaceous remains, woody fragments and varying silt content (Unit 4) was sealed by dense grey-brown silts and clays (Unit 5), merging into the modern floodplain topsoil. The overlying olive-grey silty sands at the base of the sequence (Unit 1) were probably deposited during the early-mid Holocene as relative sea levels rose, leading to channel aggradation (see Chapter 3). The grey-brown silts and clays (Unit 2) lying above this layer indicate a reduction in depositional energy and imply a shallow channel or channel edge context.

DIATOMS

Three sub-samples for diatom analysis were taken from the clay-silt deposits of Unit 5 on the eastern side of the

Table 5.3: Dendrochronological data from Barsham

Sample	Size (mm)	Rings	Sap	Date of measured sequence	Interpreted result
01	245 × 195	86	–	Undated	–
02	185 × 125	53	–	Undated	–
03	215 × 155	122	7	132BC–11BC	8 BC–AD 37
04	230 × 215	c. 40	?H/S	Unmeasured	–
05	195 × 180	66	–	Undated	–
06	180 × 180	c. 20	H/S	Unmeasured	–
07	260 × 200	c. 25	?H/S	Unmeasured	–
08	185 × 155	141	–	170BC–30BC	after 20 BC
09	210 × 190	83	–	163BC–81BC	after 71 BC
10	200 × 190	c. 40	–	Unmeasured	–
11	120 × ?	< 20	–	Unmeasured	–
12	160 × 150	c. 20	?H/S	Unmeasured	–
13	155 × 105	57	–	Undated	–
14	150 × 140	131	14	141BC–11BC	11 BC–AD 30
15	150 × 130	c. 15	5	Unmeasured	–
16	180 × 150	< 20	–	Unmeasured	–
17	140 × 140	c. 40	H/S	Unmeasured	–
18	195 × 180	86	–	119BC–34BC	after 24 BC
19	145 × 115	75	H/S	Undated	–
20	150 × 115	c. 15	?H/S	Unmeasured	–
21	160 × 95	100	27	119BC–20BC	20BC–AD 8
22	140 × 140	c. 25	H/S	Unmeasured	–
23	200 × 105	59	–	Undated	–
24	150 × ?	< 20	–	Unmeasured	–
25	140 × 130	74	–	Undated	–
26	120 × 95	c. 45	–	Unmeasured	–
28	45 × 35	< 20	–	Unmeasured	–
29	180 × 130	55	H/S	Undated	–
30	30 × ?	< 20	–	Unmeasured	–

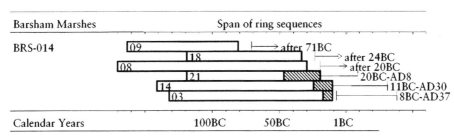

Figure 5.5: Dendrochronological dates from Barsham

trench, at depths of 0.17m, 0.27m and 0.36m. All three samples produced very low species concentrations and the majorities of the diatom frustules were heavily disarticulated or had undergone partial dissolution. This probably reflects the influence of iron oxide precipitation within the clayey silt unit due to fluctuations in redox conditions. Whilst preservation improved somewhat with depth, the limited species diversity encountered suggested preferential species preservation, with weaker biogenic silica frustules having been destroyed through post-depositional silica dissolution (Ryves *et al.*, 2001). However, the presence of disarticulated fragments of *Pinnularia* spp., *Synedra* spp. and *Epithemia* spp. indicates that the upper clay silts (Unit 5) were deposited under freshwater conditions. The records of *Diploneis bombus*, *Diploneis didyma* and *Nitzschia navicularis*, although in lower abundances, indicate some estuarine influence at this time.

RADIOCARBON DATING

The results of radiocarbon dating of the five samples from the pollen monolith are presented in Table 5.4. The uppermost three determinations of 1095±30 BP (0.20–0.30m; SUERC-22068; cal. AD 890–1020), 1155±30 BP (0.30–0.40m; SUERC-22069; cal. AD 770–980) and 1150±50 BP (0.40–0.55m; SUERC-22070; cal. AD 770–880) indicate that this part of the sequence dates to the Anglo-Saxon period. However, the two lower determinations of 3020±40 BP (0.83–0.93m; Beta-255688; 1400–1130 cal. BC) and 2430±40 BP (1.05–1.25m; Beta-255689; 760–680 and 670–400 cal. BC) display an inversion. The problems of radiocarbon dating floodplain sequences in Suffolk were highlighted previously, with evidence that *Alnus* macrofossils can be younger than the associated humic and humin fractions (see Chapter 3). It is not possible to establish which if any of these dates may

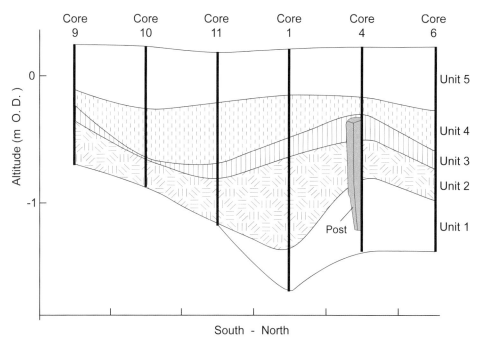

Figure 5.6: Barsham stratigraphy in relation to stake alignment

Table 5.4: Radiocarbon dates from Barsham pollen diagram

Sample depth (m)	Lab code	Sample ID	Material	$\delta^{13}C$ (‰)	Radiocarbon Age (BP)	Calibrated date (95% confidence)
0.20–0.30	SUERC-22068	BAE1822 0.20–0.30m	Wood: *Alnus glutinosa*	−29.2	1095±30	cal. AD 890–1020
0.30–0.40	SUERC-22069	BAE1822 0.30–0.40m	Wood: *Alnus glutinosa*	−29.2	1155±30	cal. AD 770–980
0.40–0.55	SUERC-22070	BAE1822 0.40–0.55m	Wood: *Alnus glutinosa*	−28.5	1150±30	cal. AD770–980
0.83–0.93	Beta-255688	BA1822 0.83m	Wood: *Alnus glutinosa*	−26.8	3020±40	1400 cal. BC–1130 cal. BC
1.05–1.25	Beta-255689	BA1822 1.25m	Wood: *Alnus glutinosa*	−26.6	2430±40	760BC–680 & 670BC–400 cal. BC

Table 5.5: Barsham percentage pollen diagram zones

Zone/ depth m	Main taxa	Interpretation
BAR-3 0.35–47.5	Cyperaceae-Poaceae-Lactuceae-*Pteridium*	Decline in *Alnus* carr & assoc-iated reduction in *Corylus* & *Pinus* wood/scrub. Expansion in open ground herb communities including local Cyperaceae (sedges) & pastoral vegetation with Lactuceae (dandelions) & *Pteridium* (bracken).
BAR-2 0.475–0.825	*Alnus-Corylus-Poaceae-Cyperaceae-Plantago lanceolata-*	*Alnus* carr on damper soils around sampling site with associated understorey vegeta-tion, scattered *Corylus* scrub with some *Pinus* growing, probably on drier soils of floodplain. Steady expansion in damp, open pastoral/meadow vegetation with Cypercaeae (sedges), Lactuceae (dandelions) perhaps at the expense of *Quercus* (oak) woodland apparent.
BAR-1 0.825–1.35	*Alnus-Corylus-Poaceae-Plantago lanceolata*	*Alnus* carr with *Corylus-Quercus* scrub, other trees including *Pinus* & *Betula* limited in extent. Pastoral vegetation with *Plantago lanceolata* & Lactuceae (dandelions) indicated.

be accurate and hence a robust chronology for sediment accumulation cannot be established, although it seems likely that the formation of the humified peat dated to the 8th–11th centuries AD.

POLLEN ANALYSES

The pollen diagram (Figure 5.7) has been divided into three local pollen assemblage zones with the prefix BAR and

Table 5.5 summarises the major features and interpretation of these zones. The diagram is notable for the relative stability of the majority of the pollen spectra until BAR-3. It is clear that *Alnus glutinosa* (alder) was dominant on and near the sampling site during BAR-1 and BAR-2. Percentages of *Corylus* (most likely to be hazel in this context) and perhaps *Quercus* indicate that these trees were growing in the wider landscape, either as scattered scrub

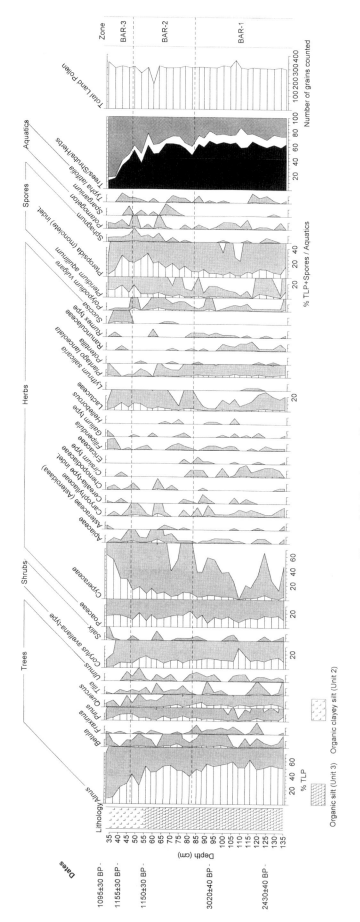

Figure 5.7: Barsham pollen diagram

Table 5.6: Summary of Barsham macrofossil analyses and associated stratigraphy

Depth/m	Macrofossils Recorded	Stratigraphy	Unit
0–0.20	–	Light grey brown organic silt	5
0.20–0.30	Damp conditions, *Phragmites australis* (common reed), *Ranunculus* (buttercups), *Urtica dioica* (nettles), *Carex* (sedges) & aquatic/muddy habitats – *Callitriche* (Water star wort). Abundant wood	Dark brown herbaceous well humified peat	4
0.30–0.40	Wet/damp conditions with *Ranunculus* spp. (buttercups), & aquatic vegetation including *Alisma* and *Eleocharis palustris/ uniglumis* (Common/slender spike rush). Abundant wood/moncots	Dark brown organic silt	3
0.40–0.55	*Mentha arvensis/aquatica, Carex* (sedge) & *Schoenoplectus lacustris/tabernaemontani* (common/grey club rush). Sparse remains but abundant wood & monocots	Dark brown organic silt	
0.55–0.90	Sparse remains. Damp/disturbed ground with *Juncus* (rushes), *Alisma, Rubus fruticosus* (brambles), *Plantago major* (greater plantain) & *Eupatorium cannabium* (Hemp agrimony)	Dark brown organic clayey silt (vivianite precipitation)	2
0.90–1.15	*Alnus* carr. Shrubs including *Betula* & *Corylus*. Aquatic vegetation including *Alisma Plantago-aquatica* (Water-plantain) & *Potamogeton* (Pond-weeds)	Dark brown organic silt with some herbaceous remains and coarse sand	
1.15–1.40	*Alnus* carr. Herbs associated with carr including *Rumex* (docks), *Chenopodium* (Fat hen) & *Lycopus europaeus* (Gypsy wort); aquatic vegetation including *Calltriche*	Dark brown organic sandy silt with some gravel	
1.40+	–	Olive-grey silty sands	1

on the drier gravel islands of the floodplain or forming more extensive woodland beyond the wetland edge. The continuous curve for the anthropogenic indicators (*sensu* Behre, 1981), *Plantago lanceolata* (ribwort plantain) and Lactuceae (dandelions), demonstrate that open pastoral vegetation was present, possibly created/maintained by grazing. Other taxa recorded sporadically including *Potentilla* (tormentil) and Caryophyllaceae (the pink family) are also apparent in the macrofossil record and are likely to reflect local herb communities on damp soils close to the river (see below).

There is little detectable change in the implied vegetation across BAR-1, although a steady rise in Lactuceae during BAR-2 suggests an expansion in meadow communities with an associated decline in the already low percentages of *Quercus* indicating that populations of this tree were affected. *Pteridium* (bracken) also increases during this zone, perhaps indicating the spread of this species onto pastureland, since a peak in *Pteridium* corresponds with a fall in *P. lanceolata* towards the close of the zone. BAR-3 records a general reduction in trees and shrubs, with *Alnus, Pinus* (Scots pine) and *Corylus* declining steadily. This is accompanied by a pronounced rise in Cyperaceae (sedges) reflecting local expansion in sedges and the demise of the *Alnus* carr. This was probably associated with a fall in local water tables, rather than human activity. The continuing record of *Pteridium* and Lactuceae imply the maintenance of pastoral vegetation with a low curve for *Succisa* (Devil's-bit scabious) perhaps also indicating the effects of grazing, since this species often grows in areas where grazing suppresses the growth of potential dominants (Grime *et al.*, 1991).

PLANT MACROFOSSILS AND INSECTS

Table 5.6 summarises the results of the macrofossil analyses alongside the stratigraphic units. Insect preservation and concentration was low and no further analyses were carried out. No identifiable plant macrofossil remains were identified within Unit 1 (inorganic olive-grey silty sand). The macrofossil samples (1.15–1.40m and 0.90–1.15m) from Unit 2 (grey-brown silts and clays) contained broadly similar plant remains indicative of aquatic vegetation and damp conditions associated with an *Alnus* carr woodland, most likely of *Alnus glutinosa-Urtica dioica* (common nettle) type (Rodwell, 1991) given the abundant fruits and seeds of these species in this sample. This confirms the evidence from the pollen diagram for the local dominance of *Alnus* during BAR-1 (see above).

Two samples (0.55–0.90m and 0.40–0.55m) are distinguished by an increase in iron oxide and other minerogenic material and an absence of *Alnus* although indeterminate wood fragments are recorded and the pollen record indicates that *Alnus* was present at least during BAR-2. The plant remains in both these samples are sparse; with that from 0.55–90m containing species associated with both damp conditions and disturbed ground. The stratigraphic transition to Unit 3 is concurrent with the beginning of a steady fall in *Alnus* and rise in Cyperaceae in the pollen record (see Figure 5.7).

The presence of iron oxide rich material in the associated macrofossil sample (0.44–0.55m) suggests that deeper water tables were quite probably responsible for both the poor preservation of macrofossil material as well as the associated local demise of *Alnus*. The lithostratigraphy of Unit 3 suggests drier conditions, probably when the channel had effectively infilled or migrated away from the sampling site, resulting in the colonisation and establishment of vegetation typical of somewhat disturbed soils.

The shift from orange-brown clayey silts to the overlying organic horizon (Unit 4) is relatively abrupt, suggesting that an erosive episode on the floodplain took place prior to biogenic sedimentation. Falling local water tables are likely to have resulted in the transition from minerogenic to biogenic sedimentation, with vegetation colonising the location, perhaps in a backswamp floodplain setting. The grey-brown silts and clays (Unit 5), which seal these deposits are interpreted as evidence for inundation of the site, perhaps as a result of overbank flooding or channel migration.

The upper macrofossil samples (0.30–40m and 0.20–30m) show an increase in taxa associated with reed swamp type vegetation and bankside habitats (Units 3 and 4). *Phragmites* (common reed) rhizomes are present in sample 0.20–0.30m with probable understory vegetation represented by the presence of *Eupatorium cannabium* (hemp agrimony). The pollen record does not extend above 0.32m but the rise in Cyperaceae recorded in BAR-3 can probably be correlated with the presence of *Carex* (sedge) nutlets in the macrofossil samples, suggesting the on-site expansion of these plants locally. Emergent or bankside habitats are indicated by the presence of *Eleocharis palustris* (common/slender spike-rush).

5.2.3 Discussion: the Barsham timber alignment

The excavations and analyses at Barsham demonstrate that an alignment of oak stakes was constructed using wood felled between 8 BC–AD 8, therefore in the very late Iron Age. It is unclear if the sampled material represents a single phase of construction or includes re-used older material, in which case the dendrochronological dates may provide a *terminus post quem*. There is no excavated evidence that the stakes supported a raised platform such as a jetty or platform, but the alignment was constructed in relatively slowly moving water at the edge of the channel of the River Waveney, with the stakes driven into and through waterlain silts. Alder carr was initially significant on the fringes of the channel, with local aquatic and bankside vegetation communities indicated, and more open wetland communities subsequently developing. The pollen record demonstrates the presence of open, pastoral habitats probably connected with the use of the floodplain as seasonal grazing, for much of the period of sediment deposition.

A subsequent fall in local water tables, perhaps as a result of a fall in the level of the river or channel aggradation, led to the growth of peat and the demise of the alder carr. The uppermost silts and clays indicate a final phase of raised water tables or flooding and the deposition of sediment in a freshwater environment, but with some tidal influence indicated by the single well-preserved diatom assemblage. Unfortunately, the lack of a robust chronology for sediment deposition hampers discussion of the timing of these events. The decayed tops of the stakes correspond to the level of the humified peat deposit, the top of which has been radiocarbon dated to 1095±30 BP (0.20–0.30m; SUERC-22068; cal. AD 890–1020). This indicates that the upper sections of the stakes had rotted off by the later Anglo-Saxon period by the very latest (although presumably much earlier than this – see below). Whilst the full extent of the site is unknown, it is possible that the Barsham and Geldeston alignments (see below) may represent the northern and southern extents of a more continuous structure and this hypothesis will be discussed further in Chapter 7.

5.3 Excavations at Geldeston, Norfolk (2011)

5.3.1 Introduction

This section describes the excavation of a third alignment site some 300m to the north-east of the site on Barsham Marshes, on the floodplain to the north of the River Waveney and hence in Norfolk, and just to the south of the village of Geldeston (see Figure 5.1). As outlined in Chapter 1, large worked stakes were discovered in 2010, again during excavation of a soke dyke as part of the programme of bank realignment by Halcrow/BESL. Heather Wallis carried out an initial excavation focusing on the disturbed area in 2010 (Site code 54133) with a subsequent season of excavation carried out by BA-E (Site code BA1254) in June 2011. The latter phase of work extended the area of investigation to the north, and was intended to better define the form and extent of the monument and to recover further samples for dating and analysis. This section presents a summary of the excavations in 2011 and synthesizes the results of dendrochronological dating of samples recovered during both the 2010 and 2011 seasons of excavation.

Archaeological methods followed those described in Chapter 1. The initial excavations in 2010 had identified an alignment of upright wooden stakes running approximately south-south-east to north-north-west (Figure 5.8). As was

Figure 5.8: Initial excavations of the Geldeston alignment by Heather Wallis

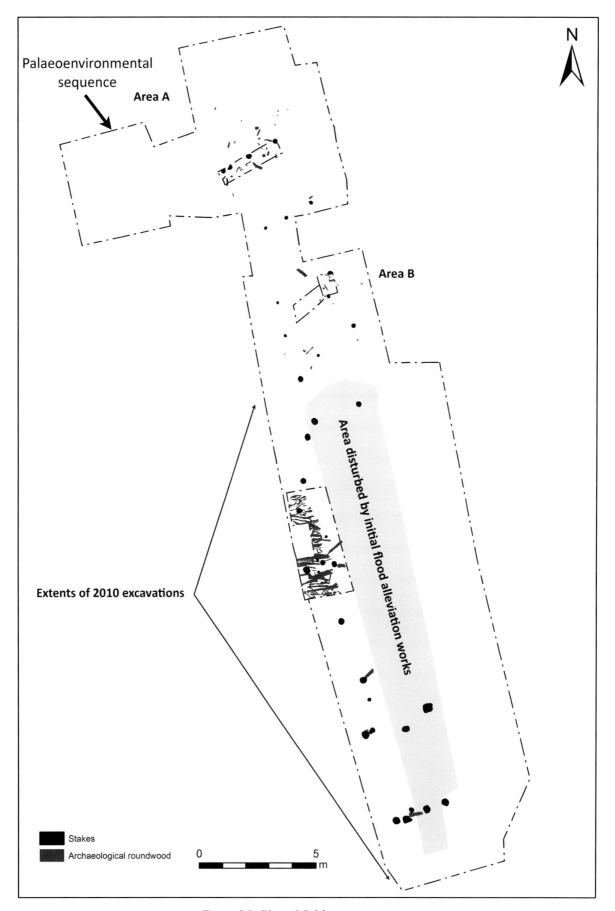

Figure 5.9: Plan of Geldeston excavations

Figure 5.10: The east–west aligned sondage within the southern part of Area A (before Areas A and B were joined) showing the alignment of stakes under excavation

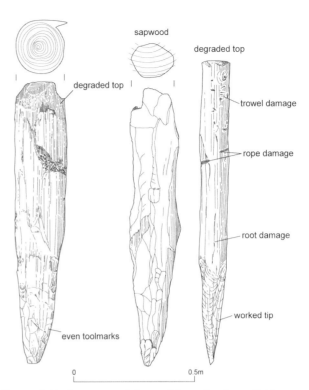

Figure 5.11: Drawings of three of the stakes from Geldeston

the case at Barsham Marshes, the machine excavation of the soke dyke had removed a number of stakes, complicating understanding of the form of the monument. Hence, the excavations in 2011 were focused on exploring the full width of the structure within an area that had not been directly disturbed by the flood alleviation works. An initial trench (Area A – see Figure 5.9)was excavated approximately 8m away from the northern extents of the 2010 excavated area (which remained open in 2011) over an area of 5.6m by 4.8m. Following the initial results, Area A was widened to both east and west but the archaeology did not extend into these areas. This trench was subsequently extended to the south (Area B – see Figure 5.9), linking the excavations with those from 2010. This provided a maximum extent of excavation of approximately 11.5 × 15m.

A sondage was excavated in Area A (see Figure 5.9), to a maximum depth of 0.80m (Figure 5.10) but rising water tables limited the depth of excavation. An additional sondage was excavated in Area B to the south (see Figure 5.9) in order to investigate the row of stakes revealed in the centre of the trench. The degraded tops of large wooden stakes were encountered at –0.68m OD (*c.* 1.0m below ground level). A total of eight stakes were recorded in the two sondages and these were box-sectioned to allow the stakes to be extracted. The upright stakes still extant from the 2010 excavations were resurveyed using the DGPS to harmonise the two phases of excavation. Wood chips were sampled in bulk from around the stakes and timber debris was recorded individually. In Area B, the tops of wooden stakes were encountered at –0.45m OD (*c.* 1.0m depth). Woodworking debris was again mostly confined within the alignment and a small amount of pottery was recovered from the southern end of the trench.

At the junction between Areas A and B a further three stakes (tops at –0.49m OD), representing a single row, were recorded. These stakes were extremely degraded in their

upper portion, which may be due to the unusually thick sapwood present resulting in less structural integrity. The majority of the pottery (SF nos 008–011) was recovered from this area (see below). The east-facing side of the soke dyke partially exposed during the 2010 excavations was further cleaned back to further expose additional stakes; a short section of horizontally laid roundwood (surface at –0.61m OD) was also exposed and was over 1.5m wide and over 4m long. A single sherd of pottery was recovered from the surface of the roundwood.

Stakes were extracted for recording from Areas A and B, each of which was hand drawn and photographed before being sampled for dendrochronological dating (e.g. Figure 5.11). A single stake was retained for subsequent recording using high-definition laser scanning (see Chapter 7). A sequence for pollen assessment was taken through the south-facing section within Area A (see Figure 5.9) using monolith tins, with a Russian corer used to recover a sequence from the bottom of the trench through to the base of the peat (total sequence 0.15–2.15m depth; –0.62 to –0.77m OD).

5.3.2 Results

Excavation

The two seasons of excavation identified 33 earthfast driven stakes, extending for around 28m south-south-east to north-north-west. As stated above, removal of an unknown number of stakes during the initial soke dyke

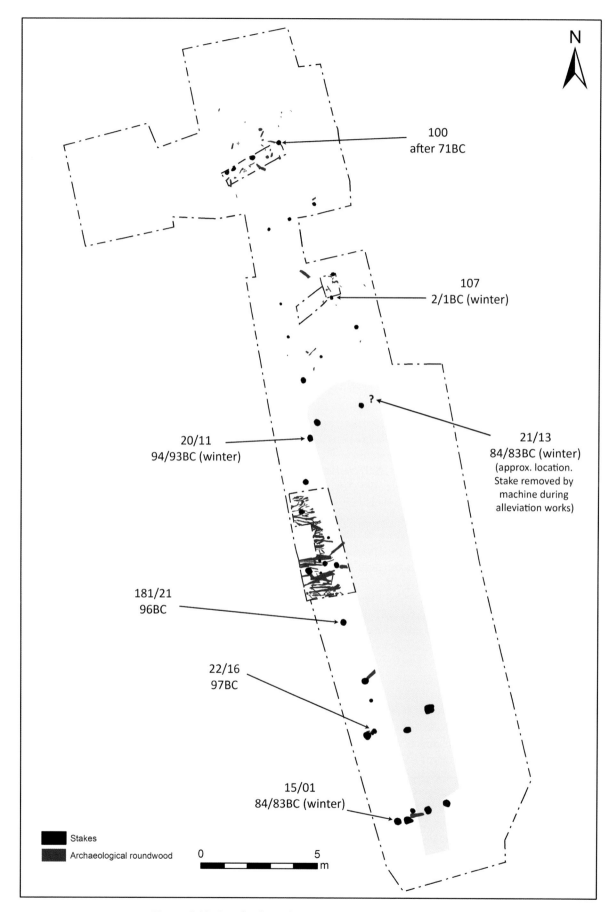

Figure 5.12: Dendrochronology sample locations at Geldeston

Table 5.7: Details of the 19 oak (Quercus spp.) dendrochronological samples from Geldeston (2010). Interpretations are given using a 10–55 ring sapwood estimate.
KEY: +B bark, season unidentifiable, +Bw bark edge, complete ring, =winter felled.

Context/sample	Rings	Sap/bark	Growth rate	Date of measured sequence	Interpreted result
15/01	61	21+Bw	1.74	144–84 BC	84/3BC winter
16/02	c. 35	–	–	not analysed	–
17/03	53	14+Bw	1.98	undated	–
180/04	c. 40	–	–	not analysed	–
16/05	64	20	2.08	undated	–
19/06	50	17+Bw	1.43	undated	–
183/08	c. 40	–	–	not analysed	–
178/09	54	25	1.30	undated	–
179/10	c. 40	–	–	not analysed	–
20/11	52	20+Bw	2.10	145–94 BC	94/3BC winter
182/12	58	–	1.82	undated	–
21/13	64	18+Bw	1.47	147–84 BC	84/3BC winter
22/16	42	21+B	1.86	138–97 BC	97BC
184/17	c. 40	–	–	not analysed	–
23/18	41	16+Bw	2.15	137–97 BC	97/6BC winter
24/19	47	15+Bw	1.96	undated	–
181/21	45	25+B	1.85	140–96 BC	96BC
177/37	c. 40	–	–	not analysed	–
25/42	c. 40	–	–	not analysed	–

excavation hampers understanding of the precise form of the monument for much of its length, but the undisturbed areas in Area A and to the southern end of the site imply a roughly triple alignment arrangement, around 2.5–3m wide with a spacing of around 1m between stakes within each triple grouping and approximately 3m between chords. The chords are not always very regular, and one double cluster of stakes and a single triple cluster of stakes are evident. The southernmost chord of stakes consisted of five relatively closely spaced pieces. The short section of horizontally lain roundwood in the western side of the 2010 trench is interpreted as a brushwood trackway or perhaps platform of corduroy construction. The structure was preserved within floodplain peats, described as brown, moderately humified with frequent monocotyledonous and fragments of wood. The upper c. 0.15m of the sequence consisted of grey-brown alluvial silts and clays. This stratigraphic sequence did not show significant variation across the site.

Dendrochronology

Samples for dendrochronological dating were submitted from both the 2010 and 2011 excavations and hence although the results of these two phases of analyses were reported separately, they are summarized in Figure 5.12. Dendrochronological analyses followed the standard methods described in Chapter 1.

The submitted material from the 2010 excavations comprised 19 oak (*Quercus* spp.) samples of which 12 contained measurable tree-ring sequences and more than 40 annual rings. These 12 samples were each measured successfully (Table 5.7). Cross-matching evidence identified that six of these individual series could be linked to other timbers from within the site (Table 5.8), and that the composite sequence constructed from these

Table 5.8: Showing t values (Baillie & Pilcher 1973) between the six matched timbers from Geldeston 2010 excavations

	11	13	16	18	21
01	4.85	5.86	4.22	2.80	4.60
11		3.83	3.60	3.52	6.43
13			5.49	4.76	4.85
16				5.62	4.78
18					4.16

Table 5.9: Showing example t values (Baillie and Pilcher 1973) between the composite sequence constructed from six timbers from Geldeston 2010 excavations, and independent site series

	Geldeston 54133 147–84 BC
London, 72–80 Cheapside (Tyers 1992)	5.64
London, Drapers Gardens/Throgmorton Ave (Tyers 2008)	6.86
London, Miles Lane/Upper Thames St (Hillam pers. comm.)	6.01
London, Pudding Lane (Hillam pers. comm.)	6.26
London, Thames St Tunnel (Hillam 1980)	5.83
Suffolk, Beccles 2006/2007 (Tyers 2007)	5.55

could be successfully matched to Beccles (see above), as well as to the regionally strong data-sets from London excavations (Table 5.9).

The results are presented in a bar diagram (Figure 5.13). All of the dated samples retained intact bark-edges. Four of the samples come from the period 97–94 BC, two of indeterminate season in 97 BC and 96 BC. In both cases this could also cover the late winter/early spring of the following year; the others were felled in the winter of 97/96 BC and winter of 94/93 BC respectively. The two remaining samples date from winter 84/83 BC.

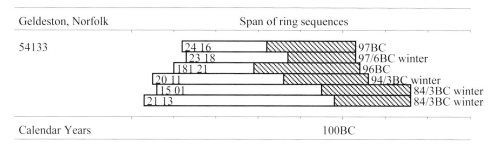

Figure 5.13: Bar diagram showing the dating position of the 6 dated oak tree-ring samples from Geldeston 2010 excavations.
Key: bars are labelled with Sample/Context, heartwood (white bars), sapwood (hatched bars).

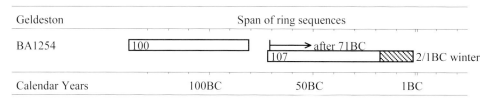

Figure 5.14: Bar diagram of dendro samples from Geldeston 2011 excavations

Table 5.10: Details of the 18 oak (Quercus spp.) dendro-chronological samples from Geldeston 2011 excavations. Interpretation of sample 100 using a ten ring minimum sapwood estimate.
KEY: +Bw bark edge complete ring, =winter felled * banded growth pattern prevented analysis.

Sample	Rings	Sap	Date of measured sequence	Interpreted result
100	59	–	139–81 BC	after 71BC
102	c. 65	–	not analysed *	–
104	< 30	–	not analysed	–
105	c. 40	–	not analysed *	–
106	54	2	undated	–
107	71	16+Bw	72–2 BC	2/1BC winter
108	81	13	undated	–
109	c. 40	–	not analysed	–
110	58	–	undated	–
111	< 30	–	not analysed	–
112	< 30	–	not analysed	–
157	< 30	–	not analysed	–
162	< 30	–	not analysed	–
185	< 30	–	not analysed	–
187	c. 40	–	not analysed	–
203	< 30	–	not analysed	–
205	< 30	–	not analysed	–
209	c. 35	–	not analysed	–

Table 5.11: Showing example t values (Baillie and Pilcher, 1973) between timbers 100 & 107 from Geldeston 2011 excavations, and samples from Barsham Marshes (Tyers, 2008).

	100	107
Barsham Marshes BRS014 Suffolk composite chronology	7.25	6.11
Barsham 03	6.43	5.49
Barsham 08	3.47	3.10
Barsham 14	3.18	5.40
Barsham 18	4.09	5.11
Barsham 21	3.56	3.92

The submitted material from the 2011 excavations comprised 18 oak (*Quercus* spp.) samples of which five contained sufficient rings for analysis, or were free of stressed growth banding. The five suitable samples were each measured successfully (Table 5.10). Cross-matching evidence identified that two of these individual series were datable (Table 5.11). The results are presented in the bar diagram (Figure 5.14), one of the dated samples (107) was intact to bark-edge and felled in the winter of 2/1 BC. Although no

sapwood survives on Sample 100, this was a roundwood timber so the latest rings are likely to be near the edge of sapwood; although this seems likely, it cannot be proven to be a different phase of activity than Sample 107. The two dated series cross-match strongly with the material from Barsham (see above), but they do not have any similarity with the samples from the 2010 excavations discussed above.

In summary, the dendrochronological evidence suggests that whilst the Geldeston timber alignment dates to the late Iron Age, there was potentially a more complex and extended period of monument construction at Geldeston compared to the Beccles and Barsham sites. However, interpretation is hampered by the fact that only seven out of the thirty-seven samples submitted yielded dates. The available chronology stretches from an initial a period of construction using wood felled in 97–94 BC, followed by the addition to, or repair of, the structure a decade or so later in 84/83 BC. The single Sample 107 demonstrates a phase of repair or extension of the structure in 2/1 BC. Other similar phases may well be present but are not identifiable in the available tree-ring data; this will be discussed further below (see also Chapter 6).

Table 5.12: Timber debris from debris scatter

No	Species	Bark/ sapwood/ heartwood	Condition score	Notes		Length (mm)	Max breadth (mm)	Max thickness (mm)
w0113/	Quercus sp.	H	3	Rad 1/2.Tan (mod)	outer surface split away	490	153	53
w0114/	Quercus sp.	SH	3	Tan		128	27	12
w0116/	Quercus sp.	SH	3	Tan	square cross section	125	21	16
w0120/	Quercus sp.	H	3	Tan		400	82	18
w0121/	Quercus sp.	H	3	boxed heart	1 end/1 dir	178	78	37
w0128/	Quercus sp.	H	4	Rad 1/3 (mod) outer	both ends/1 dir	130	95	55
w0129/	Quercus sp.	H	4	Tan	1 end/1 dir	490	82	40
w0133/	Quercus sp.	H	4	Tan	1 end/1 dir. 1 end/cross cut	200	50	
w0134/	–	SH	3	Rad 1/2		150	140	70
w0137/	Quercus sp.	H	4	Tan outer	1 end worked into partial halving lap joint	510	95	55
w0182/	–	SH	4	Rad 1/2	1 end/1 dir 1 end cross cut	250	89	60
w0232/4	Quercus sp	H	4	Rad 1/4 (mod) SQ	1 end/cross cut & worn	129	55	50

Palaeoenvironmental assessments

A monolith sequence was extracted from the open face of the trench section (1.2m) in Area A with core samples taken through the base of the trench to the underlying gravels at a depth of 2.20m providing a continuous sequence through the peats. However, subsequent palynological assessment indicated low concentrations of poorly preserved pollen, especially in the middle part of the sequence (1.50–0.70m) where assessment level counts could not be achieved. A brief summary of the results is provided here.

The data indicate that peat inception probably began in an alder fen carr with high percentages of *Alnus* (alder) and few other trees besides *Corylus avellana*-type (probably hazel) recorded in the basal samples (2.15–1.70m), indicating either woodland cover beyond the floodplain or on drier areas close-by. A marked increase in *Pinus sylvestris* (Scots' pine) just below the middle of the sequence (1.50–0.70m) may represent a phase of drying out of the site and the possible spread of this tree onto the floodplain surface or perhaps onto gravel islands in the close vicinity. This depth of the core also corresponds to the level of the later prehistoric ground surface and above, perhaps indicating that deeper water tables persisted on the site for some time.

However, there is no clear stratigraphic evidence for any marked change in sediment accumulation and no radiocarbon dates are available to infer the chronology for the hiatus in the palynological stratigraphy. Pollen preservation improved in the shallower deposits (0.70–0.20m) with tree and shrub pollen including *Alnus*, *Ulmus* (elm) *Betula* (birch) and *Salix* (willow) recorded but with herbs in the form of Poaceae (wild grasses) and relatively high counts for Pteropsida (monolete) indet. (ferns). The latter and the generally poor condition of the

grains, suggest that the pollen record has been affected by differential preservation. It can be observed that the pollen preservation in the deeper parts of the cores from Beccles was also rather poor (see Chapter 2), perhaps implying that the sedimentary environments on the Waveney floodplain during the Holocene have been inimical to pollen preservation in general.

Archaeological wood analysis

Wooden debris was 100% recorded from the two sondages in Area A, one sondage in Area B and the small areas excavated around the upright stakes to facilitate their removal. A total of 83 items were recovered from the debris scatter, which was noted as being less dense than that encountered during the excavations at Beccles (see Chapter 4). The debris scatter consisted of roundwood (5 pieces), woodworking debris (76 pieces) and two items classified as artefacts.

Three pieces of roundwood and two pieces of half split roundwood were identified. Trimmed ends/side-branches were noted in three cases. The items varied in length from 65mm to 300mm and 19–60mm in diameter. The woodworking debris consists of bark (1 piece), timber debris (12 pieces), woodchips (45 pieces) and unclassified debris (18 pieces). A single worked piece of bark (W197/1 – 74 × 36 × 15mm) with a trimmed end was recorded. Approximately one hundred unworked bark fragments were encountered but they are not discussed here in detail. Many of these fragments were fairly thick, suggesting they were derived from larger oak timbers

Twelve items (ten of which were identified as oak) were classed as timber debris (off-cuts from the reduction of larger timbers) all of which scored a 3 or 4 for condition (Table 5.12). All the items were split – six tangentially aligned, five radially aligned and a single boxed heart. Six of the items were also trimmed with two items trimmed at one end from one direction, one item trimmed at both ends from one direction, and three items trimmed at one end from one direction and cross cut at the opposite end. It is relatively unusual to encounter pieces of waterlogged wood with both original worked ends intact. A single item (W116) appears to be splitting debris – the long, slender 'streamers' that connect two opposing split surfaces during cleaving. A single item (W137) had been worked at one end into a partial halving lap, but the worked end was severely fragmented, precluding detailed recording.

Forty-five items were classed as woodchips, of which 24 (53%) were identified as oak. The items scored 1–4 for condition, with 3 being the most frequent (18 items – 40%). Twenty-seven of the woodchips were formed of heartwood only, 13 of sapwood and heartwood and two of sapwood only. There were also three 'slabs', formed of bark and sapwood and probably indicative of bark removal (Taylor, 2001: 175). Thirty-six of the woodchips were tangentially aligned and nine radially aligned. Seven items had trimmed ends; five at one end from one direction and two at both ends from one direction. There were 18 items of unclassified debris, nine of which (50%) were identified as oak. All the items were split, nine in the radial plane and nine in the tangential plane. Eight items had trimmed ends; four trimmed at one end from one direction and four trimmed at both ends from one direction.

The only items classified as timber from the wood assemblage were the oak stakes of the alignment, only three of which were converted. The oak woodchips may have derived from dressing the split surfaces of converted stakes (in both the radial and the tangential planes) and from shaping the stakes into points (in the tangential plane). There were no large non-oak timbers within the assemblage from which the 22 non-oak woodchips could have originated. This is also the case for the two pieces of non-oak timber debris and the nine non-oak pieces of unclassified debris.

Artefacts

W119 – PEG

This tangentially aligned oak item (114 × 42 × 28mm) had been split and hewn into a wedge shape and was recovered from the sondage within Trench 1. It scored a 4 for condition. The opposite end had been cross cut. The original function of this item is unknown.

W156 – ROUGH DOWEL

This item (260 × 70 × 60mm) was formed from a radial 1/8 that had been hewn into a rough dowel. One end had been trimmed from all directions into a blunt pencil point. It was positioned at approximately 45° in the sondage in Trench 2 and scored a 4 for condition. Although no evidence as to its possible original function has survived, it may have been a broken tool handle.

Figure 5.15: The roundwood structure identified on the western edge of the Geldeston alignment (facing east)

Trackway/platform structure

A roundwood structure representing a probable trackway or platform of corduroy design was identified, extending into the trench edge on the western side of the 2010 excavations and further investigated in 2011 (Figure 5.15). It was formed predominantly of 40 east–west aligned pieces of roundwood and three half-split lengths of roundwood. A small quantity of woodworking debris was also encountered in this location (a single piece of timber debris and three woodchips). The material was set around an upright stake of the alignment (W205) and a roundwood stake (W224) (Figure 5.16). The eastern edge of the structure was revealed in plan but the western edge continued out of the trench.

The only marked difference between the upright stake in the area of the structure (W205) and those from the remainder of the site is that the sharpened end has been worked from the point towards the body of the timber – the opposite direction to all the other stakes. The degraded top of the upright stake stood 0.15m proud of the surrounding horizontal material. The east–west aligned roundwood seemed to respect the upright stake, suggesting that the trackway/platform was constructed around the same time that the stake was inserted. A single roundwood stake (W224), 1.2m to the south-south-east of stake W205 was also respected by the horizontal material. The stake had been trimmed to a point at the bottom end from one direction to form a chisel point (L: 410mm, D: 45 × 50mm).

The majority of the roundwood had bark present (30 items). The condition score varied from 2–4, with the majority scoring a 3. Two pieces appear to be coppice heels and ten pieces had the straight, even stem, no side branches and central pith indicative of coppiced material (Rackham, 1977). Eight pieces were trimmed at one end from one direction, two of the items were cross-cut at one end and a single item had a side branch trimmed away. The roundwood varied in length from 100–1040mm and in diameter from 13–5mm. The original diameters of the

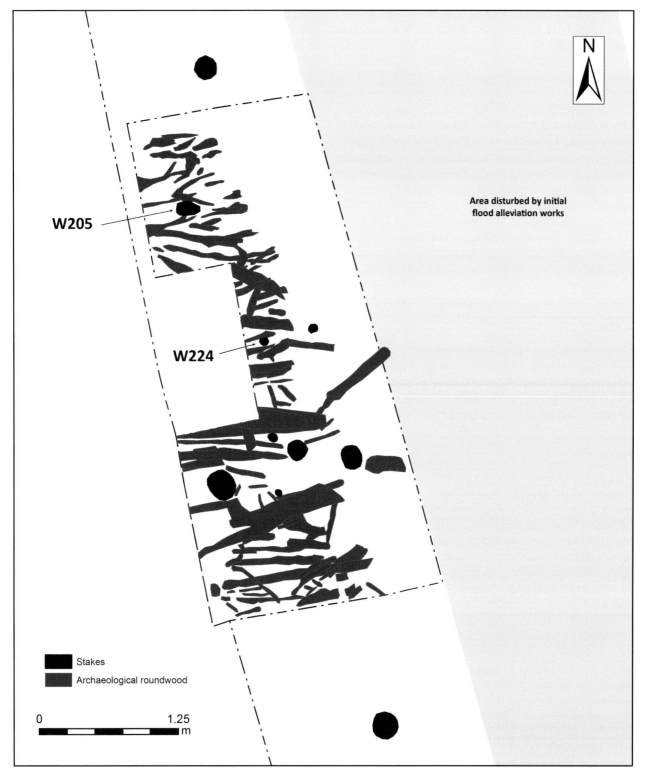

Figure 5.16: Plan of the trackway excavations showing the positions of alignment stake W205 and roundwood stake W224

half split roundwood items (30–72mm) also fitted within this range. The diameters of the roundwood and half split roundwood were relatively tightly grouped, with 71% falling between 10mm–49mm.

Ring counts were obtained from thirty-one of the pieces of roundwood. There was a broad spread of ages varying from 3–23 years of growth. This same broad spread can be seen within the eleven items that show morphological evidence of coppicing, which ranged from 4–23 years of growth. There was a broad range of species represented with seventeen items identified as alder, eleven as hazel, eight as oak and two as willow. The broad range of ring counts was also evident when considered by species. The ring counts have provided no evidence for a rotational coppicing cycle.

Given the relatively tight grouping of diameters it seems likely that roundwood stems were selected for their diameter, across a range of species present in mixed deciduous woodland. Although some of the material may have been sourced from coppiced woodland, the relatively high ring counts of several of the roundwood stems suggests that at least some of the material was sourced from naturally occurring understorey growth. The most likely scenario is that the material was gathered on an *ad hoc* basis, selected by no criteria other than a suitable diameter. The woodworking debris, in the form of both timber debris and woodchips, was predominantly oak and derived from the working of larger timbers. As such, it does not appear to be derived from the roundwood and split roundwood elements that the platform/trackway is constructed from.

Stakes

Three smaller, oak, upright stakes were identified. Stake W101: radially split, one end trimmed from one direction, side-branches trimmed away; Stake W103: radial 1/3 split, bottom end cross cut; W181: radial 1/5 split, proximal end trimmed to a point.

Pottery

A total of 40 sherds weighing 477g were recovered during excavations, the majority from the junction between Areas A and B. The pottery is all of later Iron Age date and all but one of the sherds are from a single vessel. The sherds were well-preserved, but fragmentary, with an average sherd weight of just over 11g. Two fabrics were identified: sandy with no visible inclusions and a second fabric that was similar but has small, scattered, angular flint inclusions (Table 5.13).

The sandy fabrics suggest that the pottery dates to the later Iron Age, perhaps from around 300–250 BC onwards. Rims were present from two vessels: a single out-turned rim, with rounded rim ending made of sandy fabric Q1, was found in association with the corduroy platform/trackway (see above). Rim, body and base sherds from a second vessel made of fabric Q2, were collected from ten find spots in Area B. This vessel is a small jar with a diameter at the rim of *c.* 170mm. Again the rim is out-turned with a simple rounded rim ending above a concave neck and sinuous body. The base of the vessel is simple.

Table 5.13: Quantity and weight of pottery from Geldeston by fabric

Fabric	Description	Quantity	Weight
Q1	Common, dense quartz sand	1	4 g
Q2	Common, dense quartz sand; sparse small angular white flint	39	473 g
Total	–	40	477 g

Approximately 44% of the rim survives along with *c.* 30% of the base. The shoulder of the jar is emphasised with a faint cordon. The exterior of the jar is smoothed or lightly burnished. The pottery is also similar to that from several other sites along the Waveney Valley such as Flixton FLN057 (Percival, 2004), and the sandy later Iron Age pottery from Barnham (Martin, 1993: 15) to the south-west of Beccles on the Little Ouse river.

5.3.3 Discussion: the Geldeston timber alignment

The excavations at Geldeston identified oak stakes forming a timber alignment some 28m long and *c.* 2.5–3m wide. The structure may be loosely described as a triple alignment, at least in so far as its surviving layout, similar in form to Beccles and perhaps Barsham. As at Barsham, the removal of material during the soke dyke excavation hinders understanding of the original distribution of the stakes and hence the possible form of the monument. The alignment was built across an alder carr floodplain environment, which was probably very similar to that at Beccles, but poor pollen preservation prevents detailed understanding of local or extra-local changes in vegetation during later prehistory and no other palaeoenvironmental data are available.

The dendrochronological dates demonstrate an initial period of construction during 96–97 BC, with at least one stake added a few years later in 94/93 BC and two more a decade later in 84/83 BC. It can be noted that all these dated samples were recovered from the westernmost line of stakes. The two remaining dated samples indicate the insertion of at least one stake after 71 BC and one stake in 2/1 BC. Both of these were located on the easternmost side of the monument. The range of dates indicate activity at the site over a period of nearly a century, but the relatively small number of stakes, which returned dendrochronological dates, does not permit in depth understanding of the chronology of monument construction. It is not known when the short stretch of corduroy trackway was constructed. Other surviving fragments of worked wood derive from finishing of the stakes carried out on site during construction of the monument; with other identifiable (non-oak) remains probably derived from the on-site clearance of trees and shrubs at or around the same time. Few artefacts were recovered during excavation, other than the sherds of a single Iron Age vessel, and two wooden items identified as a peg and possible broken handle. The majority of the pottery sherds represent a single broken vessel, dispersed across the excavated area of stakes. The three fragmentary vessels of comparable date from Beccles (see Chapter 4) exhibited similar dispersal patterns across the alignment (see Chapter 7 for further discussion).

Whilst the extent of the monument to the south has not been established, the alignment would appear to terminate abruptly to the north in Trench 1. The alignment does not therefore extend to the floodplain–dryland interface, which was located approximately 20m to the north of the excavated area. Alternatively, the structure may have been partially dismantled in antiquity, or the spacing between stakes might increase beyond the 5m limit that defines the gap between the final chord of stakes and the northern end of the excavated area. It is unknown whether the alignment extended into the open channel of the river or terminated at the channel edge of the floodplain, which was likely in later prehistory to have been very close to its current location.

The available data do not permit a definitive statement as to whether the triple arrangement of the extant stakes reflects the initial form of the monument. As was the case with Beccles, the upper sections of the stakes must have rotted off in antiquity, perhaps within a fairly short period of time following their insertion (see below). However, as outlined above, the available data are insufficient to determine the character or chronology of local environmental changes and relationship to human activity.

5.4 Summary: late prehistoric timber alignments at Barsham Marshes and Geldeston

This chapter has summarised the results of excavations and associated analyses of two later prehistoric wetland sites in the lower Waveney Valley on Barsham Marshes and at Geldeston. Despite the profusion of archaeological, palaeoenvironmental and geoarchaeological data that wetland sites and landscapes can generate, the basic archaeological questions of form and hence possible function of monuments can often remain just as problematic as for dryland sites. This is even more difficult when there are very few comparative excavated structures (see Chapter 7).

The Geldeston and Barsham alignments are situated on opposite sides of the River Waveney, some 300m apart, and following similar north–south alignments. The dendrochronologically dated samples demonstrate that there was a very slight chronological overlap between the two sites. For the most part, the site at Geldeston is older, with the majority of stakes (all from the westernmost line of stakes) dating to the 90s and 80s BC, although with a small number of later stakes; one of which dated to 2/1 BC (on the eastern-most side of the structure). The alignment on Barsham Marshes was constructed around a century later, with dendrochronological dates between 8 BC and AD 8, although it is possible that some of these timbers were re-used, in which case this range represents a *terminus post quem*. Some degree of contemporaneity during the final stages of activity at Geldeston and Barsham might be assumed, and hence these may have effectively formed a single monument stretching for some 800m across the River Waveney and its floodplain during their latest phases. This hypothesis could only be tested by further excavation. Given the date for a phase of construction at Geldeston around 84/83 BC, it seems likely that the stakes may have been upstanding when the main phase of activity at Beccles began (75 BC). Chapter 7 presents an integrated discussion of the form, function and broader context of all three Waveney timber alignments.

6. Assessing the Preservation of the Archaeo-Environmental Resource at Beccles and Barsham: Implications for Future Management and Preservation *In Situ*

With contributions from
Ian Panter, Emma Hopla, David Smith, Wendy Smith, William Fletcher and Ingrid Ward

6.1 Introduction

The difficulty of identifying organic archaeology within waterlogged sediments means that generally the first knowledge of such remains is when ground is broken by developments or other interventions, as was the case with the Waveney timber alignment sites. Once sites have been identified and characterised there is a related problem of determining the most appropriate response, assessing the state of preservation and determining the prospects for future preservation *in situ* (e.g. Olivier, 2013). During the past decade, a number of investigations have been carried out on archaeological sites and deposits in both rural and urban contexts in England (e.g. French, 2004, 2009; Holden *et al.*, 2006; Williams *et al.*, 2008; Kenward and Hall, 2008; Boreham *et al.*, 2011; Brunning, 2012, 2013; Malim and Panter, 2012), which are beginning to allow the efficacy of preservation *in situ* of waterlogged sites to be critically assessed (Williams, 2012).

This chapter outlines detailed decay analyses of the archaeological wood recovered during the excavations at Beccles (2009) and a more limited programme of this work at Barsham, with investigations of the associated burial environment geochemistry and the results of assessments of the preservation of the palaeoenvironmental proxies (pollen, plant macrofossils and beetles) from Beccles. A two-year programme of monitoring of the water table across the Beccles study area was undertaken in order to investigate the relationship between hydrological fluctuations in the burial environment and the state of preservation of the archaeo-environmental resource. These data provide information regarding the impact of current and past processes on the condition of the resource and inform on the prospects for the long-term preservation *in situ* of the deposits. The chapter concludes with a general discussion of the problems and potential of preserving the timber alignment sites in the face of current and possible future threats to the stability of the burial environment.

6.2 Assessing the preservation of the organic archaeology at Beccles

The condition of the archaeological wood at Beccles showed significant variation within and between trenches. As well as the semi-quantitative approach discussed in Chapter 4, other analyses also provided data regarding preservation, with some indications that the material to the southern end of the site was more degraded than that to the north. The dendrochronological studies also identified evidence for variable preservation of the stakes along the excavated length of the alignment; for example, the number of timbers identified with more than 35 rings, and complete sapwood and bark-edge totalled only four from the excavations in 2009, three of these were from Trench 1 and one from Trench 4. In contrast 14 and 11 stakes were dated from the 2006 and 2007 excavations respectively.

Table 6.1: Physical condition of wood samples (2009)

Timber no.	Trench	Species	Function	Physical condition
821	1	*Alnus* spp	horizontal	Split roundwood, 27 × 14mm. No bark, wood very soft, compressible. Rootlets growing through wood.
852-	1	*Alnus* spp	horizontal	Roundwood, 62 × 45mm. Some bark present, wood soft & compressible. Rootlets growing through wood. Longitudinal desiccation cracks on underside.
855	1	*Alnus* spp	Horizontal	Roundwood, 40 × 33mm. Some bark attached, wood soft & compressible. Rootlets growing through wood. Longitudinal desiccation crack on underside.
744	1	*Quercus* spp	Upright	Recovered in 2 sections labelled a & b (cut for dendro.), maximum diam. 680mm. No bark, 1 trimmed large side branch, worked to a point. Pith eccentric. Outer sapwood to upper end very decayed, but solid heartwood core. Desiccation cracks 250mm long from upper end. Rest of wood is solid.
1220	4	*Quercus* spp	Upright	Upright, recovered in 1 complete length, 810mm long, worked to a point. Upper end eroded, sapwood very soft & decayed. Remainder of wood better preserved by longitudinal cracks to worked facets.

The poorer preservation of the stakes excavated in 2009 was reflected in the loss of bark-edge, sapwood and outer rings so consequently these samples were below the threshold for reliable analysis. In addition, many samples displayed narrow bands around the heartwood/sapwood transition, reflecting poor growth conditions in antiquity, a few decades before the felling of the wood. These bands further reduced the number of suitable samples from the 2009 assemblage. This phenomenon was not commonly observed in the 2006 or the 2007 samples, which may also suggest that different woodland areas were being exploited for the construction of the southern part of the alignment.

It was noted during the wood species analyses of the horizontal beams in Trench 4 that the samples appeared degraded on a cellular level. In some cases, the condition was such that it was not possible to determine if the beams had been altered by preservation conditions and/or anthropogenically modified in antiquity by cleaving. There was also a higher than average degree of compression and the beams had poorer condition scores (2–4) and a higher incidence of damage caused by *Phragmites* roots in comparison to material from the other trenches. In some cases the effects of degradation were clear, such as with timber 1206, which had degraded to such an extent that the sapwood and bark remained at the lower end of the timber, whilst only the bark remained at the highest end and all the heartwood and much of the sapwood had rotted away. In the case of shallower archaeological remains, such as the brushwood trackway in Trench 1, all of the wood samples displayed damage from desiccation and penetration by *Phragmites* roots.

The data therefore implied significant variation in the state of preservation of the archaeological remains at Beccles. In order to further investigate this, samples were taken from two trenches (Trenches 1 and 4 2009) for a combination of more detailed condition assessments (see Table 6.1). These were selected to ensure integrated, multi-proxy data regarding the physical nature of the burial environments (soil chemistry), which could be linked to

the recorded preservation of palaeoenvironmental proxies (beetles, pollen and plant macrofossils).

Sampling and assessment for wood condition characterisation – methods

Detailed decay analysis was undertaken on five timbers; three horizontal (821, 852 and 855), one stake from Trench 1 (744), and one stake from Trench 4 (1220); wood species identification was carried out by Steve Allen (York Archaeological Trust). Standard condition assessment tests were also applied (Panter and Spriggs, 1996, see also Chapter 1), including a physical description of each sample, density assay, maximum water content determinations and calculation of loss of wood substance.

The samples of *Alnus* were soft and compressible, with water exuding when compressed. Rootlets had grown through many of the samples of wood indicating high levels of decay (Table 6.1). The *Quercus* stakes appeared to be better preserved, although high levels of decay were observed in the uppermost sections, presumably as a result of fluctuating water levels (see below). A pin test survey (de Jong, 1977) of all the stakes indicated similar patterns: a more decayed upper zone but better preservation with increasing depth. Several classification systems have been developed in an attempt to group wood according to decay. One early system (de Jong, 1977) grouped *Quercus* wood into three classes depending upon the maximum water content values:

Class 1 – the wood has a µmax value greater than 400% and is considered severely decayed with isolated pockets of harder wood.

Class 2 – the wood has µmax values of 185–400% and is considered to be moderately decayed with a well-preserved inner core, but softer decayed outer zones.

Class 3 – the wood has a µmax value of less than 185% and is considered to be well-preserved with much of the wood substance still present.

Using this system the wood from Beccles can be grouped as per Table 6.2, showing the full range of preservation assessments. A more recent system (Smit *et al.*, 2006) broadly classifies wood decay into two groups, again depending upon maximum water content:

- Healthy water-saturated wood with a maximum moisture content of between 60%–140%
- Highly degraded wood with a maximum moisture content of between 600%–900%

Using this latter system, the *Quercus* stakes can be broadly classified as 'healthy water-saturated wood' although the shallow surface zone (to a depth of *c.* 10mm) has undergone slightly more decay. For stake 744, the highest water contents were recorded from remaining sapwood (1040%) as well as from areas worked in antiquity. For example, the worked tip of 744 gave a value of 212%, which indicates moderate levels of decay, and the other area that gave a higher value (243%) was also taken from a worked facet. Working with a bladed tool causes disruption to the wood cell structures, exposing cellulose-rich areas to increased biological decay. A similar pattern was observed in stake 1220, where the sapwood elements were severely decayed (1192%) but preservation improved with depth, although again the worked tip of the stake was more decayed (exhibiting a maximum water content of 310%).

The three *Alnus* stakes produced very high water contents and can be classified as 'highly degraded wood' using the system of Smit *et al.* (2006). Non-*Quercus* species often exhibit higher levels of decay due to the absence of distinct heartwood zones, which are in effect 'dead' wood and hence more resistant to microbial decay. Furthermore, these stakes are from a zone where water levels are constantly fluctuating and hence prone to episodes of microbial decay (see below).

When compared with the standard quoted density for English oak (0.56), several samples extracted from the heartwood core of stakes 744 and 1220 exhibited apparent densities greater than this value. Wood density is determined and influenced by a number of factors including proportion of early to late wood cells, position of the timber within the 'parent' tree, the location of the growing tree and the presence of minerals within wood cells. Furthermore as density is defined as the mass per unit volume (g/cc) at a given moisture content, then an increase in moisture content will increase the mass of the wood at a faster rate than its volume will increase. Hence, a higher density value can be obtained for sound wood with increasing moisture content (Siau, 1984). In effect, the stakes from Beccles have undergone little or no decay, and increasing moisture content has produced density values higher than the standard value quoted for *Quercus*.

Burial environment geochemistry

Eight samples of sediment were collected to assess the suitability of the burial environment for *in situ* preservation (Table 6.3). Three samples were collected from Trench 2 and three from Trench 4 to assess depth variations, with further samples collected from around the base of stakes 744 and 1220. Each sample was stored in a re-sealable mini-grip bag at 5°C and placed in a coolbox. Analyses were performed on the liquid extracts by Derwentside

Table 6.2: Preservation of the Beccles timbers

Timber	Class
821	1
852	1
855	1
744 (sap)	1
744 (heart)	3
744 (tip)	2
1220 (sap)	1
1220 (heart)	3
1220 (tip)	2

Table 6.3: Geochemical assessment results

	Trench 1 0.35m depth (−0.78m OD)	Trench 1 0.60m depth (−1.03m OD)	Trench 1 1.15m depth (−1.58m OD)	Trench 4 0.60m depth (−1.03m OD)	Trench 4 0.80m depth (−1.23m OD)	Trench 4 1.10m depth (−1.53m OD)	Stake 744	Stake 1220
Nitrate mg/l	2.3	0.66	0.20	11	2.4	0.18	0.35	<0.10
Nitrite mg/l	<0.10	<0.10	<0.10	<0.10	<0.10	<0.10	<0.10	<0.10
Phosphate mg/l	<0.10	<0.10	<0.10	<0.10	<0.10	<0.10	<0.10	<0.10
Sulphate mg/l	240	1400	1900	130	310	1500	750	560
Sulphide ug/l	<250	<250	<500	<250	<250	<250	<250	<250
Total Sulphur mg/l	88	460	600	49	100	440	230	170
Dissolved oxygen mg/l	7.5	7.8	8.6	7.9	7.5	8.2	8.6	8.0
Ammoniacal Nitrogen mg/l	0.52	15	33	0.57	3.8	7.4	10	6.8
pH	6.7	3.4	5.3	5.2	5.3	5.5	6.4	6.3

Environmental Testing Services (www.dets.co.uk) using UKAS accredited test methods. Principal redox sensitive species usually used to characterise burial environments include sulphates, sulphides, sulphur, nitrates, nitrites, nitrogen (as ammoniacal nitrogen) and phosphates (see for example, Brunning, 2013). Dissolved oxygen and the pH of each sample were also tested.

Decay and geochemical analyses: results and discussion

The aim of these analyses was to identify which redox (oxidation-reduction) sensitive chemical species were present in the sediments to determine whether the burial environment was conducive to continued preservation of the timber structure. The principle chemical species used to characterise a burial environment are oxygen, iron (ferrous and ferric ions), nitrogen (nitrate and nitrite) and sulphur (sulphate and sulphide). These chemical species are utilised by organisms during the oxidation of organic matter based on the availability of the species and the potential energy yield. The maximum energy yield is obtained from oxygen (thereby resulting in the highest level decay) and the lowest energy yield coming from the utilisation of methane. Therefore degradation will occur in anoxic deposits, but at a much slower rate, as the energy yield is lower.

Overall, the sampled deposits can be characterised as acidic in nature, with low levels of oxygen, nitrates, nitrites, nitrogen and phosphates. The dominant species recorded were sulphur, sulphates and low levels of sulphide. The low concentrations of both oxygen and sulphide suggest that oxidation of the sediments is likely to have occurred between sampling and analysis. The presence/absence of each of these can be used to define the redox environment of the sediments (Table 6.4).

Optimum preservation conditions are to be found in those sediments that are defined as 'highly reducing', although long-term preservation is still possible where conditions are 'mildly reducing'. As stated above, there is evidence to suggest that oxidation of the sediments occurred between the time the samples were collected and subsequent laboratory processing (low levels of oxygen and low concentrations of sulphide). However, the overall low concentrations of nitrate/nitrite coupled with high concentrations of sulphur and sulphate suggest that the burial environment can be defined as 'mildly reducing'. Concentrations of sulphur and sulphate increased with depth in both Trenches 1 and 4 suggesting that hydrological conditions may be more stable at greater depth (see below).

The deposits were generally acidic although the sample

recovered from –1.03m OD in Trench 1 was highly acidic (pH 3.4). Similar highly acidic deposits have been identified at the site of Star Carr where high levels of sulphate were also encountered (Boreham et al., 2011). However, the highest concentration of sulphate (1900mg/l) at Beccles was recorded from the deepest sample from Trench 1 (–1.58m OD) where the pH was 5.3. It is feasible that this measurement may be anomalous although such a low pH value might be indicative of enhanced microbial activity.

Sulphate Reducing Bacteria (SRB) are the principle agent of decay in mildly reducing deposits. Such bacteria require anoxic conditions, the presence of sulphates and essential nutrients for growth. Potential sources of nutrients will include any organic remains associated with the structure and during growth, the SRBs will oxidise organic matter, using the sulphates as a source of energy. However, as the energy yield is low degradation will proceed at a very slow rate. The uppermost sections of timbers 744 and 1220 indicate decay in the uppermost deposits where oxygen ingress is occurring as a result of fluctuating water tables.

6.3 Assessing the preservation of the on-site palaeoenvironmental record

In addition to providing information for palaeoenvironmental reconstruction, the analyses of the proxies from Beccles (see Chapter 5) were also intended to gather data on the state of preservation of these different records. This section outlines the results of these preservation assessments and adds to a growing corpus of knowledge concerning preservation conditions of proxy records within lowland floodplain wetlands (Brunning, 2013).

Pollen

Each pollen sample was counted to a total of 300 TLP grains, with preservation of each grain classified as well-preserved or affected by biochemical or mechanical deterioration (see Table 6.5) following the protocols of Delcourt and Delcourt (1980) and Jones et al. (2007). The further sub-division of biochemical deterioration into 'corroded' or 'degraded' and mechanical deterioration into 'broken' or 'crumpled' was not employed; due to the fact that most of the grains displayed evidence for all four categories and complications occurred with quantifying the degree to which each grain had been exposed to each deterioration type. The decision was therefore taken to include biochemical and mechanical deterioration as a single category. Grains of Cyperaceae (sedges) are often folded or crumpled even when well-preserved in sub-fossil spectra; therefore the majority of Cyperaceae grains were classed as well-preserved (apart from in extreme cases) even though they had often undergone some form of mechanical deterioration. Indeterminable grains and those concealed by mineral or organic material were recorded and although fern spores were counted, they were not individually graded for preservation.

Table 6.4: General trends within redox environments

	Redox species present	Redox environment
	Oxygen	Oxidising
	Nitrate	Mildly reducing
	Iron and Sulphate	Mildly reducing
	Methane	Highly reducing

Table 6.5: Preservation categories used for identified pollen grains. After Delcourt and Delcourt (1980) and Jones et al. (2007)

Deterioration Type		Description	Processes responsible
Well-preserved		No observable deterioration	
Biochemical deterioration	Corroded	Exine pitted, etched or perforated.	Biochemical oxidation related to fungal/bacterial activity.
	Degraded	Exine thinned and/or structural features fused and indeterminate.	Chemical oxidation within aerial and sub-aerial environments.
Mechanical deterioration	Broken	Grain split or fragmented.	Physical transport of pollen grains.
	Crumpled	Grain squashed.	Compaction of grains within the sediment, particularly resulting from the progressive extrusion of water.

Preservation assessment: Trench 1

The results of the preservation analyses are presented in Figures 6.1 and Table 6.6. Preservation varied throughout the sequence with the percentage of well-preserved grains ranging from 40% at 0.71m (−1.26m OD) to 71% at 0.59m (−1.44m OD). The general trend indicates that biochemical deterioration is highest at the base of the sequence (0.97–1.09m; −1.52m to −1.64m OD) and mechanical deterioration peaks between 0.67–0.85m (−1.22 to −1.40m OD), coinciding with the main level of the archaeological deposits as represented by the debris field (see above). The percentage of total well-preserved grains maintained consistent values between 40–49% throughout this layer, but there was a sharp drop in the percentage of total mechanical deterioration above this at 0.59m (−1.14m OD), associated with an increase in well-preserved grains.

Trench 4

The results of preservation are presented in Figure 6.2 and Table 6.6. Preservation varied throughout the sequence with relatively sharp rises and declines in the percentage of well-preserved grains. Preservation appears to be generally good at the base of the sequence with *c.* 47–55% of the grains recorded as well-preserved. There is then a sharp decrease to 33% at 0.80m depth (−0.77m OD) where percentages of both biochemical and mechanical deterioration rise, suggesting deterioration associated with the main archaeological deposits as defined by the debris field (0.72–0.80m; −0.69m OD to −0.77m OD). One pattern, which is clear from Trench 4, but not apparent in Trench 1 are the coincident rises and falls in values for biochemical and mechanical deterioration.

Plant macrofossils

Indices for fragmentation and erosion/corrosion used by Jones *et al.* (2007) were also employed to assess the preservation of the plant macrofossils (Table 6.7). However, three fundamental methodological issues hindered the use of this index:

- Varying sub-sample volumes: the method employed in this study involved examination of the full one litre

of flot material, as opposed to the 250ml sample size employed by Jones *et al.* (2007). In part, the decision of the Beccles project to use the larger sample size was because the recommended sample size for the analysis of waterlogged plant remains is generally accepted as one litre; however, it also reflects that the quantity of plant remains in the Beccles samples was not particularly rich.

- A single 0.25mm sieve was used to collect the flot, whereas, Jones *et al.* (2007) used a nest of sieves (2mm, 1mm, 0.5mm and 0.25mm apertures).

- Jones *et al.* (2007) studied only 25 seeds (in the widest sense) from each of the four separate sieves utilised, whereas all of the plant macrofossils recovered from Beccles samples were scored in terms of fragmentation and erosion/ corrosion indices.

There is no one 'magic number' of plant remains that would be representative of any assemblage (van der Veen and Fieller, 1982). The choice of number will vary according to the level of accuracy desired (i.e. how likely the number of seeds selected will represent the complete assemblage) and the proportion of species within a population. Selecting a target of 250 seeds, for example, would produce results representative of an infinite population of plant remains with an accuracy of ±5% at 95% confidence, where 20% of that population could be made up of one species (van der Veen and Fieller, 1982: 296). Counts of greater than 250 would therefore, be likely to be more reliable in cases where a single taxon represents more than 20% of all identifications in an assemblage. In fact, even with four times the volume of sediment processed at Beccles (than studied by Jones *et al.*, 2007), two of the samples (Trench 1, Sample 6 and Trench 4, Sample 5) did not reach the minimum 250 'seed' target'. Conversely the Jones *et al.* (2007: 78, table 4) study was based on counts ranging from 2 seeds to the maximum 100, with nearly a quarter of the samples (six out of 28) based on 33 plant macrofossils or less.

It is clear that there are several practical limitations to the use of the fragmentation index scale for assessing macroscopic plant condition, since it is an artificial quantification of what are intuitive impressions of the state of preservation of individual plant macrofossils where:

- Fragmentation could be due to mechanical damage

Table 6.6: Pollen preservation data from Trenches 1 and 4

Note: Cyperaceae pollen is often folded or crumpled even when well preserved, therefore the majority of Cyperaceae grains were classed as well preserved (apart from in extreme cases) even though they had often undergone some form of mechanical deterioration. *Lycopodium – 55,749 grains cm³/sediment 1cm³

Sample	TLP	Pollen concentration (grains per cm³) *	Total indeter-minable grains	Total well preserved grains	Total biochemical deterioration	Total mechanical deterioration	Concealed by mineral or organic deposition	Total Pteropsida (monolete) indet. (ferns)
Trench 1 0.35m	308	100,442	48	185 (60%)	77 (25%)	46 (15%)	3	60
Trench 1 0.39m	323	56,539	56	181 (56%)	38 (12%)	104 (32%)	3	34
Trench 1 0.47m	313	64,164	67	177 (57%)	73 (23%)	63 (20%)	2	256
Trench 1 0.51m	308	54,159	34	189 (61%)	46 (15%)	73 (24%)	0	263
Trench 1 0.59m	301	52,917	58	214 (71%)	32 (11%)	55 (18%)	15	375
Trench 1 0.67m	237	54,929	77	115 (48%)	30 (13%)	92 (39%)	8	86
Trench 1 0.71m	308	41,776	43	124 (40%)	73 (24%)	111 (36%)	7	66
Trench 1 0.75m	301	24,727	52	132 (44%)	46 (15%)	123 (41%)	1	36
Trench 1 0.85m	294	70,018	51	133 (45%)	80 (27%)	81 (28%)	3	62
Trench 1 0.97m	316	133,142	43	128 (41%)	115 (36%)	73 (23%)	3	31
Trench 1 1.03m	315	40,513	45	174 (55%)	80 (26%)	60 (19%)	2	9
Trench 1 1.09m	305	85,901	48	133 (44%)	122 (40%)	52 (17%)	12	24
Trench 4 0.60m	316	63,690	49	161 (51%)	91 (29%)	64 (20%)	5	11
Trench 4 0.64m	312	90,064	33	191 (61%)	60 (19%)	61 (20%)	12	16
Trench 4 0.68m	321	45,936	52	152 (47%)	87 (27%)	82 (26%)	5	47
Trench 4 0.72m	342	116,487	62	129 (38%)	109 (32%)	104 (30%)	12	112
Trench 4 0.76m	315	119,567	49	120 (38%)	106 (34%)	89 (28%)	9	189
Trench 4 0.80m	310	95,238	59	102 (33%)	107 (35%)	101 (32%)	4	149
Trench 4 0.84m	314	82,848	43	173 (55%)	84 (27%)	57 (18%)	7	87
Trench 4 0.92m	323	74,442	55	152 (47%)	90 (28%)	81 (25%)	17	57
Trench 4 1.02m		Concentration too low for count. Some Poaceae and Cyperaceae grains recorded.						

in excavation, processing and/or sorting. Certainly different methods can result in varying degrees of damage to fragile plant macrofossils, such as the wings of birch (*Betula* spp.) seeds (e.g. Jones *et al.* 2007: 79, figure 3.). Washing material through sieves may also result in damage.

• Erosion/corrosion scores may be skewed by the loss of crucial identifiable features. For example, at Beccles, fool's water-cress (*Apium nodiflorum* (L.)

Lag.) is identifiable when the longitudinal ridges are present, but cannot be identified with certainty when these are highly eroded or absent. This would also affect identification of winged taxa, such as birch (see again Jones *et al.* 2007: 79, figure 3). Such imprecision in identification means that rather than scoring these remains as one single taxon they are scored separately. This does not alter the index for the overall assemblage, but does for individual taxa.

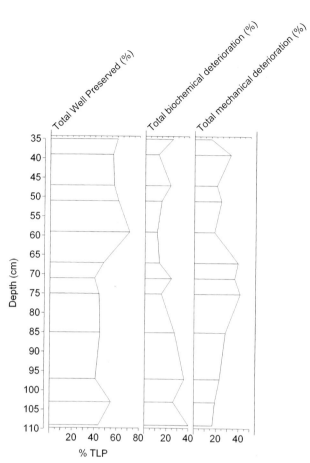

Figure 6.1: Preservations trends for Trench 1 pollen

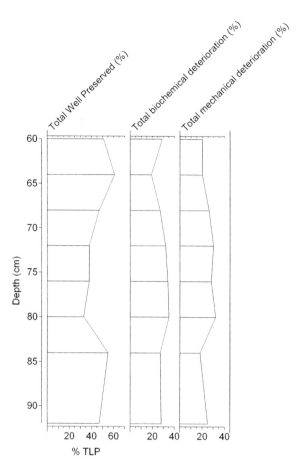

Figure 6.2: Preservation trends for Trench 4 pollen

- Many waterlogged deposits are dominated by robust taxa. Typically, the selection of a sample for analysis is based on the range of taxa present and its relative preservation. In principle an assemblage made up of elder (*Sambucus nigra* L.), alder (*Alnus glutinosa* (L.) Gaertn. and common nettle (*Urtica dioica* L.) could potentially be scored as well-preserved, but may in fact actually represent only the robust plant macrofossils that survive better than more fragile remains.
- As observed by Jones *et al.* (2007: 84) the recording of plant macrofossils in this detail is time consuming and unlikely to be justifiable for many projects.

These points were raised in Davis *et al.* (2002) in relation to the application of a 5-point preservation scale for fragmentation and erosion applied to plant macrofossils from York. The calculation of the fragmentation and erosion/corrosion indices is quantifying what is, in essence, an extremely subjective process, arguably yielding false precision to an intrinsically imprecise process (Davis *et al.*, 2002). There is a great need for analogue data on the processes of plant decay, especially from conditions mimicking archaeological situations.

Beetles

Table 6.8 records the preservation of the insect remains

recovered; the 5-point recording scheme of Kenward (in Davis *et al.*, 2002) for fragmentation, preservation and the extent of reddening of material has been employed. In this scheme 5 is very good and 1 is poor to non-existent. Table 6.8 also provides information on whether small, fragile taxa/elements are present, if scales are still mounted on weevils and if the distinctive 'pitting' of the surface of insect remains (perhaps the result of contact by fugal hyphae) were present or not.

At Beccles, there is little difference in preservation of insect remains between the two trenches and the numbers of taxa and individuals are fairly consistent between the two sequences in samples that were suitable for full analysis. Using Kenward's numerical estimation of fragmentation, preservation and colour change it seems that the majority of the faunas from both of the trenches are very well-preserved with scores in all three criteria often in the 5–4 range. In both cases, there is evidence for a slight decline in preservation within the top 0.10m of the analysed samples (i.e. Trench 1, Sample 1, between –0.85m and –0.95m OD, and Trench 4, Sample 2, between –0.63m and –0.73m OD). Small and thin elements were recovered throughout both sections and there was also no sign of 'pitting'. Many of the weevils also still had scales mounted in the material from both trenches. However, these assessments excluded samples from above –0.85m OD in Trench 1, and those

Table 6.7: Preservation of plant remains from Trenches 1 and 4

Key to preservation indices: Fragmentation: 0 = seed entire, 1 = <25% fragmented, 2 = 25–50% fragmented, 3 = >50%
fragmented (based of Jones et al. 2007: 77)
Erosion/corrosion: 1 = <25% erosion of seed testa, 2 = 25–50% erosion, 3 = >50% erosion
* the total number of taxa is likely to be somewhat inflated because less precisely identified seed coat fragments and/or internal
structures are potentially derived from taxa identified to species or genus level. † Rush (Juncus spp.) seeds were superabundant
in Trench 4 sample 2 and would have been too time consuming to fully sort. A 100ml sub-sample of the flot was fully sorted
for Juncus spp. and this score was factored up for all 550ml of flot.

Trench	1	1	1	1	1	4	4	4	4
Depth (m)	0.20–0..30	0.30–0.40	0.40–0.50	0.50–0.60	0.60–0.70	0.70–0.80	0.80–0.90	0.90–1.00	1.00–1.10
Sample	3	4	5	6	7	2	3	4	5
Sample volume (l)	1 L	1 L	1 L	1 L	1L	1 L	1 L	1 L	1 L
Total count (less unident. macrofossils)	335	363	318	215	362	5366†	530	270	177
Total taxa*	32	33	36	23	20	31	26	29	20
Total fragmentation score 0	246	287	193	166	301	4965	461	196	89
Proportion fragmentation score 0	73.43%	79.06%	60.69%	77.21%	83.15%	92.54%	86.98%	72.59%	50.28%
Total fragmentation score 1	68	46	63	27	43	391	56	48	72
Proportion fragmentation score 1	20.30%	12.67%	19.81%	12.56%	11.88%	7.29%	10.57%	17.78%	40.68%
Total fragmentation score 2	14	20	46	14	13	7	9	24	15
Proportion fragmentation score 2	4.18%	5.51%	14.47%	6.51%	3.59%	0.13%	1.70%	8.89%	8.47%
Total fragmentation score 3	7	10	16	8	5	2	4	2	1
Proportion fragmentation score 3	2.09%	2.75%	5.03%	3.72%	1.38%	0.04%	0.75%	0.74%	0.56%
Fragmentation index	0.35	0.32	0.64	0.37	0.23	0.08	0.16	0.38	0.59
Total erosion score 1	264	302	256	144	268	5003	472	226	145
Proportion erosion score 1	78.81%	83.20%	80.50%	66.98%	74.03%	93.25%	89.06%	83.70%	81.92%
Total erosion score 2	66	51	50	61	94	361	55	43	30
Proportion erosion score 2	19.70%	14.05%	15.72%	28.37%	25.97%	6.73%	10.38%	15.93%	16.95%
Total erosion score 3	5	10	12	10	0	1	3	1	2
Proportion erosion score 3	1.49%	2.75%	3.77%	4.65%	0.00%	0.02%	0.57%	0.37%	1.13%
Erosion index	1.23	1.18	1.23	1.38	1.26	1.07	1.12	1.17	1.19

above −0.63m OD in Trench 4, as these upper deposits were very dry and desiccated.

Summary: preservation of palaeoenvironmental proxies

Pollen preservation in both sequences deteriorates markedly between 0.67m and 0.97m (−1.22m to −1.52m OD) in Trench 1 and 0.70–0.82m (−0.67m to −0.79m OD) in Trench 4. This is approximately the same level as the main archaeological horizons (see above) as defined by the radiocarbon dates from Beccles Core 1 (see Chapter 2), and illustrated by the presence of the debris field and horizontal structural timbers. The poor condition of the archaeological wood (see above) implies that human activity on the floodplain was probably associated with a

period of lower water tables and the subsequent degradation of the structures closest to the floodplain surface in antiquity (see Chapter 7). It can therefore be hypothesized that the poor condition of the pollen is also connected with these conditions, rather than subsequent fluctuations in the water table (see below).

This hypothesis appears to be supported by the fact that pollen preservation improves in both sequences in the samples from the overlying peat deposits, implying that the recorded state of preservation of sub-fossil palynomorphs is more strongly associated with conditions during primary deposition. Percentages of mechanical deterioration are higher in Trench 1 and biochemical deterioration is higher in Trench 4, but it is unclear whether this reflects the impact of different micro-environmental conditions. Notably, other than in the very dry and disturbed deposits in the upper

Table 6.8: Beetle preservation data from Beccles Trenches 1 and 4.

Depth (m)	Trench 1 0.90–1.00	0.80–0.90	0.70–0.80	0.60–0.70	0.50–0.60	0.40–0.50	0.30–0.40	Trackway	Trench 4 1.00–1.10	0.90–1.00	0.80–0.90	0.70–0.80	0.60–0.70
Sample no.	7	6	5	4	3	2	1		6	5	4	3	2
No. individuals	70	73	84	33	47	61	6	57	79	48	18	42	52
No. species	44	42	39	22	27	39	6	36	48	26	17	31	27
Fragmentation	4	4	4	4	4	4	3	4	5/4	5/4	4	4	3
Preservation	5	5	5	5	5	4	4/3	5	3	5/4	5	4	3
Colour change (reddening)	5	5	5	5	5	4/5	4/3	5	2	5	5	5	4
Small/thin elements present	+	+	+	+	+	+	–	+	+	+	+	+	+
Erosion pitting present	–	–	–	–	–	–	–	–	Slight	–	–	–	–
Scales present	+	+	+	+	+	+	–	+	+	+	+	+	+

Figure 6.3: Installation of Piezometers

layers, the Coleoptera are well-preserved in both sequences whilst there is no clear correlation between the preservation of the plant macrofossils and the pollen.

6.4 Water table monitoring

The assessments of the state of preservation of the archaeo-environmental resource must be informed by an understanding of the current hydrological conditions prevailing at the site in question (Brown *et al.*, 2011). The character of the water table can provide an indication of the potential of the area for the *in situ* preservation of archaeological organic material using the approach defined by Van de Noort *et al.* (2001) and Chapman and Cheetham (2002). At Beccles, groundwater monitoring was undertaken to gather base-line data for future management of the site. A grid of 15 single tube piezometers was installed over the alignment to establish the depth of the water table in relation to the site and associated deposits (Figure 6.3 and Figure 6.4). Groundwater levels were recorded on a twice-monthly basis over two full annual water cycles (up to September 2011). Despite the unusually cold conditions in the winter of 2010, none of the piezometer tubes froze, even though the water in the adjacent drainage ditches iced over. This contrast perhaps reflects the presence of enough dissolved salts in the groundwater to prevent this; the River Waveney is tidal beyond Beccles and brackish water must contribute to the floodplain groundwater, a point

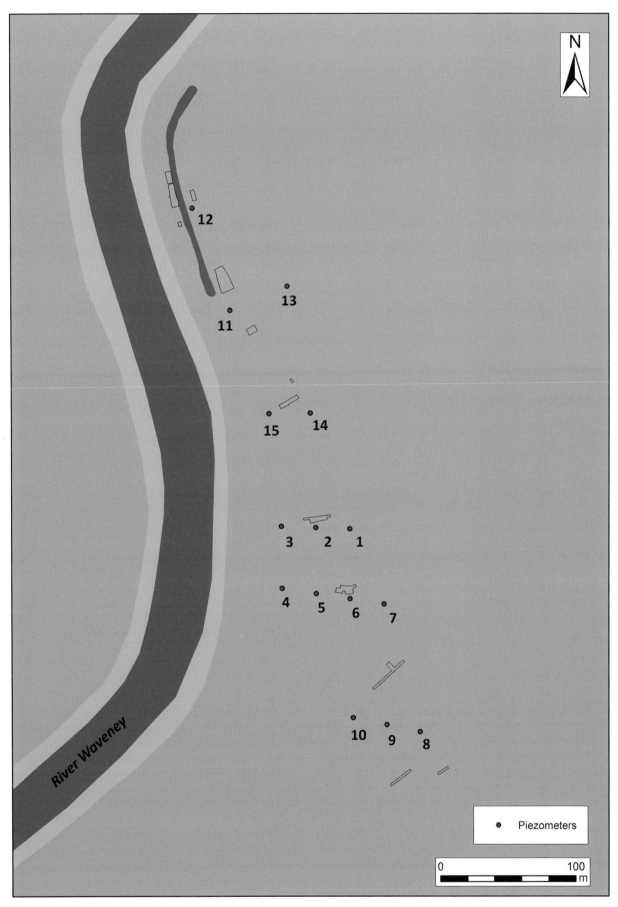

Figure 6.4: Location of Piezometers

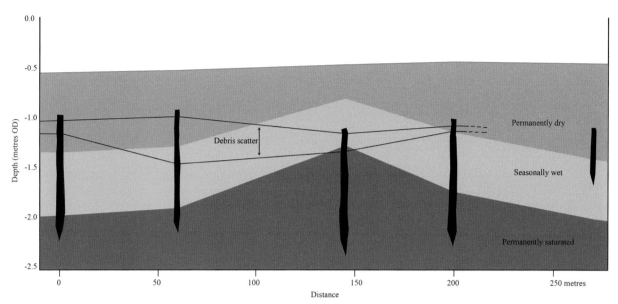

Figure 6.5: Water table minima and maxima plotted against levels of archaeological material. Distance on x-axis measured from north to south (see Figure 6.4)

corroborated by the precipitation of gypsum salts from the peat exposed on the excavation spoil heaps.

The water table height values for the entire study area were analysed using GIS to determine the 'shape' of the water table across the site, and variations in its form during the duration of study. Furthermore, the maximum and minimum values recorded at each monitoring position were utilized to provide data regarding the vertical range of the water table, to define a lower 'saturated zone', a middle 'zone of fluctuation' and an upper 'permanently dry zone' (Figure 6.5). Previous studies have demonstrated that these zones reflect variable potential for the preservation of archaeology and any associated palaeoenvironmental resource. The greatest potential for *in situ* preservation is within the saturated zone, with material above this zone at risk of long-term deterioration and associated loss of archaeological information, as demonstrated at other lowland alluvial sites such as those within the Vale of Pickering (Boreham *et al.*, 2011) and Somerset Levels (Brunning, 2013).

Trench 1

In Trench 1 (2009), the water table recorded fluctuated between –1.97m and –1.34m OD, providing a range of 0.63m. Archaeological remains within this trench included the stakes of the alignment (highest top at –0.96m OD), the debris scatter (between –1.02m and –1.12m OD) and the brushwood trackway (at –1.02 m OD). Comparison between the water table and the archaeological data shows that the upper 0.38m of the stakes are within a permanently dry zone, and that the majority of the stakes lie within the fluctuation zone (0.63m). Furthermore, the debris scatter and the brushwood trackway both lie completely within the upper 'dry' zone. Hence, it is very likely that the wet-preserved archaeology within the area of Trench 1 at the northern end of the

study area will deteriorate rapidly, with only the base of stakes below –1.97m OD surviving below the current water table.

Trench 2

To the south of Trench 1, groundwater levels are higher, with fluctuations between a maximum of –1.27m OD and a minimum of –1.88m OD, a range of 0.61m. Organic remains identified during the excavation in this trench consist of the stakes (–0.9m OD and below) and woodworking debris (between –0.97m and –1.44m OD). Here, the upper 0.63m of the stakes and the upper part of the debris scatter are permanently dry, with the lower 0.17m of the debris layer lying within the fluctuating zone. Only the basal parts of the stake stakes lie within the saturated zone, and so it is very likely that in the foreseeable future the majority of the wet-preserved archaeology will deteriorate rapidly in this area.

Trench 3

Within Trench 3, groundwater levels are highest across the site, between –0.80m and –1.26m OD, a range of 0.46m. The archaeology identified within this trench consisted of stakes (the highest at –1.09m OD), woodworking debris (top at –1.09m OD) and the roundwood structure (at –1.04m OD). Here, the top 0.29m of the stakes lie within the area of fluctuating groundwater, with most of the stakes saturated. The woodworking debris is nearly all contained within this zone of fluctuation, as is the roundwood 'planking'. Based on current data, this area has greater potential for long-term preservation of the wet-preserved archaeology compared with that in the trenches to the north; this might also explain the preservation of the roundwood 'planking'. However, only the lower sections of the stakes lie within the saturated zone and so deterioration of the remainder of the archaeological resource is extremely likely.

Trench 4

To the south of Trench 3, groundwater levels decrease slightly, between a maximum of –1.13m OD and a minimum of –1.72m OD (a range of 0.59m). The archaeology revealed in this trench consists of stakes (top at –0.99m OD), woodworking debris (top at –1.06m OD) and roundwood 'planking' (top at –1.10m OD). Here, the upper 0.14m of the stakes, the whole of the woodworking debris scatter and the roundwood 'planking' all lie within the dry zone. However, groundwater levels are higher than in Trenches 1 and 2 at the northern end of the site, which might explain the preservation of the roundwood 'planking' superstructure, but demonstrate the rapidity of likely deterioration in the future.

Trench 5

The southernmost trench revealed only stakes (tops at –1.09m OD) with no other wet-preservation of archaeological material. Here the groundwater declined to similar levels as in Trench 1 at the northern part of the site, with a maximum water level of –1.40m OD and minimum level of –1.99m OD, a total range of 0.59m. Hence the top 0.39m of the stakes were never saturated, remaining dry all year round. These stakes were relatively short (*c.* 0.3m), meaning that the majority of each remained dry, indicating that long-term *in situ* preservation is unlikely.

In summary, the 'shape' of the water table along the length of the site demonstrated higher overall levels towards the central area (Trench 3). The water table appears to deepen to the north, where it is nearer to the river and where drainage and draw-down is therefore presumably greater; to the south, the lower levels perhaps reflect proximity to the floodplain edge. The relatively high groundwater levels towards the centre of the site, within an area of rough, unfarmed land, indicate the ineffectiveness of the largely unmaintained drains in this area, and hence the greater potential for the preservation of organic remains within less well-drained parts of the floodplain. The effect of artificial land drainage in determining water tables has been noted in the Vale of Pickering with computer modelling suggesting that the insertion of under-drainage may have lowered water tables by more than half a metre in the archaeologically sensitive zone (Brown *et al.*, 2011).

The tops of the highest stakes from all trenches equate to a mean elevation of –1.01m OD, with the debris scatter at –1.03m OD and the roundwood 'planking' at –1.07m OD. The highest water table recorded provides a mean level of –1.19m OD, and a lowest mean of –1.76m OD. These figures demonstrate that, overall, the site is unlikely to be preserved *in situ* in the long term, with mean values suggesting that the archaeological remains are above the water table for most of the year. In contrast, the water table is locally higher in the centre of the site, and where the tops

of archaeological remains are locally lower, the potential for longer-term preservation is enhanced. However, the vast majority of the archaeological remains identified through excavation lie outside of the permanently saturated zone, long-term *in situ* preservation of the alignment and associated wooden remains is regarded as unlikely. The archaeo-environmental resource may thus be regarded as under significant threat.

Past and present hydrology and state of preservation

There is evidence that the state of preservation of the archaeo-environmental archive recorded at Beccles is associated with the variation in a combination of hydrological processes operating within the floodplain over a range of timescales. The poor preservation of the pollen in Trench 1 in particular appears to relate to a drier phase on the floodplain during the Iron Age, which resulted in the deterioration of the archaeological wood, oxidation of the peat and subsequent biochemical damage to the palynomorphs. It can also be observed that pollen concentration and preservation was generally poor in the SRVP cores from Beccles (see Chapter 2) and also at Geldeston (see Chapter 5) where pollen was entirely absent from many of the samples assessed. In the case of the former, this included samples from well below the current depth of the floodplain water table as established by the monitoring work described above. This may imply that conditions during antiquity have on occasion been inimical to pollen preservation in the floodplain peats of the Waveney Valley.

The phase of lower water tables that might have impacted on the preservation of pollen at Beccles during the later prehistoric period does not seem to have impacted significantly upon the state of preservation of the insect remains or plant macrofossils, although quantifying this observation in a robust manner, particularly in respect to the latter has proved problematic. The palaeoenvironmental record has been lost from the very desiccated deposits close to the current floodplain surface and clearly well above the current water table for probably all of the year. However, it is clear that there is a complex relationship between patterns and processes of hydrological fluctuation and preservation of the archaeo-environmental resource, an observation also made by Brunning (2013) in the context of the varying states of preservation of organic archaeological remains identified in the Somerset Levels.

The pollen spectra display clear evidence for poorer preservation around the level of the Iron Age land surface on the floodplain, but with scores for well-preserved pollen actually improving in the shallower deposits above this. Although a lack of base-line data hampers interpretation, these patterns represent compelling evidence for the impact of past processes on the palaeoenvironmental record. However, at Beccles, the beetle record appears to have been largely unaffected by either past or sub-recent hydrological variations other than in the shallow and very dry near surface deposits. It is unclear how long the current hydrological regime has pertained, but in terms of the archaeological record, both past and recent/sub-recent factors may account for the general absence of any structural elements that would have originally been situated well above the contemporary ground level, such as the upper extents of the stakes or any superstructure elements (although it is also possible that any wooden remains exposed on the surface of the floodplain may also have been washed away during episodes of seasonal flooding; see above Chapter 4). The only archaeological material that is generally well-preserved is the deeper extents of the stakes that are below the current water table. Remains such as the debris field and larger timbers, which were close to, or below the ground surface during prehistory have survived, albeit in generally poor condition.

The relationship between factors controlling the relative preservation of organic archaeological remains and micro- and macrofossils is on the whole, rather poorly understood (e.g. Kenward and Hall, 2000) and the results presented here would seem to confirm this impression of local complexity, stressing the importance of site-specific investigations. Whilst it is well established that preservation of organic material under waterlogged conditions is related to a complex of factors including temperature, pH and oxidation-reduction (redox) potential, recent research demonstrates that the exact parameters that control processes of microbial decay under different conditions are highly complex (e.g. see Caple, 1994; Douterelo *et al.*, 2009, 2011; Lillie *et al.*, 2012). Further study of the palaeoenvironmental record at Beccles, perhaps supported by geochemical and additional water table monitoring, has the potential to provide an on-going investigation of processes and rates of deterioration. The local growth of *Phragmites* has also damaged the archaeological wood (Figure 6.6) and may also be indirectly responsible for the anomalous radiocarbon dates previously obtained in

Figure 6.6: Phragmites damage to one of the archaeological timbers

association with the palaeoenvironmental analyses at the site (see Chapter 3).

6.5 Barsham: condition assessment of two timber stakes

Two of the timber stakes (Stakes 2 and 26) recovered during the excavations at Barsham were submitted for decay analysis in order to collect base-line data concerning the state of preservation of the archaeological wood and to inform on prospects for *in situ* preservation of the site. Selection for assessment was made after archaeological wood analysis and sampling for dendrochronology (see above). Methods followed standard condition tests (see Chapter 1) and included decay profiling using a Sibert probe and the extraction of core samples to determine maximum water content, density, ash content and percentage loss in wood substance.

Results Timber #2 (oak stake, two sections)

A full table of results for both stakes is presented in Table 6.9 and Figures 6.7 and 6.8. Both of the sections were heavily iron-stained on the surface with evidence of mineralisation. The uppermost section exhibited physical damage with rupturing to the wood fibre structure, but there was no visual evidence of collapse or desiccation. A series of Sibert decay profiles, drilled in the tangential plane, were obtained and representative examples are presented in Figure 6.7. Each profile was drilled at 5cm intervals and core samples were extracted from four locations: one from the smaller uppermost section of the stake (labelled as profile 2.2), and three from the lowermost section (labelled as profile 2.3, 2.6 and 2.9). The fourth profile (2.9, through the worked point of the stake) was too soft to register resistance and hence no profile could be recorded.

The decay profiles indicate that much of the wood was in an excellent state of preservation, with decay confined to the outermost surface zones. Profile 2.2 recorded the physical damage visible at the uppermost end of the stake (where the wood forked into two sections) at 70mm and another zone of decay just beneath the surface. Profile 2.3 exhibited similar decay at the surface, with very well-preserved wood throughout the stake. A similar profile was observed at location 2.6, although the wood appeared to be harder than modern un-decayed oak.

Maximum water content data together with decay profiling data (Table 6.9) indicate that the outermost zones have undergone slightly more decay than inner areas of the wood. Surface zone water contents range from 131% (location 2.6) to 322% (location 2.9, base of stake), whilst values from within the wood range from 83% (at location 2.6) to 115% (at location 2.3). The majority of the core samples retained their shape and form after oven drying, and no compression was observed during the coring process (decayed wood cores can often compress to half their original length during coring). The highest maximum water content value, 322%, was obtained from location 2.9 (i.e. the lowest point of the stake). This equates to an apparent density of 0.257g/cc or 54% loss in wood substance. The core sample was fibrous in nature and had little structural integrity. Ash contents ranged between 0.5% and 20%, with all samples having a red/brown hue, probably indicative of iron contamination. This indicates that iron salts have permeated throughout the wood structure.

Timber #26 (oak stake, 2 sections)

Both sections of the stake were iron-stained with mineralised deposits on the surface. No evidence of physical damage or desiccation cracks, or collapse of the wood cell structure was apparent. A series of Sibert decay profiles drilled in the tangential plane were obtained and representative examples are illustrated in Figure 6.8 with associated data presented in Table 6.9. Each profile was drilled at 5cm intervals and, following assessment, core samples were extracted from three locations: the top of the stake (26.1); the midpoint (26.8); and towards the base of the stake (26.15). Cores extracted from 26.1 and 26.15 were processed whole as the wood was fibrous, whereas core 26.8 was sub-sampled into 3 sections (outer, middle and inner zones).

The decay profiles (Figure 6.8) suggest that timber 26 has undergone more decay than timber 2. Profile 26.1 reveals pockets of hard (sound) wood but that much of the remainder of the wood is softer (less resistance to the probe) where more decay has occurred. The maximum length of the profile should be 100mm, but data was only captured for the first 40mm. This indicates that the wood was too soft for the probe to register data; the maximum water content for the entire core sample was 323%, equating to a density of 0.257g/cc and a 54% loss in wood substance.

Profile 26.8 is also similar to 26.1, with zones of less decayed wood adjacent to a more decayed zone. This heterogeneous decay pattern is typical of oak. The highest water content, 207%, was observed from the core extracted

from the outermost 200mm, which equates to a density of 0.365g/cc and 35% loss in wood substance. The decay profile from the lowermost (deepest) section of the stake, location 26.15, suggests much better preserved wood with more decay to the surface zone. The overall water content was 133%, with a density of 0.501, and 11% loss in wood substance. Ash contents ranged from 2% to 8%, and all samples were red/brown in colour. Overall ash contents for timber 26 were, on average, lower than those observed from timber 2.

Discussion

Both stakes can be described as well-preserved, although stake 2 has undergone less decay then stake 26. Both exhibited the typical heterogeneous decay patterns observed in oak from archaeological contexts, and the lower sections (i.e. the deeper buried sections) of stake 26 are better preserved than the uppermost (higher) sections. However, the reverse appears to be true for stake 2, where the highest levels of decay were observed in the lowermost sections of the stake. When compared with the standard quoted density for English oak (0.56), both stakes appear in places to have apparent densities greater than this value. Density will be determined by a number of factors including the proportion of early to late wood cells, position of timber in 'parent' tree, location of growing tree and presence of minerals within wood cells, all of which will influence the actual density of the wood. Furthermore, as density is defined as the mass per unit volume (g/cc) at a given moisture content, then an increase in moisture content will increase the mass of the wood at a faster rate than its volume will increase. Hence, a higher density value can be obtained for sound wood with increasing moisture content (Siau, 1984). In effect, the stakes have undergone little or no decay, and increasing moisture content produces density values higher than the standard value quoted for oak.

Most sound woods tend to have ash contents of

Table 6.9: Summary of Sibert probe analyses, maximum water content values, density %loss in wood substance and ash for Barsham stakes 2 and 26.
Umax – maximum water content; %LWS – percentage loss in wood substance, based on a value of 0.56g/cc for the density of modern oak (Bulletin no 50, Forest Products Research, Ministry of Technology, undated)

Sample	Sibert: depth into wood (mm)	Umax %	Density g/cc	% LWS	Ash %	Colour of ash
2.2	20	131	0.506	10	4	Deep red/brown
2.2	20–60	106	0.579	–	4	Deep red/brown
2.2	60–120	105	0.583	–	5	Deep red/brown
2.3	15	229	0.338	40	5	Deep red/brown
2.3	15–30	101	0.596	–	3	Red/brown
2.3	30–60	115	0.550	2	0.5	Pale wood, slight red
2.6	20	157	0.447	20	17	Deep red/brown
2.6	20–40	98	0.607	–	5	Red/brown
2.6	40–60	83	0.668	–	3	Red/brown
2.9	Whole	322	0.257	54	20	Deep red/brown
26.1	Whole	323	0.257	54	7	Red/brown
26.8	25	114	0.554	1	5	Red/brown
26.8	25–45	107	0.576	–	2	Deep red/brown
26.8	45–65	207	0.365	–	8	Pale red/brown
26.15	Whole	133	0.501	11	4	Deep red/brown

a

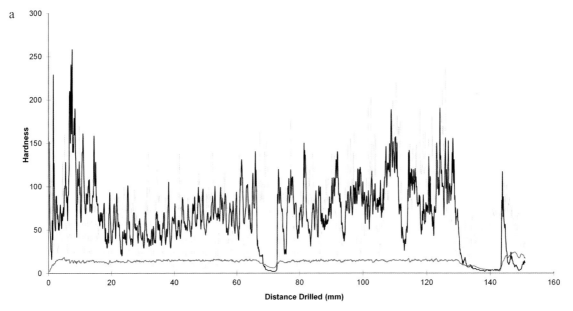

b

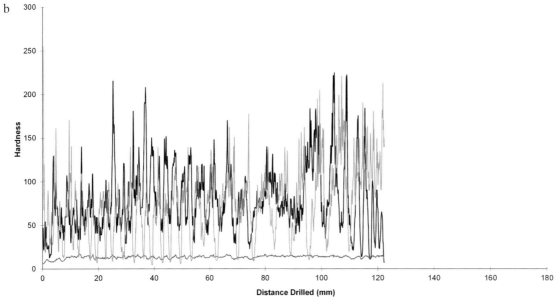

c

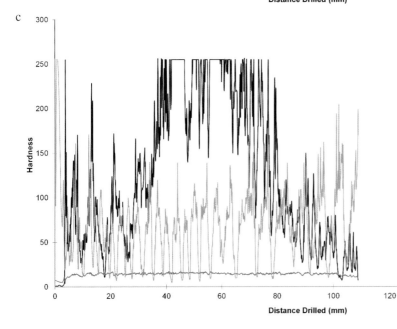

Figure 6.7: Sibert decay profiles for Barsham stake 2, profile 2 (a), 3 (b) and 6 (c); X-axis: records depth of penetration of the probe into the wood; Y-axis: records resistance encountered by probe during drilling, as "hardness" units (the more resistance, the greater the hardness, hence less decay of the wood). 5 plots are shown on each profile: pink = pressure exerted during drilling; black = hardness of the wood against distance drilled; blue = hardness for modern undecayed oak, drilled in the tangential plane. Plotting both sample and modern curves on the same chart allows for direct comparison to be made concerning the state of preservation of the wood

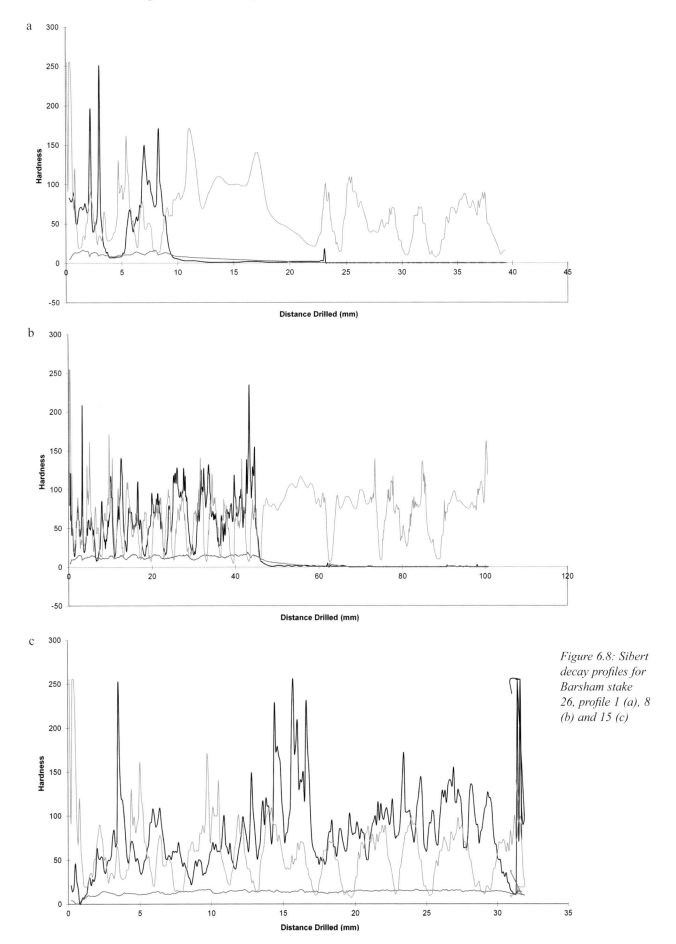

Figure 6.8: Sibert decay profiles for Barsham stake 26, profile 1 (a), 8 (b) and 15 (c)

below 1% by weight. Higher ash contents recorded from waterlogged archaeological wood are usually indicative of contamination from minerals derived from the burial environment. In this instance, given the high level of iron contamination on the surfaces of both timbers, it is highly likely that anaerobic groundwater rich in dissolved iron has percolated through the wood cell structure. Once the wood is exposed to aerobic conditions, the iron becomes insoluble and deposits will form within the wood cells and on the outer surfaces. The evidence suggests that the timbers have been buried in fully saturated deposits where reducing, or highly reducing conditions existed, which were conducive to the preservation of the organic archaeological remains. The higher level of decay recorded from the worked point of stake 2 may be a function of the burial environment, the result of physical working of the wood, or evidence of decay in antiquity before the stake was buried. Further investigation of the hydrology and geochemistry of the burial environment would be required in order to clarify this issue.

6.6 Discussion: heritage management implications

The data presented in this chapter provide base-line information regarding the state of preservation of the archaeo-environmental resource of the Beccles and to a lesser extent the Barsham timber alignments. These data have implications for the management and preservation *in situ* of the sites. This section reflects on the implications of this research for Beccles in particular, and raises concerns regarding the potential for future successful preservation *in situ* of the monument. As the site was discovered following the publication of *Monuments at Risk in England's Wetlands Survey* (MAREW), English Heritage's *Strategy for Wetlands*, and *Heritage Management of England's Wetlands* (HMEW), it was not included in the management analysis undertaken as part of those projects (Van de Noort *et al.*, 2002). How does the Beccles alignment fit into current policies and agendas regarding wet-preserved archaeological sites (e.g. Brunning, 2012, 2013; Malim and Panter, 2012; Williams, 2012)? Using the methodology developed as part of the Heritage Management of England's Wetlands projects as a reference (See Fletcher, 2003, 2011; Fletcher and Van de Noort, 2004) the management implications can be identified as:

1) The fragility of the archaeological resource

Organic archaeological remains are amongst the most fragile and sensitive of all such materials. The variable water table and agricultural improvement has apparently had an adverse impact on the preservation of the deposits in the upper horizons of the floodplain. Because the hydrology has been altered over a period of time it must be recognised that preservation *in situ* may not be feasible. The deepest extents of the site, in particular

Figure 6.9: Stake tip from Beccles with prehistoric tool marks clearly visible, demonstrating excellent preservation at depth

the tips and points of the stakes, which have remained fully waterlogged, are likely to be the best preserved components of the site and may survive the longest (e.g. Figure 6.9). As discussed above, water table fluctuation across the site has created an intermediate zone of variable and declining preservation.

The preservation issues also include groundwater contamination, nitrate input from floodwater and possible chemical contaminants from farming residues. A diversity of land uses along the site and variations in the sub-surface topography, burial environment, the levels of humification and the composition of the peat might have affected the site in different ways. Water chemistry and horizontal flow of water below ground are additional issues that this research has not considered.

2) Access, boundaries and site ownership, and maintenance of drainage

Given the site is linear and situated on a large floodplain, issues of access and ownership are complex. In particular, any alteration of the drainage pattern, which may be key to ensuring preservation of the site, would impact on various stakeholders. Safeguarding the monument through any form of groundwater manipulation would need co-operation across local ownership boundaries and from these stakeholders, and might substantially affect neighbouring areas. Although the landscape is designated by Defra (Department for Environment, Food and Rural Affairs) as an Environmentally Sensitive Area (ESA) and classed as a rare habitat, it does not necessarily follow that the current landowners will conform to the nature conservation advice for these areas. If action is required to preserve the site, agreements from all landowners together with natural environment groups will be necessary. Likewise the local hydrology is controlled in part by bodies such as the Internal Drainage Board (IDB) and the Environment Agency.

3) Conflict of interest

A largely benign and passive management regime in the past has so far ensured that the site has been preserved and as far as can be ascertained, no ploughing has taken place over the site. The uppermost deposits are likely to be, during the summer season in particular, much drier than in previous decades, and the current preservation environment may well deteriorate further under these conditions. This represents a potential conflict between archaeological resource management requirements and the preferred land-use regime of the current owners and other stakeholders.

If the Beccles alignment was to be identified as a candidate for designation then this has the potential for clear conflicts of interest at a local and possibly regional or even national level. As an ESA target area, it is eligible for Natural England's Entry and Higher Level Stewardship schemes. Changes may be required to the farming regime to gain entry to Higher Level Stewardship or ESA, which could conflict with the needs of the archaeological site; furthermore, long-term funding priorities with respect to these schemes may also change (see Brunning, 2012).

4) Knowledge and research

The site was systematically excavated as part of a research programme that included the assessment of preservation and water table modelling. This work has implications for understanding and management of similar wetland sites and deposits both in the region and further afield, and will be discussed further in Chapter 7.

The approach taken at Beccles has benefited considerably from lessons drawn from research at Sutton Common (Van de Noort *et al.*, 2007) and elsewhere (e.g. Somerset, Brunning, 2013). Research should continue to be a priority for the archaeological community, in order to inform management and guide future strategy and policies.

6.7 Summary: preservation and future management of wetland sites in the Waveney Valley

This chapter has outlined the results of quantitative and qualitative assessments of the state of preservation of the archaeo-environmental resource of the Beccles alignment and a more limited programme of study at Barsham. Whilst there is good evidence that the poor condition of elements of the Beccles archaeo-environmental resource relates to natural processes during antiquity, it is clear that recent and sub-recent changes in hydrology and land-use have also compromised the organic remains. The water table monitoring indicates that the majority of the shallower archaeological remains (upper extents of stakes, the trackways, timbers and debris field) are not presently situated within permanently saturated deposits. The assessment of the preservation of two of the stakes from Barsham indicates that this site may be located in a more stable burial environment, but further work on this site and that at Geldeston is necessary to establish the relationship between the hydrological regime and the archaeo-environmental records.

As other studies of organic preservation such as in the Vale of Pickering (Boreham *et al.*, 2011; Brown *et al.*, 2011; Milner *et al.*, 2011) and the Somerset Levels (Brunning, 2013) have found, there is a correlation between the better-preserved areas of archaeology and the levels of saturation demonstrated by the higher annual groundwater levels. Recently, Lillie *et al.* (2012) have shown how the diversity and function of microbial activity in a floodplain context can be affected by water levels during flood events, implying that short-term weather patterns may also play an important role in decay processes. It seems unlikely that the differences in the hydrological regime at Beccles are related directly to the predominant land-use *per se,* with the higher average water table recorded close to Trench 3 probably a result of the poorer drainage in this part of the floodplain. The data indicate that the upper sections and horizontal elements (e.g. trackways and planks) of the Beccles timber alignment probably cannot be preserved *in situ*, although the likely timescale for the deterioration and eventual complete loss of the archaeology cannot be reliably estimated on the basis of the current data. The already fragmentary archaeological deposits at the far southern end of the Beccles alignment (Trench 6) are perhaps at greatest threat in the short-term. Further evaluation of the site in the future will be necessary to assess the rate at which archaeological information is being lost. A management plan for the Beccles site is outlined in Appendix 1.

7. Holocene Environments, the Archaeological Record and Human Activity in the Suffolk River Valleys: Synthesis, Discussion and Conclusions

With contributions from
Mike Bamforth, Tom Hill, Clare Good, Will Fletcher, Kristina Krawiec, Michael Lobb and Eugene Ch'ng

7.1 Introduction

River valleys offer exceptional preservation potential for wetland archaeological remains and associated palaeoenvironmental deposits, but these remains are also some of the most threatened by contemporary human activity (urbanisation and associated infrastructure development, changing land use, quarrying). Understanding this resource and developing mitigation strategies that ensure the long-term management of riverine archaeology in the light of future population needs requires: (1) a baseline assessment of the character of the heritage resource, which may include archaeological remains deeply buried within the floodplain; and (2), an understanding of natural geomorphological processes and landscape evolution, which may impact on archaeological visibility, the level of preservation, and strategies for geoprospection. This monograph has presented the results of a range of archaeological and palaeoenvironmental research focusing on the post-glacial (Holocene) record of the river valleys of Suffolk and has attempted to redress the balance of previous work, which has largely focused on Palaeolithic and Pleistocene geoarchaeological records.

This chapter provides a synthesis of these different lines of evidence within the context of previous studies relating to palaeoenvironments and archaeology in this region. It also considers the excavations of a previously unknown type of late prehistoric timber alignment identified at Beccles, Barsham and Geldeston in terms of form and function of these monuments within their local, regional and national environmental and cultural contexts. The chapter concludes by reflecting on the management, future protection, preservation and prospection of wetland sites such as those of the Waveney Valley in the face of a range of societal and environmental pressures, as well as exploring some of the key outstanding research questions and research directions for the region.

7.2 Late Quaternary environments, the archaeological record and human activity in the Suffolk river valleys

Direct evidence for Upper Palaeolithic environmental changes is lacking in the studies presented in this monograph; on the whole this is because many of the investigations involved the retrieval of cores, which restrict the recovery of the coarser, clastic deposits that underlie the Holocene sediments. There were no opportunities to record or sample open sections such as those available within quarries. However, it was also a conscious decision to design a project to consider the Holocene geoarchaeological record, which had received far less attention by past workers. However, any study of the post-glacial record must begin by understanding the background to early Holocene occupation of the Suffolk landscape.

One of the earliest alluvial geoarchaeological studies

undertaken in Britain was at Sproughton, near to Ipswich, on the River Gipping, where Rose *et al.* (1980) undertook stratigraphic recording, palaeoenvironmental analyses and radiocarbon dating of a quarry section that had yielded evidence for human activity during the Upper Palaeolithic (Wymer, 1976). This sequence provides information regarding Lateglacial environments, which is otherwise largely lacking from the work presented in Chapters 2 and 3 and indeed from parts of east England in general (but see Gao *et al.*, 2007).

At Sproughton, Rose *et al.* (1980) identified the deposition of calcareous silts in a shallow lake, probably in a backswamp environment, with dates from the base of the silts (11,940±180 BP, HAR-260; 12,360–11,430 cal. BC; and 11,740±190 BP, BIRM-750; 12,090–11,250 cal. BC) indicating this body of water formed during the Windermere Interstadial. A subsequent phase of erosion and then deposition of sand and gravel followed after 11,370±210 BP (HAR-210; 11,650–10,820 cal. BC), probably associated with climatic deterioration during the Loch Lomond Stadial. This was succeeded by more stable conditions in the early Holocene, although the data suggest that the deposition of sand and gravel within an active channel continued until at least 9880±120 BP (HAR-259; 6270–6000 cal. BC), prior to the formation of peat around 9500 BP (*c.* 7550 BC). There is little other information concerning the status of rivers and floodplains in Suffolk between the end of the Lateglacial and the 7th–8th millennia BC, with more detailed investigations required to establish the nature and timing of environmental processes during this period.

Mesolithic environments and the archaeological record

The earliest radiocarbon dates (Table 7.1) obtained for the work described in this book were: the River Gipping at Stowmarket Relief Road (Chapter 3), (*c.* 31m OD; SUERC-20658; 7200–7060 cal. BC), and the River Waveney, Beccles Cores 1 and 2 (Chapter 2), 7580–7370 cal. BC (–4.57 m OD; R_Combine GrN-31118 and 31153) and 6640–6480 cal. BC (–4.28m OD; R-Combine GrN-31156 and 31121) respectively; the former dates are close to the date for peat formation reported by Rose *et al.* (1980) at Sproughton (see above). A slightly later date of 6460–6360 cal. BC (24.83m OD; R_combine GrN-31112 and 31147) was obtained from the base of the peat at the River Blackbourn at Ixworth/Mickle Mere (Chapter 2). The palaeoentomological record from Stowmarket (Chapter 3) implies a relatively high energy fluvial system during the earliest stages of sediment accumulation, with the beetle fauna in the basal sample (7200–7060 cal. BC; SUERC-20658), dominated by aquatic taxa including the 'riffle beetle' *Oulimnius* sp. indicating the proximity of fast flowing, oxygenated water (Smith and Howard, 2000). This may suggest that this sequence reflects the initial stages of aggradation of a palaeochannel. The stratigraphic

profile across the Gipping floodplain may also support this inference, indicating that the organic deposits accumulated in a pronounced channel incised into the basal sands (see Chapter 3, Figure 3.2).

Where the data are available, it would appear that there has been relatively little lateral migration of the Suffolk Rivers across the Holocene; Rose *et al.* (1980) concluded that the River Gipping has remained stable and fixed within its floodplain for around 9500 years. This pattern is also evident from the River Waveney and probably other of the rivers investigated (see below). Occasional sandy and silty laminations recorded in the sediments at Ixworth and Hengrave (Chapter 2) would also appear to indicate occasional episodes of flooding resulting in alluviation across floodplains for much of the period represented by these sequences. This picture is broadly typical of other lowland British river systems during the early Holocene (Howard and Macklin, 1999), when fine-grained sedimentation, low energy discharges and the vegetation of channel banks led to the evolution of stable, meandering and anastomosing channel systems (the 'Stable Aggrading Banks Model' of Brown and Keough, 1992), the infilling of secondary braided channels with alluvium and the subsequent smoothing of floodplain topography and potential burial of earlier land surfaces and any associated archaeology. The mid-Holocene appears to have been a period of relative ecological stability in many of the Suffolk river valleys, with the accumulation of extensive sequences of floodplain peat in backswamp environments dominated by *Alnus* fen carr. This pattern of development is typical of temperate, low energy fluvial systems (e.g. Green *at al.*, 2014)

Overall, it is probable that a range of currently poorly understood site-specific factors, such as the influence of the pre-Holocene topography, must have been significant in terms of the timing and extent of paludification, channel and floodplain aggradation across the drainage network of Suffolk. It is probable that this process was related to rising relative sea level, perhaps as a result of 'backing up' seaward draining rivers causing paludification of valley floors as has been identified for other Holocene fluvial networks in east England (e.g. The Humberhead levels, see Van de Noort, 2004) or as a result of a reduction in the rate of sea level rise. This would have enabled groundwater levels to stabilise and peat formation as the paludification of valley floors commenced.

The rapid rise in relative sea level during the early Holocene resulted in the inundation of extensive areas of coastal lowland across and into which the rivers of East Anglia drained. The analysis of some 139 sea-level index points (SLIPs) from the Fenland basin, refined by glacio-isostatic modelling, suggests that relative sea level rose from around –20m OD to –5m OD between *c.* 6000 and 3000 cal. BC (Shennan and Horton, 2002; Shennan *et al.*, 2006). However, as observed in Chapters 2 and 3, radiocarbon dates obtained from basal peat deposits (and associated intercalated freshwater peat and estuarine

Down by the river

Table 7.1: Summary of radiocarbon dates from Suffolk Rivers study areas (Chapters 2 and 3). Accurate elevation data not available for all sites

Site/sequence	Context/depth (m)	Depth m OD	Code	Calibrated date (95%)
Radiocarbon dates (basal peats)				
Beccles C1 2008, Waveney	Base floodplain peat	-4.57	R_combine GrN-31118 and 31153	7580–7370 cal. BC
Beccles C2 2008	Base floodplain peat	-4.28	R_combine GrN-31121 and 31156	6640–6480 cal. BC
Ixworth/Mickelmere, Black Bourn	Base floodplain peat	24.84	R_combine GrN-3112 and 31147	6460–6260 cal. BC
Hengrave, Lark	0.94 above peat base	17.75	R_combine GrN-31115 and 31150	410–360 cal. BC
Stowmarket, Gipping	Base peat	–	SUERC-20658	7200–7060 cal. BC
Great Blakenham, Core 4, Gipping	Basal floodplain peat, 4.98	–	Beta-281673	cal. AD 340–540
AFC Sudbury, Trench 1b, Stour	Base floodplain peat	–	Beta-263579	510–380 cal. BC
Bury Abbey, Stour, Core 26b	Base peat, 3.90	–	Beta-258112	900–790cal. BC
Bury Abbey, Core 27	Base peat, 4.92	–	Beta-258113	2910–2860 cal. BC, 2800–2750 cal. BC, 2710–2710 cal. BC
Other radiocarbon dates (selected)				
Beccles C1 2008	Top *in situ* peat 0.84	–0.81	R_combine GrN-31116 and 31151	360–50 cal. BC
Beccles C1 2008	3.3	–3.27	R_combine GrN-31117 and 31152	3500–3340 cal. BC
Beccles C2 2008	3.59	–3.57	R_combine GrN-31120 and 31155	3960–3785 cal. BC
Ixworth/Mickel Mere	0.71	26.52	R_combine GrN-31110 and 31145	cal. AD 130–340
Ixworth/Mickel Mere	1.24	25.99	R_combine 31112 and 31147	910–800 cal. BC
Hengrave	1.61	18.90	R_combine GrN-31114 and 31149	cal. AD 570–665
Great Blakenham, Core 1	Upper peat, 4.56	–	Beta-281672	cal. AD 1670–1780; 1800–1950; 1950–1960
AFC Sudbury	Peat-Silt contact	–	Beta-263580	cal. AD 660–810
Bury Abbey, Stour, Core 26b	Top peat, 2.77	–	Beta-258111	cal. AD t640–710 to 750–760
Bury Abbey, Core 27	Top peat, 2.71	–	Beta-258114	cal. AD 670–880
Sizewell Belts	Organic aggradation in channel, 1.28	–	SUERC-19651	1130–930 cal. BC
	Shift to inorganic sedimentation	–	SUERC-19649	cal. AD 440–630

silt units) in East Anglia vary spatially, hence inferring regional complexity and the likely impact of additional forcing mechanisms, such as sediment auto-compaction and palaeo-tidal amplification (Waller, 1994; Andrews *et al.*, 2000; Shennan *et al.*, 2000a; Shennan *et al.*, 2000b; Shennan and Horton, 2002).

There is a marked difference in the absolute position of the height of the basal samples relative to the associated basal radiocarbon dates at Stowmarket (31m OD), Beccles and Ixworth (see Table 7.1). At the latter two sites, peat inception began at similar times in the mid-7th millennium BC despite a vertical height difference between the two samples of nearly 30m (Beccles C2, –4.28m OD, Ixworth, 24.83m OD). At Hengrave, on the River Lark, a much later date of 410–360 cal. BC (17.75m OD; R_combine GrN-3115 and 31150) was obtained from *c.* 1m above the base (16.81m OD) of the core, but even allowing for this, the accumulation of organic deposits on the floodplain, probably in a reed swamp environment, evidently began much later in the Holocene. As much of the radiocarbon dating evidence used to quantify Holocene sea level change in East Anglia is derived from mid–late Holocene deposits, a key outstanding research question therefore relates to establishing the timing, rate and pattern of inundation

during the early to mid Holocene and more specifically, its precise relationship to environmental change in river valleys draining into the southern North Sea.

Establishing the chronology and character of environmental changes in the river valleys is also significant for addressing questions concerning the possible use of river systems as corridors of communication and access from the southern North Sea during the prehistoric period. A number of scholars (see Bradley, 2007 for a review) have discussed the importance of rivers in facilitating movement of people across Britain as well as linking to Continental Europe. It is not possible on the basis of the available data to map with confidence the age and extent of the early Holocene 'hidden landscapes' of the river valleys across the county, but the timing of the aggradation of floodplains from the 7th to the 8th millennium BC has associated implications for the visibility and preservation of archaeological sites in the River valleys of Suffolk.

By the late Mesolithic–early Neolithic, sea levels were close to (<5m) those of the present day (Shennan *et al.*, 2006), a process that in part controlled changes in the fluvial systems draining seawards. Positive sea-level tendencies are apparent between 4000–2000 cal. BC, but by *c.* 1000 cal. BC, the whole of the Fenlands experienced a negative sea level tendency, prior to a return to marine conditions towards the end of the 1st millennium BC (Brew *et al.*, 2000). Similar patterns have been recorded in the Blyth Estuary near Southwold (Brew *et al.*, 1992), although in the Yare Valley (Norfolk), there was a transition from marine to freshwater environments around 2550 cal. BC, a negative tendency was maintained until *c.* 50 cal. BC (Coles and Funnell, 1981; see also Chapter 2). The nature of sea level change is critical to our understanding of processes of environmental change and human activity within the river valleys themselves, as well as that on the coastal margins and further east in the drowned early Holocene landscapes of the southern North Sea ('Doggerland': Gaffney *et al.*, 2009). At present, nothing is known concerning the rate or nature of flooding of the areas, which are now below the southern, North Sea, but which were previously parts of the wider landscape of Suffolk.

The results of the SRVP (Chapter 2) and the work described in Chapter 3, suggest that earlier prehistoric landscapes and possibly archaeological sites, may be buried beneath the peat and alluvial deposits in the Suffolk river valleys. This archaeological potential is well illustrated for the later prehistoric period at least, by the discovery of the Waveney prehistoric alignments (Chapters 4 and 5, see further discussion below) and previously at a few other locations such as Scole Bridge (Chapter 2). In general, the aggradation of floodplains from at least the 7th millennium BC discussed above, and perhaps the initiation of stable river channels from around this time, indicates the potential for the preservation of a range of archaeological sites and artefacts in peat and alluvial deposits elsewhere in the region (see below).

A recent study of the distribution of Mesolithic sites in the lower Waveney Valley (Dewing, 2012) demonstrates an absence of early prehistoric sites from the floodplain area despite numerous flint scatters on adjacent dryland. This is almost certainly a result of the burial of earlier landscapes beneath the significant depths of peat and alluvial deposits in the valley (Dewing, 2012; see below). The aggradation of floodplains and development of wetland vegetation such as alder carr might also indicate, although this is rather speculative, that movement and travel by human communities may have been easier by water during the prehistoric period, rather than overland through potentially dense woodland of the central claylands (see Chapter 1). Generally, the potential of the River Waveney as providing an east-west corridor of movement of people during the later prehistoric period at least (see below), has been overlooked in favour of the Wash as an access point to East Anglia from the southern North Sea, due in part to the distribution of artefacts such as gold torcs and coin hoards (e.g. Hutcheson, 2007). This is perhaps also related in part to an absence of direct evidence for water transport as well as settlement patterns in Suffolk during later prehistory; this will be discussed further below in the context of the possible function of the Waveney prehistoric timber alignments.

In terms of environmental changes in the landscape beyond the river valleys, the Ixworth pollen diagram (Chapter 2) provides one of the longest and potentially most complete records of vegetation change, but its utility is limited by the low resolution of analysis. The data imply that the growth of *Betula* (birch) scrub during the earlier Holocene was followed by the spread of woodland dominated by *Tilia* (lime), *Corylus* (hazel), *Quercus* (oak) and *Ulmus* (elm). These trees formed the Holocene woodland across Suffolk, but with exact species composition varying dependent on local edaphic conditions. For example, *Ulmus* appears to have been less prevalent in the Waveney Valley (see Chapter 2, Figure 2.5) whilst *Tilia* seems to have been very significant on the central claylands around the River Blackbourn at Ixworth with percentages of this taxon reaching *c.* 40% (see Chapter 2, Figure 2.12). At Beccles, *Pinus sylvestris* (Scots' pine) seems to have persisted from the early Holocene, probably on the exposed areas of terrace sands and gravels, but declined concomitant with the *Alnus* (alder) rise, perhaps as continuing floodplain aggradation subsumed such contexts. At Ixworth, *Pinus* persisted and even flourished after the *Alnus* rise, again presumably reflecting the continuing availability of better-drained soils on terrace gravels, which were only later, subsumed by floodplain aggradation.

Pollen records from Norfolk provide comparative data for the records described in Chapters 2 and 3. The record from Hockham Mere, Norfolk (Bennett, 1983), indicates that during the early Holocene, *Betula* and *Pinus* woodland expanded initially and was subsequently replaced by mixed forest comprising *Ulmus*, *Quercus* and *Corylus* (Peglar *et al.*, 1989; Waller, 1994). In wetter areas, *Salix* (willow) formed part of this vegetational mosaic (Wiltshire and Emery, 2000) with marls deposits reflecting open water and the presence of sedge dominated fen environments (Scaife, 1990). *Tilia* and *Alnus* were the final main components of the terrestrial woodland to become established. Bennett (1983) recorded low but consistent percentages of *Alnus* at Hockham Mere from a date of 8230±150 BP (Q-2217; 7580–6890 cal. BC), with *Tilia* and *Alnus* values increasing from 7280±75 BP (Q-2219; 6270–6000 cal. BC). The presence of *Alnus* macrofossils at the Stowmarket Relief Road site (Chapter 3) in a bulk sample with a corresponding date of 8160±35 BP (SUERC-20658; 7200–7060 cal. BC) indicates that this tree species might have been present in mid-Suffolk perhaps a millennium earlier than at Hockham Mere.

The Holocene *Alnus* rise in the British Isles was evidently chronologically and spatially variable and has been the subject of some discussion (e.g. Tallantire, 1992). No associated pollen data are available from the Stowmarket site, but the presence of alder macrofossils may support Bennett's (1983) contention that this tree was present locally in East Anglia, prior to its main rise associated with the development of locally suitable conditions for its full establishment. Alder subsequently formed carr woodland on the floodplains, as demonstrated for other of the Suffolk river valleys and elsewhere in lowland England during the mid-Holocene (see Chapter 3).

Understanding the structure and character of the Holocene vegetation has a number of implications for contextualising human activity as interpreted from the archaeological record. The pollen record implies that the woodland of central Suffolk was dense with few natural openings; lime woodland for example, tends to create deep shade. Recent palaeoentomological research suggests that early Holocene lowland landscapes were perhaps not as impenetrable or densely wooded as once assumed (Smith *et al.*, 2010; Whitehouse and Smith, 2010). More open areas were probably located at ecotonal boundaries such as the wetland-dryland edge in river valleys and other areas of open water such as lakes and meres. Lithic material indicative of Mesolithic activity is relatively abundant throughout Suffolk, although the majority represents stray surface finds or small flint scatters and very few 'primary' contexts have been excavated (Austin, 1997). However, excavations and palaeoenvironmental analyses of sites elsewhere across Britain have demonstrated that Mesolithic peoples often occupied wetland edges, possibly attracted in part at least by the abundant resources available at these ecotonal boundaries (Bonsall, 2007; Milner *et al.*, 2012). Other research in Suffolk has identified Mesolithic activity close to former river channels, for example, the River Gipping at Sproughton (Wymer, 1975, 1976), the River Lark at Lackford Heath (Roberts *et al.*, 1998), West Stow (West, 1989) and Mildenhall (Tester, 2001a), and to the south of the River Great Ouse at Lakenheath (Tester, 2001b).

The Lackford Heath site produced over 5000 flint artefacts, and evidence of an 'occupation floor' with three hearths, buried beneath blown sand deposits (Roberts *et al.*, 1998). Across the Breckland in the north-west of the county, the recovery of lithic material suggests relatively widespread activity with the most prolific sites also being located around wetland margins and fen edges (Sussams, 1996), for example, at Joist Fen and Cavenham Mere (Stimson, 1979). Mesolithic artefacts have also been recovered at sites including Wangford and West Row between the River Lark and the River Great Ouse (Dymond and Martin, 1999). At Hockham Mere, the presence of microscopic charcoal identified during pollen analysis was interpreted as indicating the deliberate firing of vegetation (Wymer, 1991). Pollen analyses at a number of sites in Cambridgeshire (Smith *et al.*, 1989; French and Pryor, 1993) and Hockham Mere (Murphy, 1994a) may imply limited woodland clearance during the Mesolithic. It has been suggested that Mesolithic peoples may have manipulated natural openings possibly using fire to remove the build-up of dead plant litter and to encourage new growth and attract game to specific locations (e.g. Grant *et al.*, 2015). Further detailed studies of palaeoenvironmental records are required to determine if similar patterns can be detected in Suffolk.

Neolithic environments and the archaeological record

As in other lowland river valleys, such as the Thames (Garwood and Barclay, 2011), Severn (Garwood, 2007), Lugg (Jackson and Miller, 2011) and Trent (Knight and Howard, 2004), valley floors in East Anglia appear to have become the focus of ritual and funerary activity during the Neolithic. For example, at Fornham in the Lark valley, a complex of monuments including a Cursus, Causewayed Enclosure and Henge have been recorded by aerial photography (Oswald *et al.*, 2001). Other monuments include a Cursus at Stratford St Mary in the Stour valley (Brown *et al.*, 2002) and a causewayed enclosure at Freston in the Gipping valley. Excavation of a ring ditch at West Stow revealed an individual crouched inhumation together with 49 cremation burials (West, 1989). Recent excavations at Flixton Quarry, 12km to the west of Beccles in the Waveney Valley have revealed numerous Neolithic pits containing evidence interpreted as 'structured deposition' (Boulter, pers. comm.).

The earliest available palaeoenvironmental evidence for anthropogenic activity in East Anglia comes from a pollen sequence from Haddenham, Cambridgeshire, which Waller (1994: 105) reports as presenting: "... strong evidence for a clearance phase which was accompanied by at least some arable farming." at a date of 5420±100 BP (Q-2814; 4450–4000 cal. BC) (see also Brown and Murphy, 1997). Peat overlying sands and silts in a ditch on the edge of the River Little Ouse floodplain near Brandon has been interpreted as resulting from paludification caused by the impact of woodland clearance on local hydrology (Hall, 2006). At Sproughton in the Gipping Valley, Wymer (1976) argued that the absence of post-Neolithic settlement in an area that was occupied during the Mesolithic might have been related to increased waterlogging of the floodplain. It has also been proposed that anthropogenic catchment disturbance increased delivery of fine-grained sediments to valley floors and promoted the development of anastamosed river systems from the Neolithic onwards in eastern England (e.g. French and Pryor, 2005) but there is little direct evidence for human disturbance in the River valleys of Suffolk until later in the prehistoric period (but see below).

There is evidence for the movement of people over relatively long distances in Suffolk during the Neolithic, perhaps most clearly demonstrated by the significant number of polished stone axes derived from regions such as Cornwall and the Lake District (Dymond and Martin, 1999). There was also an increasing demand for high quality flint during the Late Neolithic, which saw a shift in raw material procurement strategies with the earlier reliance on surface flint replaced by locally mined deposits. The best-known site is that of Grimes Graves, where flint mining began around 2750 cal. BC and peaked around 2050 cal. BC (Clarke, 1971; Barber *et al.*, 1999). Whilst the overall spatial distribution of material such as pottery and axes show a higher density in north-west Suffolk, there is a small, but representative distribution of Neolithic finds from across the county, seemingly limited to river valleys and tributaries. For example, at Sproughton, Mesolithic activity on the floodplain was succeeded by a Neolithic 'long blade' industry, interpreted as evidence of continuity of occupation (Wymer, 1976).

During the Neolithic, settlement and farming also appears to have been largely confined to river valleys and adjacent better-drained hillsides. For example, in the Lark Valley at Hurst Fen, Mildenhall, the discovery of ditches, and features interpreted as storage pits and stakeholds, together with pottery and worked flint suggests a settlement with evidence for the cultivation of emmer and barley and faunal remains of oxen, swine, sheep and goat (Clarke *et al.*, 1960). Away from the river valleys, the lighter but poorer sandy soils of the Breckland appear to have been less exploited (Sussams, 1996). The recognition of a buried Neolithic land surface beneath reactivated coversands (Bateman and Godby, 2004), demonstrates that these sandy soils may be vulnerable to erosion following cultivation.

The character of environments and associated evidence of the timing and nature of human impact during the Neolithic in Suffolk is on the whole poorly understood. There is no evidence for a clear Neolithic 'elm decline' in the Ixworth diagram due to the relatively coarse sampling intervals, whilst *Ulmus* is very poorly represented in Beccles Core 1 (see Chapter 2). The 'elm decline' at Hockham Mere was dated to 6010±100 BP (Q-2221; 5210–4700 cal. BC) and attributed to the effects of disease, with the palynological evidence for Neolithic disturbance to the vegetation described as 'limited' (Bennett, 1983: 482).

There are indications in the palaeoenvironmental data from the Stowmarket Relief Road site for the presence of grazing animals on or near the floodplain during the Neolithic-early Bronze Age, with 'dung' and 'dor' beetles first recorded from an estimated date of 3630–3090 to 2370 cal. BC (Chapter 3). As these beetles are ready fliers, the precise significance of these data are unclear, but may reflect grazing animals close to or perhaps even on the floodplain. The sampling resolution of the palynological data from the SRVP sites (Chapter 2) are too coarse for detailed interpretation, but the Beccles and Ixworth diagrams indicate that the mid-Holocene dryland vegetation was dominated by *Tilia*, with *Quercus*, *Corylus* and *Ulmus* forming lesser components of the woodland. Herbs and open ground taxa are poorly represented, and mainly seem to reflect plants growing on the wetter soils close to the sampling sites.

Bronze Age environments and the archaeological record

Bronze Age activity in Suffolk is apparent from three main types of evidence: surviving earthworks such as round barrows; sites identified from aerial photography including ring ditches and barrow groups; and finds of metal work as single pieces, small groups and hoards. Over 800 barrows are known to have once existed in Suffolk the majority of which are thought to date from the Early Bronze Age (Dymond and Martin, 1999). Agricultural activity and development has significantly reduced the number of barrows that survive today to a little over 100. It has also been suggested that the *c.* 800 known barrows represented only 34% of the original number (Martin, 1981). The distribution of barrows once again shows a predisposition for the lighter soils and in proximity to the river valleys and four main concentrations have been identified: the Breckland of north-west Suffolk; the Sandlings along the coastline of east Suffolk; the Stour, Box, Brett and Glenn Valleys of southern Suffolk; and the river valleys of central and south-east Suffolk such as the Gipping.

There are few barrows on the high clay plateau of central and south-west Suffolk, which as for the Neolithic, may reflect both heavy, poorly drained soils and the possible presence of dense woodland (see above). Many barrows were grouped in close proximity to Bronze Age settlements, reserving the river terraces and valley slopes for arable and pastoral land. The location of some barrows also appears to coincide with boundaries (some of which may survive as parish boundaries), suggesting that the barrows may have been intentionally positioned to indicate the demarcation of territories and land 'ownership' (*ibid.*). Evidence of further cultural variations may also be visible in the archaeological record during the Bronze Age, with predominantly cremation burials in the south, and both inhumation and cremation burials to the north, potentially demarcating distinct cultural groupings. Few barrows have been excavated, but four barrows without external ditches were identified on Martlesham Heath and described by Martin (1975, 1976a). Finds included flint scrapers, arrowheads and early Bronze Age pottery. A similar site at the aptly named Barrow Bottom in Risby, west of Bury St Edmunds, yielded a female skeleton burial dated to 3495±30 BP (GrN-11358; 1900–1740 cal. BC) (Martin, 1976b).

Woodland clearance and agriculture seems to have intensified during the Bronze Age in Suffolk. In the Breckland, the archaeological evidence suggests that human activity was concentrated on calcareous soils. At Risby, barrow ditches contained molluscan assemblages indicative of dry grassland with unstable soil surfaces (Murphy, 1994a), which implies clearance of woodland and grazing (Sussams, 1996). There is further evidence for human activity in the valley of the River Lark; at Mildenhall for example, heat shattered flints and charcoal derived from *Alnus*, *Corylus*, *Quercus* and *Crataegus* (hawthorn) were dated to 3720±70 BP (HAR-1876; 2350–1930 cal. BC; Murphy, 1994a). A few kilometres away at West Row, a burnt *Quercus* log was dated to 3650±100 BP (HAR-5637; 2270–1830 cal. BC; Martin and Murphy, 1988) and around 10km south-east (of West Row Fen) in the valley floor at Lackford, evidence for the clearance and burning of *Alnus* carr is dated to around 3940±80 BP (HAR-2824; 2830–2150 cal. BC; Martin, 1994a); all these examples suggests a surge in human activity from the 3rd millennium BC. Other pollen evidence includes that from Core 27, Bury St Edmunds Abbey (Chapter 3), which indicates, open, damp meadow vegetation close to the River Lark by a date of 2910–2860 cal. BC (Beta-258113), and although it is tempting to implicate human activity, natural geomorphic processes might equally also be responsible for the creation/maintenance of such environments on floodplains.

Declines in *Tilia* during the Bronze Age around 1350–1050 cal. BC, are recorded in a number of pollen diagrams from the wider region, including at Holme Fen (Cambridgeshire) and in the south-east Fens (Waller, 1994). Although processes including paludification may sometimes be responsible for such reductions (see Grant and Waller, 2011), the accompanying increases in *Plantago lanceolata* (ribwort plantain) and Poaceae (grasses) in many cases imply anthropogenic woodland clearance and the spread of grassland and pastoral environments. At Scole, in the Waveney Valley, pollen analysis of palaeochannel peats imply mixed woodland with *Tilia* dominated woodland at *c.* 2000 cal. BC, after which increased charcoal levels and increases in ruderal herbs suggest localised clearance. By the end of the Bronze Age, the landscape at this location was predominantly open, herb-rich grassland (Wiltshire, in prep.).

Declines in *Tilia* and associated reductions in arboreal taxa are recorded in the SRVP pollen diagrams from Beccles Core 1 and Ixworth and although neither has been dated directly these events seem to be related to the effects of later prehistoric human activity (Chapter 2). Other data from the Suffolk river valleys provides additional evidence of Bronze Age environments; the beetle record from the Stowmarket Relief Road includes members of the Curculionidae or 'weevils' such as the Apionidae and *Sitona* spp., which imply grassland including *Trifolium* (clovers), *Vicia* (vetches) and *Rumex* (docks). This suggests the expansion of open grassland environments close to the floodplain between estimated dates *c.* 2370–1710 cal. BC. Core 26b, Bury St Edmunds Abbey (Chapter 3) also contained palynological evidence for pastoral environments from a date of 900–790 cal. BC (Beta-258112), which may indicate the effects of human activity opening up woodland environments during the later Bronze Age.

The Stowmarket Relief Road record also implies rising water tables on the floodplain of the River Gipping from *c.* 1710 cal. BC. The Fenlands experienced marine inundation and estuarine sedimentation from *c.* 2150–1750 cal. BC, before a reduction in the rate of relative sea level and fen peat development (Waller, 1994). The investigations at Sizewell Belts on the east coast (Chapter 3) indicate the accumulation of organic silts in slow flowing or standing water from 1130–930 cal. BC (SUERC-19651), perhaps reflecting the impact of this process.

Archaeological excavation of a number of previously unrecorded ring ditches, including four at Flixton quarry in the Waveney Valley, have provided evidence of three inverted biconical cremation urns and at Lakenheath, on

Figure 7.1: Must Farm Bronze Age log boat under excavation

the fen edge, a ditch with a central grave containing four inhumations was excavated in 2005 (Martin, 2006). At West Row Fen, a settlement was excavated, comprising three round-houses and numerous pits, whilst faunal remains indicated animal husbandry and seasonal cattle rearing (Martin and Murphy, 1988). Fieldwalking in Mildenhall Parish resulted in the discovery of a range of surface finds including beaker sherds, barbed and tanged arrowheads, plano-convex knives, worked/cut bone and a whetstone; subsequent full-scale excavations identified stake-ring houses, a 'flax retting' pit, water holes and a number of working areas (Martin and Murphy, 1988).

As in earlier periods, wetlands were still an important focus of activity and past discoveries indicate the potential for the preservation of archaeological material including organic remains. At Joist Fen, near Lakenheath, excavations revealed decorated beaker sherds, arrowheads, scrapers and knives (Briscoe, 1964) and at Barton Mere near Pakenham, lithic material, pottery, bronze spearheads and faunal remains (deer, pig, sheep, hare, goat and dog) suggest domestic activity at the lake edge (Jones, 1869). A wattle structure believed to be a fish basket was also recorded towards the centre of the former mere. The recent discovery of the Bronze Age logboats and features including fishtraps, at Must Farm, near Whittlesey, in the Fenland (Figure 7.1) demonstrates the potential for direct evidence of water travel and exploitation of riverine environments in East Anglia.

Other palaeoenvironmental evidence for human activity during the later Bronze Age is present in the form of the record of *Linum usitatissimum* (flax) from Stowmarket Relief Road (Chapter 3), perhaps indicating 'retting' of this crop on the floodplain or even local cultivation on the alluvial soils. Stems of the cultivated plants can be processed to produce fibres suitable for weaving linen (Murphy, 1982). Remains of cultivated flax are known from many sites in Europe from the Neolithic onwards (e.g. Zohary and Hopf, 1988) but records for prehistoric evidence for flax retting in Britain are rare. Interestingly, early Bronze Age pit features at the site of West Row Fen, Suffolk (see above, Martin and Murphy, 1988), contained plant macrofossil remains suggesting flax retting. Further work is required to establish the significance of these relatively early records for flax in the east of England.

The abundance of metalwork found in and around the Fen edge illustrates the potential social significance of wetland environments, with these finds generally interpreted as reflecting votive deposition similar to that observed in riverine locations, although recent study has drawn attention to the potential differences between deposition of material in river as opposed to bog environments (e.g. Mullin, 2012). Martin (2006) concluded that much of the metalwork found at West Row Fen was considerably later than adjacent settlements. Other finds, particularly those from the Breckland watering hole at Rymers Point, also seem to follow this pattern (Martin, 2006). The hoard discovered at Isleham in 1959 comprised over 6500 pieces (200lb) of bronze, with the bulk of the finds consisting of fragments of weapons (including Wilburton-type swords typical of the Late Bronze Age), tools, ornaments and an abundance of raw metal slab and the by-products of bronze-casting. It was suggested that this might have belonged to a metalworker (Britton, 1960), although the reasons for its deposition are unclear.

Iron Age environments and the archaeological record

Suffolk was occupied by at least two British tribes by the later Iron Age, commonly known as the *Iceni* and *Trinovantes* (Martin and Murphy, 1988). The *Iceni* settled in Norfolk and the north of Suffolk, whilst the *Trinovantes* populated southern Suffolk and Essex. Martin and Murphy (1988) attempted to reconstruct this tribal boundary, as a line that bisected the county from east to west, but it is unclear how these territories were defined or developed through the Iron Age. In common with evidence from earlier periods, the majority of Iron Age settlements were probably located on areas of lighter soils, and along the main river valleys. During the Iron Age, woodland clearance and agricultural intensification, was in part associated with an expansion of settlement onto the heavier clay soils. However, whilst palaeoenvironmental analyses of Iron Age sequences are available, the radiocarbon 'plateau effect' for the time period creates an accuracy

envelope of between 200 and 500 years per age estimate (Bryant, 1997; Wiltshire and Murphy, 1999). Although recent developments in Bayesian chronological modelling may offer increased precision (e.g. Gearey *et al.*, 2009a), to date none of the available palaeoenvironmental sequences have been re-analysed using this approach.

Bennett (1983) identified evidence of woodland clearance at Hockham Mere in the Breckland, from a date of 2660±50 BP (Q-2223; 920–780 cal. BC) hence during the late Bronze Age/early Iron Age, with cereal pollen becoming prominent around 500 years later. A reduction in arboreal pollen observed at Hockham was mirrored by an increase in grasses, ruderal plants and heather showing the development of heathland from 1980±50 BP (Q-2224; cal. AD 110–130) and hence during the early Romano-British periods. Further disturbance is recorded at Diss Mere, Norfolk, where tree pollen decreased markedly during the Iron Age with concomitant increases in Poaceae, Cyperaceae (sedges), *Artemisia* (mugwort), *Plantago lanceolata* and *Rumex*. The decline in tree pollen and major expansion of herbs suggests widespread and extensive deforestation and spread of pastoral agriculture, since cereal pollen was largely absent (Peglar *et al.*, 1989).

However, this is in part at least a result of taphonomic bias, as cultivation is reflected by charred grains and chaff of spelt, emmer and hulled barley from a settlement located on a gravel terrace at West Stow (West, 1989). Around Haddenham, Peterborough and Heybridge, open grassland environments expanded (Bryant, 2000), whilst at Scole in the Waveney Valley, the early Iron Age environment was broadly similar to that of the late Bronze Age, with a pastoral landscape and the expansion of arable agriculture in the middle Iron Age (Wiltshire, forthcoming). After the middle Iron Age, there was a brief re-expansion of woodland at Scole, but it never regenerated to the level recorded in the earlier Holocene (Wiltshire and Murphy, 1999). Certainly, by the late Iron Age/early Roman period at this site, renewed major clearance associated with cereal cultivation was occurring close to the river.

The formation of floodplain peat along the River Great Ouse at Staunch Meadow, Brandon was dated to 1950±70 BP (HAR-6475; 120 cal. BC–cal. AD 240) (Murphy and Fryer, 2005). Plough marks attributed to Iron Age activity were also recorded at the basal sand-peat interface and pollen analysis (of the peat at the sediment transition) identified abundant grassland and weed species, whereas the overlying peat was characterised by tall herb/swamp communities with limited trees and shrubs in the wider landscape (Wiltshire, 1990). Investigations at Micklemere, near Pakenham (Chapter 3), have also identified basal peats that accumulated under mixed sedge fen and open grassland habitats during the late Iron Age (Murphy and Wiltshire, 1989).

It has been suggested that the widespread paludification of valley floors in the region in later prehistory, especially well attested in Norfolk, may reflect rising water tables in part linked to changing catchment hydrology associated with deforestation and perhaps climatic deterioration (Wiltshire and Murphy, 1999). A major marine transgressive phase dated to 550 cal. BC–cal. AD 150 is also evident in the Fenlands, with estuarine silts being deposited as far inland as Redmere in north-west Suffolk (Waller, 1994). The character of this event appear to have varied regionally; in the Yare valley for example, freshwater peat accumulation was maintained throughout much of the Iron Age (Coles and Funnell, 1981) with estuarine sedimentation prevailing from *c.* 20 cal. BC–cal. AD 350 (see below and also Chapter 2).

In common with previous periods, the majority of Iron Age settlements appear to have been located on areas of lighter soil and along the main river valleys although as stated previously, there was some expansion onto the heavier clay soils. Most settlement sites were apparently unenclosed, whilst hillforts akin to those recorded elsewhere in England are generally precluded from East Anglia perhaps due to the absence of prominent hilltops, large defensive earthworks have been identified at Clare in the Stour Valley, at Burgh near Ipswich (Martin, 1988b) and at Barnham in the Breckland (Martin, 1993; Sussams, 1996) and perhaps at Holkham, on the north coast of Norfolk. The latter site has produced a comparatively small number of Roman finds, which suggested that the site was abandoned by the mid-1st century AD (Clarke, 1936). At West Stow, evidence for occupation throughout the Iron Age has been found, although activity was concentrated towards the middle and late Iron Age (West, 1989).

At Joist Fen, Lakenheath, excavations of the multi-period settlement provided evidence of domestic activity including coins (attributable to the *Iceni*) and dark grey pottery sherds (Briscoe, 1964). A number of Iron Age sites interpreted as individual farmsteads have also been identified along the Flynn and Deben valleys, all situated on high ground at around 30m OD and no more than 500m from the nearest water source (Martin, 1993). In the Breckland, farmsteads are also located at fairly regular intervals along the major river valleys such as the Lark and again may reflect dependence upon principal water sources (Sussams, 1996).

Field systems would have been a significant aspect of the Iron Age landscape and numerous examples have been recorded by aerial photography, particularly on the areas of lighter soil, although without excavation, some of these may be of earlier date. Field systems and pits of a probable Iron Age date were identified in a re-evaluation of previously excavated material from Lackford Bridge adjacent to West Stow (Tipper, pers. comm.). On the claylands, such features are less easy to identify, but a combination of field survey and study of surviving field systems suggests that exploitation of these landscapes may have been more intensive than hitherto considered (Martin and Satchel, forthcoming). In addition to field systems, a long linear embankment in the Lark valley known as the 'Black Ditches' may date to the Iron Age (Dymond

and Martin, 1999), providing another form of landscape delineation and division in this period.

There has been debate regarding the date of areas of co-axial field systems in Suffolk with some suggestion that they may have their origins in later prehistory (Williamson, 1987). These can be extensive, that of the Scole-Dickelburgh system in the Waveney Valley in Norfolk covers around 50km^2, with the main axes of the systems running up and out of the valley northwards onto the boulder-clay plateau (Williamson, 2012). In common with other areas in the south-east, evidence for Belgic influence is also present in Suffolk towards the end of the Iron Age. For example, two cemeteries at Boxford contain Belgic influenced materials one with at least 43 cremation burials in urns, some of which were accompanied with Bronze Age brooches (Clarke, 1971). In the late Iron Age and Romano-British period, eastern England also became a focus for salt making (e.g. Wilkinson and Murphy, 1995; Lane and Morris, 2001; Thomas and Fletcher, 2001).

Romano-British environments and the archaeological record

Much of the current evidence for Roman Suffolk continues to be developed from aerial photographs, surface and metal detected finds. New sites, particularly farmsteads and villas, have been identified within the last few years and a clearer picture of Roman exploitation of the landscape has begun to develop. The evidence seems to point to a spread of settlement across the county that was more widespread than during the Iron Age, but still avoided much of the central clay landscape. The presence of the Roman Military in Suffolk was relatively small-scale with only two 1st century AD forts known from Pakenham and Coddenham (Plouviez, 1999). Individual farmsteads by far make up the largest proportion of the known Roman sites (Plouviez, 1999), and also the most excavated, with approximately twenty villas excavated or investigated to date (Carr, 1991). A number of significant Romano-British 'urban' centres are known throughout the county (Icklingham, Pakenham, Long Melford, Coddenham, Stonham, Hacheston, Capel St Mary and Wenhaston) (West and Plouviez, 1976). Archaeological investigations have concentrated on Coddenham (12 excavations), Pakenham (15 excavations), Hacheston (7 excavations) and Icklingham (11 excavations; Carr, 1991). The settlement at Icklingham, located on the River Lark, produced artefacts dating from the 3rd century AD onward. In addition, this site was also an important Christian settlement during the latter part of the 4th century AD, identified through the discovery of lead tanks with Christian monograms and the presence of a large Christian cemetery (West and Plouviez, 1976).

An extensive settlement also existed at Hacheston, possibly spanning up to 30ha, from the edge of the River Deben floodplain almost to the watershed between the Deben and the River Ore to the north (Blagg *et al.*,

2004). Initial occupation is evident during the late Iron Age, with a seemingly peaceful transition into the Roman occupation. Settlement developed gradually during the early Roman period, coinciding with improving road and trade networks. The site was probably abandoned by around AD 370, possibly in response to the reduction in military presence at the coastal forts that occurred towards the end of the Romano-British period. Industrial sites existed at a number of locations across the county, particularly pottery manufacture. At West Stow, for example, on the River Lark, an active pottery-manufacturing site including five pottery kilns and numerous associated pits developed during the 1st and 2nd centuries AD over earlier Iron Age and Neolithic levels (West, 1989). Only limited evidence was found for domestic activity and settlement, with two possible buildings, although subsequent medieval occupation might have destroyed earlier features. Approximately nineteen salterns are also recorded in Suffolk from this period (Suffolk SMR). At Cavenham Mere, multi-phase occupation was recorded, with scatters of Romano-British pottery and metalwork bracelets and coins that span the 1st–3rd centuries AD (Stimson, 1979).

At West Row, located *c*. 10km down-valley from West Stow, an important hoard of 4th century AD silver dishes, goblets and spoons known as the 'Mildenhall Treasure' was discovered during ploughing in the early 1940s (Painter, 1977). The silverware was discovered in close proximity to the site of a Roman building, located *c*. 20m to the east, and may reflect the hurried burial of a wealthy settler's possessions. A second buried hoard of about 500 coins at Little Bealings was dated to AD 379–395, whilst a 4th century AD hoard containing 3100 coins is recorded from Freston near Ipswich (Clarke, 1971). However the Hoxne treasure of jewellery, coins and over 100 silver spoons (Plouviez, 1999) is probably the most famous of the Roman period hoards from Suffolk. The burial of such valuable artefacts may have been in response to the gradual breakdown of the Roman Empire's monetary economy and the onset of Saxon attacks in the region as a consequence of the Empire's demise. A Saxon Shore Fort of late Roman date is thought to have existed on the end of the Felixstowe peninsular, although this has now been lost to the sea. Evidence for Romano-British settlements is recorded along much of the coastal margin in and around Suffolk. At Hollesley Bay, stakeholes and an abundance of Roman pottery suggest continuous occupation through to the late Romano-British period, with some evidence for initial settlement during the Iron Age (Mowat, 1975). Further north, Roman settlement has long been known in the Cambridgeshire Fenlands, close to the Suffolk border. Sites at Stonea, March and Grandford are recorded from this period with evidence for salt production and animal husbandry (Hall, 1988).

However, as is the case for much of the Holocene, there is a relative lack of detailed palaeoenvironmental data for the Romano-British period in Suffolk. As mentioned above, Bennett's (1983) pollen diagram from Hockham

Mere, Norfolk, shows a pronounced increase in Poaceae and *Calluna vulgaris* (heather) from a date of 1980±50 BP (Q-2224; 110 cal. BC–cal. AD 130) and hence possibly during the 1st–2nd centuries AD, interpreted as heathland development as a result of soil deterioration following woodland clearance. The SRVP pollen sequences (Chapter 2) including Ixworth, Hengrave and Beccles cover this period, but must be used with some caution due to the chronological problems with these data. The Stowmarket Relief Road sequence also incorporates the Romano-British period, but again the analytical resolution is only sufficient to draw broad conclusions. Elsewhere in the region, palaeosol development was recorded within the Breckland dunefields near Wangford Warren at *c*. 170 cal. BC–cal. AD 110, suggesting higher water tables attributed to relative sea-level rise affecting the adjacent East Anglian fens (Bateman and Godby, 2004). Murphy and Fryer (2005) suggested that the expansion of intertidal environments was associated with a positive sea-level tendency during this period, causing drainage to be impeded throughout many lowland river valleys in East Anglia. This will be discussed further below, as will the data for later prehistoric landscape change from the site of Beccles.

7.3 The Waveney Valley later prehistoric timber alignments in context

The excavations and associated analyses at Beccles (2006–2009; Chapter 4), Barsham (2007; Chapter 5) and at Geldeston (2011; Chapter 5) have revealed a type of monument previously unknown in Suffolk. These monuments consist of alignments of upright driven stakes, commonly established in three rows, approximately 3.5m wide. At Beccles, this pattern was relatively consistent, although the arrangement of the stakes at Barsham and Geldeston were less regular, in part due to the disturbance of the archaeology by the soke dyke excavations. The Beccles alignment was at least 500m long, whilst at Barsham and Geldeston, the excavated lengths were much shorter, at 30m and 38m respectively. Six of the Beccles stakes and a single stake from Geldeston (see below) had either intact or broken cross halving lap joints (Figure 7.2, *sensu* Spence, 1994), five of which had *in situ* lateral wooden cross bars which seem to have been intended to aid insertion and/or support the upright stakes once *in situ* (Figure 7.3). There is no extant evidence that these joints functioned to support any form of superstructure and the completed form of the monuments remains open to speculation although it seems likely that the stakes must have protruded for some length above the contemporary floodplain surface (see below).

The chronology for these structures extends across the 1st century BC into the 1st century AD, hence the later Iron Age and the Romano-British periods. The earliest alignment constructed was at Geldeston, with timber felled between 97–94 and 83 BC, with a single timber indicating construction/repair in 2/1 BC. Barsham produced

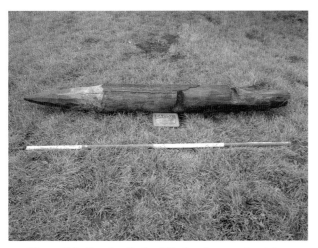

Figure 7.2: Beccles Stake 613 showing two lap joints

dendrochronological dates of between 8 BC and AD 8, thus possibly contemporary with the later phases of Geldeston, though the estimated chronology must be viewed with some caution as it is possible that the timbers were re-used. Further downstream at Beccles, the alignment was constructed using timber felled in the spring of 75 BC, hence around two decades after that at Geldeston. Given the possible longevity of driven stakes, it is possible that at least some of the earlier stakes of the former site were still standing when those at Beccles were felled. The undated samples and the double, triple, and (at Beccles) quadruple clusters of stakes, point towards phases of maintenance and repair at all the sites, with the 'stake packing' at Beccles seemingly demonstrating attempts to stabilise the stakes. The dendrochronological analyses at Beccles reflect the use of winter-felled wood. It is not known if such repairs

Figure 7.3: Reconstruction drawing showing how the lap joints might have been used to aid insertion. Drawing: Colin Edwards and Alan Bartley, Norwich

This display was produced in July 2008; illustrations by Alan Bailey; text by Jessica Tunstall; designed by Colin Edwards Graphic Design; printed by Digital Displays; display manufactured by Simon Gordon Signs.

Beccles mystery unearthed

As you walked out on to the marshes from Beccles did you notice it getting quieter as the 21st century noise of traffic faded into the background? Did you hear more birds? Did you feel in a slightly different world?

If you did, that's appropriate, because close beneath where you're standing lies a mystery trail to another world – the world of Beccles Marshes when there was no modern town, no church tower, no houses across the river, over 2000 years ago.

The River Waveney was here, following very much the same meandering course it follows today, similar marshy plants grew here and cattle or sheep grazed just as they often do today.

What else was here?
An elaborate structure of three rows of oak posts, stretching about 95 m and 3-4 m across, marking a route for pedestrians or horses and ponies.

Sixty-seven posts have been found, they were carefully finished and they stood about 1-4 m high.

could have been a combination of both.

Where were they?
The remains were found on the marshes here. If you look at the trees on the riverbank and compare them to the illustration you can see the general area of the site. The posts were preserved in the peat.

When exactly was this?
Archaeologists have dated the construction to the early spring of 75 BC, during the Iron Age.

Why were they here?
We don't have a definite answer - yet. The posts could have had a practical purpose - marking the approach to the river and a quay for loading and unloading. Or they could have marked the approach for ceremonial and boundary purposes. Or it

Fragments of pottery found at the site are typical of the shouldered Roman pot illustrated.

The 2007 dig
They have also found posts from the Roman period and some remains of Roman pottery.

Who built the structure?
Ancient Britons, probably men but possibly women as well.

How was it discovered?
In 2006 Broadland Environmental Services Ltd was working on this stretch of the Waveney as part of the Environment Agency funded Broadland Flood Alleviation Project. Following initial discoveries during the flood defence work, archaeologists from the University of Birmingham and Suffolk County Council carried out excavations of the site in 2006 and 2007. Their research is still a work in progress and they hope to carry out a further excavation to uncover more answers.

How were the posts made?

The posts came from local coppiced (cut) woodlands, showing the local people were skilled in woodland management.

Straight trees were selected, and cut using an axe. The wood was moved to the site, then shaped using a variety of iron axes.

Roughly and smoothly finished posts

From variations in the woodworking styles we can see that the work was done by several people, with differing levels of craftsmanship, using different tools and techniques.

We assume that the grooves and cross-braces we found inserted into them were used to push the posts into the ground. By twisting the wood and exerting downward pressure the uprights were worked into the softer soil.

A path to the past

Recent engineering works have exposed well-preserved evidence of the early history of Beccles, dating back to the Iron Age. Updated information will be displayed at the Beccles Museum.

Was it a ceremonial pathway, marking a boundary?

Did it have a practical purpose - a link to the river?

Keep in touch
For news of the project you can keep in touch with Beccles Museum in Ballygate, Beccles, tel 01502 715722 or www.becclesmuseum.org.uk or by visiting the Suffolk County Council Archaeological Service website at www.suffolk.gov.uk/environment/archaeology

Project Partners
Birmingham ArchaeoEnvironmental
Broadland Environmental Services Limited
Broads Authority
Environment Agency
Suffolk County Council
The University of Birmingham

Figure 7.4: Broads Authority panel showing reconstruction of the Beccles alignment (see also Figure 7.3)

were carried out on an *ad hoc* basis as individual stakes decayed, or in distinct phases reflecting distinct 'renewal' of the monuments. Taken collectively, the sites therefore represent a continued (or revisited) theme in monument, construction that continued for over 100 years at the very end of the Iron Age and into the Romano-British period.

The full extent of the alignments has not been established, although at Beccles, the site clearly extended across the full width of the southern floodplain of the River Waveney, it is not known if it continued into the river itself or across the *c.* 100m of floodplain on the northern side of the river. The southern, dryland terminus of the Beccles alignment has been identified, although desiccation and wastage of the peat at the dryland-floodplain interface has resulted in the loss of much of the archaeology with only stake tips surviving. The possible northern terminal of the structure at Geldeston was similarly identified, but in this case the site appears to terminate abruptly within the floodplain and not at the dryland edge.

Other wooden structures were also identified at Beccles, representing discrete phases of construction on the site: four ground-level structures, two of which were dated to the Iron Age (brushwood structures 06 and 07), the third (Trench 4 platform structure), probably Iron Age and with the fourth, the brushwood trackway in Trench 1 (brushwood structure 09; see Chapter 4), dating to the Romano-British period. The Bayesian analyses indicate that the construction of brushwood structure 07 pre-dated, whilst brushwood structures 06 post-dated, the felling of the timber for the alignment in 75 BC. Trench 4 revealed a series of 25 north–south aligned half split and unconverted beams (predominantly alder with occasional oak) lying along the entire axis of the alignment.

It is interesting to note that although much of the debris field (see below), and the upright stakes themselves are of oak, alder dominates in this structure. Alder wood survives well in wet environments, making it an ideal choice for use in a structure associated with a wet environment (Gale and Cutler, 2000), although the use of this wood might equally reflect its local availability. These timbers lay on the 'preservation horizon' for waterlogged wood, as attested to by the degraded upper surfaces of many of the beams and the strong correlation with height of the top of the degraded upright stakes. This relationship (Chapter 4) may hint that these stakes had rotted off before the beams were emplaced, or that the stakes of the alignment did not protrude far above ground level at this location. However, this relationship may well have resulted from disturbance to the structure by the later ditch. The beams were not particularly closely packed and would not seem to have constituted a continuous surface, but still one which may have functioned as a discrete section of trackway or perhaps a platform.

Brushwood structure 09 in Trench 1 was constructed from roundwood sourced from coppiced *Alnus* woodland, which had possibly been managed on a 4/5-year cycle. This probably functioned as a short section of trackway

which appears to be leading away west from the alignment, perhaps marking a routeway across the wetter ground towards the River Waveney. There was also evidence of a possible plank overlying a ground-level beam in Beccles Trench 3, indicating that some form of planking or surface might have originally been present (Chapter 4). However, the very poor condition of the wood prevented further analysis of this material.

The uprights stakes, wood working and technology

At Beccles, the excavations have therefore indicated that the form of the monument may have varied along its length, with evidence for a number of ground level structures. However, aside from the Romano-British trackway towards the northern end of the site at Beccles, the relationship between the stake alignment itself and the ground level features is somewhat unclear in structural and functional terms at least. Whilst the final completed form remains speculative it seems likely that the stakes originally protruded some distance above the contemporary ground surface, but there are no unambiguous archaeological data that support the hypothesis of above ground protrusion aside from the essentially functional assumption that stakes of the size and depth of insertion recorded must have been designed to extend at least some distance above the ground level (see Figure 7.4). Indeed, on the basis of depth of insertion, the height of the stakes above the contemporary ground surface seems to have varied along the length of the Beccles alignment.

However, no material that might have represented the collapsed or rotted off portions of the upright timbers was recovered from any of the sites. Given the context of erection in open water at Barsham, this is not surprising, but for Beccles and Geldeston, it implies that the dry conditions that led to the rotting of the stakes at or above contemporary ground-level must have been sustained long enough to prevent any above ground material from surviving even once it had collapsed onto the floodplain surface. Alternatively, and perhaps more likely, seasonal flooding might have washed this material away, with only the wooden remains such as the stakes and other material that was anchored, or that were more firmly embedded in the peat (perhaps through trampling) surviving *in situ*.

The uppermost sections of the stakes at all the sites were degraded and survived to a broadly similar height, dictated by a 'preservation horizon' (between –0.1m OD and –1.25m OD over 513m of alignment at Beccles), with the tops of the degraded upright stakes flush with the first recorded horizontal wooden remains. At Geldeston, this preservation horizon was identified at a higher elevation, with horizontal remains preserved between –0.40m and –0.60m OD. This clearly demonstrates the taphonomic effects of the 'preservation horizon' that has acted to essentially slice an unknown quantity of wooden material away from the top of the structures. Hence the surviving

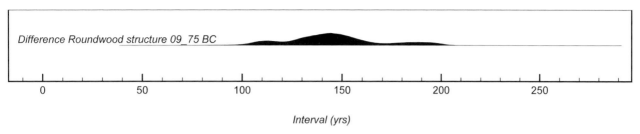

Figure 7.5: Estimated time between the construction of the timber alignment and the brushwood trackway in Trench 1 (2009)

lengths of the upright stakes at all three sites are dictated by depth of past insertion. With this in mind, it can be speculated, using a 'rule of thumb' of 1/3rd below ground to 2/3rd above ground for earthfast stakes (*cf.* Mercer, 1981; Gibson 1994, 2000). Using this approximate measure, the maximum stake lengths of 1.45–6.6m equate to potential protruding heights above ground level in antiquity of *c.* 0.97–4.4m.

The possible longevity of the alignments can be estimated using several lines of evidence. The stratigraphic position of the brushwood trackway in 2009 Trench 1 at Beccles, indicates that in this section of the monument at least, the upright stakes must have decayed by the Romano-British period at the latest. The period between the construction of the alignment and that of the brushwood trackway can be estimated using the chronological data (Figure 7.5) as *105–165 years (68% probability)* or *100–200 years (95% probability)*. These figures represent a *terminus ante quem* and it is probable that the stakes in this northern extent of the monument had rotted off sometime before the trackway was built. Anecdotal evidence indicates that timber fence stakes on Beccles Marshes currently remain serviceable for a maximum of 25 years before degrading at ground level and requiring replacement. The stakes at Beccles may thus have been starting to rot off at ground level by 50 BC. It is probable that the monument therefore survived in its original form for a period of time much shorter than the maximum of two centuries (Figure 7.5) and perhaps a span of time as short as or even less than, a single human generation. It is unfortunate that there were probable repair phases represented by the clusters of upright stakes, which did not return dendrochronological dates, although it is tempting to relate these to the 1st–2nd century AD phase of activity represented by the brushwood trackway and finds of Romano-British pottery.

The morphology of some of the uprights from Beccles may indicate that they were sourced from 'overgrown' coppice, whilst the alder timbers were likely sourced from trees, which were growing on the floodplain, perhaps even those that were cleared from the route of the alignment. In all cases the tips had been shaped from all directions to 'pencil points'; all the extracted stakes showed clear tool facets, which were generally broad and flat, suggesting the use of iron axes (e.g. see Coles and Orme, 1978). None of the sites revealed evidence of finishing or 'complex carpentry' from the relatively large wood assemblages.

With the exception of a single timber recovered from Geldeston, with a possible degraded halving lap, the only jointed timbers recorded from the three sites were relatively basic, 'rough and ready' halving laps recorded on some of the upright stakes from Beccles and Geldeston (see above).

The same can be said of the basic nature of the limited assemblage of wooden artefacts. From Beccles, these consist of a peg, a possible rope runner, three rough dowels (probably forming part of broken handles) and a single, well finished, small jointed item of unknown function that had broken in antiquity (030). Geldeston yielded a single peg and a rough dowel, whilst the enigmatic fragment 039 is perhaps the only example of 'specialised carpentry' recovered from any of the three excavations. Instead, the evidence implies a pared down, functional form of woodworking, with no clear evidence for 'specialised' woodworking. The different skills or even attitudes of individual woodworkers can probably be glimpsed within the upright stake assemblage – some were trimmed to very neat, symmetrical, aesthetically pleasing points whilst others have been worked in a much more haphazard manner. Perhaps this indicates the efforts of members of a community, some of whom were clearly very proficient in the working of wood, whilst others might have been less skilled or possibly working rapidly (see Figure 7.6 and 7.7).

As discussed above, Barsham is the only site that provides any possible evidence for the re-use of timbers, with several stakes showing signs of wet rot prior to the ends being worked into points (Chapter 5). No such evidence for re-use was recorded from either Beccles or Geldeston, indicating that all the material used in the construction of the monuments was obtained specifically for that purpose. There is some evidence for 'trial and error' within the construction process: in several cases, the timbers with halving laps cut into them also had a 'notch' present. Possibly where a woodworker had started to cut a halving lap but had then, for reasons unknown, decided to change the location of the joint. A single stake recovered from Geldeston echoes this process, with two notches of unknown function present.

The extensive debris field at Beccles can be sub-categorised by type and conversion, providing information on the character of woodworking activity (Gearey *et al.*, 2011). A total of 224 pieces of roundwood were recovered, 125 of which demonstrated morphological evidence of coppicing, generally in the form of straight, even stems

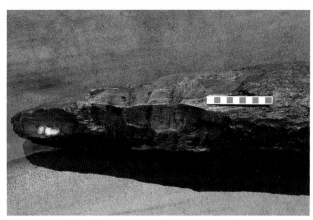

Figure 7.6: Beccles worked stake pencil point, indicating a high level of woodworking skill

Figure 7.7: Beccles worked stake pencil point, implying rapid or less skilled woodworking in comparison to that in Figure 7.6

devoid of side branches. Sixty-five items had been worked, generally displaying one or more trimmed ends, the most common form was a 'chisel' end, trimmed from one direction often with a single visible tool facet. It is possible that much of the *Quercus* and *Alnus* debris recorded on the site was a product of the construction of the triple stake row and ground level structures, but the debris derived from *Fraxinus excelsior* (ash) cannot have derived from this. An initial hypothesis regarding this debris field was that it represented primary debris from the construction of the monument, but the evidence indicates that the debris reflects the construction of wooden objects not present on site, and it is therefore possible that some or all of this material was imported to the site, possibly to stabilise the peat during the construction of the monument.

The apparent lack of specialised woodworking from these sites is notable given evidence from elsewhere that demonstrates that such skills were present even well before the Iron Age. There is evidence for specialist carpenters throughout later prehistory, from finely crafted log boats and larger craft, such as the Bronze Age Dover Boat (Arnold and Clark, 2004), through the complex multi-part Middle Bronze Age wheel recovered from Flag Fen (Taylor, 2001), to the beautiful coopered vessels that appear in the Iron Age (Earwood, 1993). No evidence of this type of high-level carpentry is present from any of the three Waveney valley sites. This may indicate construction undertaken by the community as a whole, rather than by specialised artisans, or might simply demonstrate that the form and associated function of the structures themselves did not call for the overt expression of such skills.

The small finds: pottery

The finds assemblage from Beccles composed primarily Iron Age pottery, with a single Roman vessel dating to the mid or late 1st to early 2nd century AD recovered. All of these vessels were domestic forms, comprising jars and bowls. At least two examples in the Iron Age assemblage had preserved food residues indicating that they were used for cooking. The forms compare well with those from contemporary published assemblages such as Burgh (Martin, 1988b) and West Stow (Martin, 1990). The micaceous clays used for several of the vessels suggest that these were probably locally made from clay sources available in the Waveney Valley. However, the presence of quartz-sand-tempered fabrics suggests perhaps that the vessels came from at least two sources. The later Iron Age pottery chronology broadly agrees well with the dendrochronological dates and suggests that the pottery was probably contemporary with the alignment.

At Geldeston, all but one of the 40 sherds recovered were from a single small jar, although less than half of the complete vessel was recovered. The sherds were collected from ten different find spots within a maximum area of perhaps 3 × 3m. It is possible that this represents an object that was broken on site, either through accidental or deliberate breakage. The lack of pottery from elsewhere on site, coupled with the proximity of this scatter towards the northern end of the alignment, might indicate something more deliberate, an intentional breakage and the spilling of its contents, perhaps as a libation. Within this context it is possible to consider the remains of the three fragmented vessels from Beccles as representing a similar event (see below).

The small assemblage of worked and burnt flint from Beccless also indicates knapping was occurring on site and whilst not sufficiently diagnostic to provide a date, given their association with the pottery, they are probably Iron Age. Therefore, the assemblage of material culture recovered from all three sites was relatively small; suggesting that any activities carried out have left little trace, and/or perhaps the sites were actually used for relatively short periods of time (see below). This may well fit with the evidence for the possible longevity of the upright timber stakes (see above).

The landscape context and later prehistoric environments in the Waveney Valley

The construction of these alignments must be considered within the wider cultural and environmental context of the later Iron Age and also the Romano-British period. However, overall archaeological evidence for later prehistoric and Romano-British activity in the Waveney Valley has been described as limited and "... highly fragmentary ..." (Hegarty, 2011: 7). It would appear that the River Waveney was situated within the centre of *Iceni* territory, which probably included north Suffolk and Norfolk (see above; Martin, 1988). Robinson (2007) has summarised the available evidence from the Waveney Valley: possible Iron Age cropmarks have been identified on the west side of the river close to Barsham, whilst it has been suggested that a small ring ditch and enclosure may perhaps have been an Iron Age round house.

Further upstream at Bungay (*c.* 5km upstream from Barsham), finds of Roman coins, metalwork and pottery have been found close to the postulated line of the Roman road. Also close to Bungay at Flixton quarry, is one of the few examples from the Waveney of Iron Age activity below 25–35m OD, with stakeholes, enclosure ditches and field boundaries identified. A number of ditched enclosures identified on aerial photographs some 1.5km to the east of the Beccles alignment have been tentatively interpreted as possible small agglomerate settlements of late prehistoric or Romano-British date but there is considerable uncertainty concerning these features and they are recorded as 'undated' in the SMR (Heagrty, 2011). Twenty-four single find spots and scatters of Roman period material are recorded from metal detecting in the valley, including two coins and a nail from Barsham. At St Mary South Elmham (15km upstream from Barsham), a large Roman settlement has been located on the river terrace gravels, and this site includes evidence for Iron Age activity. Overall, whilst the known sites and finds in the Waveney demonstrate activity during the later prehistoric period it would seem that this was not especially extensive. In the absence of further excavation, the precise nature and chronology of activity remains unclear.

The palaeoenvironmental investigations summarised above (Chapters 3 and 4) provide some evidence of the spatial and chronological patterns of landscape and environmental change. The Late Devensian basal sands and gravels in the lower Waveney Valley (West, 2009) are sealed beneath over 5m of floodplain sediment. This 'hidden landscape' (*sensu* Chapman and Gearey, 2013) therefore represents the Mesolithic terrestrial land surface, which began to paludify during the early Holocene by 7580–7370 cal. BC (see Chapter 2) in response to rising relative sea level. The waterlogged floodplain was shortly afterwards readily colonised by *Alnus*, leading to peat accumulation in a fen carr environment (*sensu* Rodwell, 1991: 91–101). As discussed above (see also Chapter 2), the channel of the River Waveney seems to have remained stable for much of this time (see also Coles and Funnell,

1981), hence the position of the alignment relative to the river itself was probably broadly that of the present day, although it is possible that the river has migrated south over time, given the lack of stratigraphic data from north of the present channel.

Pollen was not well-preserved in the deeper peats at Beccles (Chapter 2), but the available data suggest dense deciduous woodland in the wider landscape and the establishment of alder and willow carr on the floodplain, with Scots pine also important locally, probably on the sands and gravels of the floodplain prior to extensive paludification. The problems with radiocarbon dating of the deposits at Beccles prevent the establishment of an independent chronology for later Holocene environmental change and in particular the timing of evidence for human impact on the local environment. However, the on-site palaeoenvironmental analyses (Chapter 4) demonstrate that the floodplain vegetation during the later prehistoric period consisted of alder carr with an understory of sedge fen vegetation. The beetle record confirms the impression of a fen carr floodplain in the form of various beetles associated with dead/decaying wood and specific trees including willow, pine and alder, although the latter tree is often poorly reflected in the beetle record (see Chapter 4). The plant macrofossil record also demonstrates the presence of fen woodland with little evidence for either the wider environment or any 'cultural' plant remains.

The pollen sequences from Beccles 2009 Trenches 1 and 4 do not have independent, absolute chronologies (Chapter 4) but indicate reductions in trees and shrubs and associated rises in indicators of open grassland at a level which is coincident with local activity on the floodplain, suggesting that the Iron Age saw intensified woodland clearance and probably pastoral agriculture in the lower Waveney Valley. The presence of dung beetles in the samples preceding the main phase of activity may reflect pastoral environments on the dryland or possibly even seasonal grazing of the floodplain. As discussed above, although palaeoenvironmental data for this part of Suffolk are somewhat sparse, the impression is that the later Iron Age was in general a period of landscape scale clearance of woodland and expansion of open, pastoral environments.

Prior to the main phase of activity on the floodplain at Beccles during the later Iron Age, the palaeoenvironmental record indicates some opening up of the *Alnus* carr, the expansion of reed swamp/damp grassland and the expansion of aquatic environments. The disappearance of indications of *Alnus* from the beetle record (Chapter 4) may well reflect the clearance of the on-site fen carr and subsequent use of some of this locally derived wood as timber for the alignment stakes. Coppiced *Alnus* stools identified in the excavations in 2007 (Gearey *et al.*, 2011) certainly demonstrate the clearance of fen carr prior to the construction of the monument. The fragments of roundwood from the debris field (see above) from trees with natural growth regimes probably also derive from the clearance of trees from the floodplain at or shortly before

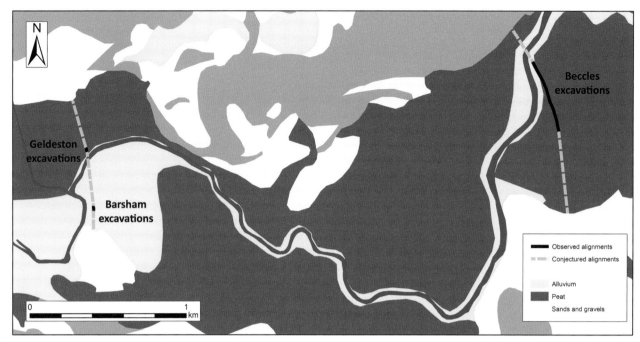

Figure 7.8: The lower Waveney valley timber alignments in relation to contemporary human geography and current extents of floodplain deposits and dryland

this time. Changes in floodplain hydrology indicated by the coleoptera and diatom records (Chapter 4) must be related in part to the influence of relative sea level during the later prehistoric period, the possible character and significance of which will be considered further below.

Despite the uncertainties regarding the form of the monuments, the palaeoenvironmental and geoarchaeological work at the sites provides important information regarding the landscape context of the sites (see below). Whilst the alignments were all situated on the later prehistoric floodplain-channel edge of the River Waveney, the local landscape contexts were actually somewhat different (Figure 7.8). At Beccles, the alignment extended from a point at the northern edge of the later prehistoric dryland, thereby taking a fairly straight route across the floodplain towards the river. The route *across* the floodplain or more precisely the destination itself was apparently significant, rather than the provision of access from the contemporary dryland to the open water of the river channel, which was located considerably closer to southern landfall of the monument (Figure 7.9). This would seem to imply that for Beccles at least, the alignment was not just intended to provide practical access directly *to* the river, as a shorter and more direct route to the open channel would have been taken directly west from the dryland. In other words, the routeway or direction taken by the alignment was significant beyond facilitating movement to and from the river.

At Barsham, the excavated section of the alignment ran parallel to the course of the river. Its projected alignment to the south extends across to the contemporary dryland edge approximately 125m away, focused on a small

embayment in the terrace gravels apparent in the British Geological Society mapping. The projected alignment to the north leads to the River Waveney directly south of the site at Geldeston, and it is possible that the structure led to or marked a crossing or fording place of the river. At Geldeston, the excavated area lay nearly 300m to the south of the current edge of the floodplain. Whilst the northern extension of the trench revealed no continuation of the structure in this direction, it is possible that the stake alignment formed the northernmost expression of a route that extended from dryland but which was 'monumentalised' at the point of reaching the river. Given the proximity of the two sites it is possible that they represent two sections of the same alignment, which crossed the river and linked the areas of dryland to the north and south (Figure 7.8). The dendrochronological dates indicate some chronological overlap: whilst the Geldeston structure is older (early 1st century BC, and hence broadly contemporaneous with the site at Beccles), later additions to the structure (dated 2/1 BC) are close to the dates for Barsham, between 8 BC and AD 8. Hence, it is possible that both represent the southern and northern ends of what was a single alignment structure, at least during this later phase.

As discussed above, a significant marine transgression affected much of East Anglia during the later 1st millennium BC; palaeoenvironmental analyses in the Flag Fen basin, Peterborough, indicate that at this location fen deposits were sealed beneath alluvial material during the later Iron Age, probably as a result of the 'ponding back' of the rivers draining the Fenland (Scaife, 2001). There is diatom evidence from the same site for the incursion of brackish waters in the later 1st millennium BC, attributed to: "… the backing up of freshwater against spring high tide conditions further to the east." (French, 2001: 403). Therefore the later 1st millennium BC witnessed a significant period of rising water tables and flooding of rivers draining into the southern North Sea across Suffolk and Norfolk.

Whilst there is some evidence that this impacted more on the northern parts of Norfolk, there is also evidence that paludification possibly related to the deposition of marine silts around this time led to the formation of freshwater meres in the southern fens (Waller, 1994; French, 2003). The palaeoenvironmental analyses of Beccles (2008) Cores 1 and 2 present similar evidence that a rise in relative sea level affected the Waveney Valley during the later prehistoric period. This has not been dated directly in Beccles Core 2 but the deposition of diatoms indicative of marine incursion is attested by 360–50 cal. BC in Core 1 (see Chapter 2). A temporary shift from peat to estuarine silt deposition occurred at Stanley Carr, just to the north-east of Beccles at 1985±40 BP (Q-2184; 90 cal. BC–cal. AD 140), before fen peat accumulation returned at 1755±40 BP (Q-2183; cal. AD 140–390 (Alderton, 1983). However, as discussed above, there is considerable spatial and chronological variation in sedimentary stratigraphy throughout the Waveney Valley and in Broadland more widely; in the Yare Valley for example, peat accumulation continued throughout much of the Iron Age (Coles and Funnell, 1981) with estuarine sedimentation between *c.* 20 cal. BC–cal. AD 350.

The Beccles alignment was constructed at a location close to the upper edge of the 'wedge' of estuarine silts (as demonstrated by the stratigraphic differences between Cores 1 and 2 from 2008; see Chapter 2) and therefore the structure extends northwards towards the head of the landward extent of the Waveney estuary during the later Iron Age. Although the data from Stanley Carr discussed above, suggests that this rise in relative sea level may date to just after 75 BC, the alignment was probably aligned on a point that defined the transition from the freshwater of the River Waveney into the open waters of the estuary and beyond this the sea. It seems likely that the landward expansion of estuarine conditions evidenced at Stanley Carr had begun sometime previously. In contrast, whilst the site at Barsham appears to have been oriented on a gravel island at the edge of the river (see Figure 7.8), this site was effectively separated from the main dryland to the south by floodplain. The British Geological Survey maps locate Barsham in an area defined as 'floodplain alluvium' although the local stratigraphic survey did not investigate beyond the immediate limits of the site and the wider context remains unknown. The excavated portion of the alignment at least at Barsham was situated in a shallow channel or channel edge context; it is possible of course that the Beccles site extended into the channel itself. Again, the possible continuation of these alignments into and across the river may significantly affect the interpretation of the monuments.

7.4 Dividing, defining or uniting the landscape? Stake alignments in prehistory

Structural parallels for the timber alignments

Brunning (2013) has recently reviewed the evidence from the sixteen known pile alignments from England and Wales as a comparison with the Late Bronze Age Harding/Harters Hill alignment, in the Somerset Levels. Although some of these sites present similar structural parallels with the Waveney alignments, the majority are of Bronze Age date with notably fewer later prehistoric examples. The function and form of prehistoric timber alignments has previously been much discussed (Allen and Welsh, 1996; Pryor 2001; Milne, 2002; Parker Pearson and Field, 2003). Some have been interpreted as including rows of upright stakes and associated ground level trackways, for example that at Flag Fen (Pryor, 2001) and Fiskerton (Parker Pearson and Field, 2003), others as bridges (e.g. Dorney, Eton Rowing Lake: Allen and Welsh, 1996) or jetties (e.g. Vauxhall: Milne, 2002). In the case of those interpreted as having supported raised structures (Dorney and Vauxhall), no unequivocal evidence for any such superstructure has survived and interpretation thus rests primarily on the stratigraphic context of the archaeology.

Other sites, which arguably echo architectural details of the Waveney alignments, include the timber alignment complex at Barleycroft Farm, near Willingham in the Cambridgeshire Fens. Whilst not a wetland site, the Barleycroft alignments were located on the floodplain of the River Great Ouse and comprised around 1000 timber stakes in nine single alignments covering some 6ha, apparently related to field systems to the north and south of the river (Evans and Knight, 2001: 87). The alignments vary from between 77m and 129m long on east–west and north–south axes with the stakes spaced roughly 0.5m to 1.1m apart. With an average diameter of 0.2m it is suggested that the stakes stood between 1m and 2m high. Although the alignments do not have an absolute date, they post-date and cut Bronze Age field systems and in the absence of Iron Age finds, have been interpreted as of Bronze Age date. There was no evidence of re-cutting of stakeholes, indicating that the monuments had a relatively short life. The stakes did not act to enclose and the lack of artefactual evidence precluded the authors from providing either a domestic or ritual interpretation. Instead, as the site is located between a group of Bronze Age ring-ditches to the west, and a group of Barrows at Over across the River Ouse to the east, it was suggested that the alignments acted as a kind of 'screen' or to 'connect' the space between the burial sites. The Beccles site shares aspects of the structural 'permeability' of Barleycroft and does not seem designed to enclose land in a conventional sense, likewise the lack of evidence for ritual deposition of metalwork, or significant evidence for domestic associations.

The Fiskerton 'causeway', Lincolnshire, on the north bank of the River Witham is a closer comparison in terms of age, architecture and landscape context. Over 100m of the causeway has been investigated, with a section first excavated in 1981 with further investigation undertaken in 2001 when the river embankment was improved. The site consisted of at least two parallel stakes alignments about 4m apart, with groups of stakes driven into the floodplain peats at right angles to the river. The predominantly oak stakes were well-preserved and were found to be 2.50–4.60 m long. Timbers were laid horizontally between these stakes and pegged into the ground to form a causeway. A third alignment of stakes, running parallel to the main causeway was also identified. This was more sparsely populated with stakes than the main structure and situated some 7–8 m to the west. Evidence for two earlier structures including a wattle structure was also recorded.

The Fiskerton causeway has been dated by dendro-chronology to between 505 BC and 339 BC, with major episodes of felling taking place between 457/456 BC and 339/338 BC (Field *et al.,* 2003: 19). The structure was repaired or consolidated approximately nine times over about 150 years of use, with the major repair events separated by *c.* 16–18 years. Finds included four iron swords, three socketed iron spearheads, an iron axe, a hammer, a file and an object described as a 'pruning hook'. Other finds included bone needles and both Iron Age and Roman pottery, whilst during the 2001 excavation two Roman log boats were recovered. Two other stake-built structures associated with the River Witham were recorded in the valley, although neither has been investigated thoroughly (see Field *et al.,* 2003: 30) but include a double stake row on the south side of the river at Washingborough, of possible Bronze Age date, and a further Iron Age timber site from close to Washingborough pumping station.

Whilst the site of Fiskerton is earlier than those within the Waveney Valley, the architecture and landscape context may be described as broadly similar. However, a significant difference is represented by the apparent growth in what may be described as ritual activity in the form of votive deposition represented by both the large quantity of metalwork deposition associated with the causeway, and the observation that the major episodes of construction appear to have coincided with a series of mid-winter solar eclipses, although doubt has been cast on this association (Ian Tyers, pers. comm.).

Other broadly similar structural parallels exist for earlier periods. For example, the later Bronze Age at Flag Fen, near Peterborough, provides a strong parallel for the use of wood to build up a wet ground surface where: "Most of the roundwood seems to have been used as foundations or makeup to build up the surface either of the platform or the walkways between the rows of the alignment ..." (Taylor, 2001: 172). As with the sites within the Waveney valley, there were also significant quantities of timber, timber debris and wood chips within these 'make-up' layers. Although the platform at Flag Fen might have been more substantial, the off-platform stretches of the

timber alignment bear some resemblance to the material recorded at Beccles.

A possible Iron Age timber causeway and platform, Strangeway's causeway or the Greylake causeway, has also been recorded in the Somerset Levels, south-west England. The initial discovery of this site was made in the late 19th century and Harold St George Gray subsequently excavated the site in 1926, identifying oak piles and wooden planks. The site was located on the northern side of Kings Sedgemoor Drain and possibly provided a north-south route across the middle of Sedgemoor. It was dated by association with features characteristic of the Iron Age, with further chronological evidence in the form of an Iron Age vessel found close to the site. This site may be interpreted as a trackway, but elements of the monument, in particular the platform and stakes rows, may point to a blurring of a strictly functional interpretation. The site may have parallels with Fiskerton (above), and the associated platform may also have similarities with Flag Fen.

Timber alignments may also share structural and contextual similarities with structures recorded in lowland mire systems in Britain and Ireland (e.g. Coles and Coles, 1986; Crockett *et al.,* 2002; Raftery, 1996). In fact, the river valleys in which most timber alignments were often located represent very different landscape contexts to ombrotrophic mires. Stake-rows are known from lowland mires in north-west Europe and date from the prehistoric as well as the medieval periods, but these appear to have been comparatively simple linear structures consisting of single rows of stakes with no evidence of associated woodworking or jointing. Some of the Irish examples may have demarcated areas of deeper or wetter peatland (e.g. Gowen *et al.,* 2005).

Brunning (2013: 150) proposed that the largely Later Bronze Age (1250–850 BC) alignments may be defined as a new class of monument, defined by six key characteristics and associated with: "... a focus on freshwater wetlands in contemporary religious activity ..." The Waveney alignments certainly incorporate five of the key characteristics (oak piles in lines, layers of worked horizontal wood, a local environment of shallow freshwater/fen, at least one end of the alignment connected to dryland, possible deposition of pottery), but differ in terms of the significantly later date and absence of ritual deposition of metalwork or human bone.

7.5 Conclusions: The function of the Waveney Valley timber alignments

Whilst ambiguity regarding the probable form of the Waveney alignments hampers understanding of the possible function(s) of the alignments, the following hypotheses can be proposed on the basis of the geoarchaeological, palaeoenvironmental and archaeological data alongside evidence derived from similar sites outlined above. The excavations have clarified the extent of the Beccles alignment and have also provided information regarding phasing, but it is unknown whether the alignment continues on the northern side of the river; the presence or absence of the structure in this location of course has implications for interpretation. Some 3km upstream of Beccles, the excavations at Barsham and Geldeston have also revealed similar structures, although their precise forms are less well understood due to the shorter sections excavated and the interference caused by the construction of the soke dykes which removed large sections of archaeology. It is possible that, in their final form at least, the sites at Barsham and Geldeston formed a single alignment crossing the River Waveney, although the evidence indicates that initial activity at Geldeston was well before that at Barsham.

The palaeoenvironmental and stratigraphic data demonstrate that, by the later prehistoric period, the dryland environment of the lower Waveney Valley was a largely open landscape, created and maintained by human clearance and pastoral farming. The river seems to have flowed in a defined single, probably diffuse channel with a wide (1.5km east–west at Beccles) alder fen carr dominated floodplain. Immediately downstream to the north-east of the Beccles alignment, the river opened abruptly out into a broad estuary, which led via confluence with the River Yare and River Bure into the southern North Sea. The palaeoenvironmental data provide indications that rising relative sea levels during the 1st millennium BC had resulted in the landward incursion of the estuary and that downstream of the alignment at Beccles, the river debouched into a wide estuary. This was to all extents and purposes probably un-fordable, although crossing by boat might have been possible.

The Beccles alignment therefore seems to have effectively marked the transitional zone between land and seascape during the Iron Age. As well as a possible impediment to movement overland, the river itself also represents a potential east-west corridor of movement by water with subsequent connection to the southern North Sea and inland to central Suffolk and Norfolk. The Beccles alignment was also located at the closest point to the east coast at which a north–south crossing of floodplain and river may have been feasible, but also at a location where journeys by the river inland, or by the estuary ultimately into the North Sea could have departed and made land. A combined landing/crossing/ferry point at Beccles would have allowed movement of people and goods overland north and south, whilst also marking the start and end of journeys by river and sea to the west and east respectively.

The River Waveney may have been an obstacle to north–south movement, but also a resource and transport link, and one that may have been important in terms of external connections to the wider North Sea region. Parker Pearson and Field (2003) have observed that the wealth and political power of communities in eastern England may have been related to broader developments within the North Sea basin. Journeys by sea between the eastern coast and the Rhine and other continental North Sea rivers were likely to have been much shorter than from central/western Britain. However, journeys by boat might have been local in scope, the quotidian movement of people and goods, as well as long distance into the North Sea for purposes of enhancing power and prestige (e.g. see Van de Noort, 2006). However, there is little archaeological evidence in the form of site or artefact distributions to imply that the Waveney Valley was significant in this sense during the later Iron Age (see Hill, 2007) with the Wash probably a more likely conduit for North Sea trade (Hutcheson, 2007).

The very thin archaeological evidence for Iron Age activity in the wider area outlined above must be considered. The apparent scarcity of widespread settlement during this period may at initial glance, be regarded as at odds with the pollen record from Beccles (Chapter 4) which, the lack of an absolute chronology aside, demonstrates a largely cleared and managed landscape during the later prehistoric period. Certainly, although the landscape around Beccles might have been devoid of extensive settlement during the later Iron Age, restricted values for tree and shrub pollen and the indicators of pastoral environments on the drier soils around the floodplain suggest a largely open, de-forested situation implying some form of continued management or human presence. This contention may also be supported by the fact that the alignment timbers may have been derived from overgrown coppice (Chapter 4).

This resonates to an extent with Hill's (2007: 22) suggestion that apparently 'empty' areas of the landscape in east England may actually have been exploited economically and agriculturally during the Iron Age. This was perhaps as part of seasonal transhumance movement of people and animals, which may have taken place over distances of up to 100km. Other social and religious as well as economic strategies could be highlighted here and the importance of accessing the coast from areas further to the west, either over land or by river. The Beccles alignment would have required an estimated 750–1000 stakes. Felling, preparing and transporting this timber thus indicates a major investment in time and resources, although this is of course dependent on the number of people involved. As Coles and Coles (1986) observed for the Neolithic Sweet Track, the Somerset Levels, the actual construction of the monument might have been a relatively rapid task compared to the time taken to gather and prepare the required materials.

In this context, the use of timber felled in spring (Chapter 4), and the likelihood that the alignment was built in a single phase, may be significant. Not only might spring have been the optimal, practical time for such an undertaking given that the floodplain would have been drier, it may also correspond to a seasonal cycle of activity that brought people and labour from the more heavily settled areas of central Suffolk across to the east coast. The probable single phase of construction of the monument sometime around 75 BC and possible short life span of this initial phase at least (see above) could also be regarded as implying some form of 'community project' (*sensu* Evans and Knight, 2001) in keeping with a seasonal coming together of different and otherwise dispersed groups.

It was proposed above that the upright stakes might have only lasted for some 25 years before they rotted through at ground level and hence the Beccles alignment may have started to collapse by *c.* 50 BC. At the slightly earlier site of Geldeston this might have happened by around 70 BC, although the range of dates indicate additions to the structure prior to this, in 84/83 BC, which themselves may have collapsed by shortly after 60 BC. The subsequent addition to the site in 2/1 BC is a little late to be considered as a replacement for these timbers, although it is possible that there were intermediate additions, which could not be dated. This evidence can be compared to the suggested periodicity of repair phases at the Iron Age site of Fiskerton (*c.* 16–18 years) (Hillam, 2003). A wider study of the maintenance regimes and the longevity of prehistoric timber structures provides a further perspective on this, concluding that many structures in wetland environments generally remained in use for less than a human generation, with instances cited of wooden structures being repaired or completely replaced at intervals of *c.* 10–30 years (Barber and Crone, 2001: 69).

The Waveney alignments might therefore be interpreted as encapsulating and integrating a range of themes, which are reflected in the interface between later prehistoric architecture, landscape and the social sphere for other aspects of the Iron Age (e.g. Hill, 1995) and indeed earlier periods. The River Waveney might be viewed as an obstacle/barrier, a resource and a link during prehistory. All three of these perceptions are probably important in terms of any interpretation of the Waveney alignments. The practical function of the sites in terms of providing or marking access to and across the river cannot be discounted, but the role of the alignments in reinforcing themes of identity and territory may also be relevant. In this sense the river during prehistory might not be regarded as an internal barrier or territorial divide, certainly it would appear that the tribal boundary in the Iron Age was not related to this geographical feature. However, the essentially monumental character of the sites in this context could also have acted as a pronounced and imposing marker of territory to anyone travelling up the river from the east coast.

Whilst the floodplain itself was a semi-terrestrial environment, it must have been subject to seasonal flooding. The physical appearance and also ease of access across the floodplain would have changed on a seasonal basis, with standing water on the floodplain in the autumn and winter and drier conditions in the spring and summer. If as has been argued, the alignment timbers protruded some distance above the contemporary floodplain, even given the likely tall reed and carr floodplain vegetation which is evidenced by the palaeoenvironmental record during the Iron Age, then the structures would have been highly visible both from the higher areas of dry ground but also from watercraft moving up and down the river. Orientation and positional sense from the perspective of boats low down on the river in the flat and largely featureless landscape, would have been problematic, with fen carr vegetation growing in and close to the channel (see Figure 7.9). The significant physical extent of the

Figure 7.9: The River Waveney near Barsham viewed from close to water level. The fringing vegetation of reeds (Phragmites), alder (Alnus) and willow (Salix) is broadly similar to that attested for the later prehistoric floodplain environment, although the present vegetation is restricted by drainage and cultivation to a narrow corridor along the banks of the river, in prehistory such vegetation would have characterized the entire c. 1–2km wide floodplain

alignments might thus have functioned in essentially two main ways: as a symbolic and also functional marker of a landing point to be seen from the river as well as a routeway from the river to dryland.

It has been suggested that significant social changes occurred in the later Iron Age of southern Anglia (Hill, 2007). Hutcheson (2007: 369) has argued that these changes in Norfolk and north Suffolk in the later 1st century BC/1st century AD: "… may have been related to a coming together of the tribe-or federation of tribes – that the Romans subsequently labelled the *Iceni*." It is possible to see the Waveney alignments as a particular manifestation of this broader process, a marking and affirmation of territory at the easternmost edge and transition from land to sea. As Willis (2007: 121) has observed in the context of Iron Age shrines in Britain: "The point where rivers met the sea was clearly of considerable symbolic importance …" Other aspects of landscape context might also be significant, for example as has been observed for other rivers such as the Thames (see York, 2002; Mullin, 2012), the River Waveney flows east towards the rising sun.

The Waveney alignments display certain parallels with other similar sites, Fiskerton in particular, especially in terms of the floodplain context, the motif of triple stake rows and the continuation of activity into the Romano British period. However, the general arrangement of the timber stakes, and perhaps also scale of construction of both monuments may be regarded as echoing themes previously identified at Flag Fen. It can be noted that both Flag Fen and the Beccles site in particular were constructed in locations affected by prolonged episodes of rising waters and flooding. Pryor (2001: 431) has suggested that: "… the alignment [at Flag Fen] can … be seen as a symbolic weir or dam against the inexorable rise [of the waters to the northeast]." The pottery sherds from Beccles were in the main recovered from the western side of the alignment, hence on the 'landward' edge of the monument. Again this parallels Flag Fen where symbolic acts seem to have taken place on the southern side of the alignment interpreted as the 'safe' side of the barrier (Pryor, 2001: 430). Although Flag Fen had ceased to be maintained as a working timber platform, the monument was visited into the Iron Age with votive deposits made through this period.

Viewed from this perspective, Beccles might have been constructed as a response to the steady encroachment of the sea during later prehistory. Whilst no metalwork indicative of 'ritual' deposition has been recovered, there is no immediate reason that this might militate against an essentially symbolic role for the Waveney alignments but one that was inseparable from other 'practical' functions of marking and defining access and territory. The merging of the 'ritual' and domestic spheres of life during later prehistory may be highlighted here (see Bradley, 2003). This theme is a tempting one, although the evidence for rising relative sea level is rather at odds with the construction of the site at or around the time of a distinct phase of deeper water tables on the floodplain; poor understanding of the relative chronology of environmental changes hampers further consideration of the relationship of these processes to human activity and the archaeological record.

This interpretation stresses the monumental character of the Beccles alignment, its close physical and chronological relationship with the westwards creeping head of the estuary and possibly an attempt to both mark and perhaps 'hold back' this process during the later Iron Age. The practical function of the alignments as facilitating access is not necessarily negated through this interpretation, but stresses instead that the alignments were constructed for a range of interrelated practical and symbolic reasons. The subsequent evidence for Romano-British activity can therefore be explained as re-use, or continuing use, of the site as a crossing/landing point, with the occasional evidence for the insertion of the undated additional stakes, probably reflecting a later attempt to maintain the line of a routeway across the floodplain. However, this is rather speculative, it is possible that the site was viewed and used in a very different way in this later period.

The Geldeston and Barsham alignments are even more of an enigma, not least because the chronologies are somewhat more complex than at Beccles, but the Barsham site was clearly in use during the very end of the Iron Age and into the Romano-British period. Whilst there is little other sign of Romano-British settlement in the close vicinity of these alignments, there is considerable evidence of Roman activity further up but close to the River Waveney at Flixton (*c.* 5km west of Bungay), where two aisled buildings, multiple burials and pottery kilns were excavated; one of the kilns was last fired at the end of the 1st century AD and the second between the 3rd and 5th centuries AD (Robinson, 2007). This settlement was thus likely contemporary with Barsham at least and possibly the later phase of activity at Beccles; but beyond this observation it is difficult to propose any direct links between the sites.

7.6 Wetland archaeology: testing novel techniques for the 21st century

In addition to exploring the nature of the later prehistoric structures in the Waveney valley, the investigations provided the opportunity to apply and test a range of technological developments. These focused on the application of new geophysical prospection techniques (Chapter 4) and on the application of laser scanning for the documentation, recording and analysis of wet-preserved archaeological wood.

Geophysics: spectral induced polarisation

As outlined in Chapter 4, wetland environments have long been particularly challenging in terms of geophysical approaches owing to high water tables and the problem of distinguishing archaeological material from the organic peat matrix – a problem related to the lack of contrast between the target and the surrounding deposit (Coles and Coles, 1996). The development of new approaches applying Induced Polarisation (IP) demonstrated the capacity to distinguish the cellular structure of wood within peat (Schleiffer *et al.,* 2002). This technique was trialled at Beccles, alongside the traditional techniques of magnetometry, earth resistance, electrical imaging and ground-penetrating radar for comparison. The results from this showed some correlation with known features, which indicates the potential of the approach, although none of the techniques provided unambiguous evidence for the presence of the alignment. Further work is required to refine the use of SIP and other techniques such as GPR in wetland contexts (see also Weller and Bauerochse, 2013).

Digital recording, display and curation: laser scanning of waterlogged archaeological wood

Archaeology is traditionally subjective rather than objective in its recording methods, with the focus being on the understanding of material culture rather than its assiduous recording. Archaeology is therefore reliant on interpretive drawings and plans rather than the objectivity of the data captured through techniques such as laser scanning (Blake, 2010). A danger of such high-resolution recording is of 'documentation for the sake of it' which can impact negatively on the resources available for a project (Andrews *et al.*, 2007). However, benefits of such an approach can be seen through the ability to capture highly accurate models of the surfaces of objects or other heritage assets that might degrade unless conserved (Paquet and Viktor, 2005). Such recording of high-resolution virtual models can also allow the monitoring of degradation over time (Lobb *et al.*, 2010) and provide remote access to an object or site via a virtual copy (Paquet and Viktor, 2005).

These 'virtual copies' can be used for artefact analyses (e.g. Grosman *et al.*, 2008; Karasik and Smilansky, 2008; Kovács and Hanke, 2012), and have formed the foundation for the creation of virtual reference collections (e.g. Niven *et al.*, 2009) and virtual museums (e.g. Virtual Hampson Museum – Center for Advanced Spatial Technologies, 2014; Eton Myers Collection Virtual Museum – VISTA Centre 2014) allowing access to artefacts which are physically or culturally sensitive, remotely located or which are no longer represented physically as a single collection (Chapman *et al.*, 2010). The metric data collected through laser scanning can also allow the reproduction of the artefact through the use of 3-dimensional printing, or physical interaction with the virtual copy via haptic technology (Chapman *et al.*, 2013).

Laser scanning has been used in various ways in wetland archaeology: Lobb *et al.* (2010) applied optical triangulation scanning to samples of Anglo-Saxon waterlogged worked wood recovered from Shardlow Quarry in Derbyshire. The project proposed the use of laser scanning as a method both of recording waterlogged wood and aimed to assess the viability of long-term storage techniques. The recording of waterlogged wood had previously been carried out subjectively, by hand-made drawings and photography. Sands (1997) trialled the use of dental moulding putty to create 3D models of worked wood from crannog sites, but no true metric technique had previously been applied. Kovács and Hanke (2012) similarly used data collected from an optical triangulation scanner to perform hydrologic analysis of tool marks, providing insights not only into the type of hand tool used, and the shape and size of its facets, but using the model to provide information on how the wood was physically worked. Recent projects in the Shannon and Fergus estuaries in Ireland have seen the application of terrestrial laser scanning to the recording of inter-tidal archaeology, specifically that of fishweirs (Shaw and Devlin, 2010). Here the technology was used for the detailed recording of the fishweirs within a challenging environment for survey, with the results providing visualisation of the data in point cloud form and translation of the structure's metrics into a wider landscape context through the use of GIS.

Long-term storage of waterlogged archaeological wood is problematic whilst conservation of such material is often prohibitively expensive. Storage and curation may also alter the morphology of an artefact following extraction from waterlogged deposits (Lobb *et al.*, 2010), and it is therefore advisable that a record of the wood be made as soon as possible following its excavation. Laser scanning can be used to create a high-resolution digital record of waterlogged wooden artefacts, which can be further interrogated to provide metric analysis of tool marks and morphology. This method was explored using a Leica HDS6000 scanner to produce volumetrically accurate digital replicas of stakes from both Geldeston and Beccles (e.g. Figure 7.10a–d). Whilst valuable for analytical and 'virtual archiving' purposes, these images also provide a digital mechanism by which the heritage value of waterlogged archaeological wood can be communicated and presented to the general public. This is arguably a significant challenge facing wetland archaeology in the 21st century.

7.7 Public engagement with the archaeology of the Waveney Valley

The Beccles project has engendered a considerable amount of local support, positive engagement and a sense of ownership, with site open days resulting in visits by upwards of 300 people (Figure 7.11). This programme of outreach that was delivered as part of the work has demonstrated the level of local interest and support for wetland sites. The excavations were well supported by Beccles Town Council, through local societies and by the Broads Authority who commissioned and installed the interpretation panel that is sited on the flood bank that overlooks the northern end of the site (Figure 7.12, see also Figure 7.4 for detail). A final output from the project is a permanent exhibition in the Beccles Museum, the centrepiece of which is the display of one of the Beccles stakes, conserved by York Archaeological Trust (Figure 7.13).

As discussed above, a problem with most wetland sites in terms of public promotion and appreciation is of course the lack of above ground remains and the expense and technical challenges of presenting/conserving such remains. Flag Fen is the only location in the UK where exposed, *in situ* wetland archaeological remains are on permanent display. The display in the local museum is at least one way of leaving a community legacy, and hopefully promoting a better understanding of the value of wetland archaeology amongst the general public. This aspect of archaeology will become increasingly important as heritage agendas come under pressure from a range of economic and environmental drivers in the 21st century.

Another possible solution to the problem of public promotion and appreciation of wetland sites due to the lack of above ground remains is through digital reconstruction. Whilst it is possible to create physical reconstructions of

Figure 7.10: laser scans of two of the timbers from Geldeston showing high-resolution models of prehistoric tool marks (each shown both with and without colour texturing)

archaeological sites, the generation of virtual, interactive reconstructions provides the opportunity to access the site from multiple places in addition to enabling alternative interpretations to be presented (*cf.* Ch'ng *et al.,* 2015).

The 'virtual reconstruction' of the site at Geldeston was built using the archaeological plans and informed by palaeoenvironmental data (Figure 7.14). For the model, the heights of stakes above ground were based on the formula outlined above, with each stake being reconstructed from 3D polygons with appropriate textures mapped onto them. The data were integrated within a gaming engine environment using Unity 3D software. In addition to modelling the environment surrounding the site, other effects were added which included water reflections, the swaying of vegetation to simulate mild wind conditions and sound effects from fauna such as birds and insects. Furthermore, shafts of sunlight simulate radial light scattering when the virtual sun is partly obscured by objects such as the timber poles. Aerial perspective effects were also added to add a depth-of-field camera effects to distance objects. All virtual objects are light-mapped for an appropriate contrast between light and shadows after virtual light sources are positioned. As there are thousands of 3D objects in the virtual reconstruction, Occlusion Culling, a technique to optimise a 3D scene for faster and smoother real-time exploration was applied. These effects enhance the 'experience', giving users a sense of time and space through the sensory experience of sight and hearing in a landscape.

The value of such a reconstruction arguably lies in its ability to engage audiences by revealing interpretations of the site in an interactive way. Such engagement is possible within different environments, from the public spaces of museums to online access from a user's home computer or portable device. Whilst only one reconstruction was generated for Geldeston, the process of digital reconstruction using gaming engines provides

Figure 7.11: Local engagement: site open day at Beccles (Trench 2, 2009)

the opportunity to generate models showing alternative interpretations. As a mode of engagement, the uses of digital technologies are growing rapidly (e.g. Parry, 2013). For wetland archaeological sites and landscapes, such applications could be of increasing importance in the future in terms of communicating and presenting the appearance of sites which are difficult to appreciate once excavations have ceased.

Figure 7.12: The Broads Authority display board (Figure 7.5) on the banks of the River Waveney looking north. The alignment extends across the pastureland to the right of the picture

7.8 Summary and conclusions: the Suffolk river valleys in the past and the future

The research outlined in this monograph has included a comprehensive assessment of the Holocene archaeo-environmental history of East Anglia, in addition to identifying and excavating a new class of archaeological monument for Suffolk at Beccles, Barsham and Geldeston. The research at Beccles has again demonstrated the importance of an integrated approach to understanding, managing and promoting the value of wetland sites. This monograph began with the observation that the Holocene river valleys of Suffolk had seen little coherent archaeo-environmental research, especially in comparison to the intensive study of the Palaeolithic record in East Anglia and the Fenlands. It is hoped that the work presented here has gone some way towards redressing this situation and demonstrating that Suffolk has a rich and to date largely unrealised, potential, which places it on a par with the neighbouring Fenlands of Norfolk and Cambridgeshire. The SRVP and various commercial projects (Chapters 2 and 3) have provided evidence that river valleys of this county preserve deposits of significant archaeo-environmental potential. In particular, certain reaches such as the Gipping at Stowmarket, the Blackbourn at Ixworth, and the lower Waveney Valley at Beccles contain valley fills that provide near continuous Holocene sequences. Early Holocene deposits preserving evidence of Neolithic and Bronze Age

Figure 7.13: Conserved stake from Beccles on display within Beccles Museum

Figure 7.14: Digital reconstruction of Geldeston timber alignment

environments are also found at various locations such as on the east coast at Sizewell, in Ipswich and on the floodplain of the River Lark in Bury St Edmunds. The latter site is especially interesting, as the evidence indicates that the Abbey grounds adjacent to the river may preserve medieval organic archaeological remains *in situ*.

The palaeoenvironmental analyses have generated a range of information regarding Holocene environmental change, human activity and the archaeological record. Further work is necessary to establish the broader distribution, date and character of deposits associated with the various Suffolk Rivers. and a number of outstanding research questions specifically relating to the Holocene record can be identified:

• Refining understanding of the relationship between fluctuations in Holocene relative sea level and geomorphological processes, particularly patterns of sedimentation and erosion within the perimarine estuaries and freshwater rivers.

• The implications of these processes for human activity, especially during the earlier prehistoric periods. In particular, the character of the mid Holocene woodland and the nature of human activity during the Mesolithic and Neolithic periods.

• The timing and nature of alluviation within the river valleys away from the coastal margins and its relationship to other drivers of landscape change, such as vegetation, land-use and climatic change.

• The potential of alluviation, particularly during the early and Middle Holocene, to have buried significant archaeological remains and palaeolandsurfaces within the major valley floors.

• The potential of non-invasive techniques such as airborne remote sensing and newly developed geophysical techniques that can prospect within 'wetland' environments, to identify and characterise such remains.

• The relationship between the dryland and wetland environments of Suffolk and human interaction between these zones and elucidation of the apparently 'empty' interior, particularly in later prehistory.

• To consider the long-term future of valley floor remains in the face of increasing societal and natural environmental pressures, and to design and implement strategic frameworks that enable sustainable resource management.

The radiocarbon dating programme of the SRVP (Chapter 2) led to some unplanned but ultimately worthwhile investigations of the problems of establishing robust chronologies for alluvial contexts such as floodplains. The multiple fraction radiocarbon dating programme has demonstrated that the formation processes of floodplain sediments are in general poorly understood and that radiocarbon dating of these environments must be approached with caution. This is also demonstrated by the results of the radiocarbon dating of the palaeoenvironmental sequence from the site of Barsham. The use of single entity macrofossils may produce very different but apparently equally conformable chronologies compared to humin and humic fractions. Despite the commonplace application of radiocarbon dating to peats and other organic sediments and increasingly sophisticated methods provided by developments in Bayesian chronological modelling, further research is required into the formation processes of different

Figure 7.15: The excavation of the Ludham medieval boat

sedimentary systems and the implications for building precise and robust chronologies for palaeoenvironmental records.

Preservation of palaeoenvironmental proxies (Chapters 2, 3 and 5) has been demonstrated to be somewhat variable across sites, but this is perhaps to be expected with organic floodplain sediments where highly local factors such as groundwater chemistry, deposit formation processes and hydrological fluctuations through time may result in differential destruction of sub-fossil material. The complexity of such processes is well illustrated by the research at Beccles, with analyses suggesting that the preservation of both archaeological and palaeoenvironmental remains may be related to fluctuations in the water table both in the past and in sub-recent times (Chapter 5). In addition, the research at Beccles also implies that there can be spatial variations in the preservation environment. Disentangling the relative influence of these changes across spatial and temporal scales presents a challenge for the future management and preservation *in situ* of wetland sites and deposits.

Archaeological excavations were not initially planned or envisaged when the SRVP was first formulated and in this sense the discovery of the late prehistoric timber alignments at Beccles, Barsham and Geldeston (Chapter 4) was serendipitous if unanticipated, clearly illustrating the wetland archaeological potential of the region, and in the process demonstrating the problems of identifying

and mitigating for such discoveries. Given the continuing programme of river bank realignment and soke dyke re-profiling planned for the Broadlands over the next 20 years, it seems inevitable that there will be further discoveries of wetland sites and associated deposits of high palaeoenvironmental potential. This was also demonstrated by the discovery of a Medieval boat in palaeochannel deposits at Ludham, Norfolk (Figure 7.15, see Krawiec and Gearey, 2010).

The timber alignments of the lower Waveney Valley are rather enigmatic structures and despite the profusion of data that such wetland sites can provide, archaeological interpretation still relies heavily on an understanding of form and context. This is further complicated by the lack of evidence for Iron Age settlement in this part of Suffolk. The current interpretation implies that the alignments may be best interpreted as providing access to and from the river and across the floodplain, but also as highly visible markers of identity and territory at a time of marked social change across East Anglia. The association of the Beccles alignment with a period of marine transgression and rising water tables across the region may also echo ideas of a symbolic 'defence' proposed for earlier sites such as Flag Fen. The absence of metalwork may not necessarily be fatal to this argument; indeed it is entirely possible that any such votive deposits were made into the River Waveney itself.

It can also be observed that the palaeoenvironmental evidence for human activity during the later prehistoric period is rather muted in the on-site pollen records from the excavations at Beccles. This might be related in part to the fact that this alignment may actually have been built quickly and used for a relatively short period of time and the palynological signal of the clearance of the floodplain and associated felling of a significant area of oak trees is hence not resolved in the sampling intervals of the on-site palaeoenvironmental data. This presents a *caveat* for palaeoenvironmental interpretation and inference regarding the nature and extent of human activity from such records. In the absence of the wetland archaeological record, there would be no clear indication in the palaeoenvironmental records for local human activity and these data might thus be interpreted in a very different way. Thus again, the palaeoenvironmental record has provided valuable additional evidence and future researchers should not neglect this resource when examining the palimpsest of landscapes that exist within East Anglia.

References

Alderton, A. 1983. *Flandrian Vegetation and Sea Level Change in the Waveney Valley.* Cambridge: Ph.D. Thesis, University of Cambridge.

Allen, S. and Welsh, K. 1996. Eton Rowing Lake – Bronze Age Bridge? *Current Archaeology* 148, 124–27.

Andrews, D., Bedford, J., Blake, W. H., Clowes, M., Crispe, A., Papworth, H. and Santana Quintero, M. 2007. Partnership in learning: English Heritage & the Raymond Lemaire International Centre for Conservation. *International Archives of the Photogrammetry, Remote Sensing and Spatial Information Sciences* 34, 57–70.

Arnold, B. and Clark, P. (eds) 2004. *The Dover Bronze Age Boat in Context: society and water transport in prehistoric Europe.* Oxford: Oxbow Books.

Ashwin, T. and Tester, A. forthcoming. *A Romano-British Settlement in the Waveney Valley: excavations at Scole, 1993–1994.* Norwich: East Anglian Archaeology.

Aspinall, A., Gaffney, C. and Schmidt, A. 2008. *Magnetometry for Archaeologists.* Walnut Creek CA: Altamira Press.

Aspinall, A. and Lynam, J. T. 1970. An induced polarisation instrument for the detection of near-surface features. *Prospezioni Archeologiche* 5, 67–75.

Astin, T., Eckardt, H. and Hay, S. 2007. Resistivity imaging survey of the Roman barrows at Bartlow, Cambridgshire, UK. *Archaeological Prospection* 14, 24–37.

Austin, L. 1997. Palaeolithic and Mesolithic. In N. Brown and J. Glazebrook (eds), *Research and Archaeology: a framework for the Eastern Counties, 1. Resource assessment*, 5–11. Dereham: East Anglian Archaeology Occasional Paper 3.

Baillie, M. G. L. 1991 Suck in and smear: two related chronological problems for the 90s. *Journal of Theoretical Archaeology* 2, 12–16.

Baillie, M. G. L. and Pilcher, J. R. 1973. A simple cross-dating program for tree-ring research. *Tree-Ring Bulletin* 33, 7–14.

Bamforth, M. and Pryor, F. 2010. (eds) *Flag Fen, Peterborough: excavation and research 1995–2007.* Oxford: Oxbow Books.

Barber, J. W. and Crone, B. A. 2001. The duration of structures, settlements and sites: some evidence from Scotland. In B. Raftery, B. and J. Hickey (eds), *Recent Developments in Wetland Research*, 69–86. Dublin: UCD, Department of Archaeology WARP Occasional Paper 14.

Barber, M., Field, D. and Topping, P. 1999. *The Neolithic Flint Mines of England.* Swindon: English Heritage.

Bateman, M. D. and Godby, P. 2004. Late-Holocene inland dune activity in the UK: a case study from Breckland, East Anglia. *Holocene* 14(4), 579–88.

Behre, K.-E., 1981. The interpretation of anthropogenic indicators in pollen diagrams. *Pollen et Spores* 23, 225–43.

Bennett, K. D. 1983. Devensian late glacial and Flandrian-vegetational history at Hockham Mere, Norfolk, England, 1. Pollen assemblages and concentrations. *New Phytologist* 95, 457–87.

Bennett, K. D., Whittington, G. and Edwards, K. J. 1994. Recent pollen nomenclature changes and pollen morphology in the British Isles. *Quaternary Newsletter* 73, 1–6.

Blagg, T., Plouviez, J. and Tester A. 2004. *Excavations at a Large Romano-British Settlement at Hacheston, Suffolk in 1973–4.* Ipswich: East Anglian Archaeology 106.

Blake, W. H. What is the future of metric heritage documentation and its skills? *Proceedings of the ISPRS Comission V Mid-Term Symposium 2010*, International Archives of Photogrammetry, Remote Sensing and Spatial Information Sciences, Vol. XXXVIII, Part 5 Commission V Symposium, Newcastle upon Tyne, UK. 2010, pp 98–102.

Boismier, W. A., Gamble, C. and Coward, F. (eds) 2012. *Neanderthals among Mammoths: excavations at Lynford Quarry, Norfolk UK.* Swindon: English Heritage.

Boismier, W. A., Schreve, D. C., White, M. J., Robertson, D. A., Stuart, A. J., Etienne, S., Andrews, J., Coope, G. R., Green, F. M. L., Keen, D. H., Lewis, S. G., French, C., Rhodes, E., Schwenninger, J. L., Tovey, K., Donahue, R. E., Richards, M. P. and O'Connor, S. (2003). A Middle Palaeolithic site at Lynford Quarry, Mundford, Norfolk: interim statement. *Proceedings of the Prehistoric Society* 69, 315–24.

Bonsall, C. 2007. Human–environment interactions during the Late Mesolithic of the Cumbria coastal plain: the evidence from Eskmeals. In P. J. Cherry (ed.), *Studies in Northern Prehistory: essays in memory of Clare Fell*, 25–43. Kendal: Cumberland and Westmorland Antiquarian and Archaeological Society.

Boreham, S., White, T. S., Bridgland, D. R., Howard, A. J. and White, M. J. 2010. The Quaternary history of the Wash fluvial network. *Proceedings of the Geologists Association* 121, 393–409.

Boreham, S., Boreham, J. and Rolfe, C. 2011. Physical and chemical analyses of sediments from around Star Carr as indicators of preservation. *Journal of Wetland Archaeology* 11, 20–35.

Bradley, R. 2007. *The Prehistory of Britain and Ireland.* Cambridge: Cambridge University Press.

Bradley, R. 2003. A life less ordinary: the ritualization of the domestic sphere in later prehistoric Europe. *Cambridge Archaeological Journal* 13(1), 5–23.

Brayshay, B. A. and Dinnin M. H. 1994. Integrated palaeo-ecological evidence for biodiversity at the floodplain-forest margin. *Journal of Biogeography* 26, 115–31.

Brennand, M. and Taylor, M. 2003. The survey and excavation of a Bronze Age timber circle at Holme-Next-Sea, Norfolk, 1998–1999. *Proceedings of the Prehistoric Society* 69, 1–84.

Brew, D. S. 1990. *Sedimentary Environments and Holocene Evolution of the Suffolk estuaries*. Norwich: Unpublished Ph.D. Thesis, University of East Anglia.

Brew, D. S., Funnell, B. M. and Kreiser, A. 1992. Sedimentary environments and Holocene evolution of the lower Blyth estuary, Suffolk (England), and a comparison to other East Anglian coastal sequences. *Proceedings of the Geological Association* 101(1), 57–74.

Brew, D., Holt, T., Pye, K. and Newsham, R. 2000. Holocene sedimentary evolution and palaeocoastlines of the Fenland embayment, eastern England. In I. Shennan and J. Andrews (eds), *Holocene Land-Ocean Interaction and Environmental Change around the North Sea*, 253–73. London: Geological Society Special Publication 166.

Bridgland, D. R., Howard, A. J., White, M. J. and White, T. S. 2014. *Quaternary of the Trent*. Oxford: Oxbow Books.

Briscoe, G. 1964. Bronze Age pottery from Joist Fen, Lakenheath. *Proceedings of the Cambridge Antiquarian Society* 56, 1–5.

Britton, D. 1960. The Isleham Hoard, Cambridgeshire. *Antiquity* 34, 279–82.

Brock, F., Higham, T., Ditchfield, P. and Bronk Ramsey, C., 2010. Current pretreatment methods for AMS radiocarbon dating at the Oxford Radiocarbon Accelerator Unit (ORAU). *Radiocarbon* 52(1), 103–12.

Brock, F., Lee, S., Housley, R. A. and Bronk Ramsey, C. 2011. Variation in the radiocarbon age of different fractions of peat: A case study from Ahernshöft, northern Germany. *Quaternary Geochronology* 6, 550–5.

Bronk Ramsey, C., 1995. Radiocarbon calibration and analysis of stratigraphy: the OxCal program. *Radiocarbon* 37, 425–30.

Bronk Ramsey, C., 1998. Probability and dating. *Radiocarbon* 40, 461–74.

Bronk Ramsey, C., 2000. Comment on 'The use of Bayesian statistics for ¹⁴C dates of chronologically ordered samples: a critical analysis'. *Radiocarbon* 42, 199–202

Bronk Ramsey, C., 2001. Development of the radiocarbon calibration program OxCal. *Radiocarbon* 43, 355–63.

Bronk Ramsey, C., 2009. Bayesian analysis of radiocarbon dates. *Radiocarbon* 51, 337–60.

Bronk Ramsey, C., Higham, T. and Leach, P. 2004. Towards high precision AMS: progress and limitations. *Radiocarbon* 46(1), 17–24.

Brown, A. G. 2009. *The Environment and Aggregate-related Archaeology*. Oxford: Oxbow Books.

Brown, A. G. and Keough, M. 1992. Holocene floodplain metamorphosis in the Midlands, United Kingdom. *Geomorphology* 4, 433–45.

Brown, A. G., Keough, M. and Rice, R. J. 1994. Floodplain evolution in the East Midlands, United Kingdom: the Lateglacial and Flandrian alluvial record from the Soar and Nene valleys. *Philosophical Transactions of the Royal Society of London* A348, 261–93.

Brown, N. and Glazebrook, J. (eds) 2000: *Research and Archaeology: a framework for the Eastern Counties, 2: research agenda and strategy*. Norwich: East Anglian Archaeology Occasional Paper 8.

Brown, N. and Murphy, P. 1997. Neolithic and Bronze Age. In J. Glazebrook, *Research and Archaeology: a Framework for the Eastern Counties, 1. resource assessment*, 5–11. Norwich: East Anglian Archaeology Occasional Paper 3.

Brown, N. and Murphy, P. 2000. Neolithic and Bronze Age. In N. Brown, and J. Glazebrook (eds), *Research and Archaeology: a framework for the Eastern Counties, 2. research agenda and strategy*, 12–22. Norwich: East Anglian Archaeology Occasional Paper 8.

Brown, N., Knopp, D. and Strachan, D. 2002. The archaeology of Constable Country: the crop-marks of the Stour Valley. *Landscape History* 24, 5–28.

Brown, T., Bradley, C., Grapes, T. and Boomer, I. 2011. Hydrological assessment of Star Carr and the Hertford Catchment, Yorkshire, UK. *Journal of Wetland Archaeology* 11, 36–55.

Brun, C., Dessaint, F., Richard, H. and Bretagnolle. F. 2007. Arable weed flora and its pollen representation: a case study from the eastern part of France. *Review of Palaeobotany and Palynology* 146, 29–50.

Brunning, R. 2012. Partial solutions to partially understood problems – the experience of *in situ* monitoring and preservation in Somerset's peatlands. *Conservation and Management of Archaeological Sites* 14, 397–405.

Brunning, R. 2013. *Somerset's Peatland Archaeology. Managing and Investigating a Fragile Resource*. Oxford: Oxbow Books.

Bryant, S. 1997. Iron Age. In J. Glazebrook (ed.), *Research and Archaeology: a framework for the Eastern Counties, 1: resource assessment*, 17–27. Norwich: East Anglian Archaeology Occasional Paper 3.

Bryant, S. 2000. Iron Age. In N. Brown, and J. Glazebrook, J. (eds), *Research and Archaeology: a framework for the Eastern Counties, 2. research agenda and strategy*, 23–34. Norwich: East Anglian Archaeology Occasional Paper 8.

Buckland, P. C. and Dinnin, M. H. 1993. Holocene woodlands the fossil insect evidence. In K. J. Kirby and C. M. Drake (eds), *Dead Wood Matters: the ecology and conservation of saproxylic invertebrates in Britain*, 6–20. Peterborough: English Nature Science 7.

Bullock, J. A. 1993. Host plants of British beetles: a list of recorded associations. *Amateur Entomologist* 11a, 1–24.

Bunting, M. J., Armitage, R., Binney, H. A. and Waller, M. P. 2005. Estimates of relevant source area of pollen assemblages from moss polsters in two Norfolk (UK) wet woodlands. Holocene 15, 459–65.

Caple, C. 1994. Reburial of waterlogged wood, the problems and potential of this conservation technique. *International Biodeterioration and Biodegradation* 34, 61–72.

Caple, C. 1996. Parameters for monitoring anoxic environments. In M. Corfield, P. Hinton, T. Nixon and M. Pollard (eds), *Preserving Archaeological Remains In Situ*. 111–23. London: MoLAS.

Caple, C. and Dungworth, D. 1998. *Waterlogged Anoxic Archaeological Burial Environments*. Swindon: English Heritage, Ancient Monuments Laboratory Report 22/98.

Cappers, R., Bekker, R. and Jans, J. 2006. *Digitalezadenatlas Van Nederland*. Groningen: Barhuis.

Carr, R. D., Tester, A. and Murphy, P. 1988. The Middle Saxon settlement at Staunch Meadow, Brandon. *Antiquity* 62, 371–7.

Center for Advanced Spatial Technologies. 2014. *The Virtual Hampson Museum* [Online]. Available: http://www.cast.uark.

edu/home/research/archaeology-and-historic-preservation/ archaeological-geomatics/archaeological-laser-scanning/ hampson-museum.html

Challis, K. 2006. Airborne laser altimetry in alluviated landscapes. *Archaeological Prospection* 13, 103–27.

Challis, K. and Howard, A. J. 2006. (eds) *Remote Sensing and Environmental Modelling in Alluvial Archaeological Landscapes. Archaeological Prospection* 13(4) special issue.

Challis, K. and Howard, A. J. 2014. Preservation and prospection of alluvial archaeological remains: a case study from the Trent Valley, UK. In E. Meylemans, M. De Bi, K. Cordemans, J. Poesen, Ph. Van Peer and G. Verstraeten (eds), *The Archaeology of Erosion, the Erosion of Archaeology*, 117–215. Brussels: Relicta Monografieën.

Chapman, H. P. 2006. *Landscape Archaeology and GIS*. Stroud: Tempus.

Chapman, H., Baldwin, E., Moulden, H. and Lobb, M. 2013. More than just a sum of the points: re-thinking the value of laser scanning data. In E. Ch'ng, V. Gaffney and H. Chapman (eds), *Visual Heritage in the Digital Age*, 15–31. Dordrecht: Springer.

Chapman, H. P. and Cheetham, J. L. 2002. Monitoring and modelling saturation as a proxy indicator for *in situ* preservation in wetlands: a GIS-based approach. *Journal of Archaeological Science* 29, 277–89.

Chapman, H. P. and Gearey, B. R. 2003. *Predictive Modelling of Archaeological Site Locations in Raised Mires: Final Report*. Hull: University of Hull, Unpublished Report to English Heritage.

Chapman, H. P. and Gearey, B. R. 2013. *Modelling Archaeology and Environment in a Wetland Landscape: the hidden landscape archaeology of Hatfield and Thorne Moors*. Oxford: Oxbow Books.

Chapman, H., Gaffney, V. L. and Moulden, H. L. 2010. The Eton Myers Collection Virtual Museum. *International Journal of Humanities & Arts Computing* 4, 81–93.

Chatwin, C. P. 1948. *East Anglia and Adjoining Areas*. London: HMSO, British Regional Geology Series.

Cheetham, J. L. 2004. *An Assessment of the Potential for in situ Preservation of Buried Organic Archaeological Remains at Sutton Common, South Yorkshire*. Hull: Ph.D. thesis. University of Hull.

Ch'ng, E., Chapman, H. and Gaffney, V. 2015. From product to process: new directions for digital heritage. In H. Din and S. Wu (eds), *Digital Heritage and Culture: strategy and implementation*, 219–44. Singapore: World Scientific.

Clark, J. 1996 SQUID Fundementals. In H. Weinstock (ed.) *SQUID Sensors: fundamentals, fabrication and applications*. NATO ASI Series 329, 1–62.

Clark, J. G. D., Higgs, E. S. and Longworth, I. H. 1960. Excavations at the Neolithic site at Hurst Fen, Mildenhall, Suffolk, 1954, 1957 and 1958. *Proceedings of the Prehistoric Society* 26, 202–45.

Clarke, H. 1971. Regional Archaeologies: *East Anglia*. London: Heinemann Educational Books Ltd.

Clarke, R. R. 1936. Holkham Camp, Norfolk. *Proceedings of the Prehistoric Society* 2, 231–3.

Clarke, W. G. 1913. Some Barnham palaeoliths. *Proceedings of the Prehistoric Society of East Anglia* 1, 300–3.

Coles, B. P. L. 1977. *The Holocene Foraminifera and Palaeogeography of Central Broadland*. Norwich: Ph.D. Thesis, University of East Anglia.

Coles, B. P. L. and Funnell, B. M. 1981. Holocene palaeo-

environments of Broadland, England. *Special Publication of the International Association of Sedimentologists* 5, 121–31.

Coles, J. and Coles, B. 1986. *Sweet Track to Glastonbury*. London: Thames and Hudson.

Coles, J. and Coles, B. 1996. *Enlarging the Past – the contribution of wetland archaeology*. Exeter: Wetland Archaeology Research Project and the Society of Antiquaries of Scotland.

Coles, J. M., Orme, B. J., Caseldine, A. E. and Morgan, R. A. 1985. A Neolithic jigsaw: the Honeygore Complex. *Somerset Levels Papers* 11, 51–61.

Collins, P. E. F., Worsley, P., Keith-Lucas, D. M. and Fenwick, I. M. 2006. Floodplain environmental change during the Younger Dryas and Holocene in North-West Europe: Insights from the lower Kennet Valley, south central England. *Palaeogeography, Plaeoclimatology, Palaeoecology* 233, 113–33.

Conyers, L. 2004. *Ground-Penetrating Radar for Archaeology*. Maryland: AltaMira Press.

Corfield, M. 1993. Monitoring the condition of waterlogged archaeological sites. In P. Hoffman (ed.), *Proceedings of the 5th ICOM Group on Wet Organic Archaeological Materials conference*, 423–36. Paris: International Council of Museums.

Corfield, M. 1996. Preventive conservation for archaeological sites. In A. Roy and P. Smith (eds), *Archaeological Conservation and its Consequences*, 32–7. London: International Institute for Conservation.

Corfield, M. 1998. The role of monitoring in the assessment and management of archaeological sites. In K. Bernick (ed.), *Hidden Dimensions: the cultural significance of wetland archaeology*, 302–18. Vancouver: UBC Press.

Cowell, R. W. and Innes, J. B. 1994. *The Wetlands of Merseyside*. Lancaster: Lancaster University Press.

Cox, M. L. 2007. *Atlas of the Seed and Leaf Beetles of Britain and Ireland*. Oxford: Pisces Publications.

Cox, M., Earwood, C., Jones, E. B. G., Jones, J., Straker, V., Robinson, M., Tibbett, M. and West, S. 2001. An assessment of the impact of trees upon archaeology within a relict wetland. *Journal of Archaeological Science* 28, 1069–84.

Crockett, A. D., Allen M. J. and Scaife R. G. 2002 A Neolithic Trackway within peat deposits at Silvertown, London. *Proceedings of the Prehistoric Society* 68, 185–213.

Crutchley, S. and Crow, P. 2009. *The Light Fantastic: using airborne laser scanning in archaeological survey*. Swindon: English Heritage.

Darvill, T. and Fulton, A. K. 1998. MARS: *The Monuments at Risk Survey in England 1995. Main Report*. Bournemouth and London: Bournemouth University and English Heritage.

David, A. 1995. *Geophysical Survey in Archaeological Field Evaluation*. Swindon: English Heritage Research and Professional Services Guideline 1.

David, A., Linford, N. and Linford, P. 2008. *Geophysical Survey in Archaeological Field Evaluation*. London: English Heritage.

David, A., Linford, N., Linford, P., Fassbinder, J. W. E., Stanjek, H. and Vali, H. 1990. Occurrence of magnetic bacteria in soil. *Nature* 343, 161–3.

David, A., Cole, M., Horsley, T., Linford, N., Linford, P. and Martin, L. 2004. A rival to Stonehenge? Geophysical survey at Stanton Drew, England. *Antiquity* 78, 341–58.

Davis, M., Hall, A., Kenward, H. and Oxley, J. 2002. Preservation of urban archaeological deposits: monitoring and characterisation of archaeological deposits at Marks and Spencer, 44–5 Parliament Street, York. *Internet archaeology*

11, http://intarch.ac.uk/journal/issue11/oxley_index.html. Access date 22/02.2011.

de Jong J., 1977. Conservation techniques for old waterlogged wood from shipwrecks found in the Netherlands. In A. H. Walters (ed.), *Biodeterioration Investigation Techniques.* London: Applied Science Publishers.

Delcourt, P. A and Delcourt, H. R. 1980. Pollen preservation and Quaternary environmental history in the south-eastern United States. *Palynology* 4, 215–31.

Dewing, E. A. 2012. *Mesolithic Coastal Community Perception of Environmental Change in the Southern North Sea Basin.* Southampton: Unpublished PhD Thesis, University of Southampton.

Dinwoodie, J. W. 1989. *Wood: nature's cellular polymeric fibre-composite.* London: Institute of Metals.

Douterelo, I., Goulder, R. and Lillie, M. 2009. Response of the microbial community to water table variation and nutrient addition and its implications for in situ preservation of organic archaeological remains in wetland soils. *International Biodeterioration and Biodegradation* 63(3), 795–805.

Douterelo, I., Goulder, R. and Lillie, M. 2010. Soil microbial community response to land-management and depth, related to the degradation of organic matter in English wetlands: implications for the *in situ* preservation of archaeological remains. *Applied Soil Ecology*, Volume 44, Issue 3, 219–227.

Duff, A. 1993. *Beetles of Somerset: their status and distribution.* Taunton: Somerset Archaeological and Natural History Society.

Dymond, D. and Martin, E. 1999. *An Historical Atlas of Suffolk: Revised and Enlarged Edition.* Ipswich: Suffolk County Council, Environment and Transport.

Earwood, C. 1993. *Domestic Wooden Artefacts in Britain and Ireland from Neolithic to Viking times.* Exeter: University of Exeter Press.

Edwards, K. J. and Whittington, G. 1990. Palynological evidence for the growing of *Cannabis Sativa* L. (hemp) in medieval and historical Scotland. *Transactions of the Institute of British Geographers* 15, 60–9.

English Heritage 2004. *Dendrochronology: guidelines on producing and interpreting dendrochronological dates.* Swindon: English Heritage.

English Heritage 2008. *Geophysical Survey for Archaeological Field Evaluation* (2nd edn). Swindon: English Heritage.

English Heritage 2012, The National Heritage Protection Plan. http://www.english heritage.org.uk/publications/nhpp-plan-framework/. Accessed 7/10/14.

European Commission 2000. *Directive 2000/60/EC. Establishing a framework for community action in the field of water policy.* Luxembourg: European Commission PE-CONS 3639/1/100 REV 1.

Evans, C. and Knight, M. 2001. The 'community of builders': the Barleycroft post alignments. In J. Brück (ed.), *Bronze Age landscapes: tradition and transformation*, 83–98. Oxford: Oxbow Books.

Fassbinder, J. W. E. and Stanjek, H. 1993. Occurrence of bacterial magnetite in soils from archaeological sites. *Archaeologia Polona* 31, 117–28.

Faulkner, S. P., Patrick, W. H. and Gambrell, R. P. 1989. Field techniques for measuring wetland soil parameters. *Soil Science Society of America Journal* 53, 883–90.

Field, N. and Parker Pearson, M. 2003. *Fiskerton: an Iron Age timber causeway with Iron Age and Roman votive offerings.* Oxford: Oxbow Books.

Finzi-Contini, G. 2001. Resistivity/IP tomographies near ancient boats embedded and preserved by fluvial sediments in an undiscovered ancient harbour, Pisa (Italy). *Proceedings of the 7th Meeting, Environmental and Engineering Geophysics (EEGS-ES),Birmingham, England*: 46–7.

Fletcher, W. 2003. *Flag Fen Archaeological Management Plan, Heritage Management of England's Wetlands Project Report for English Heritage.* Exeter: University of Exeter.

Fletcher, W. 2011. *Valuing Archaeology; exploring the reality of the heritage management of England's wetlands.* Exeter: Ph.D. thesis.

Fletcher, W. and Van de Noort, R. 2004. *Sutton Common Management Plan. Heritage Management of England's Wetlands Project Report for English Heritage*, Exeter: University of Exeter.

Foster, G. 2000. *A Review of the Scarce and Threatened Coleoptera of Great Britain. Part 3. Water Beetles.* Peterborough: UK Joint Nature Conservation Committee.

Freeze, R. A. and Cherry, J. A. 1979. *Groundwater.* New Jersey: Prentice Hall.

French, C. A. 2001. The development of the prehistoric landscape in the Flag Fen Basin. In F. Pryor, *The Flag Fen Basin*, 400–4. Swindon: English Heritage.

French, C. A. 2003. *Geoarchaeology in Action.* London: Routledge.

French, C. 2004. Hydrological monitoring of an alluviated landscape in the Lower Great Ouse Valley at Over, Cambridgeshire: results of the gravel extraction phase. *Environmental Archaeology* 9, 1–12.

French, C. 2009. Hydrological monitoring of an alluviated landscape in the Lower Great Ouse Valley at Over, Cambridgeshire: the quarry restoration phase. *Environmental Archaeology* 14, 62–75.

French, C. A. I. and Pryor, F. M. M. 1993. *The South-west Fen Dyke Survey Project, 1982–1986.* Cambridge: East Anglian Archaeology 59.

French, C. A. and Pryor, F. M. 2005. *Archaeology and Environment of the Etton Landscape.* Cambridge: East Anglian Archaeology 109.

French, C. and Rackham, J. 2003. Palaeoenvironmental Research Design for the Witham Valley. In S. Catney and D. Start (eds), *Time and Tide: the archaeology of the Witham Valley*, 33–42. Lincoln: Witham Valley Archaeological Research Committee.

Friday, L. E. 1988. *A Key to the Adults of British Water Beetles.* London: Field Studies 7.

Fulford, M. and Nichols, E. 1992. (eds) *Developing Landscapes of Lowland Britain. The archaeology of the British gravels: a review.* London: Society of Antiquaries Occasional Paper 14.

Gaffney V., Fitch S. and Smith D. 2009. *Europe's Lost World: the rediscovery of Doggerland.* York: Council for British Archaeology Research Report 160.

Gale, R. and Cutler, D. 2000. *Plants in Archaeology.* Otley: Westbury Publishing.

Gao, C., Boreham, S., Preece, R. C., Gibbard, P. L. and Briant, R. M. 2007. Fluvial response to rapid climate change during the Devensian (Weichselian) Lateglacial in the River Great Ouse, southern England, UK. *Sedimentary Geology* 202, 193–210.

Garwood, P. 2007. Late Neolithic and Early Bronze Age funerary monuments and burial traditions in the West Midlands. In P. Garwood (ed.), The Undiscovered Country: the earlier prehistory of the West Midlands, 134–65. Oxford: Oxbow Books.

Garwood, P. and Barclay, A. 2011. Making the dead. In G. Hey, P. Garwood, M. Robinson, A. Barclay and P. Bradley, *The Thames Through Time: volume 1, section 2; earlier prehistory*, 383–432. Oxford: Oxford Archaeology.

Gearey, B. 2009. *Palaeoenvironmental sampling at AFC Sudbury: Kings Marsh stadium, Sudbury, Suffolk: recommendations for assessment*. Birmingham: University of Birmingham, BAE report AFH-01-09.

Gearey, B., Grinter, P. and Tetlow, E. 2010a. *The Holocene fluvial development of the River Gipping, Stowmarket, Suffolk, from coleopteran and plant macrofossil analyses*. Birmingham: University of Birmingham, BAE report to SCCAS. No code.

Gearey, B. R., Marshall, P. and Hamilton, D. 2009. Correlating archaeological and palaeoenvironmental records using a Bayesian approach: a case study from Sutton Common, south Yorkshire, England. *Journal of Archaeological Science* 36, 1477–87.

Gearey, B., Hopla, E.-J., Grinter, P. and Reilly, E. 2010b. *Palaeoenvironmental assessment of deposits at AFC Sudbury, Kings Marsh stadium, Sudbury, Suffolk*. Birmingham: University of Birmingham, BAE report AFH-01-10.

Gearey, B. R., Hall. A. R., Kenward, H., Bunting, M. J., Lillie, M. C. and Carrott, J. 2005. Recent palaeoenvironmental evidence for the processing of hemp (*Cannabis sativa* L.) in eastern England during the medieval period. *Medieval Archaeology* 49, 317–22.

Gearey, B. R, Chapman, H.C, Howard, A. J., Krawiec, K., Bamforth, M., Fletcher, W. G. Hill, T. C. B., Marshall, P, Tetlow, E. and Tyers, I. 2011.The Beccles triple post-alignment, Beccles Marshes, Suffolk: excavation and palaeoenvironmental analyses of an Iron Age wetland site. *Proceedings of the Prehistoric Society* 77, 231–50.

Gibbard, P. L., Pasenan, A. H., West, R. G., Lunkka, J. P., Boreham, S. Cohen, K. M. and Rolfe, C. 2009. Late Middle Pleistocene glaciation in East Anglia, England. *Boreas* 38, 504–28.

Gibson, D., Knight, M. and Allen, M. 2010. The Must Farm timber alignments: an archaeological and environmental evaluation. post-excavation assessment. Cambridge: Cambridge Archaeological Unit CAU Report 935.

Girling, M. A. 1985. An 'old forest' beetle fauna from Neolithic and Bronze Age peat deposit at Stileway. *Somerset Levels Papers* 5, 25–32.

Glazebrook, J. 1997. *Research and Archaeology: a framework for the Eastern Counties*. Norwich: East Anglian Archaeology Occasional Paper 3.

Godwin, H. 1968. Studies of the post-glacial history of British vegetation: XV. Organic deposits of Old Buckenham Mere, Norfolk. *New Phytologist* 67, 95–107.

Grant, M. J. and Waller, M. 2011. The *Tilia* deline: vegetation change in lowland Britain during the mid and late Holocene. *Quaternary Science Reviews* 20, 394–408.

Grant, M. J., Stevens, C. J., Whitehouse, N. J., Norcott, D., Macphail, R. I., Langdon, C., Cameron, N., Barnett, C., Langdon, P. G., Crowder, J., Mulhall, N., Attree, K., Leivers, M., Greatorex, R. and Ellis, C. 2015. A palaeoenvironmental context for Terminal Upper Palaeolithic and Mesolithic Activity in the Colne Valley: Offsite records contemporary with occupation at Three Ways Wharf, Uxbridge. *Environmental Archaeology* 19(2), 131–52.

Green, C. P., Batchelor, C. R., Austin, P. J., Brown, A. D., Cameron, N. G. and Young, D. S. 2014. Holocene alluvial environments at Barking, Lower Thames Valley, London, UK. *Proceedings of the Geologists Association* 125, 279–95.

Grime, J. P. 1988. *Comparative Plant Ecology*. London: Chapman and Hall.

Grimm, E. 1991. TILIA and TILIA*GRAPH. Springfield: Illinois State Museum.

Grosman, L., Smikt, O. & Smilansky, U. 2008. On the application of 3-D scanning technology for the documentation and typology of lithic artifacts. *Journal of Archaeological Science* 35, 3101–10.

Hall, D., Wells, C. and Huckerby, E. 1995. (eds) *The Wetlands of Greater Manchester*. Lancaster: Lancaster University.

Hall, D., Evans, C., Hodder, I. and Pryor, F. 1987. The Fenlands of East Anglia, England: survey and excavation, in J. M. Coles and A. J. Lawson (eds), *European Wetlands in Prehistory*, 169–202. Oxford: Clarendon Press.

Hall, N. 2006. *Archaeological Monitoring of Ground Reduction at the Lignacite Works, Brandon, Suffolk*. Heckington, Lincolnshire: Archaeological Project Services, Report 190/05.

Hall, V. A. 1988. The role of harvesting techniques in the dispersal of pollen grains of Cerealia. *Pollen et Spores* 30, 265–70.

Hansen, M. 1987. *The Hydrophilidae (Coleoptera) of Fennoscandia and Denmark Volume 18 – Fauna Entomologyca Scandinavica*. Leiden: Brill/Scandinavian Science Press.

Haslam, S. M. 2003. *Understanding Wetlands: fen, bog and marsh*. London: Taylor and Francis.

Haslett, S. K., Davies, P., Curr, R. H. F., Davies, C. F. C., Kennington, K., King, C. P. and Margetts, A. J. 1998. Evaluating the late-Holocene relative sea-level change in the Somerset Levels, southwest Britain. *Holocene* 8, 197–207.

Hawkes, C. F. and Hull, M. R. 1947. *Camulodunum*. London: Report of the Research Committee of the Society of Antiquaries of London 14.

Heathcote, J. 2012: Strategy for Water and Wetland Heritage, English Heritage www.english-heritage.org.uk/professional/protection/national-heritage-protection-plan/plan/activities/3a5

Hegarty, C. 2011. *The Aggregate Landscape of Sufffolk: The Archaeological Resource Areas 4 and 5: The Waveney Valley*. ASCCAS/ALSF Report to English Heritage 3987.

Hewett, D. G. 1964. *Menyanthes trifoliata* L. *Journal of Ecology* 52(3), 723–35.

Hill, J. D. 1995. How should we study Iron Age societies and hillforts? A contextual study from Southern England. In J. D. Hill and C. G. Cumberpatch (eds) Different Iron Ages: Studies of the Iron Age in Temperate Europe Oxford: British Archaeological Report Supplementary Series 602, 45–66.

Hill, J. D. 2007. The dynamics of social change in Later Iron Age eastern and south-eastern England. In C. Haselgrove and T. Moore (eds), *The Later Iron Age in Britain and Beyond*, 16–41. Oxford: Oxbow Books.

Hill, T. C. B. 2006. *The Quaternary Evolution of the Gordano Valley, North Somerset, UK*. Bristol: Ph.D. Thesis, University of the West of England.

Hill, T. C. B. 2007a. *The Cedars Park Anglian water pipeline: a palaeoenvironmental assessment of floodplain deposits around the River Gipping*. Birmingham: University of Birmingham, BAE report SCCAS-39-07.

Hill, T. C. B. 2007b. *Eastgate St, Bury St Edmunds: a palaeoenvironmental assessment of deposits encountered during ground investigations*. Birmingham: University of Birmingham, BAE report SCCAS-33-07.

Hill, T. C. B. 2007c. *Rushbrooke to Nowton water pipeline: a palaeoenvironmental assessment of deposits encountered during ground investigations*. Birmingham: University of Birmingham, BAE report SCCAS-32-07.

Hill, T. C. B. 2007d. *Ipswich triangle west: a palaeoenvironmental assessment of deposits encountered during ground investigations.* Birmingham: University of Birmingham, BAE report SCCAS-40-07.

Hill, T. C. B. 2007e. *Ipswich Mills: summary of site visit and proposals for further work.* Birmingham: University of Birmingham, BAE report SCCAS No Code.

Hill, T. C. B. 2008. *Palaeoenvironmental evaluation of borehole deposits from the Stowmarket relief road, Suffolk.* Birmingham: University of Birmingham, BAE report SCCAS-61-08.

Hill, T. C. B. and Gearey, B. R. 2008. *Sizewell, Suffolk: A palaeoenvironmental evaluation of deposits encountered along the proposed Leiston substation 132kV cable route.* Birmingham: University of Birmingham, BAE report SCCAS-54-08.

Hill, T. C. B. and Tetlow, E. 2007. *University site, Ipswich: a palaeoenvironmental assessment of deposits encountered during ground investigations.* Birmingham: University of Birmingham, BAE report SCCAS-31-07.

Hill, T., Fletcher, W., Gearey, B. and Howard, A. 2007. *The Suffolk River Valleys Project: an assessment of the potential and character of the palaeoenvironmental and geoarchaeological resource of Suffolk river valleys affected by aggregate extraction.* Birmingham: University of Birmingham, BAE report for ALSF/English Heritage.

Hill, T. C. B., Gearey, B. R., Fletcher, W. and Howard, A. J. 2008a. *The Suffolk River Valleys Project Phases I and II: Final Report.* Birmingham: University of Birmingham, BAE report for ALSF/English Heritage.

Hill, T. C. B., Gearey, B. and Smith, D. 2008b. *Sizewell, Suffolk: A Palaeoenvironmental Assessment of Deposits Encountered along the proposed Leiston Substation 132kV Cable Route.* Birmingham: University of Birmingham, BAE report SCCAS-56-08.

Hoffman, P. 1981. Chemical wood analysis as a means of characterizing waterlogged wood. In D. W. Grattan (ed.), *Proceedings of the ICOM Waterlogged Wood Working Group Conference,* 73–83. Ottawa: ICOM (International Council of Museums).

Holland, D. G. 1972. *A Key to the Larvae, Pupae and Adults of the British Species of Elminthidae.* London: Freshwater Biological Association Scientific Publication 26.

Holden, J., West, L. J., Howard, A.J., Maxfield, E., Panter, I. and Oxley, J. 2006. Hydrological controls on *in situ* preservation of archaeological deposits. *Earth Science Reviews* 78, 59–83.

Hoper, S. T., McCormac, F. G., Hogg, A. G., Higham, T. F. G. and Head, M. J. 1998. Evaluation of wood pretreatments on oak and cedar. *Radiocarbon* 40, 45–50.

Hopla, E-.J. and Krawiec, K. 2010. *A palaeoenvironmental assessment of deposits in the Stour Valley, Wixoe.* Birmingham: University of Birmingham, BAE report no code.

Hopla, E.-J., Smith, D. and Smith, W. 2010. *Great Blakenham Highways Depot Palaeoenvironmental Assessment.* Birmingham: University of Birmingham, BAE report Entec-BA2103-2010.

Hopla, E-.J., Gearey, B. R., Tetlow, E. and Grinter, P. 2008. *Palaeoenvironmental assessment of deposits from the River Gipping floodplain, Stowmarket relief road, Suffolk.* Birmingham: University of Birmingham, BAE report SCC-1850-08.

Howard, A. J. and Macklin, M. G. 1999. A generic geomorphological approach to archaeological interpretation and prospection in British river valleys: a guide for archaeologists investigating Holocene landscapes. *Antiquity* 73, 527–41

Howard, A. J. Gearey, B. R., Fletcher, W., Hill, T. and Marshall, P. 2009. Fluvial sediments, correlations and palaeoenvironmental reconstruction: the development of robust radiocarbon chronologies. *Journal of Archaeological Science* 36, 2680–8.

Howard, A. J., Carney, J. N., Greenwood, M. T., Keen D. H., Mighall, T., O'Brien, C. and Tetlow, T. 2011. The Holme Pierrepont sand and gravel and the timing of Middle and Late Devensian floodplain aggradation in the English Midlands. *Proceedings of the Geologists Association* 122, 419–31.

Hunt, C. O., Lewis, S. G., Rose, J. and Wymer, J. J. 1991. Lackford, Suffolk (TL 815704). In S. G. Lewis, C. A. Whiteman and D. R. Bridgland (eds), *Central East Anglia and the Fen Basin Field Guide,* 85–92. London: Quaternary Research Association.

Hutcheson, N. 2007 An archaeological investigation of later Iron Age Norfolk: analysing hoarding patterns across the landscape. In C. Haselgrove and T. Moore (ed.) *The Later Iron Age in Britain and Beyond.* Oxford: Oxbow Books (2007): 358–370.

Hyman, P. S. 1992. *A review of the Scarce and Threatened Coleoptera of Great Britain, Part 1* (rev. and updated M. S. Parsons). Peterborough: UK Joint Nature Conservation Committee.

Jackson R. and Miller D. 2011. Wellington Quarry, Herefordshire (1986–96). Investigations of a landscape in the Lower Lugg Valley. Oxford: Oxbow Books.

Jennings, J. N. and Lambert, J. M. 1955. Alluvial stratigraphy and vegetational succession in the region of the Bure valley Broads 1: Surface features and general stratigraphy. *Journal of Ecology* 39, 106–48.

Jessop, L. 1996. *Coleoptera: Scarabaeidae. Handbooks for the Identification of British Insects* 5(11). London: Royal Entomological Society of London.

Jones, J., Tinsley, H. and Brunning, R. 2007. Methodologies for assessment of the state of preservation of pollen and plant macrofossil remains in waterlogged deposits. *Environmental Archaeology* 12, 71–86.

Jordan, D. 2009. How effective is geophysical survey? A regional review. *Archaeological Prospection* 16, 77–90.

Karasik, A. and Smilansky, U. 2008. 3d Scanning technology as a standard archaeological tool for pottery analysis: practice and theory. *Journal of Archaeological Science* 35, 1148–68.

Kenward, H. K. 1975. Pitfalls in the environmental interpretation of insect death assemblages. *Journal of Archaeological Science* 2, 85–94.

Kenward, H. K. 1978. *The Analysis of Archaeological Insect Assemblages: a new approach.* York: Archaeology of York 19/1.

Kenward, H. K. and Hall, A. R. 1995. *Biological Evidence from Anglo-Scandinavian Deposits at 16/22 Coppergate.* York: Archaeology of York. 14/7.

Kenward, H. K. and Hall, A. R. 1997. Enhancing bioarchaeological interpretation using indiactor groups: Stable manure as a paradigm. *Journal of Archaeological Science* 24, 663–73.

Kenward, H. and Hall, A. R. 2000. Decay of delicate organic remains in shallow urban deposits: are we at a watershed? *Antiquity* 74, 519–25.

Kenward, H. and Hall, A. R. 2008. Urban organic archaeology: an irreplaceable palaeoecological archive at risk. *World Archaeology* 40, 584–96.

Kenward, H. K., Hall A. R. and Jones, A. K. G. 1980. A tested set of techniques for the extraction of plant and animal macrofossils from waterlogged archaeological deposits. *Scientific Archaeology* 22, 3–15.

Knight, D. and Howard, A. J. 2004. *Trent Valley Landscapes.* Kings Lynn: Heritage Marketing and Publications.

Knight, M. 2009. Excavating a Bronze Age timber platform at Must Farm, Whittlesey, near Peterborough. PAST 63, 1–4.

Knox, J. C. 1972. Valley alluviation in southwestern Wisconsin. *Annals of the Association of American Geographers* 62, 401–10.

Koch, K. 1989a. *Die Kafer Mitteleuropas: Ökologie Band 1.* Krefeld: Goecke and Evers.

Koch, K. 1989b. *Die Kafer Mitteleuropas: Ökologie Band 1.* Krefeld: Goecke and Evers.

Koch, K. 1992. *Die Kafer Mitteleuropas: Ökologie Band 3.* Krefeld: Goecke and Evers Verlag.

Kovács, K. & Hanke, K. 2012. Hydrologic and feature-based surface analysis for tool mark investigation on archaeological finds. *ISPRS-International Archives of the Photogrammetry, Remote Sensing and Spatial Information Sciences* 1, 565–70.

Krawiec, K. and Gearey, B. R. 2010. *A palaeoenvironmental assessment of deposits associatd with the Ludham Boat, Norfolk.* Birmingham: BAE report.

Krawiec, K., Hopla, E.-J. and Gearey, B. 2009. *A palaeo-environmental assessment of deposits from the Abbey Gardens and Nursery site, Bury St Edmunds.* Birmingham: University of Birmingham, BAE report no code.

Krawiec, K., Gearey, B., Chapman. H. P., Bamforth, M., Hopla, E. and Griffiths, C. 2011. Triple post alignments in the Waveney Valley, Suffolk: excavations at Barsham Marshes. *Journal of Wetland Archaeology* 10, 46–71.

Lane, T. W. 1993. *The Fenland Project Number 8: Lincolnshire Survey, The Northern Fen-Edge.* East Anglian Archaeology 66.

Lane, T. and Morris, E. L. (eds) 2001. *A Millennium of Saltmaking: Prehistoric and Romano-British Salt Production in the Fenland.* Lincolnshire Archaeology and Heritage Report Series 4.

Latalowa, M. 1998. Botanical analysis of a bundle of flax (*Linum usitatissimum* L.) from an early medieval site in northern Poland: a contribution to the history of flax cultivation and its field weeds. *Vegetation History and Archaeobotany* 7, 97–107.

Lewis, S. G, Whiteman, C. A. and Bridgland, D. R. (eds) 2000a. *Central East Anglia and the Fen Basin Field Guide.* London: Quaternary Research Association.

Lewis, S. G., Whiteman, C. A. and Preece, R. C. (ed.) 2000b. *The Quaternary of Norfolk and Suffolk. Field Guide.* London: Quaternary Research Association.

Lewis, S. G., Ashton, N., Parfitt, S. A. and White, M. 2000. Hoxne, Suffolk (TM 176769). In S. G. Lewis, C. A. Whiteman and R. C. Preece (eds), *The Quaternary of Norfolk and Suffolk Field Guide.* London: Quaternary Research Association.

Lillie, M., Soler, I. and Smith, R. 2012. Lowland floodplain responses to extreme flood events: long-term studies and short-term microbial community response to water environment impacts. *Conservation and Management of Archaeological Sites* 14, 126–49.

Limbrey, S. and Evans, J. G. 1978 (eds) *The Effect of Man on the :andscape: the lowland zone.* London: Council for British Archaeology Research Report 21.

Lindroth, C. H. 1974. Coleoptera: Carabidae. *Handbooks for the Identification of British Insects* 4(2). London: Royal Entomological Society.

Lindroth, C. H. 1986. *The Carabidae (Coleoptera) of Fennoscandia*

and Denmark – Fauna Entomologyca Scandinavica* 15(2). Leiden: Brill/Scandinavian Science Press.

Linford, P. 2005. An automated approach to the arrangement of post-pits at Stanton Drew, *Archaeological Prospection* 12(3), 137–150

Linford, N. 2006. The application of geophysical methods to archaeological prospection. *Reports on Progress in Physics* 69, 2205–57.

Loke, M. H. 2004. 2-D and 3-D electrical imaging surveys. www.geoelectrical.com (accessed 21 May 2009).

Losito, G., Mazzetti A. and Trova, A. 2001. Frequency electrical behaviour of soils and archaeological woods at laboratory and field scale in Roman boat area of Pisa–San Rossore (Italy). *Geophysical Research Abstracts 3, European Geophysical Society (EGS) 26th Assembly.* Nice: SE 17.01.

Lowe, J. J. and Walker, M. J. C. 1997. *Reconstructing Quaternary Environments.* Harlow: Longman.

Lott, D. A. 2003. *An Annotated List of Wetland Ground Beetles (Carabidae) and Rove Beetles (Staphylinidae) Found in the British Isles Including a Literature Review of their Ecology.* Peterborough: English Nature Report 488.

Macklin, M., Jones, A. F. and Lewin, J. 2010. River response to rapid Holocene environmental change: evidence and explanation in British catchments. *Quaternary Science Reviews* 29, 1555–76.

Malim, T. and Panter, I. 2012. Is preservation *in situ* an acceptable option for development control? Can monitoring prove the continued preservation of waterlogged deposits? *Conservation and Management of Archaeological Sites* 14, 429–4.

Mannerkoski, I., Hyvärinen, E., Alexander, K., Büche, B. and Campanaro, A. 2010. *Xylophilus corticalis.* The IUCN Red List of Threatened Species. Version 2014.3. <www.iucnredlist.org>. Accessed on 14 November 2014.

Mansell, L., Whitehouse, N., Gearey, B. R., Barratt, P. and Roe, H. 2014. Holocene floodplain palaeoecology of the Humberhead Levels and implications for regional wetland development. *Quaternary International* vol 341, 91–109.

Martin, E. A. 1975. The Excavation of Barrow I, Martlesham Heath. In: *East Anglian Archaeology* 1, 00–00.

Martin, E. A. 1976a. The excavation of Barrows II, III and IV, Martlesham Heath, 1974. In *East Anglian Archaeology* 3, 17–41.

Martin, E. A. 1976b. The excavation of a tumulus at Barrow Bottom, Risby, 1875. In *East Anglian Archaeology* 3, 43–62.

Martin, E. A. 1981. The Barrows of Suffolk. In A. J. Lawson, E. A. Martin and D. Priddy (ed.), *The Barrows of East Anglia.* Norwich: East Anglian Archaeology 12.

Martin, E. A. 1988. *Burgh: Iron Age and Roman Enclosure.* Ipswich: East Anglian Archaeology 40.

Martin, E. 1990. Commentary on the illustrated Iron Age pottery. In S. West, *West Stow, Suffolk: the Prehistoric and Romano-British Occupations.* Ipswich: East Anglian Archaeology 48.

Martin, E. A. 1993. *Settlements on Hill-Tops: Seven Prehistoric Sites in Suffolk.* Ipswich: East Anglian Archaeology 65.

Martin, E. A. 2006 (ed.). Site Summaries. *Proceedings of the Suffolk Institute of Archaeology* 41, 231–260.

Martin, E. A. and Murphy, P. 1988. West Row Fen, Suffolk: a Bronze Age fen-edge settlement site. *Antiquity* 62 (235), 353–8.

Martin, E. and Satchell, M. (forthcoming). *Wheare most Inclosures be: East Anglian Fields, History, Morphology and Management.* Ipswich: East Anglian Archaeology.

Mayer, L. M., Jorgensen, J. and Schnitker, D. 1991. Enhancement of diatom frustule dissolution by iron oxides. *Marine Geology* 99, 263–6.

Meddens, F. M. 1996. Sites from the Thames estuary wetlands, England, and their Bronze Age use. *Antiquity* 70, 325–34.

Meddens, F. and Beasley, M. 1990. Wetland use in Rainham, Essex. *London Archaeologist* 6(9), 242–8.

Menzies, I. S. and Cox, M. L. 1996. Notes on the natural history, distribution and identification of British reed beetles. *British Journal of Entomology and Natural History* 9, 137–62.

Meyer, C., Ullrich, B. and Barlieb, D. M. 2007. Archaeological questions and geophysical solutions: ground-penetrating radar and induced polarization investigations in Munigua, Spain. *Archaeological Prospection* 14, 202–12

Milne, G., 2002. The Vauxhall piled structure. In J. Sidell, J. Cotton, L. Rayner, and L. Wheeler (eds), *The Prehistory and Topography of Southwark and Lambeth*, 29–30. London: MoLAS Monograph 14.

Milner, N., Lane, P., Taylor, B., Conneller, C. and Schadla-Hall, R. T. 2011. Star Carr in a Postglacial Lakescape: 60 years of research. *Journal of Wetland Archaeology* 11, 1–19.

Mook, W. G. 1986. Business meeting: recommendations/resolutions adopted by the twelfth International Radiocarbon Conference, *Radiocarbon* 28, 799.

Mook, W. G. and Steurman, H. J. 1983. Physical and chemical aspects of radiocarbon dating. In W. G. Mook and H. T. Waterbolk (eds), *Proceedings of the First International Symposium ¹⁴C and Archaeology*, 31–55. PACT 8.

Mook, W. G. and Waterbolk, H. T. 1985. *Radiocarbon Dating, Handbook for Archaeologists*. Strasbourg: European Science Foundation.

Moore, G. E., Burdick, D. M., Peter, C. R. and Keirstead, D. R. 2012. Below ground biomass of *Phragmites australis* in coastal marshes. *Northeastern Naturalist* 19(4), 611–26.

Moore, P. D., Webb, J. A. and Collinson, M. E. 1991. *Pollen Analysis* (2nd edn). London: Blackwell.

Moorlock, B. S. P. 2000. *Geology of the Country around Lowestoft and Saxmundham: Memoir for 1:50,000 Geological Sheets 176 and 191*. Nottingham: British Geological Survey.

Morigi, T., Schreve, D., White, M. and Hey, G. 2011. *The Thames through Time: the archaeology of the gravel terraces of the upper and middle Thames. The formation and changing environment of the Thames Valley and early human occupation to 1500 BC*. Lancaster: Thames Valley Landscapes Monograph 1.

Mullin, D. 2012. The river has never divided us: Bronze Age metalwork deposition in western Britian. *Oxford Journal of Archaeology* 31, 47–57.

Murphy, P. 1982. *Mollusca, peat section, charred crop plants and weed seeds from Brandon, Suffolk*. Swindon: English Heritage Anient Monuments Laboratory Report Old Series 3637.

Murphy, P. 1994a. *Environmental archaeology in East Anglia 1977–1980: a review*. Norwich: UEA Centre of East Anglian Studies.

Murphy, P. and Fryer, V. 2005. Valley sediments and plant macrofossils. In Tester, A., Anderson, S., Carr, R. and Riddler, I. (eds), *A High Status Middle Saxon Settlement on the Fen Edge: Staunch Meadow, Brandon*, 313–329. Ipswich, East Anglian Archaeology 151.

Murphy, P. and Wiltshire, P. E. J. 1989. *Pakenham, Suffolk (PKM 028): Environmental and Economic Studies*. London: HBMC Ancient Monument Laboratory Report Series 99/89..

Murphy, P. L. and Wiltshire, P. J. 1994. A proposed scheme for evaluating plant macrofossil preservation in some archaeological deposits. *Circaea* 11, 1–6.

Needham, S. and Macklin, M. G. (ed.) 1992. *Alluvial Archaeology in Britain*. Oxford: Oxbow Monograph 27.

Neighbour, T., Strachan, B. A. and Hobbs, B. A. 2001. Resistivity imaging of the linear earthworks at the Mull of Galloway, Dumfries and Galloway. *Archaeological Prospection* 8, 157–62.

Nilsson, A. N. and Holmen, M. 1995. *The Aquatic Adephaga (Coleoptera) of Fennoscandia and Denmark II.Dytiscidae – Fauna EntomologycaScandinavica*. Leiden: Brill

Niven, L., Steele, T. E., Finke, H., Gernat, T. and Hublin, J. J. 2009. Virtual skeletons: using a structured light scanner to create a 3d faunal comparative collection. *Journal of Archaeological Science* 36, 2018–23.

Olivier, A. 2013. International and national wetland management policies. In F. Menotti and A. O'Sullivan (eds), *The Handbook of Wetland Archaeology*, 687–703. Oxford: Oxford University Press.

Olivier, A. and Van de Noort, R. 2002: English Heritage Strategy for Wetlands, London: English Heritage www.english-heritage.org.uk/upload/pdf/wetlands_strategy.pdf.

Oswald, A., Dyer, C. and Barber, M. 2001. T*he Creation of Monuments: Neolithic causewayed enclosures in the British Isles*. Swindon: English Heritage.

Out, W. A., Vermeeren, C. and Hänninen, K., 2013. Branch age and diameter: useful criteria for recognising woodland management in the present and past? *Journal of Archaeological Science* 40, 4083–97.

Painter, K. S. 1977. *The Mildenhall Treasure: Roman silver from East Anglia*. London: British Museum Publications.

Panter, I. and Spriggs, J. 1996. Condition Assessments and conservation strategies for waterlogged wood assemblages. In P. Hoffman (ed.), *Proceedings of the 6th ICOM Group on Wet Organic Archaeological Materials Conference*, 185–200. York: ICOM (International Council of Museums).

Paquet, E. and Viktor, H. L. 2005. Long-Term preservation of 3-d cultural heritage data related to architectural sites. *Proceedings of the ISPRS Working Group* 4. http://www.isprs.org/default.aspx.

Parfitt, S. A., Berendegt, R. W., Breda, M., Candy, I., Collins, M. J., Coope, G. R., Durbidge, P., Field, M. H., Lee, J. R., Lister, A. M., Mutch, R., Penkman, K. E. H., Preece, R. C., Rose, J., Stringer, C. B., Symmonds, R., Whittaker, J. E., Wymer, J. J. and Stuart, A. J. 2005. The earliest record of human activity in northern Europe. *Nature* 438, 1008–12.

Parfitt, S. A., Ashton, N. M., Lewis, S. G., Abel, R. L., Coope, G. R., Field, M. H., Gale, R., Hoare, P. G., Larkin, N. R., Lewis, M. D., Karloukovski, V., Maher, B. A., Peglar, S. M., Preece, R. C. Whittaker, J. E. and Stringer, C. B. 2010. Early Pleistocene human occupation at the edge of the boreal zone in northwest Europe. *Nature* 466, 229–33.

Parry, R. 2013. *Museums in a Digital Age*. London: Routledge.

Parker Pearson, M. and Field, N. 2003. The construction and appearance of the causeway. In N. Field and M. P. Pearson, *Fiskerton: an Iron Age timber causeway with Iron Age and Romanvotive offerings, the 1981 excavations*, 133–4. Oxbow, Oxford Books.

Passmore, D. G. and Waddington, C. 2012. *Archaeology and Environment in Northumberland: Till-Tweed Studies volume 2*. Oxford: Oxbow Books.

Pearce, E. J. 1957. *Handbooks for the Identification of British*

Insects IV part 9: Pselaphidae. London: Royal Entomological Society.

Peglar, S. M. 1993. The mid-Holocene *Ulmus* decline at Diss Mere, Norfolk: a year by year pollen stratigraphy from annual laminations. *Holocene* 3(1), 203–22.

Peglar, S. M., Fritz, S. C. and Birks, H. J. B. 1989. Vegetation and land-use history at Diss, Norfolk, UK. *Journal of Ecology* 77, 203–22.

Percival, J. 1918. *Agricultural Botany* (5th edn). London: Duckworth.

Peterken, J. 2007. Some new aspects of Roman Broadland. *Bulletin of the Norfolk Archaeological and Historical Research Group* 16, 23–35.

Plater, A. J., Horton, B. P., Haworth, E. Y., Appleby, P. G., Zong, Y., Wright, M. R. and Rutherford, M. M. 2000. Holocene tidal levels and sedimentation using a diatom-based palaeoenvironmental reconstruction: the Tees estuary, northeastern England. *Holocene* 10(4), 441–52.

Plouviez, J. 1999. The Romans. In D. Dymond and E. Martin (eds), *An Historical Atlas of Suffolk: revised and enlarged edition*. Ipswich: Suffolk County Council, Environment and Transport.

Prehistoric Ceramic Research Group, 2009 *The Study of Later Prehistoric Pottery: General Policies and Guidelines for analysis and Publication*. Occasional Papers 1–2 (3rd edn) www.pcrg.org.uk

Pryor, F. 1980. *Excavation at Fengate, Peterborough, England: the 3rd report*. Northampton: Northamptonshire Archaeological Society Monograph 1/Royal Ontario Museum Archaeological Monograph 6.

Pryor, F. 1992. Current Research at Flag Fen. *Antiquity* 66, 439–57.

Pryor, F. 2001. *The Flag Fen Basin*. Swindon: English Heritage.

Pryor, F., French, C., Crowther, D., Gurney, D., Simpson, G. and Taylor, M. 1985. *The Fenland Project No. 1: Archaeology and Environment in the Lower Welland Valley Volume 1*. Cambridge: East Anglian Archaeology Report 27.

Rackham, O. 1977. Neolithic woodland management in the Somerset Levels: Garvin's, Walton heath, and Rowland's tracks. *Somerset Levels Papers* 3, 65–71.

Rackham, O. 1986. *The History of the Countryside*. London: Dent.

Rackham, O. 2001. *Trees and Woodland in the British Landscape*. London: Orion.

Raferty, B. 1996. Trackway excavations in the Mountdillon bogs, Co. Longford, 1985–1991. *Irish Archaeological Wetland Unit, Transactions* 3. Dublin: Crannog Publications.

Raiswell, R. 2001. Defining the burial environment. In D. R. Brothwell and A. M. Pollard (eds), *Handbook of Archaeological Sciences*, 595–603. Chichester: Wiley.

Reimer, P. J., Baillie, M. G. L., Bard, E., Bayliss, A., Beck, J. W., Bertrand, C. J. H., Blackwell, P. G., Buck, C. E., Burr, G. S., Cutler, K. B., Damon, P. E., Edwards, R. L., Fairbanks, R. G., Friedrich, M., Guilderson, T. P., Hogg, A. G., Hughen, K. A., Kromer, B., McCormac, G., Manning, S., Bronk Ramsey, C., Reimer, R. W., Remmele, S., Southon, J. R., Stuiver, M., Talamo, S., Taylor, F. W., van der Plicht J. and Weyhenmeyer, C. E. 2004. IntCal04 terrestrial radiocarbon age calibration, 0–26 cal kyr BP. *Radiocarbon,* 46, 1029–58.

Renfrew, J. M. 1973. *Palaeoethnobotany. The prehistoric food plants of the Near East and Europe*. London: Methuen.

Roberts, A. J., Barton, R. N. E. and Evans, J. 1998. Early Mesolithic mastic: radiocarbon dating and analysis of organic residues from Thatcham III, Star Carr and Lackford Heath. In N. Ashton, F. Healy and P. Pettitt (eds), *Stone Age Archaeology: essays in honour of John Wymer,* 185–92. Oxford: Oxbow Monograph 102/Lithic Studies Society Occasional Paper 6.

Robinson, L. 2007. *The Aggregate Landscape of Suffolk: the archaeological resource*. Unpublished SCCAS Report.

Robinson, M. A. 1981. The Iron Age to Early Saxon Environment of the Upper Thames Terraces. In M. Jones and G. Dimbleby (eds), *The Environment of Man: the Iron Age to the Anglo-Saxon period,* 251–86. Oxford: British Archaeological Report 87.

Robinson, M. A. 1983. Arable/pastoral ratios from insects. In M. Jones (ed.), *Integrating the Subsistence Economy,* 19–47. Oxford: British Archaeological Report S181.

Robinson, M. A. 1993a. Pre-Iron Age environment and finds. In T. G. Allen and M. A. Robinson (eds), *The Prehistoric Landscape and Iron Age Enclosed Settlement at Mingies Ditch, Hardwick with Yelford, Oxon,* 7–16. Oxford: Oxford Archaeological Unit.

Robinson, M. A. 1993b. The scientific evidence. In T.G. Allen and M. A. Robinson (ed.), *The Prehistoric Landscape and Iron Age Enclosed Settlement at Mingies Ditch, Hardwick with Yelford, Oxon,* 101–17. Oxford: Oxford Archaeological Unit.

Robinson, M. A. 2002. *English Heritage Reviews of Environmental Archaeology: Southern Region Insects*. Swindon: English Heritage Centre for Archaeology Report 39/2002.

Rodwell, J. S. (ed.) 1991. *British Plant Communities. Volume 1: Woodlands and Scrub*. Cambridge: Cambridge University Press.

Rolfe, J. 2007. *Land East of Station Road, Stowmarket*. Unpublished SCCAS Report 2007/074.

Rose, J. 2009. Early and Middle Pleistocene landscapes of eastern England. *Proceedings of the Geologists' Association* 120, 3–33.

Rose, J., Turner, C., Coope, G. R. and Bryan, M. D. 1980. Channel changes in a lowland river catchment over the last 13,000 years. In R. A. Cullingford, D. A. Davidson and J. Lewin (eds), *Timescales in Geomorphology,* 159–75. London: Wiley.

Sands, R. 1997. *Prehistoric Woodworking: the analysis and interpretation of Bronze and Iron Age Toolmarks*. London: Institute of Archaeology.

Scaife, R. 1990. *Pilot Pollen Analysis of Methwold*. Southampton: Unpublished report. Department of Geography, University of Southampton.

Scaife, R. 2001. Flag Fen: the vegetation and environment. In F. Pryor *The Flag Fen Basin*, 351–81. Swindon: English Heritage.

Schleifer, N., Weller, A., Schneider, S. and Junge, A. 2002. Investigation of a Bronze Age plankway by Spectral Induced Polarization. *Archaeological Prospection* 9, 243–53.

Schofield, J. E and Waller, M. P 2005. A pollen analytical record for hemp retting from Dungeness Foreland, UK. *Journal of Archaeological Science* 32, 715–26.

Scollar, Tabbagh, A., Hesse, A. and Herzog, I. 1990. *Archaeological Prospection and Remote Sensing: topics in remote sensing*. Cambridge: Cambridge University Press.

Scott, E. M., 2003. The third international radiocarbon intercomparison (TIRI) and the fourth international radiocarbon intercomparison (FIRI) 1990–2002: results, analyses, and conclusions, *Radiocarbon* 45, 135–408.

Shaw, R. and Devlin, G. 2010. 3-D surveying – terrestrial laser scanning. In A. O'Sullivan, M. Dillon, R. Sands,

C. McDermott, R. Shaw and G. Devlin 2010. *The Fergus Estuary and Islands: discovering a maritime historic landscape in Co Clare*, 17–20. Dublin: University College Dublin in Association with the Discovery Programme. Report to the Heritage Council.

Shennan, I., Lambeck, K., Horton, B., Innes, J., Lloyd, J., McArthur, J. and Rutherford, M. 2000a. Holocene isostasy and relative sea-level changes on the east coast of England. In I. Shennan and J. Andews (eds), *Holocene Land-Ocean Interaction and Environmental Change around the North Sea*, 275–98. London: Geological Society Special Publication 166.

Shennan, I., Lambeck, K., Flather, R, Horton, B., McArthur, J., Innes, J., Lloyd, J., Rutherford, M. and Wingfield, R. 2000b. Modelling western North sea palaeogeographies and tidal ranges during the Holocene. In I. Shennan, I. and J. Andews (eds), *Holocene Land-Ocean Interaction and Environmental Change around the North Sea*, 299–319. London; Geological Society Special Publication 166.

Shennan, I. and Horton, B. P. 2002. Holocene land-and sea-level changes in Great Britain. *Journal of Quaternary Science* 15, 511–26.

Shennan, I., Bradley, S., Milne, G., Brooks, A., Bassett, S. and Hamilton, S. 2006. Relative sea-level changes, glacial isostatic modelling and ice-sheet reconstructions from the British Isles since the Last Glacial Maximum. *Journal of Quaternary Science* 21, 585–99.

Siau, J. F. 1984. *Transport Processes in Wood*. New York: Springer.

Singer, R., Gladfelter, B. G. and Wymer, J. J. 1993. *The Lower Palaeolithic at Hoxne, England*. Chicago: University of Chicago Press.

Slota Jr, P. J., Jull, A. J. T., Linick, T. W. and Toolin, L. J. 1987. Preparation of small samples for ^{14}C accelerator targets by catalytic reduction of CO. *Radiocarbon* 29, 303–6.

Smit, A. van Heeringen, R. M. and Theunissen, E. M. 2006. *Archaeological Monitoring Standard*. Amersfoort: Nederlandse Archaeologische Rapporten 33.

Smith, D. N. and Howard, A. J. 2004. Identifying changing fluvial conditions in low gradient alluvial archaeological landscapes: can coleoptera provide insights into changing discharge rates and floodplain evolution? *Journal of Archaeological Science* 31, 109–20.

Smith, D. N. and Whitehouse, N. J. 2005. Not seeing the trees for the woods: a palaeoentomological perspective on Holocene woodland composition. In D. N. Smith, M. B. Brickley and K. W. Smith, (eds), *Fertile Ground: papers in honour of Susan Limbrey*, 53–67. Oxford: Oxbow Books.

Smith, A. G., Whittle, A., Cloutman, E. W. and Morgan. L.A. 1989. Mesolithic and Neolithic activity and environmental impact on the south-east fen edge in Cambridgeshire. *Proceedings of the Prehistoric Society* 55, 207–49.

Smith, D. N., Whitehouse, N, Bunting, M. J. and Chapman, H. 2010. Can we characterise 'openness' in the Holocene palaeoenvironmental record? Analogue studies from Dunham Massey deer park and Epping Forest, England. *Holocene* 20, 215–29.

Smith, P. J. 1997. Graham Clark's new archaeology: the Fen Research Committee and Cambridge prehistory in the 1930s. *Antiquity* 71, 11–30.

Stace, C. 2010. *New Flora of the British Isles* (3rd edn). Cambridge: Cambridge University Press.

Stockmarr, J. 1971. Tablets with spores used in absolutre pollen analysis. *Pollen et Spores* 13, 615–21.

Stuiver, M. and Kra, R. S. 1986. Editorial comment. *Radiocarbon*, 28(2B), ii.

Stuiver, M. and Polach, H. A. 1977. Reporting of ^{14}C data. *Radiocarbon* 19, 355–63.

Suffolk County Council 2008. Minerals and Waste Development Framework. Minerals Core Strategy Adapted Version. http://www.suffolk.gov.uk/environment-and-transport/planning-and-buildings/minerals-and-waste-development-framework/minerals-core-strategy-dpd/.

Sussams, K. 1996. *The Breckland Archaeological Survey 1994–1996: a characterisation of the Archaeology and Historic Landscape of the Breckland Environmental Sensitive Area*. Suffolk: Suffolk County Council.

Tallantire, P. A. 1953. Studies in the Post-glacial history of British vegetation XIII. Lopham Little Fen, a Late-glacial site in central east Anglia. *Journal of Ecology* 41, 361–73.

Tallantire, P. A. 1954. Old Buckenham Mere – Data for the study of Post-glacial history XIII. *New Phytologist* 53, 131–40.

Tallantire, P. A. 1992. The alder (*Alnus glutinosa* (L.) Gaertn.) problem in the British Isles: a third approach to its palaeohistory. *New Phytologist* 122, 717–31.

Taylor, M. 2001. The wood. In F. Pryor, *The Flag Fen Basin*. Swindon: English Heritage.

Taylor, M., 2003. The wood. In N. Field and M. P. Pearson (eds), *Fiskerton: an Iron age timber causeway with Iron Age and Roman votive offerings, the 1981 excavations*, 38–48. Oxford: Oxbow Books.

Taylor, M. 2010. Wood from excavations at the site of the moat for the New Visitor Centre. In F. M. M. Pryor and M. Bamforth (eds), *Flag Fen, Peterborough, Excavation and Research 1995–2007*, 79–80. Oxford: Oxbow Books.

Tester, A. 2001a. *Unpublished Report: Eriswell Evaluation Report, 2001/56a* Suffolk County Council Archaeological Service, Bury St Edmunds.

Tester, A. 2001b. *Consolidated Support Compex RAF Lakenheath ERL116: A Report on the Archaeological Evaluation*. Suffolk: Suffolk County Council Archaeological Service 2001/56.

Tetlow, E. A. 2003. A 'wildwood' insect fauna from Goldcliff East, Gwent. *Archaeology in the Severn Estuary* 14, 41–47.

Tetlow, E. A. 2007a. *The Insect Remains Southampton French Quarter*. Birmingham: University of Birmingham BAE OA-49-07.

Tetlow, E. A. 2007b. Insect assemblages and the environment of the lower and upper peats at Goldcliff East, in M. G. Bell (ed.), *Prehistoric Coastal Communities*. York: Council for British Archaeology Research Report 149.

Thomas, G. and Fletcher, W. 2001. Prehistoric and Romano–British saltmaking in the Lincolnshire Marsh. In S. Ellis, H. Fenwick, M. Lillie and R. Van de Noort (eds), *Wetland Heritage of the Lincolnshire Marsh*, 215–230. Hull: Humber Wetlands Project.

Thompson, I. 1982. *Grog-tempered 'Belgic' Pottery of South-eastern England*. Oxford: British Archaeological Report 108.

Tooley, M. J. 1982. Sea-level changes in northern England. *Proceedings of the Geologists Association* 93(1), 43–51.

Tottenham, C. E. 1954. *Coleoptera. Staphylinidae, Section (a) Piestinae to Euaesthetinae*. London: Royal Entomological Society Handbooks for the identification of British Insects IV, 8(a).

Turner, C. and Gibbard, P. L. 1996. Richard West – an appreciation. *Quaternary Science Reviews* 15, 375–89.

Van de Noort, R. 2004. *The Humber Wetlands: the archaeology of a dynamic landscape*. Sheffield: Windgather.

Van de Noort, R. 2006. Argonauts of the North Sea– a social maritime archaeology for the 2nd millennium BC. *Proceedings of the Prehistoric Society* 72, 267–87.

Van de Noort, R. and Ellis, S. 1997. *Wetland Heritage of the Humberhead Levels. An Archaeological Survey*. Swindon: English Heritage.

Van de Noort, R. & Ellis, S. 1998. *Wetland Heritage of the Ancholme and Lower Trent Valleys. An Archaeological Survey*. Hull: Humber Wetlands Project.

Van de Noort, R. and Fletcher, W. 1998. Bronze Age human ecodynamics in the Humber Estuary, In G. Bailly, R. Charles and N. Winder (eds), *Human Ecodynamics*, 47–54. Oxford: Oxbow Books.

Van de Noort, R., Fletcher, W., Thomas, G., Carstairs, I. and Patrick, D. 2002. *Monuments at Risk in England's Wetlands*. Exeter: University of Exeter Report for English Heritage.

Van de Noort, R., Chapman, H. P. and Cheetham, J. L. 2001. *In situ* preservation as a dynamic process: the example of Sutton Common, UK. *Antiquity* 75, 94–100.

Van de Noort, R., Chapman, H. P. and Collis, J. 2007. *Sutton Common: The Excavation of an Iron Age 'Marsh Fort'*. York: Council for British Archaeology Research Report 154.

Vandeputte, K., Moens, L. and Dams, R., 1996 Improved sealed-tube combustion of organic samples to CO_2 for stable isotope analysis, radiocarbon dating and percent carbon determinations, *Analytical Letters* 29(15), 2761–7.

van der Veen, M. and Fieller, N. 1982. Sampling Seeds. *Journal of Archaeological Science* 9, 287–98.

VISTA Centre 2014. Sacred and Profane – the Eton Myers Collection. http://www.vista.bham.ac.uk/3D%20LS/Eton_Myers.htm

Vos, P. C. and de Wolf, H. 1988. Methodological aspects of palaeo-ecological diatom research in coastal areas of the Netherlands. *Geologie en Mijnbouw* 67, 31–40.

Waller, M. 1994. *The Fenland Project, Number 9: Flandrian Environmental Change in Fenland, Cambridge*. Cambridge: East Anglian Archaeology 70.

Ward, G. K. and Wilson, S. R. 1978. Procedures for comparing and combining radiocarbon age determinations: a critique. *Archaeometry* 20, 19–31.

Weller, A. and Bauerochse, A. 2013. Detecting organic materials in waterlogged sediments. In F. Menotti and A. O'Sullivan (eds), *The Handbook of Wetland Archaeology*, 421–32. Oxford: Oxford University Press.

West, R. G. 1988. Harry Godwin 1901–1985. *Bibliographical Memoirs of Fellows of the Royal Society* 34, 1–33.

West, R. 2009. *From Brandon to Bungay: an exploration of the geology and landscape history of the Little Ouse and Waveney rivers*. Ipswich: Healeys.

West, S. E. 1989. *West Stow: The Prehistoric and Romano-British Occupations*. Ipswich: East Anglian Archaeology 48.

West, S. E. and Plouviez, J. 1976. *The Romano-British Site at Icklingham*. Ipswich: East Anglian Archaeology 3.

White, T. S., Bridgland, D. R., Westaway, R., Howard, A. J. and White, M. J. 2010. Evidence from the Trent terrace archive, Lincolnshire, UK, for lowland glaciation of Britain during the Middle and Late Pleistocene. *Proceedings of the Geologists' Association* 121, 141–53.

Whitehouse, N. and Smith D. 2010. What is "natural"? forest composition, open-ness and the british "wildwood": implications from palaeoentomology for Holocene develop-ment and landscape structure. *Quaternary Science Reviews* 29, 539–53.

Wilkinson, T. J. and Murphy, P. L 1995. *The Archaeology of the Essex Coast, Volume 1: The Hullbridge Survey*. Chelmsford: East Anglian Archaeology 71.

Williams, J., Martin Bacon, H., Onions, B., Barrett, D., Richmond, A. and Page, M. 2008. The second Shardlow boat – economic drivers or heritage policy. In H. Kars and R.M. van Heeringen, (eds), *Preserving Archaeological Remains In Situ*, 317–25. Amsterdam: Vrije University.

Williams, J. 2012. Thirty years of monitoring in England – what have we learnt. *Conservation and Management of Archaeological Sites* 14, 442–57.

Williamson, T. 1987. Early co-axial field systems on East Anglian boulder clay. *Proceedings of the Prehistoric Society* 53, 419–31.

Williamson, T. 2012. *Landscape in Early Medieval England: time and topography*. Woodbridge: Boydell.

Willis, S. 2007. Sea, coast, estuary, land and culture in Iron Age Britain. In C. Haselgrove and T. Moore (ed.) *The Later Iron Age in Britain and Beyond*. Oxford: Oxbow Books (2007): 107–30.

Wiltshire, P. E. J. 1988. *Microscopic analysis of sediments taken from the edge of Micklemere, Pakenham, Suffolk*. London: HBMC Ancient Monuments Laboratory Report 209/88.

Wiltshire, P. E. J. 1990. *A palynological analysis of sediments from Staunch Meadow, Brandon, Suffolk*. London: HBMC Ancient Monuments Laboratory Report 73/90.

Wiltshire, P. E. J. and Emery, P. A. 2000. *Report on an Archaeological Watching Brief at Riverside, Norwich*. Unpublished Norfolk Archaeological Unit, Report 354.

Wiltshire, P. E. J. and Murphy, P. L. 1999. Current Knowledge of the Iron Age Environment and Agrarian Economy of Norfolk and Adjacent Areas. In J. Davies and T. Williamson, (eds), *Land of the Iceni: the Iron Age in northern East Anglia*. 132–61. Norwich: Centre of East Anglian Studies.

Woodland, A. W. 1970. The buried tunnel-valleys of East Anglia. *Proceedings of the Yorkshire Geological Society* 37, 521–78.

Wymer, J. J. 1975. Two barbed points from Devil Wood's Pit, Sproughton. In *East Anglian Archaeology* 1, 1–14.

Wymer, J. J. and Rose, J. 1976. A long blade industry from Sproughton. In *East Anglian Archaeology* 3, 1–15.

Wymer, J. J. 1985. *The Palaeolithic Sites of East Anglia*. Norwich: Geobooks.

Wymer, J. J. 1991. Mesolithic occupation around Hockham Mere. *Norfolk Archaeology* 41, 212–3.

Wymer, J. J. 1999. *The Lower Palaeolithic Occupation of Britain. Volumes 1 and 2*. Salisbury: Wessex Archaeology and English Heritage.

Wymer, J. J. and Singer, R. 1993. Flint industries and human activity. In R. Singer, B. G. Gladfelter and J. J. Wymer (eds), *The Lower Palaeolithic at Hoxne, England*, 74–128. Chicago: University of Chicago Press.

Xu, S., Anderson, R., Bryant, C., Cook, G. T., Dougans, A., Freeman, S., Naysmith, P., Schnabel, C. and Scott, E. M. 2004. Capabilities of the new SUERC 5MV AMS facility for ^{14}C dating. *Radiocarbon* 46, 59–6.

York, J. 2002. The life cycle of Bronze Age metalwork from the River Thames. *Oxford Journal of Archaeology* 21, 77–92.

Zohary, D. and Hopf, M. 1988. *Domestication of Plants in the Old World*. Oxford: Clarendon Press.

Appendix 1:
Beccles Timber Alignment Management Plan

W. Fletcher and B. R. Gearey. March 2013

This plan was developed as part of management outcomes from the excavations and associated analyses of the timber alignment site on Beccles Marshes. It is based on a format developed for the final stage of the English Heritage funded Heritage Management of England's Wetlands project (HMEW Prn 3476 and 3610). This project in turn was derived from English Heritage's 2002 Strategy for Wetlands (see Olivier and Van de Noort, 2002). Subsequently the strategy has been updated (see Heathcote, 2012) and advocacy for the management of sites has been placed with the National Heritage Protection Plan (see English Heritage, 2012). The information generated through the development of this work has been used to generate a Statement of Significance for the Beccles timber alignment under the NHPP Activity for the 'Identification of Wetland and Waterlogged Site (3A5.101 Exceptional Waterlogged Heritage).

Statement of Significance for the Beccles Later Prehistoric Timber Alignment

Part 1: Description
1.0   *Information on Archaeological and Cultural History*
1.0.1   Archaeology
1.0.2   Palaeoenvironmental history
1.0.3   Land use history
1.0.4   Public interest
1.0.5   Monitoring
1.1   Implications for Management

Part 2: Evaluation and Objective
2.0   *Research potential and status*
2.0.1   Archaeology
2.0.2   Palaeoenvironmental
2.1   Site in wider perspectives
2.2   Management Objectives
2.3   Factors Influencing Management
2.3.1   Natural Trends
2.3.2   Human
2.3.3   External
2.4   Management Options

Part 3: Prescriptions
3.1   Projects

Part 1: Description

1.0 Information on archaeological and cultural history

The Beccles triple timber alignment is one of England's most recently discovered and investigated wet preserved archaeological sites. The site was entirely unknown prior to 2005 and it has therefore been analysed and assessed in a modern, stake-*PPG16* archaeological context. It is one of the best-preserved and most substantial prehistoric timber alignment structures in the country.

The site consists of a well preserved triple timber timber alignment, associated structural elements including short sections of ground level wooden trackways and platforms, a substantial assemblage of worked wooden debris and some cultural artefacts in the form of pottery. The timber alignment itself was probably built in a single phase during the late Iron Age, but the structure arguably belongs to a tradition of wooden linear structures that can be traced back to the early Bronze Age. There is also evidence for human activity on site during the Romano-British period.

The site is located on the south side of the river Waveney in a large floodplain wetland, although the river was canalised in the 18th century with a subsequent programme of drainage and reclamation of the associated 'marshlands'. In terms of cultural value, the archaeological and environmental contexts present represent strong evidential, historical and communal value (see Drury and McPherson, 2008). This is a significant site with high archaeological interest and the potential to inform understanding of material culture, aspects of prehistoric cultural interaction and exchange, past human interaction with, and impact on, the local and extra-local landscapes. The evidential and historical value of a wetland context such as this can be separated in to four parts:

- Organic (structural) archaeological remains;
- Cultural material associated with the structures;
- The palaeoenvironmental sequences;
- The wider landscape setting of the Waveney valley and the Norfolk Broads

1.0.1 Archaeology

Three seasons of excavation in 2006, 2007 and 2009 have established that the main feature at the site is a triple timber alignment *c.* 513m in length. A total of 109 upright stakes were recorded across eight trenches. Excavation has also identified the southern, dryland terminus of the structure, although desiccation and wastage of the peat at the dryland–wetland interface has resulted in the loss of much of the archaeology with only stake tips now surviving. It is unclear how far the upright stakes protruded above the contemporary floodplain surface or if they ever supported a structure (discussed further below). A second feature of the site is the wooden debris field, which is found in close proximity to the alignment. In addition, four discrete

structures were identified, including brushwood bundles and large wooden beams, which appear to have formed short sections of trackway or platform on the contemporary ground surface of the floodplain. The large timbers of the alignment were largely *Quercus* (oak) and have been dated using dendrochronology to the spring of 75BC. Although not all samples were datable, timbers of this date are recorded across and along the alignment, suggesting the site was built in a single phase. Radiocarbon dates from the discrete trackways, other ground level structures and elements of the debris field indicate that these also date to the Iron Age, although a brushwood trackway feature at the southern end of the site was dated to the 1st century AD. The date and stratigraphic position of this trackway is significant in that the feature overlies the top of one of the stakes of the alignment, indicating that in this part of the site at least, the above ground portion of these upright stakes must have rotted off by the early Romano-British period.

Finds included the wooden debris and three possible wooden artefacts: a broken handle, a rope runner and a square peg. Other inorganic material included a few crude and simple worked flint flakes and flake cores which were identified as later prehistoric, possibly Iron Age and hence perhaps contemporary with the timber alignment. Later Iron Age pottery from the excavations represented a domestic assemblage consisting of at least eight sand-tempered vessels all of a similar date which probably also concurs with the dendrochronological date (75BC) for the construction of the timber alignment. Roman-dated finds included pottery in the form of sherds of a single vessel, possibly a bottle or flask of mid- or late 1st to early 2nd century date, made in a local micaceous coarseware fabric.

1.0.2 Palaeoenvironmental evidence

Previous attempts to establish the chronology of peat accumulation at Beccles using radiocarbon dating had resulted in a number of anomalous determinations. A subsequent re-evaluation using duplicate multi-fraction analyses indicated that the floodplain peats at this location appear to have been affected by a variety of processes, which complicate the establishment of a robust radiocarbon chronology (Howard *et al.*, 2009). The palaeoenvironmental sequences from the site do not therefore have independent, absolute chronologies. However, a number of general observations regarding the timing of floodplain aggradation can be made on the basis of previous work. Peat accumulation probably resulting from paludification of the basal sands and gravels began during the early Holocene (7735 ± 35 BP, 6640–6480 cal. BC; R_combine GrN-31120 and 31155) and seems to have continued within a fen carr floodplain context into the mid-Holocene (Hill *et al.*, 2008). The problems associated with radiocarbon dating of the peat means that the 'on site' palaeoenvironmental sequences discussed below do not have absolute chronological control.

There is no evidence from wider stratigraphic investigation on the eastern side of the river for movement of the channel of the River Waveney during this time, although less information is available from the west side of the river and it is possible that the course of the river was further west of its current position in the past. Radiocarbon dates from a depth of 0.84m in Beccles core 1 of 2142±32 BP (360–50 cal. BC; R_combine GrN-31116 and 31151) broadly confirm the archaeological evidence (discussed above) for the depth of the later prehistoric horizon. It seems likely that later drainage of the floodplain has led to shrinkage and probably loss of more recent peat accumulation and the upper peat deposits are highly desiccated and disturbed (see hydrological monitoring, below).

1.0.3 Land use history

The on-site environmental archaeological analyses (Trench 2 and 4) demonstrate that the floodplain was dominated by *Alnus* (alder) fen carr for much of the mid-late Holocene. The pollen diagrams are characterised by relatively low percentages of tree or shrub taxa other than *Alnus*, with oak the best represented at a maximum of little over 10%. This probably reflects the localised pollen source area for floodplain peat deposits accumulating within a fen carr with plants growing on and close to the sampling site dominating the record. Macrofossil and beetle analyses of the peat confirms the presence of wet conditions and fen vegetation on and around the sampling site with *Alnus* remaining significant throughout, although there are differences within the data which reflect probably spatial variation in the vegetation as well as taphonomic factors.

The wider landscape may have been largely de-forested by the later prehistoric period, certainly the presence in the pollen record of ribwort plantain, dandelions and bracken, suggest open grassland habitats on the dryland soils beyond the floodplain edge. Although the Trench 4 sequence is closer to the contemporary dryland edge than Trench 2, there are no marked differences in total tree and shrub percentages that might reflect this spatial gradient. There are a few indications of disturbed environments in the beetle record in the form of 'dung' beetles, which might reflect grazed areas beyond the floodplain edge.

Pollen preservation deteriorates markedly at approximately the same level as the archaeological horizons (see above) as defined by the presence of the worked wood fragments of the debris field and horizontal structural timbers in each trench. The generally poor condition of much of the archaeological wood indicates that human activity on the floodplain was probably associated with a period of deeper water tables during antiquity and the subsequent degradation of the structures closest to and on the surface of the floodplain.

1.0.4 Public interest

Public interest in archaeology continues to increase and there is a widespread recognition both of the cultural and social value that archaeology delivers and its role in shaping heritage and cultural learning. The archaeology of northeast Suffolk is perhaps less well known than other similar landscapes. There are few publically accessible prehistoric sites in particular. The site therefore has the potential to develop and sustain interest in the archaeology of this region. However, the effects of development, drainage and external factors such as climate change upon the visible components (i.e. flora and fauna) of wetlands are perhaps easier for the public to appreciate than the 'invisible' impact upon buried archaeology and palaeoecological remains. Wet preserved archaeological sites such as this therefore have the potential to be employed to enhance awareness and understanding not only of archaeology, but of closely inter-related issues such as conservation and the possible effects of climate change on heritage.

1.0.5 Hydrological monitoring

The hydrological regime and water chemistry of the Beccles site are critical factors in understanding the current condition of waterlogged archaeological and palaeoenvironmental remains and the prognosis for the future *in situ* preservation of the site. The floodplain peat has provided a burial environment since later prehistory that has led to the exceptional preservation of organic remains, although the evidence (discussed above) also indicates that there was also a period of deeper water tables during the later prehistoric period, which resulted in some degradation of the archaeological and associated palaeoenvironmental resource.

Subsequent canalisation, drainage, development and the recent excavations have led to a degree of disturbance to this burial environment and possibly to changes in the hydrology. The University of Birmingham in conjunction with English Heritage therefore implemented a programme of hydrological monitoring in 2009. Details of this work can be found in Gearey *et al.* (forthcoming) and only a brief summary of the results is presented here:

The monitoring of the water table was carried out using a network of 15 piezometers across the site with readings taken every two weeks for a total of two years. The results indicate that the majority of the shallower archaeological remains (upper extents of the stakes, the trackways, timbers and debris field) are not presently located within permanently saturated deposits. It seems unlikely that the observed differences in hydrological regime across the site are related directly to the predominant land-use *per se,* with the higher average water tables recorded close the central section of the site seemingly more a result of poorer drainage in this part of the floodplain. The site cannot therefore ultimately be preserved *in situ*, although the likely timescale for the deterioration and eventual complete loss of the archaeology cannot be reliably estimated on the basis of the current data. The already fragmentary archaeological deposits at the far southern end of the alignment are probably at greatest threat in the short term. Further evaluation of the site at some point in the future would be necessary to assess the rate at which archaeological information is being lost.

1.1 Implications for Management

• *Lack of visibility of the resource*
◦ No surface archaeological remains are visible; hence in management terms, the knowledge generated by the excavations will need to be employed to address both the known and the unknown 'potential' of the resource.

• *Fragility of the resource*
◦ Organic archaeological material is in general very fragile and its continuing survival owes much to the conditions at the time of burial being maintained. Floodplain sequences must also be considered within this context as they represent the best opportunity for the discovery of future archaeological finds, and also the greatest potential for palaeoecological and geoarchaeological research.

• *Conflicts of interest*
◦ Conflicts of interest include may include land use change, drainage, agricultural and conservation needs verses maintenance of the optimal conditions for the archaeological remains.

• *Sustainable preservation and maintenance of significance*
◦ Due to the fragile nature of the resource and the variation in surface and burial environments, long-term survival of the archaeology cannot be assured. The programme of hydrological monitoring suggests that much of the site is currently located above the water table and hence may not be preserved *in situ* in the medium to long term.

• *Research*
◦ The site has potential for further archaeological and palaeoenvironmental research (see below).

• *Boundaries and site ownership*
◦ The site is situated across land in multiple ownerships and this land is currently managed in a variety of ways. Much of the land is owned by Beccles Town Council, and is under pastoral agriculture. The southern extent of the site is situated on land that is owned by an unknown third party. A small part of the site is located within the premises of Beccles Amateur Yacht club.

Part 2: Evaluation and objective

2.0 Research potential and status

Whilst the excavations at the site have provided detailed understanding of the spatial extent and nature of the archaeological sequences, a number of outstanding research

questions can be identified. These include site-specific questions as well as issues concerning the history and development of the landscape of Suffolk and the Norfolk Broads.

2.0.1 Archaeology

Whilst the southern terminus of the site has been located, it is not known whether the alignment is continued in any way onto the contemporary dryland. The location of the northern terminus of the structure is unknown, but is probably situated below the river embankment and further directs archaeological interventions in this area are unlikely. It is not known whether the alignment continues on the northern side of the River Waveney. Certain of the brushwood structures associated with the alignment extended beyond the excavated area and it is not clear how far these may extend. There is a reasonable possibility that other wet-preserved archaeological sites are present in this area. This must be considered in advance of any developments or disturbance to the floodplain.

2.0.2 Palaeoenvironment

The associated peat deposits present opportunities for further stratigraphic and palaeoenvironmental study of local floodplain development and wider landscape change. In particular, there is some stratigraphic evidence that the alignment was situated close to the point at which the channel of the River Waveney opened up into a wider estuary, with no evidence for peat deposits found below Beccles. This landscape context is critical for understanding the possible functions of the site and there is the potential for further work to investigate the architecture of the Waveney floodplain in four dimensions. The deep peat deposits also present opportunities for detailed investigations of Holocene landscape change and human impact on the environment.

2.1 Site in wider perspectives

• Archaeology
◦ This site has high evidential, historical and communal values with potential for the recovery of organic and inorganic remains. These remains are considered to be of national importance but have additional local and regional significance.

• Palaeoecology
◦ The deposits here have high evidential value with local, regional and national significance.

• Cultural Landscape
◦ The site has significant evidential value for understanding past cultural interactions and human eco-dynamics. It provides important contextual information for the wider landscape of the Norfolk Broads.

• Historical Landscape

○   Local and regional significance of the site in the context of canalisation, drainage and reclamation. This encompasses aspects of the use of pre-enclosure common land.

2.2 Management objectives

•   Objectives for management can be defined as the following:

•   To conserve and retain the primary archaeological and palaeoenvironmental sources.

○   The long-term preservation of organic and inorganic archaeological remains is essential to preserve evidential and cultural value

•   To preserve and enhance the current condition of the site to prevent further desiccation and deterioration of the resource.

•   Continued research into the organic archaeological remains. Research will play an important role in the informing future strategies and should be targeted to the areas of need identified:

○   To devise a research framework that continues to explore the potential of the Beccles site to inform future management;

○   Contribute to a greater understanding of the local history and cultural land use.

•   To enhance the education and outreach value of the site and landscape, by raising interest and awareness of the evidential and cultural significance of the site:

○   Continue the emphasis on education and dissemination of knowledge through promotion of the heritage value of the Suffolk River valleys:

○   Provide publications that present the results the excavations at Beccles. Other intellectual publications including leaflets may be considered appropriate. Web-based resources can be tailored for education at differing levels and offer an opportunity to raise the profile.

•   Provide greater accessibility and appreciation of the resource:

○   This should be undertaken through a combination of research, publication and outreach agendas. This might also include managed access and information provided through way the way marked 'marsh trails' which are close by. The presence of a display board which was commissioned and installed on the river bank adjacent to the site by the Broads Authority should ensure that the site continues to remain 'visible' for the local community and visitors to the area.

○   Accessibility does not have to be site based and wider participation is possible through broader dissemination, through the local museums or websites.

2.3 Factors influencing management

2.3.1 Natural trends

•   Hydrological fluctuations – through broader climatologically driven changes or localised factors such as drainage.

•   Colonisation by vegetation. The southern end of the site is currently waste ground and grazing does not control vegetation succession. Eventually, tree species will probably colonise this area, leading to further 'draw down' of the water table. This may have significant deleterious effects on the preservation of this part of the site.

2.3.2 Human

•   Current conservation policy and operational objectives
•   Past conservation policy and operational objectives
•   Public access
•   Boundaries and inter agency co-operation, numerous land owners
•   Conflict of interest between conservation and archaeological needs

2.3.3 External

•   Hydrological fluctuations due to water extraction
•   Funding and costs

2.4 Management options

Options for management are limited by the nature of the feature, the scale and size of the timber alignment and the multiple variations in ground condition and land use. Operational, political and practical difficulties aside, options for improved management of the resource could include.

•   Change of land use, to ensure a more consistent and benign land use that favour conservation of the archaeological resource

•   Change in the management of the drainage, which would restrict drainage, and manipulate the water levels on land surrounding the archaeology to encourage a higher average water table

•   Further condition monitoring of the archaeological resource

•   Preservation by record

•   A combination of approaches

Part 3: Prescriptions

3.1 Projects

- To ensure the long-term preservation of organic and inorganic archaeological remains, with special attention to be paid to the upper youngest sequences which are at the greatest risk of desiccation:
  - English Nature rewetting strategy with combined objectives, and monitoring of water quality and chemistry, with additional policies controlling chemical use on the mire e.g. only acidic herbicides for controlling birch.

- Continuing research into the organic and inorganic archaeological and palaeoenvironmental remains, their management and preservation:
  - Research should be focused on the upper/youngest sequences with predictive modelling in line with English Heritage policy and the 'Strategy for Wetlands' (Olivier and Van de Noort, 2002).
  - Contextualisation of the resource in the wider landscape
  - Focused projects of monitoring and predicting arch-aeology, (note success of project on Hatfield Moors (Chapman and Gearey, 2003).
  - Develop an over arching research framework to explore the wider implications as well as on-site issues (see also above)
  - Encourage access for schools and universities with active participation in research projects and PhD's (e.g. Southampton University PLUSPEAT & PALPEAT).

- Education
  - Continued emphasis on broadening the understanding of the main themes of natural and cultural history of floodplains, their past and present land use and value in palaeoenvironmental terms. This should utilise opportunities made available through schools and universities.

- Providing access to the resource
  - Project for English Nature in collaboration with partners such as English Heritage, Broads Authority, Wildlife Trusts to provide better access, information boards, walks, leaflet guides. This should not be solely on-site, but also utilising nearby major tourism centres such as Norwich and also on-line web based resources.

Index

Numbers in *italic* denote pages with figures, numbers in **bold** denote pages with tables.

Italic text is used for titles of publications and Latin plant names.

Place names are in Suffolk, except Geldeston (Norfolk), unless indicated otherwise.